LATE HARVEST

LATE HARVEST

RURAL AMERICAN WRITING

By Edward Abbey, Wendell Berry, Carolyn Chute, Annie Dillard, William Gass, Garrison Keillor, Bobbie Ann Mason, Wallace Stegner, and Others

Edited by David R. Pichaske

SMITHMARK

This edition published in 1996 by
SMITHMARK Publishers
a division of US Media Holdings, Inc.
16 East 32nd Street, New York, NY 10016

SMITHMARK books are available for bulk purchase for sales,
promotion, and premium use. For details, write or call the
manager of special sales, SMITHMARK Publishers
16 East 32nd Street, New York, NY 10016 (212)-532-6600.

Library of Congress data is available upon request

Printed in the United States of America

ISBN: 0-7651-9735-9

10 9 8 7 6 5 4 3 2 1

CONTENTS

PART 2: THE SMALL TOWN

PART 3: THE WILDERNESS

Acknowledgments

Edward Abbey, "Water" from *Desert Solitaire* (Ballantine Books, 1968). Reprinted by permission of Don Congdon Associates, Inc. Copyright © 1968 by Edward Abbey. All rights reserved.

Sherwood Anderson, "Adventure." From *Winesburg, Ohio* by Sherwood Anderson. Copyright © 1919 by B. W. Heubsch. Copyright renewed by Eleanor Copenhaver Anderson. Reprinted by permission of Viking Penguin, a division of Penguin Books USA, Inc.

Wendell Berry, "The Boundary" from *The Wild Birds*. Copyright © 1986 by Wendell Berry. Published by North Point Press and reprinted by permission. All rights reserved.

Norbert Blei, "Meditations on a Small Lake" from *Meditations on a Small Lake* (Ellis Press, 1986). Copyright © Norbert Blei. All rights reserved. Reprinted by permission of the author.

Carol Bly, "Letter from the Lost Swede Towns" from *Letters from the Country*. Copyright © 1971, 1981 Carol Bly. Reprinted by permission of Harper & Row, Publishers, Inc.

Frederick Busch, "Widow Water," from *Hardwater Country* by Frederick Busch. Copyright © 1979 by Frederick Busch. Reprinted by permission of Alfred A. Knopf, Inc.

Carolyn Chute, "Lizzie, Annie and Rosie's Rescue of Me with Blue Cake" from *The Beans of Egypt* by Carolyn Chute. Copyright © 1985 by Carolyn Chute. Reprinted by permission of Houghton Mifflin Company.

Leo Dangel, "A Farmer Prays," "What Milo Saw," "After Forty Years of Marriage, She Tries a New Recipe for Hamburger Hot Dish,"

Linda Hasselstrom, selections from *Windbreak: A Woman Rancher on the Northern Plains* (Barn Owl Books, 1987). Copyright © Linda Hasselstrom. All rights reserved. Reprinted with the permission of the author.

Jim Heynen, "Scar Tissue," "You Know What Is Right," and "Bat Wings" from *You Know What Is Right*. Copyright © 1985 by Jim Heynen. Published by North Point Press and reprinted by permission. "The Man Who Kept Cigars in His Cap," "The Man Who Sharpened Saws," "The Breeding Circuit," "Bloating and Its Remedies," and "The First-Calf Heifer" from *The Man Who Kept Cigars in His Cap*. Copyright © Jim Heynen. All rights reserved. Reprinted by permission of Graywolf Press.

Bill Holm, "The Music of Failure" from *The Music of Failure* (Plains Press, 1985). Copyright © Bill Holm. All rights reserved.

Greg Keeler, *Seven Songs of Modern Montana*. Copyright © Greg Keeler. Reprinted by permission of the author.

Garrison Keillor, "Home" from *Lake Wobegon Days*. Copyright © 1985 by Garrison Keillor. All rights reserved. Reprinted by permission of Viking Penguin, Inc.

Verlyn Klinkenborg, "Making Hay." Copyright © 1986 by Verlyn Klinkenborg. All rights reserved. Reprinted by arrangement with Lyons and Burford, Publishers, Inc.

William Kloefkorn, Poems number 1, 2, 4, 9, 11, 28, 35, and 60 from *Alvin Turner as Farmer* (Windflower Press, 1974). Copyright © William Kloefkorn. Reprinted with the permission of the author.

Mark Kramer, "The Farmerless Farm" from *Three Farms*. Reprinted by permission of Georges Borchardt, Inc. for the author. Copyright © 1977, 1979, 1980 by Mark Kramer.

Maxine Kumin, "Life on a Hill." From *In Deep* by Maxine Kumin. Copyright © 1987 by Maxine Kumin. Reprinted by permission of Viking Penguin, a division of Penguin Books USA, Inc.

Patricia Penton Leimbach, "A Double Harness." Excerpt from *All My Meadows* by Pat Leimbach. Copyright © 1977 Patricia Penton Leimbach. Reprinted by permission of Harper and Row, Publishers, Inc.

Meridel LeSueur, "Harvest," from *Harvest & A Song for My Time* (West End Press, 1977). Copyright © Meridel LeSueur. Reprinted with the permission of the author. All rights reserved.

Barry Holstun Lopez, "Buffalo." Reprinted with permission of Charles

Scribner's Sons, an imprint of Macmillan Publishing Company from *Winter Count* by Barry Lopez. Copyright © 1981 Barry Holstun Lopez.

Bobbie Ann Mason, "The Rookers." From *Shiloh and other Stories* by Bobbie Ann Mason. Copyright © 1982 Bobbie Ann Mason. Reprinted by permission of Harper and Row, Publishers, Inc.

Noel Perrin, "Low Technology in the Sugarbush" from *Third Person Rural* by Noel Perrin. Copyright © 1983 by Noel Perrin. Reprinted by permission of David R. Godine, Publisher.

Gary Snyder, "Lookout's Journal" from *Earth House Hold*. Copyright © 1962 by Gary Snyder. Reprinted by permission of New Directions Publishing Corporation.

Wallace Stegner, "Wilderness Letter" from *The Sound of Mountain Water*. Copyright © 1969 by Wallace Stegner. Reprinted by permission of Brandt and Brandt Literary Agents, Inc.

Ann Zwinger, from the "The Streams" from *Beyond the Aspen Grove*. Reprinted by permission of Frances Collen, agent. Copyright © 1970 by Ann Zwinger.

LATE HARVEST: Foreword
Eugene J. McCarthy

THIS ANTHOLOGY is more than a comprehensive gathering and compiling of writings classifiable as "rural." The editor (probably he should be called "the author") possesses not only a sweeping knowledge of the field of rural writings and experience and sensitivity to rural life, but also the power to interpret and communicate the significance, meaning, and cultural vitality of rural life and thought. In achieving this, he transcends the limits of mere collector and editor to achieve the creative synthesis of an author.

In *Late Harvest*, the reader finds surrender neither to romanticism nor to false idealization of the simple primitive virtues and values of rural life. The pieces chosen for this book are realistic, hard, clean, and unsophisticated. They report the bearing of land and nature upon human life: crops and cattle, rain and hail, blizzards and tornadoes, droughts and floods, debts and mortgages, foreclosures and forced sales; deaths of people and animals spin out as the warp and weft of mortal experience in this book, as they do in rural life in America. From the days of Jean de Crèvecoeur to those of contemporary farmers and ranchers, the lives and thoughts of men, women, and children ripen out in the traditional bounty of a harvest. This harvest shows the reaping of chaff as well as of the rich grain.

Unusual in collections of rural writing is a proper emphasis on life in small towns, which cannot be separated economically or culturally from life in the surrounding and supporting farm areas. The entire rural community consisting of farmers, ranchers, and town-dwellers—doctors, lawyers, merchants, and others—is an eminently worthy subject matter for this volume, which is most creditably compiled.

Preface

THIS BOOK GREW DIRECTLY out of my life, teaching, and writing over the past decade and a half. Around the mid-seventies, when I was teaching a course at Bradley Polytechnical Institute on "The Poetry of Rock," I began developing another course called "Midwest Authors." An Easterner by birth, I was fascinated by my adopted home, by the rhythms of its speech and the comparative largeness of its people, which I attributed to their relatively rural upbringing. I became convinced that what is peculiarly American evolved outside of the cities of the East Coast, first on the colonial plantations and later in the small towns and farming communities of the Midwest, the West, or wherever the largely mental rural geography happened, at any given historical moment, to locate itself.

Gradually "Midwest Writers" became "Rural Writers," and I moved to Southwest State University, a small liberal arts college masquerading as a state university in the amplitudes of southwestern Minnesota farmland where fifteen thousand people make a metropolis. In small-town Minneota, Minnesota, I surrounded myself with corn and bean fields, and began my study of country living first hand. In an essay titled "Lost in Elburn," Norb Blei made a reference to visiting me one winter and thinking he'd landed on the moon in February. I was very proud. "Rural Literature" became "Literature and Humanities: Rural Studies," part of SSU's Rural Studies Program, an "out-state" answer to the University of Minnesota's Urban Studies Program.

In retrospect, I realize, my experience replicated that of many others who came of age during the golden sixties, then moved out of the troubled cities and boring suburbs, emulating Henry Thoreau, or Bob Dylan, or the Woodstock crowd. This retreat to the country was probably *the* major movement, physical and philosophical, of the 1970s (the Yuppie phenomenon is a direct philosophical counterresponse to this movement). It flowered nationally in *A Prairie Home Companion*, made country music as ubiquitous as it is banal, and elected (twice) to the presidency "Cowboy" Ronald Reagan, born in small-town Tampico, Illinois, and educated in nearly as small-town Eureka, Illinois, embodiment of all the small-town virtues—and vices. The United States Department of Agriculture yearbook, *Living on a Few Acres*, described in detail the lifestyles of 4.3 million "suburbanites and city people [who] have moved to the country" between 1970 and 1976. The origins of *Late Harvest* are strictly personal, but its appeal may be to a whole generation.

This book grew specifically out of the Rural Writers Festival hosted at Southwest State in 1986 by Phil Dacey, and out of conversations with Paragon editor Ken Stuart. When we first discussed the idea of a collection of rural American writing, I had in mind some great anthology balanced by region and gender, ethnicity and genre, time and place: the great collection of classic American rural writing. Wrestling with the problem of contents during an August spent in Michelle Payne's cabin across the street from the Custer (South Dakota) Lumber Company, I decided, finally, to emphasize the new fruits of a renaissance in rural writing largely unknown around the country. I wanted also to tie that writing to a tradition extending far back in American literary history, since the new writers were spinning variations on classic themes. It also occurred to me for the first time that "rural" meant different things to different people. I identified three distinct possibilities: wilderness of one degree or another, the farm or ranch, and the small town. The book's structure followed easily, and selections became—with some attention to balance and some very useful suggestions from editors and readers of the manuscript—a matter of taste and availability. This book is a celebration of a rapidly transforming—and possibly dying—culture in which the celebrants can speak for themselves.

I am very much in debt, of course, to the authors of selections contained in this book, for their writing (which has sustained me and many others), for their kind permission to reprint, and in many cases for their friendship. I am in debt to others as well, people whose work is, for one reason or another, not here; I would not want their absence to be perceived as any kind of "statement" at all, except as a reflection of limited space and multiple opinions on selection. Among the Old Ones, I have long been partial to Henry Thoreau, Sherwood Anderson, Willa Cather, Hamlin Garland, and O. E. Rolvaag, truth-tellers all of the highest order. Among the New Ones, I wish especially to thank Dave Etter and Norb Blei, Linda Hasselstrom, John Knoepfle, Bill Kloefkorn, Leo Dangel, Wendell Berry, Bill Holm, Paul Gruchow, the remarkable Tom McGrath, and the equally remarkable Meridel LeSueur, Greg Kuzma, Jerry Klein, Jim Heynen, Thom Tammaro, Mark Vinz, Bob Schuler, John Judson, and Ralph J. Mills, a Chicago poet who is really a rural writer but just doesn't know it.

General Introduction

DIRECTLY ABOVE MY TELEVISION SET hangs a framed United States Department of the Interior geological survey map, 7.5 minute series, of the Granite Falls Quadrangle, Minnesota. Based on aerial photographs taken in 1964 and field checked in 1965, the map shows in remarkable detail the topographical features of my world: the meandering Minnesota River on whose banks I live, the small wooded areas along shoreline intimately familiar to me, the city of Granite Falls where I buy groceries—even man-made features like roads, railroads, drainage ditches, and field lines. Every building in this quadrangle is marked by a small black square or rectangle, including, three miles out of town, the house in which I live, the old farmhouse across the drive, and the greenhouse out back. And, just down the road, a building about which I have always been curious, identified as Pejuhutazizi Church, and another small frame building now used as a sawmill identified simply as "Indian Church." My map locates Minnesota Falls, the Northern States Power plant, the Spartan State Wildlife Management Area, and the Upper Sioux Indian Community. Its serpentine pattern of blue river explains why I need three hours to canoe what on Highway 67 is the three miles of valley between my home and Upper Sioux Agency Park. The graceful arcs of elongated blue splotches suggest the present Minnesota River has frequently changed its course from one side of the valley to the other, leaving in its path chains of oblong blue lakes, diminishing with time to sloughs and marshes. It reflects dramatically the strength of the old Minnesota River which carved this valley, two miles wide in places (the present river is not a hundred feet across), scouring right down to bottom-of-the-continent bedrock granite with waters from Lake Agassiz, a puddle of glacial melt water which covered most of Minnesota, North Dakota, Saskatchewan, and Manitoba and would have dwarfed present-day Lake Superior. The map is, in short, a manual of the natural and sociological history of the world in which I live.

The television beneath this map is also, of course, a conduit of information, but information of another sort. My own home, for example, has never appeared on its screen . . . nor has Indian Church or the town of Granite Falls or the Upper Sioux Indian Community or, come to think of it, anything on this map, including the Minnesota River Valley itself. Not even on public television programs. On television I get a curious kind of made-up information: sitcoms and cartoons and movies set either in a studio geography or a universe remote from my personal experience. I often watch baseball games, some of them played in parks I have visited in person. But I do not get a sense of television replicating my experience at the ball yard; instead I sense another made-up adventure. Not only is television presenting unreality, it seems to be transforming elements of the real world into artifice. Every time I enter the Metrodome to watch the Minnesota Twins play baseball, I feel I have entered the insides of a television set: the stadium itself feels like a giant pinball machine wired for sound and complete with television commercials playing between innings. Television news broadcasts leave me with the same feeling of make-believe. It seems to me that an increasing percentage of the information I get on those broadcasts is news about media non-people: which actor just recently died, what movie grossed how many dollars, what voice of what cartoon character died or entered the Hollywood hall of fame.

In other words, while the map and the television, both second-hand sources of information, present two very different worlds, the specifics of one are palpable, hard, tied to my day-to-day life in a way that the specifics of the other are not. The world of television is stylish and mesmerizing, but somehow its artificiality offends me. Possibly, I tell myself, I'm out of touch with the new American truth; like other rural people, I live as I live and I write as I write, and my life is simply not mainstream. But I'm unwilling to dismiss matters so easily. That television world is style without matter . . . and "form without content," I have been telling creative writing students for over a decade, "is just bullshit." I am a creature of mass and density. I have more in common with the hills and lakes and railroad lines marked by the geological survey map than with the unrealities of television, even of television news. The history whispered by the map, although it is hard and distant and in some respects quite inorganic, seems more compelling than the tales told on the television screen. I feel an affinity with the geological and sociological stories recorded on that map that I do not feel for the glitzy tales of television.

Maybe this is just me, although if it is, I have met a lot of people lately who would prefer the map of the natural world to the televised representation of modern life. One of these is my own son, Stephen, just returned from three weeks of survival training in Colorado, all keen on camping and the amplitudes of the wilderness. I think of Michelle Payne, who first introduced me to the Black Hills of South Dakota and the great wastelands of Wyoming, how happy she was with her job fighting fires for the National Park Service, how her dad once said that with Michelle and a couple of hands like her, he could have managed a fifteen hundred cow ranch.

I think of some of the writers in this book—Ed Abbey, Dave Etter, Sue Hubbell, Norbert Blei—who did not grow up small town or country, who left their urban-suburban worlds for life in the country. I think of many other writers in this book who *did* grow up in the country or small town, who escaped to urban insanity, then returned to the rural environment they once so happily left: Robert Bly, who escaped small-town Minnesota for the green fields of Harvard and thence New York, who returned to "his crumbly little place" (his phrase) to write the poems of *Silence in the Snowy Fields*. I think of Bob Dylan, who first escaped the North Country to make it big time in New York with songs like "Subterranean Homesick Blues" and "Stuck Inside of Mobile," only to return to rural music and mystique in albums like *Nashville Skyline* and *New Morning*:

> *Build me a cabin in Utah,*
> *Marry me a wife, catch rainbow trout;*
> *Have a bunch of kids who call me "Pa,"*
> *That must be what it's all about. . . .*
>   "Sign in the Window"

I think of Linda Hasselstrom, with her bum leg (still not right from when the horse threw her) sticking it out on that South Dakota ranch when she could have a soft writer-in-residence job at some university. I think of Jack Kerouac (have you read *The Dharma Bums* lately?). I think of

Ernest Hemingway and Orson Welles's fictitious *Citizen Kane*, the multi-millionaire who could have bought anything, anybody in the world . . . whose only real desire, emblematized by his old wooden sled named "Rosebud," was to return to the simplicity he had known as a youth in the rural West. And I think of John Muir and Henry Thoreau, and I conclude that this preference—albeit one point in our life—for the rural, natural world over the urban, man-made world has been going on for a very long time.

I cannot explain satisfactorily from whence this impulse derives, although my suspicion is that our national experience has something to do with America's impulse toward the rural. While most of the world's population live rural lives, Americans especially have, until very recently, lived country, on farms, in villages, and even in the wilderness. For a long time we congratulated ourselves for being an agrarian people. Nineteenth-century Americans, weary of complacent Frenchmen and Brits proclaiming that an unhealthy climate and bad diet made Americans sickly and both physically and mentally underdeveloped, had formulated a contrary argument: urban (European) man, enfeebled by what William Blake called "the mind-forg'd manacles" (of London, in Blake's case), would, transplanted in the American wilderness, grow healthy and robust—spiritually, mentally, and physically. The argument helped assuage the national inferiority complex, and worked well in a nation that was mostly space. It survived well into the twentieth century, when even city folk kept horses, raised chickens, and tended small gardens, thus maintaining ties to a rural, agricultural way of life. I am no psychologist or sociologist, but I suspect that what has been bred into the species for hundreds, no thousands of years is not easily forgotten. We believe, even today, in the benefits of country life.

Our American fondness for the countryside becomes especially strong in moments of stress . . . which, perhaps not accidentally, have increased in frequency and severity as America developed centers of urban civilization comparable to nineteenth-century London and Paris. Conditioned perhaps by our own rhetoric, we reach instinctively in a crisis for the proven agrarian past. Two stories come immediately to mind. One is Hamlin Garland's "God's Ravens" from *Main Travelled Roads* (1891):

> *Chicago has three winds that blow upon it. One comes from the*
> *East, and the mind goes out to the cold gray-blue lake. One from the*

*North, and men think of illimitable spaces of pinelands and maple-clad
ridges which lead to the unknown deeps of the arctic woods.*

*But the third is the West of Southwest wind, dry, magnetic, full of
smell of unmeasured miles of growing grain in summer, or ripening
corn and wheat in autumn. When it comes in winter the air glitters
with incredible brilliancy. The snow of the country dazzles and
inflames in the eyes; deep blue shadows everywhere stream like stains of
ink. Sleigh bells wrangle from early morning till late at night, and
every step is quick and alert. In the city, smoke dims its clarity, but it
is welcome. . . .*

*There are imaginative souls who are stirred yet deeper by this
wind—men like Robert Bloom, to whom come vague and very sweet
reminiscences of farm life when the snow is melting and the dry ground
begins to appear. To these people the wind comes from the wide
unending spaces of the prairie West. They can smell the strange
thrilling odor of newly uncovered sod and moist brown plowed lands.
To them it is like the opening door of a prison.*

Bloom, who has been withering away in a Chicago newspaper office,
cannot work—he can only dream. And his dreams are all escape. Returning to his wife in the evening, he proposes a plan:

> *"Mate, let's give it up."*
> *"What do you mean?"*
> *"The struggle is too hard. I can't stand it. I'm hungry for the
> country again. Let's get out of this."*

So Bloom gets out. He and his wife return to his native town in Wisconsin, where they find the country people at first quaintly attractive, then
small and petty and . . . well, rural. Bloom suffers a nervous breakdown.
The rural people minister to him. He blooms, recovering his health, his
sanity, his life. End of story.

A more recent bit of literary evidence is Arthur Miller's classic American tragedy *Death of a Salesman*. Toward the end of his play, Miller has
Willie Loman, the American Everyman living in Brooklyn, New York,
contemplate his own suicide while planting, in the shadows of the
encroaching high-rises, a garden which, he knows, will never grow. The
planting of this garden is taken by wife and family to be an indication of
Willie's insanity. It is in fact an indication—the only indication, really—

that Willie finally has realized he has missed something, lost his way, lost *the* way. In planting his garden, Willie seeks a lost Eden he can only half sense. Unlike Bloom, Loman dies before he can escape. His son Happy promises to stay in New York, fighting Willie's fight; son Biff projects rebirth and personal renewal somewhere out of Brooklyn, somewhere in the country, where he can find some land and work the soil. In this somewhat perplexing conclusion to his tragedy of the average American, Miller was absolutely right: the impulse, especially when an individual or a segment of American society or a generation feels it has made a mistake and needs to return to hard truths, is to return to the root. The compulsion to reclaim a lost rural experience is part of our genetic heritage and part of our national heritage.

There are, then, two great themes in rural writing: the theme of departure and the theme of return. These themes are peculiarly Christian, especially when the paradise lost is a rural paradise, and written accounts of American experiments in rural living often reiterate, consciously or unconsciously, the story of Eden and The Fall. True, the paradise to be regained is described often as the *City* of God, but in point of fact the Garden of Eden has been, for Americans, a far more compelling symbol than the jewelled city described, for example, in the book of Revelation. What Dorothy really wants is not the Emerald City but—do you believe it?—Kansas.

Whether our historical reverence of the countryside stems from our national theology, or our theological preferences stem from realities of history and geography, is difficult to say. Clearly, however, Americans attach a peculiar *moral* glory to the countryside. So strong was the association of Rural with Good that in only a few books James Fenimore Cooper was able to reverse a centuries-old Puritan tradition which associated all wilderness with the Devil himself. In developing Natty Bumpo, outdoorsman, as a Noble Savage, Cooper was assisted philosophically by Transcendentalist thinkers and writers, who found their gods not in the white clapboard churches of town and city, but in a shagbark hickory or the pickerel of Walden Pond. Besides, the dictates of necessity make self-reliance more likely in the countryside than in the city, and nineteenth-century American writers—Ralph Waldo Emerson to Thoreau to Walt Whitman himself—were grand proponents of self-reliance. Similarly, the work ethic seems particularly strong in rural writers, not only fiction writers like Willa Cather and Ole Rolvaag, but among the immigrants themselves, who in letters to the Old Country boasted fondly that what took a week or a month to accomplish in Europe could be done in America in a day or two or three. Finally, the moral superiority of country life derives to a large extent from its daily contact with what appears to be a higher reality. Urban splendors, while mighty, are vaguely insubstantial, even artificial (like the television programs of which I wrote earlier) and fragile. While we can easily imagine (and have indeed seen) the destruction of whole cities by fire, war, or natural disaster, it's nearly impossible to imagine an earthquake that would level the Rocky Mountains. Man in nature, surrounded by and often contending with the great primordial forces, develops a clearer sense of time and space, of his own physical limits and of the limits set by our environment. Rural man has a stronger sense of the vanity of human desires (and the bankruptcy of modern civilization), and becomes, for that knowledge, the stronger individual.

Thus Hemingway was obsessed with fishing, and sports, and a code of behavior forged in fishing and fighting and the other essential qualities of rural living. (I suspect that those most critical of Hemingway's code, and those most pleased when it failed him at the end, were in fact those apologists for the urban tradition who were more offended by Hemingway's preference for wilderness over "civilization" than by his language or his life.) Whether or not we share the specifics of Hemingway's world view and code, we are more than likely to share his view—and Thoreau's—that a code can best be worked out in Nature, where important business can be transacted "with the fewest distractions."

Rural literature, it seems to me, is a direct and relatively unadorned literature, prone to value content over style, and always a little apologetic for its lack of polish, which it associates somehow with urban and Eastern (and more recently Californian) writing. Exceptions abound, of course, especially among those modern writers who came to the country from more cosmopolitan environments, but Cooper (a veritable compendium of "literary offenses," as Mark Twain pointed out) and Sherwood Anderson (always a little ashamed of his own clumsiness at telling the tale) are models: they're easy to make fun of, easy to feel superior to, easy to dismiss, and sometimes painfully, embarassingly awkward. Clumsy or not, however, the tale stands on its own truth. As Hamlin Garland phrased it in articulating his credo of literary realism, "truth [is] a higher quality than beauty."

The simplicity of most rural writing is not to be mistaken for simple-mindedness, or even as a weakness. Often it is a great strength. Writing in *The Nation* at the height of the second great harvest of rural American writing (April 17, 1920), H. L. Mencken, with all his usual overstatement, made the case:

> *Scarcely a book of capital importance to the national literature has come out of the town for a generation. Nearly every work of genuine and arresting originality published in the United States during that time, nearly every work authentically representative of the life and thought of the American people, from George Ade's "Fables and Slang," to Edgar Lee Masters' "The Spoon River Anthology," and from Frank Norris's "McTeague" to Theodore Dreiser's "Sister Carrie," has been put together in the hinterland and by a writer wholly innocent of metropolitan influence.*

Mencken wrote over half a century ago. Many literary battles have since been won and lost, and there is no Mencken around today to speak for the hinterlands. Many rural writers today are aware that in presenting not-much-adorned truths about out-of-the-way places they run serious risks of being written off (that is the term: "written off," because there is nothing more damning) as "regionalists." The very word is anathema to any rural writer. Wallace Stegner observed in 1975, "I don't think there is any reason why Fred Manfred, writing in a strictly regional tradition, can't reach larger themes, any more than Jane Austen couldn't with her little English country towns." In his book *Home State*, under "Notes on Regionalism," Dave Etter offered the following somewhat defensive observations:

> *A regional writer is one who knows his or her territory—witness Faulkner, Hardy, Anderson, Frost, Joyce, Cather, Warren, and so many more. The lifeblood of any nation's literature has always come from writers who write primarily about one region, one state, one slice of familiar real estate, and I hope and trust that this will always be true.*
>
> *Yes, I'm pleased to be called regional. After all, William Carlos Williams, that superb regionalist, spoke the truth when he said, "The local is the universal." So that's the end of that. Case is closed. Ten-four. Over and out.*

Whether the steadfastly rural writer is in fact more regional than the steadfastly urban writer, is an interesting question: in a day-long seminar at Illinois Wesleyan University, small town poet Etter and Chicago story-teller Harry Petrakis concluded that an urban ethnic neighborhood is in most respects very much like a rural village, and the urban ethnic writer is often dismissed with the same excuses used to condemn rural writers to literary oblivion.

Another fear lurking in the back of many rural writers' minds is a nagging suspicion that acceptance comes only at the price of pandering to the prejudices of a literary establishment which is absolutely urban-suburban and has yet to discover that country people are not all charac-ters out of the "Dukes of Hazzard." They fear that popularity comes at the price of cliché, or half truth, or much left unsaid. The very prefer-ence for simple truth, tied to the particulars of time and place (and to the idiom of that time and place), locks a writer firmly into a region, and unless that region happens to be New York or Los Angeles, that writer will be a regionalist. But New York and Los Angeles are not by any definition rural. Neither are any of the nation's now enormous suburban-urban megalopolises. *Anything* rural will thus find its time and place outside the mainstream of American culture, and any chronicler of rural life will of necessity be a regionalist.

But it is precisely the country's alternatives to urban and suburban norms which constitute its attractiveness to readers from all American cultures. As Etter wrote (also in *Home State*), "You tell me how it goes in New Hampshire or Tennessee and I will tell you how it goes in Illinois."

In all this a paradox becomes increasingly obvious: rural people are both the morally and physically superior saviors of a nation diving headlong into decadence, and they are naive primitives, too graceless, too socially and politically conservative to take seriously. Although Willa Cather, in *My Antonia*, proclaimed hired girls from the country superior to the town girls on all points, Linda Hasselstrom remembers learning at age seventeen that "boys don't date girls who live thirty miles from town." Similarly, rural writers are both the strength of the national literary tradition, and either ignored or denigrated by custodians and guardians of that tradition's canon. Too bad Cooper, Carl Sandburg, Vachel Lindsay, Anderson, and Etter couldn't write. They should have taken Columbia University Master of Fine Arts degrees. Like rural people, rural writers feel cause to boast, feel compelled to apologize. Like rural people, rural writers don't seem to fit easily or comfortably into mainstream American culture; they are different, know they're different, and know they pay a price for being different.

Politically, the rural writer is still a populist, a firm believer that those who consume should also produce, that those who consume most should produce most, that hard work never hurt anyone. Among writers, at least, the old liberal traditions and the old liberal heroes remain strong. Writers who work hard are esteemed more than writers who do not, and writers who "go soft" are excoriated. The proper place for writers, it is assumed, is not in front of a word processor. They belong out in nature, out among people. The best training for writers is not necessarily a university creative writing program. Sometimes rural writers are so suspicious of work not done with the hands that they suspect their own vocations: a writer who is also a rancher, a poet who is also state champion hog-caller scores more points than one who sits daily in front of a word processor. As often as not, the writer is both propagandist and populist, since any split between thought and action is suspect. The delicate balance between hermit and crusader, first struck by Thoreau, finds contemporary embodiment in a writer like Wendell Berry. In some cases, however, splits have developed between those who understand their human limitations as rendering direct political action futile at worst, a distraction at best, and those who believe, with Hamlin Garland, that "to spread the reign of justice should everywhere be the design and intent of the artist."

Stylistically, as we have said, most rural writing opts for simplicity (the preference dates at least to Geoffrey Chaucer: contrast the style of his urban, courtly "Knight's Tale" with the plain, country directness of his "Miller's Tale"). Sherwood Anderson is a case in point, reluctant always to work a scene or hold the note, his stories almost in the nature of a folktale, spoken in the very recognizable (and plain) voice of the narrator, with appropriate slips and awkwardness and artless rough edges the likes of which Henry James would never have approved:

> *Joe himself was small of body and in his character unlike anyone else in town. He was like a tiny little volcano that lies silent for days and then suddenly spouts fire. No, he wasn't like that—he was like a man who is subject to fits, one who walks among his fellow men inspiring fear because a fit may come upon him suddenly and blow him away into a strange uncanny physical state in which his eyes roll and his legs and arms jerk. He was like that. . . .*

Rural writers' preference for a low style reflects many elements of their artistic credo: the preference for content over form, refusal to disesteem the truth with excessive and unnecessary elegance, suspicion that artifice is often a lie and always a distraction, a refusal to become too full of the self (deriving from a sense of human limitation), inability to separate rural style from rural form, a pose that is in fact an assertion of the self thrust so simply and directly to center stage.

Beyond a general simplicity of language and directness of presentation, two features of rural writing are prominent: a fondness for the first person singular, and a preference for non-fiction over fiction and poetry.

Rural writing seems to prefer the first person speaker, either first person direct or first person thinly disguised. Wrote Thoreau in mock apology, "I should not talk so much about myself if there were anybody else whom I knew as well. Unfortunately, I am confined to this theme by the narrowness of my experience." His followers have been legion. The other side of the coin, however, was also articulated by Thoreau: inquiries had been made concerning his manner of living, and he thought it only fitting that he should answer them, not that others should adopt his mode of life or thought, but that they should have a model for their own independence. Subsequent rural writers have found themselves in much the same position: "What is it like," people frequently ask, "living as an exile in Dairy land?" "In a town so small you don't even need a street address on your mail?" "On a ranch in western Dakota?" "In one of those old farm houses half way up the hill?" The truest, most direct answer always begins with the first person singular pronoun. "I had a farm in Africa." The first person rural pronoun is honest and simple. It contains an element of self-reliance, and yet there is not much ego in the rural first person, for usually the rural writer assumes that what he or she has done, you too might just as easily have managed, had you but set your mind to it. The writers, like the people and places of which they write, are very much for real, even the interlopers who have come out themselves for a season, short or long, in the wilderness.

The most interesting question surrounding rural writing is, I believe, the degree to which it can satisfy vicariously a reader's need for the actual rural experience. To a degree more than any other kind of literature, I believe, it does not. I know of no serious readers of Thoreau who have not been impelled, at one time or another in their lives, to try something more or less resembling his two-year stay at Walden. Here we confront a final paradox: the more people seek the countryside, the more the countryside resembles what they left behind, the less countryside remains. Witness the small towns and cornfields transformed into "country estates" (suburban developments) which surround virtually all major American cities. When the rush is to wilderness, those problems increase geometrically: national parks during the summer now resemble nothing so much as instant cities of tents and mobile homes (complete with television, motor bikes, refrigerators, and noise, noise, noise). Most of the New Jersey sea shore was long ago converted into a jungle of motels, restaurants, amusements, and shops not significantly different from the communities vacationers left behind in Philadelphia and New York. Maine and New Hampshire are going bonkers . . . and the whole Southwest, not to mention upper Minnesota, Wisconsin north of the Dells, rural Tennessee, and inland Florida. And the less country resembles country, the more necessarily we rely on accounts—past and present—of others. Which do not satisfy.

Where this all ends, I do not know, but I suspect the current flowering of rural writing may be a late harvest in more ways than one. To change metaphors slightly, this book contains salt water, although the taste is sweet. Drink at your own risk.

.1.
The Farm

Introduction

"EVEN IN A BAD YEAR we were almost independent," writes Meridel LeSueur (born in 1900) of her early years on the farm. "We had to buy (or exchange work or produce for) only kerosene, wood, coffee, and flour, although we could make flour from acorns or our own corn. . . ." Shelter came with the territory or could be built from materials at hand (even today in the countryside one still sees log cabins or old frame buildings studded with hand-hewn timbers and sided with home-cut boards, their edges untrimmed). Food was home-grown and home-preserved. Clothing was made from home-grown fibers or sometimes from cut, bleached, and dyed feed sacks (which were a coarse linen, not burlap as today). Farm power was horse- and oxen-power. It reproduced itself free of charge, and it fertilized crops and trimmed grass. All in all, life on a yeoman's farm was pretty easy. . . .

This ideal was perhaps most clearly articulated by Jean de Crèvecoeur in the second of his *Letters from an American Farmer*. Crèvecoeur's farmer is free from debt and bows to no one: he is, in fact, "inferior only to the emperor of China." He is physically healthy because a little hard work never killed anyone, and he lives off the sweat of his brow: "Every year I kill from 1,500 to 2,000 weight of pork, 1,200 of beef, half a dozen of good wethers; fowls my wife has always a great stock of; what can I wish more?" A coin might rest weeks, months on the bureau, unspent. Economic independence breeds a mental independence as well, so the American farmer is strong of mind, too. Proximity to Good Mother Earth helps: Crèvecoeur's farmer's child, brought out of the house to plow with his dad, is "exhilarated" by the "odoriferous furrow," looks "more blooming" for breathing the earthy air. The farmer's pleasures are simple and ever more exquisite for their simplicity. He leaves the farm but involuntarily. No operation of farm life is not in some way pleasant. His slow but steady pace and careful attention to detail naturally evoke a dozen daily "useful reflections" which escape city-dwellers who lack the natural advantages of being born and raised on a Virginia farm. The yeoman farmer is stable, and thus sane, in a world of instability and insanity. The twentieth century migration of farmers to urban and suburban centers, coupled with increasing mechanization of larger and larger farms, has made the self-sufficient yeoman farmer remembered by LeSueur and best described by Crèvecoeur virtually extinct. Probably the habits of patience, care, and closeness to the earth that conferred on him a peculiar sanctity have also passed with the McCormick reaper, making the honest husbandman, in the words of William Gass, "an old lie of poetry." But in this, as in so much else, American mythology lags; most of us still hold the farmer morally, if not economically or intellectually, superior to his city cousin. Rural Americans especially cling to the faith.

The unfolding twentieth century splintered virtually every timber undergirding Crèvecoeur's farmer's world. This American government no longer "requires but little of us"; there are taxes to be paid, and they are always more than a mere peppercorn. If the farm is situated close to suburbia, those taxes can be ruinously high, since the land is taxed not on its agricultural use but on its potential for other purposes. (The injustice of such taxation was once memorably explained to me by this analogy: "Suppose you are a high school chemistry teacher making $25,000 a year, but your government returns your tax forms with a note: since you could potentially earn $70,000 annually as a research chemist instead of just being content with teaching high school chemistry, you're being taxed on that potential earning.) Crèvecoeur's farmer's heirs slaughter not for themselves alone, but for the market, to pay mortgages, taxes, and ever-increasing operating expenses. They are businessmen whether they like it or not. Says Linda Hasselstrom candidly of her South Dakota ranching operation, "We're in the business of transforming grass into beef."

Most American homesteaders west of the Ohio were foreign immigrants brought by Yankee merchants to labor in a market economy. Even as they homesteaded they were saddled with heavy operating cash expenses which made the life of a yeoman farmer the impossible dream.

This market economy was an open invitation to those who, in Hamlin Garland's classic metaphor, "farm the farmer": bankers, equipment and lumber salesmen, mill and elevator operators, haulers of grain and warehousers of wheat. "Plunderers, desecrators, gamblers" (this is LeSueur now), "burglars, speculators, human weevils, hoarders, thieves, world eaters enemies [who] invade the root with the cold insolence of buying and selling what they never loved." Market economy meant mechanized farming, which usually meant specialization since few farmers can afford expensive, specialized equipment for crops as diverse as tomatoes, sugar beets, livestock, and soybeans. Lately, mechanized farming has also come to require heavy chemicals—chemicals to kill last year's corn lest it sprout in this year's soybeans and clog the heads of combines, chemicals to kill rootworm, chemicals to control quackgrass and broadleaf, chemicals to fertilize depleted cropland. Chemicals that must be bought, since they cannot be "exchanged for work or produce." Chemicals which, along with bills for seed and fuel, mortgage this year's crop even as it is planted . . . necessitating crop insurance and even more bills. As much as he may subscribe to the myth of the yeoman farmer, and as eager as he may be to wrap himself in the husbandman's garb, the modern American farmer or rancher is indeed impelled by all the logic of necessity in the direction of agribusiness. No time for honeybees. Keep the kids away from machinery; it's dangerous. Better yet, get them a computer so they can help dad with cost-income projections. When they sit down to negotiate bank loans, modern farmers find cash flow a more persuasive hammer than reputation as honest individuals. And as for communion with nature. . . .

Farming in the twentieth century is hard, even in the good years. "You'll struggle," a (town) lawyer tells Patricia Leimbach's husband, "but in the end you'll make out." As always, there's more struggling than making out, and more struggling on the farm than in the law office. "There is always the rock," writes William Kloefkorn at the beginning of his portrait of Alvin Turner as farmer. The rock is, like all good symbols, multi-faceted. It represents natural hardships like rabbits and weather, and unnatural hardships like a government which allows hog prices to plummet while feed corn prices spiral upward. It represents the toughness of farm work and the toughness of the farmer himself. Clearly Turner's life is not as luxurious as that of Crèvecoeur's farmer. A sense of reality has intruded.

Kloefkorn is a realist. Leimbach is also a realist in her chronicle of farm life from a woman's perspective: long hours in the field plowing or discing or harvesting; equally long hours spent inventing ways to increase income to meet payments on more and even more land; recycling denim weathered by sweat, dirt, laundry detergent and patches atop patches; the work of loading and hauling and unloading heavy bags of potatoes to various markets; $13,780 in salary earned but not paid. Hasselstrom's diary of ranching in western Dakota, Leo Dangel's description of farm life further east are realistic accounts full of sweat, flies, heat, dirt and drudge. Natural disasters are made more difficult by government and merchant classes, by the lawyers who (always for a fee) encourage land acquisition and bankers who (always for interest) underwrite it, by city kids who think they're superior to farm kids, by a social wisdom that says women do not work except for farm girls, who are allowed all the work they want and some they don't. By an equipment dealer who sells a nearly bankrupt farmer a tractor with a cracked engine block. By passing trains dispersing cinders which start prairie fires the ranchers of Hermosa struggle all night to control. A calf jolted to life with a mouthful of manure, Hasselstrom decides, is just getting an early taste of reality. (By coincidence I was passing through Hermosa, South Dakota, when the July 1989 *Life* magazines containing Hasselstrom's article on ranching were being tucked in ranchers' mailboxes. The postmaster's parting words were, "I sure hope the *Life* article brings something good into her life. She deserves something good after all she's been through.") Consensus seems to be that, finally, there is a "making out okay" (Leimbach again), that "Payment Received" exceeds "Amount Earned," but farming sure is a dickens of a way to get through life.

Realism intrudes in other areas as well. One cornerstone of romantic farmlife doctrine is that although farmers are notoriously rugged individuals (and notoriously difficult to organize for collective action), community is stronger on the farm than among suburbanites, who may or may not know the family next door, or urbanites, who each night double-deadbolt-lock their doors against the neighbors. Jim Heynen's gang of boys clearly consider themselves as a community within a community, a kind of oppressed class of youth. Greater Hermosa gathers regularly, sometimes from emergency (prairie fires, blizzards, disasters), sometimes on more auspicious occasions like County Fair time. However, community seems not as strong as we might have been led to believe. The children of Dangel's *Old Man Brunner Country* are actually surprised to see their fathers passing the orange in a PTA evening competition, embracing, "becoming a team, winning the race." Cooperation is not, apparently, a norm in this community. Even among the high school boys themselves, the word "friend" is not often used, although friends is probably what these kids are. Hasselstrom reenacts the old rituals of County Fair precisely because they are threatened, because the threads of community appear to be unraveling. In one of her letters from Madison, Carol Bly speculates that if promised absolute secrecy and given a vote, large percentages of the rural community would resent gatherings of extended family, the community for which the countryside is so celebrated, and would prefer to gather next year just three times instead of four or five. Who really feels like being polite to a guy who'd sell a tractor with a cracked block?

If the modern farmer feels his sense of community threatened, he also doubts his vocation. He lives in even more isolation than his brother in the city and is generally reluctant about expressing opinions. Wendell Berry has been especially careful in analyzing the disintegration of Crèvecoeur's working harmony of farmer, wife, family, animals, and land. Like increasing numbers of rural Americans, Berry is suspicious of highly technological solutions to problems precipitated by high technology . . . solutions that inevitably promise more problems which will require more technology to solve. Technology, Berry has argued repeatedly, intrudes on social harmony by replacing animals with machines, isolating individuals within (expensive) machinery, by forcing the land to pay for itself at least once each generation (at today's high prices, Berry argues, this is impossible without overextending and depleting the land), and by running the farmer finally into bankruptcy and the family off the farm. It is the strain of foreclosure, of course, that brings real problems: internalized guilt over a personalized failure, dependence on public assistance or a second income become sole income (usually a wife's income, since she was the half of the partnership which had time to "take a job in town" when the farm economy started going bad ten years ago), retraining for the job no farmer really wants, resultant alcoholism and sometimes wife- and child-abuse, resultant family stress—the stories are complex and messy. Writes one farm wife, "My husband became very distressed as he watched his community and our lives disintegrate around him. He was spending more time on the phone trying to get financing than on the tractor. You could see it draining him. He became very physically abusive, and the target was me. The social worker said it was because he felt so helpless. Finally the pressure was so great, he had a nervous breakdown and was hospitalized." Every modern farm family knows at least three neighbors or former neighbors who have been through these problems.

Interestingly, in a story that is not particularly new, Meridel LeSueur identifies a very similar problem and a very similar demon. In "Harvest," Winji confronts a clear choice: his wife's affection and a new machine. As the machine's hold on Winji's imagination grows stronger, Ruth's grasp (and the grasp of their unborn child) on her husband diminishes. Our last glimpse of Winji, through Ruth's eyes, is of a distant figure, mounted happily on his new machine, waving, waving, waving goodbye. Honest, hard-working, far-sighted and ambitious, Winji has made the technological decision, a decision for income over affection, an informed and sensible decision (the machine is associated with a "lust for knowing": this story reenacts an old, old fall). It is the logically correct decision, economically cost-effective in the long range. Yet it is a choice, LeSueur warns, against life, a choice "against her and against him," a choice against the community of man, wife, family, land, and animals. It is, finally, the wrong choice, although generations of farm wives have told similar tales of their husbands' choices for newer buildings and better machinery instead of home comforts, until the animals live better than the family. In its way, Winji's decision for a new machine is not unlike Ed and Paul Leimbach's decision to buy more land. "But life inflicts its ironies on hard-working men like Paul and Ed," concludes Patricia. "I have a feeling born of long observation that in the end they will have the 'struggle'—and their widows will 'make out.'"

Increasingly farm writers have become anti-technological. Three essays in this section, each telling a slightly different story, reflect the new anti-technological bias: Verlyn Klinkenborg's essay on hay-making in Montana, Mark Kramer's description of the farmerless tomato farm in California's San Joaquin Valley, and Noel Perrin's report on maple syrup production in Vermont.

The Forty Bar Ranch in Big Hole, Montana, has been growing and harvesting hay for generations now. The operation is a curious mixture of man and machine, not technology-free, but not exactly high tech. To raise hay the Forty Bar way, Klinkenborg tells us, we'll need at least seven different pieces of equipment, including "a Cat to move the beaverslides." We'd also need tractors to pull mowers and hayforks to load haywagons. But only the Cat and the tractors are not actually made in Big Hole, so in an odd way the technology sustains the community.

Further innovation is resisted and Big Hole is "squarely at odds with the agricultural advice apparatus in this country," which condemns roundly these practices of irrigation, planting, mowing. The arguments of new technologists, Klinkenborg admits, "make sense in an office" and might even figure on a calculator, but they don't make much sense on the haying fields, which have not failed within living memory to produce hay more than sufficient to ranching needs. The old way works, so why fix it?

The California tomato harvest described by Kramer is a technologist's dream: it happens, we're told, "nearly without people," and with complete disregard to night and day. Yet the more we examine this curiously Orwellian world of a hundred million tomatoes slouching their way toward Del Monte, the more insane the operation looks . . . and the less efficient. The idea, Kramer is told, is to run the sorter belt just a little too fast, so the sorters miss just a few bad tomatoes, so that "the right percentage" of bad fruit reaches the canneries in Fullerton. Of course the sorters don't know this, just as they don't know that a more efficient machine will soon displace them entirely. (The machine will allow its operator to program an acceptable level of bad tomatoes.) Truck drivers are encouraged to push limits of speed and safety—but not to get caught and not to get in serious trouble. The tomatoes themselves, as all of us know, are bred for easy planting, quick growth, and mechanized harvest; they don't really taste like tomatoes at all. The larger farms are supposedly more efficient because, among other reasons, they allow longer rows, which allow the harvesting machines to run further between turns, which means less time lost in turning. But some guy up the road with a smaller operation breaks even at eighteen tons of tomatoes per acre, while the larger, more mechanized farm breaks even at twenty-four tons per acre. "Why? Because we're so much bigger." Presumably the bigger and better machines will not only displace more workers (the cost of their retraining, or welfare support if they're not retrained, is not figured into this equation), but make the farm effective at twenty-nine tons per acre.

The maple syrup operation Perrin describes is quite the opposite to Kramer's tomato operation. It's low technology all the way: a lot of hand labor and a few buckets bought used at an auction, buckets which already had twenty years of use on them. Yes, maple syrup can be produced using high technology: plastic buckets, special tubing, vacuum pumps, oil-fired burners. However, the rise in oil prices and the slow growth of maple trees render new technologies less efficient than old methods of collection and boiling off. Hand-carried buckets actually prove easier than plastic pipes, as well as cheaper. Power tapping drills, steam hoods, reverse osmosis equipment prove "unnecessary expenses," more helpful to those farming the farmer than to the farmer harvesting maple syrup. Operations run with old, make-shift equipment, by a single individual, on a shoestring budget, prove to be the backbone of the industry. Which, Perrin concludes, is a hopeful sign for all of us.

We all hope, secretly, that the low technology people win this battle, perhaps because we too recognize the threat technology poses to our community and our sense of vocation. Perhaps we feel a certain affection for hand labor and animal labor. Nostalgia for the old, the proven, and the safe is strong among the pieces in this section. It is evident in Donald Hall's recollection of childhood on a New England farm and his recollection of a stereotype now all but disappeared, the hired hand, Anson Freedom. Out of his setting, Freedom would be grotesque, hopelessly simple and simple-minded. He is rescued from oversimplification by Hall's use of haying to embody a harmony he obviously admires and misses—a harmony that passed with his adolescence and the older man's death, the harmony of farmer, hired man, extended family, animals, land, and simple home-made machinery.

Nostalgia underlies Maxine Kumin's retreat to one of the old New England hillside farms built a century ago by some "modest in-betweener" without resources for top-of-the-hill scenery or bottom land fertility. Like Donald Hall, who did in fact return to his parents' farm to write and live, Kumin has made a deliberate choice for the relatively rural life, although in her case she has not returned to a place with strong family ties. She sought—and found—a small fragment of the old life . . . and with it a small fragment of the social harmony that went with it, "the camaraderie of other halfway hill people."

It is Wendell Berry's "The Boundary," however, which most perfectly articulates the old values continued into a twentieth century context. The story is a kind of parable containing a modern American agrarian idyll, Berry's depiction of farm life as it ought to be. The very repetitiveness of farm work, so irksome to others, becomes a virtue: in the act of walking fence one more time, Mat confirms his relationship with the land, the legion of those who have walked this line before him (his younger self included), and those who will walk it in the future. The small job well done becomes, like the small life well lived, a measure of blessedness—for Berry as for Crèvecoeur. As Crèvecoeur's farmer tended the 370 acres his father had shaped for him, Mat tends his land—a sense of custodianship is present, and a sense of order and stability. Marriage symbolizes that custodianship to Berry, as do the smaller ceremonies of tending the symbolically broken but not yet lost stone grail, of recreating imaginatively the past within the present, of dining, of tending garden and house, of carrying on through hardship. Berry sees virtue in the simple, the repetitive, and the familiar. There is nourishment—water, garden, produce, a waiting meal—in little things well tended. The farmer is absorbed into his community and is blessed, even in his death.

Especially in his death.

And money is not even a consideration.

·1·

Letter II from an American Farmer

Jean de Crèvecoeur

On the Situation, Feelings, and Pleasures of an American Farmer

As you are the first enlightened European I had ever the pleasure of being acquainted with, you will not be surprised that I should, according to your earnest desire and my promise, appear anxious of preserving your friendship and correspondence. By your accounts, I observe a material difference subsists between your husbandry, modes, and customs and ours; everything is local; could we enjoy the advantages of the English farmer, we should be much happier, indeed, but this wish, like many others, implies a contradiction; and could the English farmer have some of those privileges we possess, they would be the first of their class in the world. Good and evil, I see, are to be found in all societies, and it is in vain to seek for any spot where those ingredients are not mixed. I therefore rest satisfied and thank God that my lot is to be an American farmer instead of a Russian boor or an Hungarian peasant. I thank you kindly for the idea, however dreadful, which you have given me of their lot and condition; your observations have confirmed me in the justness of my ideas, and I am happier now than I thought myself before. It is strange that misery, when viewed in others, should become to us a sort of real good, though I am far from rejoicing to hear that there are in the world men so thoroughly wretched; they are no doubt as harmless, industrious, and willing to work as we are. Hard is their fate to be thus condemned to a slavery worse than that of our Negroes. Yet when young, I entertained some thoughts of selling my farm. I thought it afforded but a dull repetition of the same labours and pleasures. I thought the former tedious and heavy, the latter few and insipid; but when I came to consider myself as divested of my farm, I then found the world so wide, and every place so full, that I began to fear lest there would be no room for me. My farm, my house, my barn, presented to my imagination objects from which I adduced quite new ideas; they were more forcible than before. Why should not I find myself happy, said I, where my father was before? He left me no good books, it is true; he gave me no other education than the art of reading and writing; but he left me a good farm and his experience; he left me free from debts, and no kind of difficulties to struggle with. I married, and this perfectly reconciled me to my situation; my wife rendered my house all at once cheerful and pleasing; it no longer appeared gloomy and solitary as before; when I went to work in my fields, I worked with more alacrity and sprightliness; I felt that I did not work for myself alone, and this encouraged me much. My wife would often come with her knitting in her hand and sit under the shady tree, praising the straightness of my furrows and the docility of my horses; this swelled my heart and made everything light and pleasant, and I regretted that I had not married before.

I felt myself happy in my new situation, and where is that station which can confer a more substantial system of felicity than that of an American farmer possessing freedom of action, freedom of thoughts, ruled by a mode of government which requires but little from us? I owe nothing but a peppercorn to my country, a small tribute to my king, with loyalty and due respect; I know no other landlord than the lord of all land, to whom I owe the most sincere gratitude. My father left me three hundred and seventy-one acres of land, forty-seven of which are good timothy meadow; an excellent orchard; a good house; and a substantial barn. It is my duty to think how happy I am that he lived to build and to pay for all these improvements; what are the labours which I have to undergo, what are my fatigues, when compared to his, who had everything to do, from the first tree he felled to the finishing of his house? Every year I kill from 1,500 to 2,000 weight of pork, 1,200 of beef, half a dozen of good wethers in harvest; of fowls my wife has always a great stock; what can I wish more? My Negroes are tolerably faithful and healthy; by a long series of industry and honest dealings, my father left behind him the name of a good man; I have but to tread his paths to be happy and a good man like him. I know enough of the law to regulate my little concerns with propriety, nor do I dread its power; these are the grand outlines of my situation, but as I can feel much more than I am able to express, I hardly know how to proceed.

When my first son was born, the whole train of my ideas was suddenly altered; never was there a charm that acted so quickly and powerfully; I ceased to ramble in imagination through the wide world; my excursions since have not exceeded the bounds of my farm, and all my principal pleasures are now centred within its scanty limits; but at the same time, there is not an operation belonging to it in which I do not find some food for useful reflections. This is the reason, I suppose, that when you were here, you used, in your refined style, to denominate me the farmer of feelings; how rude must those feelings be in him who daily holds the axe or the plough, how much more refined on the contrary those of the European, whose mind is improved by education, example, books, and by every acquired advantage! Those feelings, however, I will delineate as well as I can, agreeably to your earnest request.

When I contemplate my wife, by my fireside, while she either spins, knits, darns, or suckles our child, I cannot describe the various emotions of love, of gratitude, of conscious pride, which thrill in my heart and often overflow in involuntary tears. I feel the necessity, the sweet pleasure, of acting my part, the part of an husband and father, with an attention and propriety which may entitle me to my good fortune. It is true these pleasing images vanish with the smoke of my pipe, but though they disappear from my mind, the impression they have made on my heart is indelible. When I play with the infant, my warm imagination runs forward and eagerly anticipates his future temper and constitution. I would willingly open the book of fate and know in which page his destiny is delineated. Alas! Where is the father who in those moments of paternal ecstasy can delineate one half of the thoughts which dilate his heart? I am sure I cannot; then again, I fear for the health of those who are become so dear to me, and in their sicknesses I severely pay for the joys I experienced while they were well. Whenever I go abroad, it is always involuntary. I never return home without feeling some pleasing emotion, which I often suppress as useless and foolish. The instant I enter on my own land, the bright idea of property, of exclusive right, of independence, exalt my mind. Precious soil, I say to myself, by what singular custom of law is it that thou wast made to constitute the riches of the freeholder? What should we American farmers be without the distinct possession of that soil? It feeds, it clothes us; from it we draw even a great exuberancy, our best meat, our richest drink; the very honey of our bees comes from this privileged spot. No wonder we should thus cherish its possession; no wonder that so many Europeans who have never been able to say that such portion of land was theirs cross the Atlantic to realize that happiness. This formerly rude soil has been converted by my father into a pleasant farm, and in return, it has established all our rights; on it is founded our rank, our freedom, our power as citizens, our importance as inhabitants of such a district. These images, I must confess, I always behold with pleasure and extend them as far as my imagination can reach; for this is what may be called the true and the only philosophy of an American farmer.

Pray do not laugh in thus seeing an artless countryman tracing himself through the simple modifications of his life; remember that you have required it; therefore, with candour, though with diffidence, I endeavour to follow the thread of my feelings, but I cannot tell you all. Often when I plough my low ground, I place my little boy on a chair which screws to the beam of the plough—its motion and that of the horses please him; he is perfectly happy and begins to chat. As I lean over the handle, various are the thoughts which crowd into my mind. I am now doing for him, I say, what my father formerly did for me; may God enable him to live that he may perform the same operations for the same purposes when I am worn out and old! I relieve his mother of some trouble while I have him with me; the odoriferous furrow exhilarates his spirits and seems to do the child a great deal of good, for he looks more blooming since I have adopted that practice; can more pleasure, more dignity, be added to that primary occupation? The father thus ploughing with his child, and to feed his family, is inferior only to the emperor of China ploughing as an example to his kingdom. In the evening, when I return home through my low grounds, I am astonished at the myriads of insects which I perceive dancing in the beams of the setting sun. I was before scarcely acquainted with their existence; they are so small that it is difficult to distinguish them; they are carefully improving this short evening space, not daring to expose themselves to the blaze of our meridian sun. I never see an egg brought on my table but I feel penetrated with the wonderful change it would have undergone but for my gluttony; it might have been a gentle, useful hen leading her chicken with a care and vigilance which speaks shame to many women. A cock perhaps, arrayed with the most majestic plumes, tender to its mate, bold, courageous, endowed with an astonishing instinct, with thoughts, with memory, and every distinguishing characteristic of the reason of man. I never see my trees drop their leaves and their fruit in the autumn, and bud again in the spring, without wonder; the sagacity of those animals which have long been the tenants of my farm astonish me; some of them seem to surpass even men in memory and sagacity. I could tell you singular instances of that kind. What, then, is this instinct which we so debase, and of which we are taught to entertain so diminutive an idea? My bees, above any other tenants of my farm, attract my attention and respect; I am astonished to see that nothing exists but what has its enemy; one species pursues and lives upon the other: unfortunately, our king-birds are the destroyers of those industrious insects, but on the other hand, these birds preserve our fields from the depredation of crows, which they pursue on the wing with great vigilance and astonishing dexterity.

Thus divided by two interested motives, I have long resisted the desire I had to kill them until last year, when I thought they increased too much, and my indulgence had been carried too far; it was at the time of swarming, when they all came and fixed themselves on the neighbouring trees whence they caught those that returned loaded from the fields. This made me resolve to kill as many as I could, and was just ready to fire when a bunch of bees as big as my fist issued from one of the hives, rushed on one of these birds, and probably stung him, for he instantly screamed and flew, not as before, in an irregular manner, but in a direct line. He was followed by the same bold phalanx, at a considerable distance, which unfortunately, becoming too sure of victory, quitted their military array and disbanded themselves. By this inconsiderate step, they lost all that aggregate of force which had made the bird fly off. Perceiving their disorder, he immediately returned and snapped as many as he wanted; nay, he had even the impudence to alight on the very twig from which the bees had driven him. I killed him and immediately opened his craw, from which I took 171 bees; I laid them all on a blanket in the sun, and to my great surprise, 54 returned to life, licked themselves clean, and joyfully went back to the hive, where they probably informed their companions of such an adventure and escape as I believe had never happened before to American bees! I draw a great fund of pleasure from the quails which inhabit my farm; they abundantly repay me, by their various notes and peculiar tameness, for the inviolable hospitality I constantly show them in the winter. Instead of perfidiously taking advantage of their great and affecting distress when nature offers nothing but a barren universal bed of snow, when irresistible necessity forces them to my barn doors, I permit them to feed unmolested; and it is not the least agreeable spectacle which that dreary season presents, when I see those beautiful birds, tamed by hunger, intermingling with all my cattle and sheep, seeking in security for the poor, scanty grain which but for them would be useless and lost. Often in the angles of the fences where the motion of the wind prevents the snow from settling, I carry them both chaff and grain, the one to feed them, the other to prevent their tender feet from freezing fast to the earth as I have frequently observed them to do.

I do not know an instance in which the singular barbarity of man is so strongly delineated as in the catching and murthering those harmless birds, at that cruel season of the year. Mr. _____, one of the most famous and extraordinary farmers that has ever done honour to the province of Connecticut, by his timely and humane assistance in a hard winter, saved this species from being entirely destroyed. They perished all over the country; none of their delightful whistlings were heard the next spring but upon this gentleman's farm; and to his humanity we owe the continuation of their music. When the severities of that season have dispirited all my cattle, no farmer ever attends them with more pleasure than I do; it is one of those duties which is sweetened with the most rational satisfaction. I amuse myself in beholding their different tempers, actions, and the various effects of their instinct now powerfully impelled by the force of hunger. I trace their various inclinations and the different effects of their passions, which are exactly the same as among men; the law is to us precisely what I am in my barnyard, a bridle and check to prevent the strong and greedy from oppressing the timid and weak. Conscious of superiority, they always strive to encroach on their neighbours; unsatisfied with their portion, they eagerly swallow it in order to have an opportunity of taking what is given to others, except they are prevented. Some I chide; others, unmindful of my admonitions, receive some blows. Could victuals thus be given to men without the assistance of any language, I am sure they would not behave better to one another, nor more philosophically than my cattle do.

The same spirit prevails in the stable; but there I have to do with more generous animals, there my well-known voice has immediate influence and soon restores peace and tranquillity. Thus, by superior knowledge I govern all my cattle, as wise men are obliged to govern fools and the ignorant. A variety of other thoughts crowd on my mind at that peculiar instant, but they all vanish by the time I return home. If in a cold night I swiftly travel in my sledge, carried along at the rate of twelve miles an hour, many are the reflections excited by surrounding circumstances. I ask myself what sort of an agent is that which we call frost? Our minister compares it to needles, the points of which enter our pores. What is become of the heat of the summer; in what part of the world is it that the N. W. keeps these grand magazines of nitre? When I see in the morning a river over which I can travel, that in the evening before was liquid, I am astonished indeed! What is become of those millions of insects which played in our summer fields and in our evening meadows; they were so puny and so delicate, the period of their existence was so short, that one cannot help wondering how they could learn, in that short space, the sublime art to hide themselves and their offspring in so perfect a manner as to baffle the rigour of the season and preserve that precious embryo of life, that small portion of ethereal heat, which if once destroyed would destroy the species! Whence that irresistible propensity to sleep so common in all those who are severely attacked by the frost? Dreary as this season appears, yet it has, like all others, its miracles; it presents to man a variety of problems which he can never resolve; among the rest, we have here a set of small birds which never appear until the snow falls; contrary to all others, they dwell and appear to delight in that element.

It is my bees, however, which afford me the most pleasing and extensive themes; let me look at them when I will, their government, their industry, their quarrels, their passions, always present me with something new; for which reason, when weary with labour, my common place of rest is under my locust-trees, close by my bee-house. By their movements I can predict the weather and can tell the day of their swarming; but the most difficult point is, when on the wing, to know whether they want to go to the woods or not. If they have previously pitched in some hollow trees, it is not the allurements of salt and water, of fennel, hickory leaves, etc., nor the finest box, that can induce them to stay; they will prefer those rude, rough habitations to the best polished mahogany hive. When that is the case with mine, I seldom thwart their inclinations; it is in freedom that they work; were I to confine them, they would dwindle away and quit their labour. In such excursions, we only part for a while; I am generally sure to find them again the following fall. This elopement of theirs only adds to my recreations; I know how to deceive even their superlative instinct; nor do I fear losing them, though eighteen miles from my house and lodged in the most lofty trees in the most impervious of our forests. I once took you along with me in one of these rambles, and yet you insist on my repeating the detail of our operations; it brings back into my mind many of the useful and entertaining reflections with which you so happily beguiled our tedious hours.

After I have done sowing, by way of recreation I prepare for a week's jaunt in the woods, not to hunt either the deer or the bears, as my neighbours do, but to catch the more harmless bees. I cannot boast that this chase is so noble or so famous among men, but I find it less fatiguing, and full as profitable; and the last consideration is the only one that moves me. I take with me my dog, as a companion, for he is useless as to this game; my gun, for no man you know ought to enter the woods without one; my blanket; some provisions; some wax; vermilion; honey; and a small pocket compass. With these implements, I proceed to such woods as are at a considerable distance from any settlements. I carefully examine whether they abound with large trees; if so, I make a small fire on some flat stones in a convenient place; on the fire I put some wax; close by this fire, on another stone, I drop honey in distinct drops, which I surround with small quantities of vermilion, laid on the stone; and then I retire carefully to watch whether any bees appear. If there are any in that neighbourhood, I rest assured that the smell of the burnt wax will unavoidably attract them; they will soon find out the honey, for they are fond of preying on that which is not their own; and in their approach they will necessarily tinge themselves with some particles of vermilion, which will adhere long to their bodies. I next fix my compass, to find out their course, which they keep invariably straight when they are returning home loaded. By the assistance of my watch, I observe how long those are returning which are marked with vermilion. Thus possessed of the course, and in some measure of the distance, which I can easily guess at, I follow the first, and seldom fail of coming to the tree where those republics are lodged. I then mark it; and thus, with patience, I have found out sometimes eleven swarms in a season; and it is inconceivable what a quantity of honey these trees will sometimes afford. It entirely depends on the size of the hollow, as the bees never rest nor swarm till it is all replenished; for like men, it is only the want of room that induces them to quit the maternal hive. Next I proceed to some of the nearest settlements, where I procure proper assistance to cut down the trees, get all my prey secured, and then return home with my prize. The first bees I ever procured were thus found in the woods, by mere accident; for at that time I had no kind of skill in this method of tracing them. The body of the tree being perfectly sound, they had lodged themselves in the hollow of one of its principal limbs, which I carefully sawed off and with a great deal of labour and industry brought it home, where I fixed it up in the same position in which I found it growing. This was in April; I had five swarms that year, and they have been ever since very prosperous. This business generally takes up a week of my time every fall, and to me it is a week of solitary ease and relaxation.

The seed is by that time committed to the ground; there is nothing very material to do at home, and this additional quantity of honey enables me to be more generous to my home bees, and my wife to make a due quantity of mead. The reason, sir, that you found mine better than that of others is that she puts two gallons of brandy in each barrel, which ripens it and takes off that sweet, luscious taste, which it is apt to retain a long time. If we find anywhere in the woods (no matter on whose land) what is called a bee-tree, we must mark it; in the fall of the year when we propose to cut it down, our duty is to inform the proprietor of the land, who is entitled to half the contents; if this is not complied with, we are exposed to an action of trespass, as well as he who should go and cut down a bee-tree which he had neither found out nor marked.

We have twice a year the pleasure of catching pigeons, whose numbers are sometimes so astonishing as to obscure the sun in their flight. Where is it that they hatch? For such multitudes must require an immense quantity of food. I fancy they breed toward the plains of Ohio and those about Lake Michigan, which abound in wild oats, though I have never killed any that had that grain in their craws. In one of them, last year, I found some undigested rice. Now, the nearest rice fields from where I live must be at least 560 miles; and either their digestion must be suspended while they are flying, or else they must fly with the celerity of the wind. We catch them with a net extended on the ground, to which they are allured by what we call tame wild pigeons, made blind and fastened to a long string; his short flights and his repeated calls never fail to bring them down. The greatest number I ever caught was fourteen dozen, though much larger quantities have often been trapped. I have frequently seen them at the market so cheap that for a penny you might have as many as you could carry away; and yet, from the extreme cheapness you must not conclude that they are but an ordinary food; on the contrary, I think they are excellent. Every farmer has a tame wild pigeon in a cage at his door all the year round, in order to be ready whenever the season comes for catching them.

The pleasure I receive from the warblings of the birds in the spring is superior to my poor description, as the continual succession of their tuneful notes is forever new to me. I generally rise from bed about that indistinct interval, which, properly speaking, is neither night nor day; for this is the moment of the most universal vocal choir. Who can listen unmoved to the sweet love tales of our robins, told from tree to tree? Or to the shrill catbirds? The sublime accents of the thrush from on high always retard my steps that I may listen to the delicious music. The variegated appearances of the dewdrops as they hang to the different objects must present even to a clownish imagination the most voluptuous ideas. The astonishing art which all birds display in the construction of their nests, ill-provided as we may suppose them with proper tools, their neatness, their convenience, always make me ashamed of the slovenliness of our houses; their love to their dame, their incessant careful attention, and the peculiar songs they address to her while she tediously incubates their eggs, remind me of my duty could I ever forget it. Their affection to their helpless little ones is a lively precept; and in short, the whole economy of what we proudly call the brute creation is admirable in every circumstance; and vain man, though adorned with the additional gift of reason, might learn from the perfection of instinct how to regulate the follies and how to temper the errors which this second gift often makes him commit. This is a subject on which I have often bestowed the most serious thoughts; I have often blushed within myself, and been greatly astonished, when I have compared the unerring path they all follow, all just, all proper, all wise, up to the necessary degree of perfection, with the coarse, the imperfect systems of men, not merely as governors and kings, but as masters, as husbands, as fathers, as citizens. But this is a sanctuary in which an ignorant farmer must not presume to enter.

If ever man was permitted to receive and enjoy some blessings that might alleviate the many sorrows to which he is exposed, it is certainly in the country, when he attentively considers those ravishing scenes with which he is everywhere surrounded. This is the only time of the year in which I am avaricious of every moment; I therefore lose none that can add to this simple and inoffensive happiness. I roam early throughout all my fields; not the least operation do I perform which is not accompanied with the most pleasing observations; were I to extend them as far as I have carried them, I should become tedious; you would think me guilty of affectation, and perhaps I should represent many things as pleasurable from which you might not perhaps receive the least agreeable emotions. But, believe me, what I write is all true and real.

Some time ago, as I sat smoking a contemplative pipe in my piazza, I saw with amazement a remarkable instance of selfishness displayed in a very small bird, which I had hitherto respected for its inoffensiveness. Three nests were placed almost contiguous to each other in my piazza: that of a swallow was affixed in the corner next to the house; that of a phoebe in the other; a wren possessed a little box which I had made on purpose and hung between. Be not surprised at their tameness; all my family had long been taught to respect them as well as myself. The wren had shown before signs of dislike to the box which I had given it, but I knew not on what account; at last it resolved, small as it was, to drive the swallow from its own habitation, and to my very great surprise it succeeded. Impudence often gets the better of modesty, and this exploit was no sooner performed than it removed every material to its own box with the most admirable dexterity; the signs of triumph appeared very visible: it fluttered its wings with uncommon velocity, an universal joy was perceivable in all its movements. Where did this little bird learn that spirit of injustice? It was not endowed with what we term reason! Here, then, is a proof that both those gifts border very near on one another, for we see the perfection of the one mixing with the errors of the other! The peaceable swallow, like the passive Quaker, meekly sat at a small distance and never offered the least resistance; but no sooner was the plunder carried away than the injured bird went to work with unabated ardour, and in a few days the depredations were repaired. To prevent, however, a repetition of the same violence, I removed the wren's box to another part of the house.

In the middle of my parlour, I have, you may remember, a curious republic of industrious hornets; their nest hangs to the ceiling by the same twig on which it was so admirably built and contrived in the woods. Its removal did not displease them, for they find in my house plenty of food; and I have left a hole open in one of the panes of the window, which answers all their purposes. By this kind usage they are become quite harmless; they live on the flies, which are very troublesome to us throughout the summer; they are constantly busy in catching them, even on the eyelids of my children. It is surprising how quickly they smear them with a sort of glue, lest they might escape; and when thus prepared, they carry them to their nests as food for their young ones. These globular nests are most ingeniously divided into many stories, all provided with cells and proper communications. The materials with which this fabric is built they procure from the cottony furze, with which our oak rails are covered; this substance, tempered with glue, produces a sort of pasteboard which is very strong and resists all the inclemencies of the weather. By their assistance, I am but little troubled with flies. All my family are so accustomed to their strong buzzing that no one takes any notice of them; and though they are fierce and vindictive, yet kindness and hospitality has made them useful and harmless.

We have a great variety of wasps; most of them build their nests in mud, which they fix against the shingles of our roofs as nigh the pitch as they can. These aggregates represent nothing, at first view, but coarse and irregular lumps; but if you break them, you will observe that the inside of them contains a great number of oblong cells, in which they deposit their eggs and in which they bury themselves in the fall of the year. Thus immured, they securely pass through the severity of that season, and on the return of the sun, are enabled to perforate their cells and to open themselves a passage from these recesses into the sunshine. The yellow wasps, which build underground, in our meadows, are much more to be dreaded, for when the mower unwittingly passes his scythe over their holes, they immediately sally forth with a fury and velocity superior even to the strength of man. They make the boldest fly, and the only remedy is to lie down and cover our heads with hay, for it is only at the head they aim their blows; nor is there any possibility of finishing that part of the work until, by means of fire and brimstone, they are all silenced. But though I have been obliged to execute this dreadful sentence in my own defence, I have often thought it a great pity, for the sake of a little hay, to lay waste so ingenious a subterranean town, furnished with every conveniency and built with a most surprising mechanism.

I never should have done were I to recount the many objects which involuntarily strike my imagination in the midst of my work and spontaneously afforded me the most pleasing relief. These may appear insignificant trifles to a person who has travelled through Europe and America and is acquainted with books and with many sciences; but such simple objects of contemplation suffice me, who have no time to bestow on more extensive observations. Happily, these require no study; they are obvious, they gild the moments I dedicate to them, and enliven the severe labours which I perform. At home, my happiness springs from very different objects; the gradual unfolding of my children's reason, the study of their dawning tempers, attract all my paternal attention. I have to contrive little punishments for their little faults, small encouragements for their good actions, and a variety of other expedients dictated by various occasions. But these are themes unworthy your perusal, and which ought not to be carried beyond the walls of my house, being domestic mysteries adapted only to the locality of the small sanctuary wherein my family resides. Sometimes I delight in inventing and executing machines which simplify my wife's labour. I have been tolerably successful that way; and these, sir, are the narrow circles within which I constantly revolve; and what can I wish for beyond them? I bless God for all the good He has given me; I envy no man's prosperity, and with no other portion of happiness than that I may live to teach the same philosophy to my children and give each of them a farm, show them how to cultivate it, and be like their father, good, substantial, independent American farmers—an appellation which will be the most fortunate one a man of my class can possess so long as our civil government continues to shed blessings on our husbandry. Adieu.

Eight Short Prose Pieces

Jim Heynen

The Man Who Kept Cigars in His Cap

One man kept cigars in his cap. When the boys sneaked up behind him during threshing and tipped it off, the cigars fell on the ground. This was very funny to everyone, until one day the man put a rat in his cap. It was a rat the man had fed eggs so it was friendly to him.

When the boys tipped off his cap this time, the rat jumped to the ground and frightened them so that they screamed and looked foolish.

The boys said, He can't do this to us! We're boys from Welcome #3! Which was their township and schoolhouse number.

So they found a big tom cat that liked to kill rats. They took a striped engineer's cap like the cigar man wore and put a rubber rat under it and taught the tom cat to find the rat.

After a while they went walking toward the threshing machine where the man was working. One of the boys carried the tom cat on his shoulder, and no one paid attention when they walked behind the man. The tom cat saw the engineer's cap and jumped at it as the boys had taught him to do.

But instead of a rat, the man had put a skunk under the cap. It was an orphan skunk the man had fed milk when it was a baby, so the skunk was friendly to the man.

When the tom cat landed on the man's hat, the skunk let go its spray in the cat's eyes and on the heads of the boys. Everybody laughed at the boys as they ran away to the stock tank screaming and crying.

When the boys had cleaned themselves, the biggest one said, He has made us look like fools again. Let's do something to keep him from making everyone laugh at us.

So they started practicing with their sling shots and practiced until they could hit a tin can from 30 yards. They crawled behind a fence where no one could see them.

The man had put an owl under his hat, thinking that this time the boys would have a weasel. It was an owl he had helped in winter when its eyes were frozen shut so the owl was friendly to him.

When the man was not expecting it, the boys shot their stones at his cap. The stones hit the cap, some going through the cloth and through the feathers of the owl, killing it.

No one scolded the boys for killing the owl. Everyone agreed that the man had been asking for trouble right from the start when he put cigars in his cap.

The Man Who Sharpened Saws

His old green truck had a soft bump to it when it came down the drive, but the man who sharpened saws was cruel. He'd kick cats or feed steel shavings to the chickens, if they bothered him. Usually they didn't—the boys cleared his way of chickens and hid the cats.

More than cruel, he was a communist. The boys heard that was how he really made his money so they made him a song:

Bumpity bumpity
Here comes the commie
In his old green chevy.

Nobody asked him to come, but when he did, everybody brought their saws and watched him file in his easy way. That sound was music to the boys. At least, the nearest they had ever heard to a violin.

When he finished his filing, he charged a dollar. Once he forgot even that.

That's how everybody knew he was a communist. And there were his tracts the boys might never accept, ones with big pictures of men with picks and shovels.

He's rotten to the core, said one of the men.

But the boys noticed how pure the saws glistened and they'd celebrate his leaving by sawing wood. Any wood. It all was butter to them then.

By spring, when he was almost off their minds, the saws got dull, and the boys could hardly cut a willow branch to make a whistle. So they sang

Bumpity bumpity
      NOW where's that commie
            In his old green chevy!

It was hard going with a dull saw, but one spring even the men talked about putting up signs to keep him away. And they would have, if they could have found saws sharp enough to make the signs.

The Breeding Circuit

Every springtime for many years this man took his stallion Bayard on a breeding circuit. They'd stop at the same farms yearly, the man leading his stallion from one place to the next where the mares would be waiting.

Bayard was a magnificent beast, muscular and spirited and noble in his carriage, yet gentle with the mares. He was the most famous horse in the county, and farmers on his circuit were as proud of the mares Bayard bred as Bayard's master was of his fine stallion. It was said that in time every young horse in the area would look a little bit like Bayard.

And it must have been happy work leading that stallion on the breeding circuit because Bayard's master was always smiling when they left one farm for the next.

When tractors came, farmers started selling their horses for dog and mink feed. A few kept their mares a few years just to have them bred by Bayard, but pretty soon the breeding circuit was a lonely walk. Farmers working the fields with their tractors would see the man and his stallion slowly moving along the road, often stopping to stare at the empty pastures. It was very sad.

Then one year only Bayard's master was walking along the road. One farmer whose mare had been a regular customer in the old days was in the back of his field when he saw the man approaching his farmyard. The farmer felt sorry for him and wondered what had happened to Bayard but did not have the time to leave his field work. Later, when the farmer drove his tractor home for dinner, Bayard's master was just leaving down the driveway to his farm. He was heading toward the next farm on the circuit, still smiling the way he had in the old days.

Bloating and Its Remedies

One night the cows broke through the fence and got into the alfalfa field. In the morning they were lying in the field bloated. Their stomachs were big mounds, and the hair on their sides looked like grass on a steep hill.

The neighbors came with their remedies. One with a sharpened metal tube which he stuck into the paunch to let the air out. Another with a small hose which he covered with grease and inserted into the anus. Another with a solution of soda and soap which he made the sick cows swallow.

The boys watched the men working on the bloated cows. Soon they wanted to help. But the men would only let them work on one they already had given up for dead. One boy pulled the tail. Another pulled the tongue. The others ran and leaped onto the swollen body. Jumped on it. Kicked. Fought for a place on the top.

The men pointed and laughed at the boys' foolish efforts. But then the cow exploded, belching and farting and coming back to life in gusts of hot alfalfa fumes. Leaping to its feet, bucking and throwing one of the boys into the air. Then it stood there looking mixed up, shaking, and letting the boys stroke its back and rub its ears.

The boys and cow stood there a while, looking at each other, and the boys almost cried at the sight of this resurrection.

Then the men reminded them to go to the house and wash themselves so that they would not smell of it in school.

The First-Calf Heifer

There was a young heifer that was trying to have her first calf. She lay in the barn tossing her head, heaving, and stiffening her legs, but nothing came out.

The boys stood behind her watching for the front hooves to appear, the tongue between them, and then the nostrils. They had helped lots of calves come into the world before, taking hold of the front feet and pulling when the cow heaved, one time helping with the block-and-tackle when one was too long in coming.

But this one was different. There were no feet showing to take hold of or tie on to. When the heifer pushed hard, they could see part of the calf—a black and white Holstein—but no front feet. They couldn't tell for sure what part of the calf was showing through the heifer's small opening.

After a few hours the men were there trying to figure out what to do. One man with small hands worked his arm in when the heifer was not pushing. He couldn't figure it out. Things were twisted around and none of the parts were the way they should be for a calf to be born. One hoof was pointed up against the spine, and the man with small hands couldn't move it.

Pretty soon it looked as if the heifer was going to die. She quit trying and lay there waiting for the men to do something.

This calf doesn't want to be born! shouted the man with small hands, and he pulled as hard as he could at the wedged parts. Then he went in with his jackknife and started cutting parts of the calf off and pulling them out.

We're going to have two dead ones if I don't get this out of there, he said. He hurried with his jackknife, cutting off parts that were stuck, pulling them out and putting them into a feed sack which the other men had brought. When all the stuck parts were cut off, what was left slipped out like an egg yolk. The men put this into the sack too. As soon as the heifer looked all right, the men went to the house for coffee.

The boys stayed with the heifer a while, waiting for the afterbirth to come. But instead, the heifer heaved once and the head of another calf appeared. The boys grabbed its front legs and pulled. This calf came out so fast that the two boys fell over backwards and the calf landed on their laps. The boys laughed to see a calf that was not all cut up into pieces. They rubbed the new calf with straw and let it suck their fingers. It was a healthy bull calf, and they led it to the heifer's teats. It was very hungry from waiting all this time to get out.

When the new calf had drunk its fill, the boys decided to play a joke on the men. They carried the calf outside and called, Come look! Come look! One of the boys had emptied the sack behind the barn so he was holding a bloody empty sack for the men to see.

When the men ran out to see what was happening, the oldest boy said, We decided to put that calf back together! Then they put the new calf down and it walked.

But the men were not fooled for a minute. By God, she had twins, the man with the small hands said.

Still, it was a good joke, and the boys teased the men with it for a long time after that.

Bat Wings

On summer nights when the sun was just setting and things were starting to get boring, the men sometimes went outside with their shotguns to shoot bats. On good nights the bats circled and dived for insects over the men's heads. The men swung their guns wildly and took quick shots from the hip. But other times the bats hovered high overhead, giving the men a chance to take careful aim. That is when they found out just how good the bats' radar is, because the bats moved so quickly that the shot missed them. At those times they seemed to jump in midair, looking more like hummingbirds than bats.

The shotguns were an awfully noisy way not to get bats, and it was the boys who thought of a quieter way. Fishing for them. They took some of the grown-ups' fly rods and started casting the flies into the sky.

When the hunting isn't good, you should try fishing, said the oldest boy to the men. The men put their guns down to watch. Soon one of the boys lured a bat by casting the fly rod. The bat dived for the fly and was caught. The boy reeled the bat in from the sky while the men watched, looking surprised with their quiet guns across their knees.

Pretty soon the men tried it too and sometimes had the same good luck the boys were having.

After they caught a half dozen bats like this, they noticed that the bats never had the hook in their mouths. It was always stuck in the bats' wings.

If they have such good radar, said one of the men, why don't they catch the fly in their mouths?

Maybe their wing is just like a hand and they have to catch the fly first, said the littlest boy.

No one paid attention to the youngest boy, because his idea sounded so silly, but many years later—at thousands and thousands of dollars expense—somebody in a laboratory, using infrared cameras, found out that bats really do catch their food in their wings, using them like hands to feed themselves.

You write the moral to this story:

Scar Tissue

He stopped chewing on his cigar and laid it down next to the lantern. It simmered there on the burnt spot where he had laid other cigars. He picked out an egg from the bucket and rubbed at a spot with the damp dishcloth. He would start talking now. The boys sat at the edge of the hoop of lantern light and looked up at his face.

Well, I'm a pretty old farmer, he said. I can remember the days before rat poison. There was as many rats back then as good stories. Good talkers and good workers. In those days you could tell the speed of a man's hands by checking the scar tissue on his legs.

He held an egg up to the lantern light, as if he could tell this way which ones would be culled out at the hatchery.

One time we was shelling corn. Corn shelling. Five or six of us shoving corn in the hopper. We was going for a thousand bushels. Big crib. And big rats. I don't know how many. Lots of them. They was legion. We seen their tails slickering in the corn. They was digging right ahead of our scoops.

He laid an egg down and wiggled his short forefinger as if he could make it look like a rat's tail. He picked up his cigar, chewed on it, and laid it down on the burnt spot again.

First thing you gotta know about rats is they're dumb, but they know when they're in trouble. The second thing you gotta know is that when they're in trouble, they don't run for light—they run for dark.

He adjusted the wick on the lantern. The egg bucket was not quite half empty. The boys leaned back on their hands.

So we was almost to the bottom of this corn when we run into them rats. First one trickles out. Then the whole works. Like when one ear of corn falls out of the pile and then it all comes down. So we start stomping. I must of stomped a dozen of them when the fella next to me misses one when he stomps. And that rat swickers around real quick and comes at me from the side where I can't see him. He is looking for a dark tunnel. And he finds it. My pants leg! He saw that little tunnel over my shoe and up he comes. I had on wool socks, the thick kind that gives rat claws something good to dig into. Good footing. So he gets his claws in my wool socks, looks up the tunnel, and don't see daylight. He must of thought he was home free for sure.

He paused and rubbed his chin while the boys squirmed.

Well, you know, in those days, rats was always running up somebody's leg. Specially during corn shelling. I guess it was just my turn. You just had to figure on it a little bit during corn shelling. Like getting stung when you're going after honey. You was always hearing somebody yelling and seeing him kick his leg like crazy in a corncrib or pulling his pants off so fast you'd think he got the instant diarrhea.

Now let me show you the scar that critter give me.

He pulled up his overalls. His leg was white and hairless. Just below the knee, on the inside calf, was a set of jagged scars.

That's how fast my hands was, he said. I grabbed that sucker before he could clear my shoestrings. He rubbed the scars with the tip of his finger, gently, as if they were still tender.

There's the top teeth. And there's the bottom, he said. I grabbed and I squeezed. And I squeezed. And the rat bites. And he bites. I felt his rib cage crack, but his teeth stayed in me like they was hog rings. I guess we both got our way. Now he's still hanging there dead inside my pants while we killed the rest of them rats. Then I pried him loose with my pocketknife. Stubborn sucker. But he knew a dark tunnel when he seen one.

There were only two eggs left in the bucket. He rinsed the washcloth and took one more chew on his cigar. He picked up an egg and rolled it over in his hand looking for spots.

Now almost any old farmer can tell you his rat story. They've all had a rat or two up their pants. But just ask him to show you his scar tissue. I can wager you this—the ones with slow hands won't show you where they got theirs.

The boys giggled a little as he put the last egg into the crate with his careful hands. It was time to make their escape. The door to the shed was open.

Watch out for the dark now, he said as the boys filed out, their shirttails fluttering behind them into the night.

You Know What Is Right

Before the boys went into town on Saturday nights, the grown-ups always warned them to stay out of trouble by saying, You know what is right. Always those words: *You know what is right*. After hearing the same warning over and over many times, the boys figured they really must know what is right. But when they were on the downtown streets, it was not always so easy.

One Saturday night the first thing that happened was some town boys gave them the finger and yelled,

Hey, Stinkeroos,
You got cowshit on your shoes!

The oldest boy answered quickly by giving them the finger too and yelling,

Oh yeah, city fellow?
Your underpants is yellow!

The youngest boy said, Yelling at them like that, was that right?

The other boys were not sure. They walked away from the town boys thinking about it. Was that right? Was that right? they said over and over to themselves. A little later they stopped in front of a new car show window. They leaned against the glass and looked up and down the streets, wondering what might happen next.

Stop leaning against that window! shouted the sales manager. The boys knew the man could tell by their work shoes and overalls that they were from the farm. Inside, the man was showing new cars to a well-dressed couple who looked as if they must be town folks. Let's do a stinkeroo, said the oldest boy.

The boys made their plan. They got into the next car that the well-dressed couple would be looking at. The boys who could passed gas. Then they all slipped out and closed the car doors behind them. They watched from across the street as the couple got into the stinky car. The man looked at the woman and said something. Then the woman spoke to the man with an angry look on her face. They were blaming each other for the smell, all right. Then they got out and looked at the sales manager as if maybe he were the one who made the car stink. They shook their heads and left.

The boys tried not to laugh in front of the couple, but then the youngest boy said, But was that right?

This made one boy laugh aloud, and soon they were running down the street laughing loudly. Stop! said one of the boys. I'm going to wet my pants!

But would that be right? asked another. Now they all laughed so hard that they were all afraid of wetting their pants.

The gas station john! one of them shouted. They ran toward it to relieve themselves. The oldest boy was the first one to the urinal.

Inside the urinal was a handful of change. It was the kind of urinal that has a few inches of water in the bottom, like a cup. Someone had dropped the change into the urinal and then urinated on it. If anyone flushed the urinal, the change would go too. But for anyone to get the change he would have to stick his hand into someone else's urine.

The boys looked at each other, and it was as if for the first time that night a clear light went on in their minds.

The oldest boy reached into his pocket for some change, dropped it into the urinal, then stepped closer and urinated over the raised ante.

Me too, said the next boy, stepping up politely. And so, in turn, each gave his share of money and urine until the mound of coins glowed like a collection plate.

Now *that* was the right thing to do, said the last boy as he buttoned up.

·3·

In Double Harness
Patricia Penton Leimbach

Not Another Farm!

The way of farm life today is by acquisition. One man dies or moves to town and his neighbor buys up the property. Every farmer knows the pattern and every farmer's wife agonizes with it.

Paul always coveted the Schuster farm: "Best soil in the area." His father had said the same thing of "the Schuster place," and his grandfather and his great-grandfather. In an era when land was cheap and tilling a field something of an extravagance, some Schuster forebear had dug up the place and painstakingly and properly drained it. The heroics of the effort were not lost on the Leimbachs.

Paul never drove past the place in midsummer without assessing the abundance of the crops, and the envy in his remarks was ill-concealed. He really took spiritual possession of that farm years ago. Farmers are a matter-of-fact lot, and they don't rhapsodize about it, but good land means more to them than almost anything else.

When the three old Schuster brothers worked it no longer, Paul was vexed at the disuse of good cropland. It was painful for him to watch it grow up in thistles and glory vines. He was prompt to respond to a request by an heir to come over and mow the place. I should have known then that he wouldn't be happy till he owned it.

Farmer's wives, who are inclined to measure wealth by fluid assets, don't get as carried away by this drive for land acquisition, so when the property was finally offered for sale, I fought the purchase all the way.

"We already have more land than I've found time to walk over," I protested. "Don't you realize you're going to be ninety and ten years dead when that property's paid off?"

Paul had found himself an ally in his farming partner, Ed. They sat down with their record books and Ed's little calculator and figured that they could make it.

"What are we gonna do with another old house and all those barns?" I argued.

"We'll sell them. Just keep the land. People are dying to get a little place in the country that they can fix up."

"The only way you could fix up that house is with a bulldozer!" I said. I might as well have saved my breath. I was a voice crying in the wilderness. With farmers the land instinct is deeper than reason.

They discussed the matter with their lawyer, who shared their optimism. "You can't go wrong," he said. "You'll struggle for a while, but in the end you'll make out." All they heard was the "make out." All I heard was the "struggle."

So we bought the Schuster place. Paul and Ed are as happy as clams. They go with their shovels and repair the drain tiles; they mow and trim and lay out plans of the crops to come.

I stay home and wring my hands and think of ways to increase the income to meet the payments. But life inflicts its irony upon hardworking men like Paul and Ed. I have a feeling born of long observation that in the end they will have the "struggle"—and their widows will "make out."

One Man's Junk

With the present mania for recycling, "getting rid of" may soon be an idiom gone from the language. Certainly getting rid of anything down on the farm these days is next to impossible.

For years now Paul has been wanting to burn the kettle house, a little vine-covered shack in the backyard, containing a great kettle built into a brick fire pot used once for rendering lard and making apple butter.

"Don't you dare touch that!" I say. "It's a period piece—irreplaceable!" And besides, I need it. It's crammed with old newspapers and pop bottles and flower pots and push lawn mowers and dozens of other things awaiting recycling.

Forty feet south of the kettle house is the ice house crowded with antique tools and household implements and Great-great-grandfather Leimbach's gilt-framed portrait. The seed house, forty feet to the north, houses a wealth of old doors and windows and lumber and porch swings and butter churns and discarded appliances "somebody might need sometime."

The horse barn, in addition to motorcycles and bicycles, shelters old harnesses and horse collars and wagon wheels.

That's just the beginning. There's also the granary, the chicken coop, the hay barn, and the "big barn"; then there's Newberry's barn (when you buy a neighbor's farm his fields and buildings traditionally carry his name ad infinitum); Newberry's milk house, and Newberry's toolshed. And every weathered building has its cache of farm treasures.

For a hundred years the Leimbachs have prevailed on this site, enlarging, expanding, acquiring, with neither a sale nor a fire. The accumulation is overwhelming.

Every time I get ready to do a good cleaning job, some yahoo comes around blabbing, "Don't throw THAT away! They're paying fabulous prices for that stuff." Where, I ask, are all these people paying "fabulous prices" for barn siding, mason jars, old bottles, rusty nails, wavy window panes, hand-hewn beams, and—are you ready for this one?—worn and faded blue denim?

Yup! I was just fixin to go down cellar and make a clean sweep of those dusty old overall jackets I inherited when we bought the Newberry place, and then I read it right there in *Time:* Saks Fifth Avenue was selling old denim jackets for twenty-six bucks! And bikinis made of old denim go for twenty. Wow! If Nelson Newberry thought his overall jackets might be resurrected as bikinis, he'd have himself reincarnated!

Odd as it seems, there's justice in placing such value on genuinely faded blue denim. (It seems they try to simulate the faded effect, but imitations don't command the price of the real McCoy.) In order to achieve the desired quality, blue denim needs to do a lot of bending in the sun and whipping in the wind. It needs to be dunked in farm ponds and ground into the slag of playgrounds. It needs to fall from horses or motorcycles or bicycles a few dozen times, and be forgotten on a fence post for a while. It should kick around in a dusty pickup truck a couple of weeks. Most of all it needs to be soaked repeatedly in sweat. It has to lie in dirty laundry piles on damp cellar floors and hang for long spells on clotheslines. It needs to be shortened and lengthened again and mildewed in the mending, nursed back to health with patches.

Then, and only then, does a garment of blue denim have integrity. And believe me, it's worth more than any city slicker's money can pay.

I wonder idly, while I'm pondering the new values, if there's any market for a retread farmer's wife in her late forties who can bake bread in an old black stove, make apple butter in one of those old kettles, can tomatoes (she raised herself) in those old mason jars, make butter in a stomp churn, and manufacture faded blue denim as a matter of course.

Subterfuge

You can "smell" a new tractor coming two or three years ahead. The first thing a wife notices is that the thrill is gone. (The thrill of the old tractor.) He no longer fondles the fenders, caresses the hood. No more does he run in the face of a storm to get 'er under cover. A crumpled muffler may lean into the wind for months on end. The vinyl seat splits and he seems not to notice. Foam oozes from the rupture and is carelessly obscured beneath a feed bag. Gone is the pride that once moved him to slyly detour visitors through the tractor shed. It doesn't seem very important anymore who drives the old thing—the wife even gets a crack at it.

"Give you any trouble?" he'll ask casually at lunch. Then as he chomps down on a cob of corn he'll move into phase two of the buildup: innuendo and suggestion.

"Been startin' a little hard lately. Thought maybe you'd notice. . . . Shifts a little rough, don't you think?" You can agree or disagree. The psychological workup is in progress. The seeds of disturbance have been sown.

"D'ja notice how much oil that tractor's been burning?" he'll say to his son one day, making sure you're within earshot. And then he'll interrupt his bookkeeping some early morning by walking into the kitchen (ostensibly for a snack) and remarking, "Guess how much we spent for repairs on the 706 last year?" And then go on to name a figure half again as high as the household budget.

"What!" you shriek. "On that new tractor?"

"That 'new tractor' is ten years old."

"You're kidding!"

"I am not kidding. We bought it the year the willow tree fell on the outhouse. Remember? I'll tell you how long we've had that tractor. We've had it so long it's paid for."

The next thing you know, there's a tractor dealer coming by on trumped-up charges, hanging around the gas pump, leaving slick four-color brochures in your kitchen, "giving" your husband the kind of time he's charging ten dollars an hour for back at the shop.

Someplace in the campaign you'll be treated to the "poor lil' ol' me" routine.

"Russ and Chuck traded their John Deeres in on a coupl'a 4-wheel-drive Cases two years ago. Don, Lenny, George, and Bob—they've all had a complete tractor turnover since we bought that 706. . . ."

Then there's the scare technique: "Parts are gettin' harder and harder to locate for that machine. Wouldn't surprise me a bit if they quit making them altogether."

About this time you'll find a list of figures on a scratch pad conveniently placed to catch your eye—over the sink next to the telephone, on the back of the john. You think at first it's an inventory of all your holdings.

"Is this anything you want to keep?" you ask.

"Oh that—that's just something the tractor dealer jotted down for me. Uhhh . . . Some figures on a tractor—and a plow. New tractor takes a new plow. Says he'll take my old tractor on trade and give me just what I paid for it ten years ago. That takes'er down to about fourteen thousand."

"Fourteen thousand dollars! Holy cow! We don't want to buy the business. We just need a tractor!"

You realize suddenly that it's all over.

Disking Dilemma

As tractor work goes, disking is about as low on the skill scale as you can go. Any ten-year-old can do it, and that's my problem. Every time I begin to think I've developed some proficiency at the business, I have a ten-year-old growing up to take over the job.

The disk and cultipacker operation aims to break up and smooth the soil immediately ahead of the planting. It isn't essential that it be done in perfectly straight passes, but why do my swaths always curve at the ends like fetal backbones? Why do I always finish with a pie-shaped wedge at the land center? How is it that I only remember the turning brakes when I've made three curvaceous rounds that resemble canoe paddles?

Paul drives past and shakes his head. I know he's hoping nobody from the Soil Conservation Service will come over for aerial photography until he gets a chance to straighten out the kinks with his planting.

It's a complex business of throttling down, raising the disk, applying the turning brake, and turning simultaneously. It really shouldn't be too challenging for a woman who has driven in a kindergarten car pool with an old stick shift. All I know is that it's a lot simpler for a ten-year-old with an uncluttered mind than a romantic in middle age who gets carried away with the scent of wild blackberry.

By the time I've coordinated all four actions I'm three feet into the adjacent wheat field. If I'm lucky, it's the neighbor's wheat field; more often it's my own.

That's just the routine part of the job. It's the less routine things that defeat you, like looking back and discovering you're carrying along a boulder, your disk is riding four feet off the ground, and you've piled up what amounts to an Olympic ski jump. You *know* it's gonna take three years of fitting and planting to level that hump.

You hop down to deal with the problem and dirt sifts into your shoes. Sometimes you have to dig through a mass of weeds and cornstalks with your hands to free it from the disk. I wouldn't be caught dead lifting that rock if there were anyone within half a mile, but with all the grace and grunt of a TV wrestler I hoist it up onto the disk. These are the times when you ask yourself why you didn't marry a bookkeeper, or why you married at all.

Overconfidence is an ever-present hazard. Get absorbed in studying cloud patterns, and you're likely to "awake" to find you've ripped out three fence posts and a mile of barbed wire.

The supreme aggravation is looking back to discover that you lost the cultipacker someplace in the last round. I have even heard tales from women who said they were approaching something big and black in the field and discovered it was the disk. At all events, this involves passing around again, backing up the disk, and hoisting the half-ton cultipacker into place. This may be child's play to a ten-year-old, but I seldom accomplish it without an "(expletive deleted)."

Without that little shot of adrenaline provided by the expletive, no woman could ever move the tongue of the son-of-a-gunning cultipacker three inches to the left without getting a hernia. Then . . . when herculean effort has finally accomplished the miracle of bringing one hole above the other, you realize that you forgot to look for the connecting pin!

There is one hazard about this disking business which I have not yet faced. The thought of it often wakes me up nights in a cold sweat. On the occasion when I turn too short and hang the whole rig up on a telephone pole, I'm going to hoof it for the barn and turn in my Slow-Moving Vehicle sign.

And what do you suppose runs through the mind of a farmer's wife when she's out there on that tractor disking for endless hours? Ah, she has her dreams. And one of them, I suppose, is of being some day a truly liberated woman. But I can promise you one thing—after twenty-five years of bouncing up and down with a disk across a rutted field, I'm not going out and burn MY bra!

Rye Is Renewal

A field is a field is a field, I suppose, until you've planted one and tended it and seen it yield in such abundance that you know the mysteries of the universe are working together for your increase. And then a field is a quiet miracle.

I knew it tonight as we came down the lane in the November twilight. All afternoon I had turned under with a disk the last of the spent potato fields while Paul followed with the grain drill. Vegetable ground is sown with a cover of rye as we finish with the crops from early September through early November. Most of our fields are already secured under its lush carpet.

All along the lane the staggered plantings are in varying stages of emergence. If the weather is warm and the soil damp, it comes through in four or five days, first in a haze of reddish-brown shoots almost indistinguishable from the soil. Then the scattered shoots become yellow-green rows. It's a thrill to watch, especially if you have been party to the sowing.

The secrets of the sower are soon evident in those ever more distinct drill rows. You see where he doubled over, or ran out of seed, or skipped a little teardrop section in turning. As the shoots thicken and grow longer the sower's errors are obscured in the mass of chartreuse.

Sun shining on rye against a frame of flaming woods or fencerow is magnificent, as it was tonight. The last of the gold light washed over the rye fields. The long shadows fell over the newly sown field, neatly grooved by the grain drill, like chocolate frosting scored with fork tines.

I thought back to the spring when Paul and I came out with our seed potatoes and fertilizer to tackle this last field. There it lay with those same orderly grooves, formed by the disk that time, ready for the commitment of seed.

How much work has gone between that day and this—the planting, the harrowing, the spraying, the hilling, the weeding, the irrigating, the harvesting. The barns are full to overflowing, truckload after truckload has gone down the road to the city. This last planting will emerge under the warmth of snow, put down a root structure to hold and aerate the soil, then nourish and loosen it when plowed under as humus in spring. The earth gives up its fullness, the farmer takes his yield, and rye is renewal.

Work Is for Women and Horses

Part of the traditional conditioning of growing up female is acceptance of the admonition that a woman shouldn't do any heavy lifting. This, of course, is a bunch of hooey, and goes a long way toward locking women into the "helpless little female" image.

It goes without saying that nobody, man or woman, should do any heavy lifting if he or she has never done any. The man who lifted the cow, after all, went out and lifted the calf every day. And each body has a physical limit that is not too difficult to ascertain. I learned at the age of sixteen that I could not lift a 100-pound sack of cement, though I'm sure there are women around who could work up to the job.

Girls who grow up on the farm are often exempt from the weight-lifting stigma. They get a steady diet of lifting experience on fertilizer bags, hay bales, feed sacks, tomato baskets, and cabbage crates. In my own case (growing up in apples, marrying into potatoes) the transition was a simple one. Moving down from crates (which weigh seventy-five pounds) to bags (which weigh fifty) was no trick.

So because it is a job I can manage and enjoy, I spend a lot of my days on the highways delivering potatoes. The men who run supermarkets and roadside stands are often thrown into panic when a woman appears with a load of potatoes, until they realize that I can hold up my end of the unloading detail.

I always feel a bit sorry for the guys with genuine problems. "Gee, I'd like to help you, but I've got a bad back," or "I wish I could help, but I'm recovering from a heart attack" are apologies I hear often. Considering the stereotype of the physical superiority of men, it has to be humiliating for a man to watch a woman unload a truck of potatoes.

That isn't my intention. If I ever felt sorry for myself as a workhorse, I have long since revised my sympathies. And as I push on into middle age and hear more and more of these back and heart reports, I feel better and better.

One day it was a woman who gave me a heart-attack story with apologies. Then she stood there smoking as I unloaded my fifty bags of potatoes.

"You poor kid," she mumbled.

"Gosh," I said, "You don't have to feel sorry for me. After all, it isn't everybody who can do this work!"

Left After Taxes

"Hey, make me up a list of what you earned last year," hollers my husband from the next room where he's winding up his six weeks' dalliance with the income tax.

Well, let's see. What did I earn last year? A skilled homemaker should be worth at least $3 an hour, and she invests about 12 hours a day. Of course, I wasn't here every day and Sundays were light. . . . Say 300 days at $36 a day. That's $10,800 to start with. And then a farmer's wife has "hired man" tasks to lengthen most of her days. I went to work with my thinker and my eighth-grade math and I drew up my list. Amount earned:

Skilled homemaker	$10,800.00
Labor foreman (equally skilled)	1,280.00
Tractor driver (mediocre)	450.00
Truck driver (fantastic skill)	450.00
Purchasing agent (reputation—"Scotch")	500.00
Sales clerk, real estate agent, phone operator, social secretary (gracious, knowledgeable, witty)	300.00
	$13,780.00

I laid it on the bookkeeper's desk and left. In a calculated few moments there was a roar. "That's not what I wanted!"

"But you asked me what I earned. I thought my estimate was conservative, considering my education and experience."

"Would you please make me up a list of what you actually got," he said in exasperation.

"Ohhh . . . what I actually got . . . Well, that's something else. . . ."

Much later I slipped in and laid my second list on his desk: Payment Received for Services Rendered:

> sunrise over the valley about 300 times (No failure with the sun.
>   I was absent a few times.)
> sunset over Schmalz's barn
> a picture frame of barn siding
> picnics in the pasture
> two dogs working a woodchuck hole
> rain coming across the potatoes in August
> new peas on counter, June 10
> sweet corn on counter, July 10
> new potatoes on counter, August 10
> a banana cream pie (from scratch) from a son on Sunday
>   morning
> swamp buttercups in May
> rural free delivery
> an oriole in the pear tree
> hot buttered rum by a hearthfire in a blizzard
> a wrought-iron kettle restored by a son
> lunch alone with my honey on weekdays
> sons coming in to supper from working with their father
> a golden gingko tree in October
> little kids in leaf piles
> impromptu visits with neighbors
> a chipmunk on the back steps
> one perfect coal bin full of wood, coal, and a neat stack of
>   kindling (Beautiful!)
> walking down the road on a starry night
> bare branches against the moon and the winter sky

wheat emerging under snow
more love, support, concrete assistance, and encouragement
    than I deserved

Total value: Incalculable.

And to it I affixed the following note:

I found it impossible to assign a value to these things, and I suppose it's just as well. If the IRS figures a way to tax our real wealth, we'll be bankrupt. No matter how you slice it, "Payment Received" exceeds "Amount Earned."

4

Haying, a Horse, and a Hired Man

Donald Hall

IN MY SUMMERS ON THE FARM, I saw only a few remnants of the flourishing low-life of former years. Once when we were riding in the buggy my grandfather pointed out a whole clan squatting vacantly on the dirt in front of an old chicken coop. Their heads turned to watch us, but they showed no expression. "That's what's left of the Turpinses I've told you about," he said.

The only representative of the four families whom I really knew was Anson Freedom, and he was an exception. In fact, he was at least negatively good, for he didn't steal or drink or lech. He was half-witted, but he could work at simple chores, and he was my grandfather's hired man. I knew him first the summer I started haying. In my last summers on the farm, my grandfather and I did the work by ourselves; when I wasn't there my grandfather mowed and raked and brought in the hay by himself. But in my first years of haying there were three of us, and Riley the old horse. I thought of haying as something that my grandfather and Anson and Riley and I did together. Anson's silly grin and Riley's bony rib-cage belong to those hot afternoons in the cut fields, as much as the teasing and story-telling voice of my grandfather.

Anson had been a hired man for my grandfather and Benjamin Keneston thirty years earlier, and he was the clown of my mother's childhood, too. He was the most hideous man I have ever seen. His face, of which the features were cramped together in a squat triangle, was always burned red, but his enormous bald head was as white as soap. The skull was wide but not high; it shot back flatly over the four deep lateral wrinkles that crossed above his eyes. His small eyes were surrounded by lines so deep that they looked like make-up. His nose was boneless and flattened between protruding cheekbones. His mouth usually curved upward in an empty-headed grin which created more of the thick, muscular ropes of wrinkles. When he walked he stooped so much he seemed hunchbacked, and his arms swung loosely at his sides.

When my mother was a girl, during the first war, Anson's cousin Lewis induced him to leave the farm for a war job, which could not have been more complicated than sweeping up. Anson did not return until 1939. I heard of it that spring in Connecticut, and I had listened to so many stories about him that it was as if Tom Sawyer had moved into the next block. My grandmother had simply looked out her window, one morning, to see Anson Freedom with twenty years added to him come shuffling up the driveway. At least he seemed to remember that he had left abruptly, for he was afraid to come close enough to knock. He had returned, they learned later, because Lewis had refused to feed him any longer. My grandmother leaned out the door and told him to go to the barn, where Wesley was cleaning the tie-up after milking.

"Hullo," said Anson to my grandfather. My grandfather told me later that he was so surprised he nearly dropped the hoe through the floor to the pile of manure under the barn, but of course he wouldn't let Anson know it. "Why Anson Freedom," he said slowly, "I thought you were dead."

"Now don't yew start plaguin' me!" The pattern that I was to hear so often during our afternoons of haying—the teasing and the half-serious rage which had begun so many years before—had started immediately. One of the subjects on which Anson could be teased was death; I once saw him bend down below the window of a car to avoid seeing a cemetery.

"You come back to work or watch me working?" said my grandfather.

"Kin I work?"

My grandfather thought for a minute. "The truth is I don't have any money to pay you with, Anson." Milk was fetching him up to twenty dollars a month, and he had no other regular cash crop. Eggs paid for the grain he fed the hens, and the chicks and lambs paid his taxes.

"I got to work."

"A dollar and a half a week, board and room?"

"That's fine." And my grandfather handed Anson the hoe to finish scraping the manure.

I had been prepared even for the way he talked by my grandfather's imitations of him. It was pathetic to think that he had changed so little. There is a story I remember about his boasting. He had gone hunting deer with another cousin, and when he came back he told everyone that he had shot a buck right through the eye. My grandfather knew that Anson couldn't hit Ragged Mountain point blank, but he said nothing until one noon when he had a sudden intuition. My grandfather said, "Now Anson Freedom, didn't your cousin shoot that buck and then tell you to go up to it and shoot it through the eye after it was dead, just so you could tell folks about it? Or maybe because he'd already shot one himself, and one was all he could shoot on his license?"

Anson's mouth dropped open wider than ever. "He said he wouldn't tell nobody, the old fuel!"

In the summers when I knew him, he fished occasionally, but I never knew him to do anything else but his chores. He seemed to have only one bodily desire. He was a glutton for candy bars. Most of his salary, which increased with war prosperity to three dollars a week, was spent on Milky Ways, Powerhouses, and Baby Ruths. His closet was littered with empty cases. At night after supper he would slink off to bed and lie in the dark peeling off the wrappers and sucking toothlessly at the chocolate bars.

At noon he would come into the sitting room, when my grandparents listened to the news and weather from a Concord radio station. One of my summers with him, he became obsessed by a thirty-second advertisement for Peter Paul's Mounds which an announcer read between the news and the weather. The rest of us learned not to hear the hired, yum-yumming voice, but Anson believed in the emotion the voice claimed to represent, and his jaws worked sensually as he listened. "Mus' tas' awful good," he said each day.

The problem was that none of the local stores carried Peter Paul's Mounds. Henry Powers, whose little store was post office, gas station, and grocery for West Andover, asked his distributor for a box at Anson's request, but the box never came. Anson began to talk about them at the supper table, during haying, and while he and my grandfather were milking. "Mus' tas' awful good," he would say. One time he found me alone. "Donnie," he said, "you hain't never eaten those Peter Paul's Mounds?" I told him I thought I had, back home in Connecticut, and that I remembered liking them. It was as if I had mentioned to a French teacher who had never left White River Junction, Vermont, that I was a personal friend of Marie Antoinette's.

Once every summer I would spend a day by myself in Concord or Franklin. I would take the Peanut in the morning, leaving at 7:05, and return by the Peanut in the evening, at 7:30. My grandfather would take me down and pick me up in the buggy. In the city, I would wander around the business section, working my way through the news stands, lending libraries, and the book store. I would always end up exhausted in the public library reading the new books. This particular year my big errand was accomplished quickly. The first drug store I came to sold me a box of Peter Paul's Mounds, and I had to carry the box all day.

Anson ran up the stairs with it when I got back and I suspect that he ate all twenty-four bars before the morning chores. He never mentioned them again, but when the ad came over the radio he would look at me and smile with our secret.

The summer of 1939 I was ten. Anson had returned the April before. I remember the first day I helped in the haying, a hot afternoon in late June. My grandfather was haying on the fields of a widow who lived a mile and a half north on the main road. She gave her hay to the farmer who would do a neat job, for she hated the look of a field that was left with hay untrimmed around the rocks, and with the scatterings unraked. My grandfather had hay on his own fields, but he liked to help the old lady.

Mornings were for mowing. In the early hours before the hay was dry enough to cut, Anson and my grandfather milked the cows and turned them out to pasture, cooled the milk, fed the hens, picked up the eggs, and set the milk out for the truck. A rainy day was good for repairs to the wagons and machinery, or for splitting wood. A day that threatened rain, or a day when the hay was drying after a rain, might be good for salting the sheep or for paying a visit to the heifers. But if the day was good, Anson would hitch Riley to the mowing machine at nine-thirty or ten, and he could cut a two-acre field by noon. He was a good workman at a job he had done often. My grandfather loved a scythe, and he would trim, coming close to the rocks without ever denting the edge of his blade. In the breast pocket of his work shirt he carried a blue-gray whetstone, and I loved to watch the fast sweeping motion with which he sharpened his blade, leaning the end of the handle in the dirt at his feet. Later, when I was fourteen, he taught me how to use a scythe, and he sharpened an old scythe for me so that I could help him trim.

At noon they usually returned for lunch and a brief rest before the afternoon haying. On the day I was to start my life's haying—doing what my grandfather had done for fifty years—lunch was a special occasion. Since I was not old enough to mow, I would help in the afternoons only. My Aunt Caroline was home that week, and at twelve o'clock we packed a huge laundry basket full of lunch into her car and drove to the widow's field. Near the house itself were a few fruit trees, and under one of them we spread an old quilt. There were a Thermos of coffee and a Thermos of milk, hard-boiled eggs, pork sandwiches, cheese sandwiches, an onion sandwich especially for me, pickles, cake, cookies, and a custard pie.

The brilliant orange and yellow paint brushes grew wild at the edge of the road, and beside the widow's house the lilacs were still blooming. The sky was bright, with only a few clouds, and there was a light breeze from the south. "Good day for haying," said my grandmother.

"I'll *say* it's a good day," said my grandfather.

I noticed that my grandmother had on a new apron, and my grandfather's blue work shirt had the creases of a shirt that has never been washed. He was the most excited of us all. He hummed little songs in his tuneless way, and his eyes were sharp with the occasion. His sweat made the dark shirt darker under his shoulders and in the middle of his chest. His lean arms were burned, and his bald head was pale when he took off the cloth cap he always wore in the sun. He told how he had helped out, a hired boy, for ten cents a day when he had been my age. The farmer had threatened to charge him for drinks of water, out of the horse trough at the barn, when they brought in their loads of hay. "It's a mighty deep well," the farmer had said, "but you look like to drink it dry, Wesley Wells."

When we had eaten the last pickle and had shaken the crumbs from the quilt, Caroline and my grandmother packed the empty basket and the quilt into the Studebaker. My grandmother told me to watch I didn't take too much sun, and to make sure that Gramp was careful when he turned from the field onto the macadam on the way home. Then they drove off.

I walked back to the apple tree, where my grandfather was stretched out in the shade, taking a shortened version of his rest after lunch. Anson was sitting cross-legged, chewing on a piece of grass. He smiled at me, and I think he was excited too. I sat down beside him.

In a moment my grandfather leapt to his feet, standing so quickly that it seemed there was no intermediate position between lying down and standing up. "Well, now, you jackrabbits!" he said. "Anson, you go draw some water for Riley. Donnie, you come with me and we'll hitch Riley up to the rake." We strode off to the other side of the field, through the swathes of cut hay, to the tree where Riley was tied. Just beyond was a stone fence that separated the field from an old pasture which was growing up with brush and young pine. Riley was old and thin in 1939; his ribs stuck out and there was a sore on his left hip. My grandfather hated to work him, but he had no alternative, and he tried to make up to Riley with apples and sugar and praise.

Now, after he cooed a little at him, he untied Riley's rope and led him over to the big metal horse-rake, and backed him between the shafts. The mowing machine was next to it, leaning on its shafts like two long stiff arms, and the hayrack was just beyond.

My grandfather buckled the leather straps of Riley's harness, and I looked up to see Anson trudging across the field with a big pail of water. Riley leaned his neck into the pail and drank in long, rhythmic swallows. "You'll lose it, old baby, pulling out there in the sun," said my grandfather, and when Riley lifted his dripping jaws from the bucket, my grandfather climbed into the saddle-shaped metal driver's seat, beside the handle which controlled the rake, and moved off to the cut hay.

He raked the hay into even strips, thirty feet apart, that crossed the field parallel to the road. After he had completed three trips up and down, Anson began to rake the strips into small haystacks. He used the bullrake, a great wooden rake about five feet wide with teeth a foot long and four inches apart. I took the tiny rake and trimmed around rocks and trees, getting the hay which my grandfather missed. When I had gathered enough to carry, I pulled it to the nearest strip or haystack. After I had finished with the trimming, I sat in the shade and chewed on pieces of grass.

There were no sounds but the whirr of an occasional car, and the shouts of my grandfather to Riley, "Whoa! Back! Get up!" The sun was high and I was already sweating, but the breeze cooled me off as I sat in the shade. I practiced noticing the details of texture and color around me. That summer I had a theory that if you looked at anything closely enough, it would be beautiful. I examined a blade of grass, its stringy construction and the layer of gray which seemed to underlie the green.

Soon little haystacks spotted the whole field. My grandfather finished making his long strips before Anson could pile more than a third of the hay, so he drew the rest into piles with the quicker horserake. It took about forty-five minutes to do all the raking.

My grandfather drove Riley next to the hayrack and climbed down from his metal perch. He took his cap off and wiped the sweat from his face and neck and head with a huge handkerchief. "Don't have any hair to catch the sweat with," he said, as I had heard him say often. Riley was finishing the pail of water. My grandfather sat down for a moment in the shade of the hayrack, until Anson walked up to us, pulling the bullrake. "Hot in the sun," my grandfather said. Then he stood and unfastened Riley from the rake and backed him into the shafts of the hayrack. "Time to pull some more hay, old Riley, old baby," he said, and he fastened the straps.

Anson climbed into the hayrack and clucked to get Riley moving toward the nearest pile of hay. "You'll rake after," my grandfather said to me. "You pull the bullrake after us now, and I'll show you what you'll be doing." We walked together to the first haystack. Anson handed my grandfather his pitchfork. My grandfather sank it expertly into the pile of hay and lifted most of it up to Anson, who placed it where he wanted it for his load. The rest of the haystack followed, leaving a scattering of hay too small to be picked up by a fork. Anson clucked, and Riley automatically began to move toward the nearest stack.

My grandfather let his fork drop. "Now this is what you do, boy," he said. He took the bullrake and in a few turns of the rake he had skillfully gathered the strands of hay left at the site of the pile. "See how to hold it?" he said. I thought I did, but when I first held the rake, he had to rearrange my hands for me. The difficulty was to keep the long teeth flat on the ground, neither pointing up and missing the hay nor pointing down and losing the hay in bounces. I managed to pull the wisp of hay over to the next pile, where Anson, who had jumped down from the wagon to pitch on, incorporated it in his next forkful. Then Anson climbed back up, my grandfather finished pitching the new pile on the rack, and I raked after, while they moved on. I was careful not to miss a single fragment, and I caught up with them just in time for my grandfather to pitch up what I had scavenged.

Anson packed and stowed and treaded the hay with the rote skill of forty years, building the load at the edges evenly back and front, so that the hay leaned out way over the rails, but was fastened securely by forkfuls treaded into the middle. The floor of the rack was only one plank wide near the front where it was cut by wells into which the wheels banked on a sharp turn. The single plank rested on the beam which was the wagon's main support, and to which the axles were attached. (I remember, from my early childhood, the late spring when my grandfather and Washington Woodward built the hayrack; the floor was thick boards bought from a lumber mill, but the rails were split birch, and the spokes which joined the rail to the floor were sticks with the bark still on them.) In loading the hay, it was tricky to cover the wells so that you could walk over them without losing hay, or even falling through yourself. At least it was tricky for me, when in later years I loaded for my grandfather.

Fifteen of the piles filled the old rack. Anson treaded the last two into the middle as binders, and we were ready to take the load home to the cow barn. I must have been hurrying with my raking, for I had forgotten to pay attention to what I was doing; when my rake stuck, I tugged at it and one of the foot-long teeth broke off. For a moment, in my chagrin, I wanted to hide it, but I knew that there would be no hiding it for long. I raked over to my grandfather. "I broke a tooth. The rake stuck in a skunk hole or something."

He laughed. "I reckon we'll have to take it out of your wages." He put the broken tooth in his long overall pocket and I went back to raking after the last pile. When I finished, my grandfather picked up the whole rake and swung it over his head, so that the hay didn't fall from it, and laid the final strip of hay across the back of the load, like a narrow fringe of curls on a girl's forehead.

We left the rake and the rest of the equipment behind us, along with considerable hay, and climbed into the wagon by the hub and the rim of a huge front wheel. For this ride, my grandfather handled the reins, while Anson dangled his legs over the back of the rack and sucked on a piece of hay. My grandfather said he loaded himself there to keep the rest of the hay in place. Only a few pieces of hay scattered behind us as we started home, leaving a trail which the cars soon dispersed. Riley walked deliberately, and needed no direction. The cars zipped past us impatiently, but we paid no attention to their haste. It was the opposite of everything in Connecticut, to sit, sinking, in a pile of hay, while a bony old horse pulled a load of hay in a home-made rack along a New Hampshire road at three miles an hour. The smell of the hay was as great a pleasure as the softness of it, and I was full of the joy of haying.

My grandfather was happy, too. He kept talking about the significance of the day, as if he were one of the preachers of his childhood who read great meanings into common events. He talked about raking after when he was a boy, and pointed to fields across the valley in which he had pulled a bullrake. When we reached, finally, the yard in front of the farmhouse, old Riley stopped without orders beside the kitchen door. My grandmother and Aunt Caroline were sitting on the porch. "I'll start the coffee, Wesley," said my grandmother. "And how do you take to haying?" she said to me. "Did he do a man's work?" she asked my grandfather.

"I guess he *did*," said my grandfather. "And you see how much quicker we're through." Then he told me to go inside where it was cool, while he and Anson pitched off in the barn. Pitching off took only two men, and I was scarcely big or strong enough to be one of them.

Inside, my grandmother had drawn a pitcher of cold water from the deep well behind the house. The faucet was fed by a shallow well up the hill, and the water was not exceptionally good. The water from the deep well was the best I ever tasted, but it was hard to draw; we had to prime the pump and spill out several gallons before we had the real essence of it. The sides of the pitcher were frosted from the cold water, and I poured myself a tumbler and drank it in sips to prolong the pleasure. I waited in the dark, cool sitting room for my grandfather and Anson to finish pitching off. Then they came in to drink their coffee.

Soon we were off again, riding back to the widow's field in the empty hayrack. Anson drove, while my grandfather and I sat in the back and dangled our legs. We brought in two more loads that day, and I broke another tooth in the bullrake. After supper, my grandfather found a good piece of wood in the shed, and he sat on the chopping block and carved two teeth out of it, while I watched him. Even though I had made him extra work, I was happy because he was so happy. He told a dozen stories while he was carving. Anson was already up in his room over the kitchen. The light was out, and he was probably lying in the dark with his candy bars. It was really the start of something, and all that summer, six days a week except when it rained, I pulled a bullrake in my grand-father's fields.

In later years, I learned to pitch on and to load, as well as to rake after, but I never learned to handle myself as well as my grandfather. He had his own particular pitchfork, which he had used as long as he could remember. Old black tape was wrapped around the wood where it joined the steel, to prevent a split from widening. The upper part of the handle, where his hands had slipped for many decades, shone as smooth as glass. He knew its moving balance as he knew how to walk or to milk a cow.

It was loading that I loved the most. I loaded when Anson had left the farm again, or when I could persuade him to trade with me and rake after. Of all the sensations retained from my summers, the most clear is this: I stand on top of a load of hay in the July sun; the load builds well out over the sides; my grandfather is catching his breath, so for a moment I stand still; I am high enough to catch the wind which is coming from the lake at my back, while the sun continually pushes down at me; the heat of the sun and the cool of the wind mingle, and neither is right without the other; a light sweat, always drying in the air, covers my bare back, and the chaff clings to it like the down on my face.

Each afternoon we pitched, loaded, and raked, and we usually brought in three loads to pack away in the dark barn. If it looked like rain we might hurry to bring in four, and keep the long line of Holsteins waiting outside the barn, milk dripping from their swollen udders. If we had to travel far for the hay, we might make two huge loads instead of three regular ones. In particular there was a single acre, beyond the boys' camp on the other side of the lake, which was solid with clover and sweet grass. Whenever we hayed there, my grandfather said, "Oh, but the cattle will love to eat *this* load!" I don't know why the land was so rich, but the tangle of growth was so thick that it was hard to walk through. And woodchucks had dug so many holes that we had to lead Riley among them by the bridle, walking in front to survey the mined land. It was so far away that we built the load far out on each side—nearly as wide as the dirt road we traveled on—and finished the acre in two afternoons of two loads each.

Sometimes our hay was poor, especially if it had stood too long uncut after it had turned ripe. The juice drained out, and in the winter the cattle would turn up their great pink-and-black noses at it. There was a meadow in back of the Blasingtons' which was thick enough—your foot sank in the soft turf—but in which the weeds and the wild flowers grew as grossly as the pungent grass. Often when we brought in a load from the Blasington meadow we stored it in the lofts of the sheep barn and spared the finicky cattle. For one thing, sheep didn't have milk to be off-flavor on the doorsteps of Manchester.

The greatest enemy was rain, unless there was no rain at all, and then drought was the enemy. What you wanted was a nice rainy Sunday, after you had cleaned a big field on Saturday afternoon, and before you cut another on Monday morning. When it rained and we had no hay down, I had a good lazy day and was glad of it; I read and wrote all day while my grandfather chopped wood and mended tools. But if hay was down when it rained, I was as gloomy as anyone. The stacks had to be torn apart and the hay spread to dry, and then turned over to dry on the other side, and then stacked again. Sometimes we would just finish stacking the hay a second time, when a thundershower would soak it again. If it was three times wet, even the best hay turned into a mud-colored and odorless straw. We could either throw it away or pass it off on the poor sheep.

We saw a lot of Merrimack County, haying, because my grandfather owned parcels of land in odd places, and because we sometimes took in someone else's hay, like the widow's. We talked in the rack, going and coming, and we talked even when we hayed. When I teased to pitch on, after Anson had left, it was partly because my grandfather would have more breath for talking if he loaded. But even while he pitched—and I stood above him taking in the sun—his soft voice kept on in the intervals between forkfuls. I heard so much about the past that the hayrack seemed a machine which took us into another century; or more as if it were big enough to contain the summers of his whole life at once. I lived with him when he was my age, and through all of his seven decades.

In the first years of haying, when Anson was with us, there was a part of me that assumed that I would spend the rest of my life haying. I could clearly see the three of us in the same fields of summer until the end of time, with the same bony Riley pulling the same frail hayrack—old man, half-wit, horse, and boy, locked in a scene where they repeated the same motions under the same skies. This tableau existed alongside the knowledge of death, that perpetual elegy which began earlier than I can remember, and which grew in the end to color everything I saw of the farm. The two feelings contradicted each other, but lived together like old brothers who had not spoken for forty years.

Anson and I were children together of the same old farmer. We giggled together when my grandfather joked. In order to bring Anson into the conversation, and probably in order to work off the irritations he must have felt, my grandfather often teased him. It was like teasing a four-year-old, because Anson never responded to a provocation until it had been rehearsed for him several times. The exchanges during our after-noons of haying followed a few known paths; every choice in the conversation limited the choices of the answer, until the final sentences resembled a *déjà vu*.

Anson would be loading while my grandfather pitched on, and my grandfather would say, "Now Anson, why can't you handle these forkfuls any faster? I'm spending all afternoon down here waiting for you to make room for me."

Anson would fume. "Yew jist sind up all yew kin sind up and I kin take ceer of what yew kin sind up."

So my grandfather, who had chosen the time for his teasing to coincide with our arrival at a big stack, would strain to lift an immense forkful onto the wagon. He would aim it so that the weight of it would catch Anson on the chest, staggering him back.

Anson would turn red and shout, "Yew don't have to knock me clean off the rack, yew old fuel!" (His special pronunciations were a delight to me. He could never say "garage," but had to say "aw-mo-beel gaage." I used to puzzle myself inventing questions which would require him to use "garage" in the answer.)

My grandfather would laugh, and while Anson was still too enraged to dispose of the last forkful, he would send up another and another—until Anson humiliated himself by asking for a chance to catch up. Or Anson's abuse would grow wilder, and my grandfather would pretend to be angry. "Well, now, young man, we can't have you talking like that!" he would say, and he would stab his pitchfork into the ground and vault into the rack with sudden agility.

Anson would cower toward the opposite end of the wagon—though my grandfather had never touched him—and he would giggle and whine, "I never said nothin', Wesley."

When Anson pitched on and my grandfather loaded, which happened when his shoulder felt stiff, my grandfather had a trick which made Anson angriest of all. Anson's forkful of hay would come riding up, and my grandfather would plunge his own fork into the middle of it, twist it a little, and snap Anson's fork out of his hands. Then he would ask Anson innocently, "Why did you pitch up this old fork, boy?"

Anson would stare up at the rack empty-handed. "Wesley, yew old fuel, what yew take my fork for? I'm goin' to climb right up there and whup yew."

Once my grandfather answered, stiff shoulder or not, by making an immediate leap from the wagon to land with both forks in front of

Anson. Anson turned as white as his skull, and he didn't even listen to my grandfather's, "Yes, sir. Here you are, sir. At your service, sir."

Most of the time we worked in silence or to the quiet narrative of my grandfather's stories, which Anson appeared to enjoy too. There were two of my grandfather's Lyceum poems which Anson preferred, and would beg him to recite. He could never remember the titles, but would ask for them by a word or two from somewhere in the poem. "Kin yew say the 'blue-eyed boy' one?" If my grandfather forgot a line or a stanza, Anson would object, but he could never help by remembering a word or a line.

It was in the winter, in 1942, that Lewis took Anson away for the last time. My grandmother wrote me in Connecticut to tell me, but said that she expected him to return in the spring. Then April came without Anson, and my grandfather spread cow manure on the garden and the corn field, and plowed it under, and planted his seed, and cultivated the growing fields—all by himself. By the time I arrived in June, he had already begun to hay alone.

I helped him, and the summers began when the two of us worked in the fields alone. We expected Anson to return until we heard Lewis's motive in taking him away, and then we knew that he would never work on the farm again. Anson had turned sixty-five, and Lewis had filed his name for a pension. Anson owned no property, and the state sent him a check every month, which Anson signed and turned over to Lewis in return for his cot, his turnip greens, his salt pork, and a candy bar on Saturday nights in Franklin.

The summer of 1942 I stayed late, because a polio epidemic had made the Connecticut schools unhealthy congregations. We finished our haying the day before Labor Day. We had cut less than we wanted to, and a late spring in 1943 would mean buying hay. We had done only two loads a day, much of the time, because I was still not as strong as a man and because Riley was lame on two legs, and moved in a pain which it was pain to watch. His hair was patchy and his breath irregular and there were sores on his sides.

After the hay was stowed away, my grandfather cut the field corn and hauled it to the barn, and an ensilage crew came to the farm for one exciting day. They chopped it up in a putt-putting gasoline-driven machine and stowed it in the silo which was inside the barn—next to the stall where old Riley had trouble rising to his feet, now, after he had lain down. When they had left, my grandfather harnessed Riley once more and put the rack and the mowing machine away for the winter, under the dry roof of the shed next to the sheep barn. It was time to begin thinking about wood for the winter.

The next day my Aunt Nan, who was staying at the farm until school opened, suddenly became very interested in showing me the attic. It was a narrow loft above the room which we called the back chamber, which was also a place of storage. The attic had been filled when my mother was a little girl. We took a candle with us and set it carefully on an old, cracked plate. We climbed up the rickety ladder. In the gloomy hodge-podge we made out old toys, broken dolls, and the wooden model of a tugboat. Disorder heaped worn quilts on top of handleless chamber pots, broken stools beside cracked mirrors, and a pile of schoolbooks under a mound of old hats. I found a jack-in-the-box which still worked, though the cloth had worn from the spring. Wedging our way far in, digging through things saved like archaeologists searching for Troy, past bundles of letters and photographs and an album inscribed with poems, we saw in the far corner, its huge front wheel propped at an angle so that its spokes looked like an enormous spider web, an ancient bicycle.

We must have looked around for an hour, carrying our candle and coughing in the dust we raised. Then I heard my grandmother call from the back chamber, standing at the foot of the ladder, "You going to come down now?" Aunt Nan picked up the candle, and I followed her down to the kitchen. Everyone was there, and no one would look at me. My grandfather was white. He took me into the living room while everyone else kept busy in the kitchen, and he told me that he had shot and buried Riley.

The horse's graveyard was across the railroad, on a sandy bank which overlooked the lake. My grandfather had loaded his shotgun with a slug, and had led the lame horse across the fields which Riley had plowed and reaped for so many years. He carried his gun and his shovel in his left hand, and he whispered love into the horse's ear. He had dug the grave while the old horse stood with rheumy eyes, and he had shot him so that he fell into the grave.

5

Ten Poems from
Old Man Brunner Country

Leo Dangel

A Farmer Prays

My bank loan overdue,
that tractor I bought
had a cracked block.
Lord, you know
I'd never wish anyone dead,
but when the time is up
for that bandit
John Deere dealer,
let him be showing off
a new manure spreader.
Let him fall
into the beaters
and be spread
over half the township,
amen.

What Milo Saw

We worried about our neighbor Milo.
After the hail pounded his corn crop
into the ground, Milo said
he would shoot himself. Milo's wife raved.

She cried into her greasy apron and worried.
Milo's six runny-nosed kids were scared quiet
for a change. Milo took his beat-up
Chevy truck and ran off to town
twice a week and got drunk. Late at night,
on the way home, Milo somehow kept the Chevy
between the fences.

The drought came and dried up Milo's pasture.
Milo was down to his last cow.
He got drunk three times a week and still
managed to keep the Chevy between the fences,
but one night he scraped the machine shed
door a little and tore off a fender.
Milo said he would shoot himself.
Milo's wife hid the shotgun in the cellar
on a shelf, behind the pickle jars.

One day Milo's old watering tank fell apart.
Milo and the six kids dragged an old bathtub
out of the grove so that the one last cow
would have a place to drink.
Milo drove the beat-up Chevy to town.

The next morning, Milo found the one last cow
drowned in the bathtub—flat on her back, legs
sticking straight up, milk bag and tits
sort of floating just under the water.

Years later, Milo told somebody, if a man
was going to kill himself, just show him
a drowned cow in a bathtub.

After Forty Years of Marriage, She Tries A New Recipe for Hamburger Hot Dish

"How did you like it?" she asked.

"It's all right," he said.

"This is the third time I cooked
it this way. Why can't you
ever say if you like something?"

"Well if I didn't like it, I
wouldn't eat it," he said.

"You never can say anything
I cook tastes good."

"I don't know why all the time
you think I have to say it's good.
I eat it, don't I?"

"I don't think you have to say
all the time it's good, but once
in awhile you could say
you like it."

"It's all right," he said.

Gaining Yardage

The word friend *never came up*
between Arlo and me—we're farm neighbors
who hang around together, walk beans,
pick rocks, and sit on the bench
at football games, weighing the assets
of the other side's cheerleaders.
Tonight we lead 48 to 6, so the coach
figures sending us both in is safe.
I intercept an underthrown pass
only because I'm playing the wrong position,
and Arlo is right there to block for me
because he's in the wrong place,
so we gallop up the field, in the clear
until their second string quarterback
meets us at the five-yard line,
determined to make up for his bad throw.

Arlo misses the block, the guy has me
by the leg and jersey, and going down,
I flip the ball back to Arlo, getting up,
who fumbles, and their quarterback
almost recovers, then bobbles the ball
across the goal line, and our coach,
who told even the guys with good hands
never to mess around with laterals,
must feel his head exploding,
when Arlo and I dive on the ball together
in the end zone and dance and slap
each other on the back.
They give Arlo the touchdown, which rightly
should be mine, but I don't mind,
and I suppose we are friends, and will be,
unless my old man or his decides to move
to another part of the country.

If Old Man Brunner Were God

Baling wire keeps the bumper
on Old Man Brunner's truck,
the muffler on his tractor.
Old Man Brunner can fix anything
with baling wire:
a wagon tongue, an iron gate,
a split seam in his overalls,
his reading glasses.
If Old Man Brunner had made
the world, baling wire coils
would spark the lightning
in the clouds. Baling wire
would keep the continents
from sinking, twisted strands
would hold the planets
in orbit. Baling wire

would grow like grass.
Old Man Brunner's universe
would be a rusty paradise
where anything could be fixed
with a pair of pliers.

No Question

There was no question,
I had to fight Arnold Gertz
behind the high school that Friday.
All fall he kept throwing pool balls
at me in the rec room.

There was no question,
I was scared spitless at the mere sight
of his grimy fists and bull neck.
When we rolled on the cinders
and grappled and thumped each other,

there was no question,
I was actually winning
when the principal broke us up.
And when Arnold went hunting pheasants
on Sunday, everybody said

there was no question,
he was a damn fool to climb through
a barbed wire fence with a loaded shotgun.
There were exactly eight of us guys
who were classmates of Arnold so

there was no question,
I had to be one of the pall bearers,
even though I never liked Arnold,
never would have, but I was sorry
the accident happened,

there was no question,
and if he hadn't got himself shot,
I wonder if he finally would have let me alone.
There is no question,
I wonder about that.

My Father in the Distance

You crossed the pasture to the cornfield.
I cultivated toward the end of the row
where you waited in your faded overalls,
your hand resting on a fence post.
Your hand, only once, had rested on my head,
while we stood at the parlor window
and watched sparrows hopping on the porch.
As the corn rows shortened between us,
I saw again man and boy photographed
on glass, framed in the window.

Your hand dropped from the post.
I thought you had come with new orders.
Go home and fix the well pump?
Grind some hog feed?
I stopped the tractor and climbed down.
We talked. Talked about how the cockleburs
were almost gone, how the field
looked greener after that last rain,
how the corn should be knee high
by the 4th of July—important things.

How to Take A Walk

This is farming country.
The neighbors will believe

you are crazy
if you take a walk
just to think and be alone.
So carry a shotgun
and walk the fence line.
Pretend you are hunting
and your walking will not
arouse suspicion.
But don't forget
to load the shotgun.
They will know
if your gun is empty.
Stop occasionally.
Cock your head and listen
to the doves you never see.
Part the tall weeds
with your hand and inspect
the ground.
Sniff the air as a hunter would.
(That wonderful smell
of sweet clover is a bonus.)
Soon you will forget
the gun in your hands,
but remember, someone
may be watching.
If you hear beating wings
and see the bronze flash
of something flying up,
you will have to shoot it.

Gathering Strength

I looked over my shoulder
at the bedroom mirror and flexed my biceps.
I inspected my body and studied
the body of Charles Atlas in a comic book.

One time, Old Man Brunner winked
and told me how to build muscles—
every day carry a calf for ten minutes
until it's a cow and you're a gorilla.
In the barn, I bent over the calf,
put my left arm under the neck,
my right arm behind the back legs,
and stood up, the calf across my chest.

I marched in giant steps around the pen.
I dreamed about the people who would come
from all over to watch. The headlines
would say: Boy Carries Full-Grown Steer.

But through the dusty window, I looked
hard at the steers in the feedlot,
their blocky shoulders bumping for space
at the feedbunk. I set the calf down.

Passing the Orange

On Halloween night
the new teacher gave a party
for the parents.
She lined up the women
on one side of the schoolroom,
the men on the other,
and they had a race,
passing an orange
under their chins along each line.
The women giggled like girls
and dropped their orange
before it got halfway,
but it was the men's line
that we watched.
Who would have thought
that anyone could get them

to do such a thing?
Farmers in flannel shirts,
in blue overalls and striped overalls.
Stout men embracing one another.
Our fathers passing the orange,
passing the embrace—the kiss
of peace—complaining
about each other's whiskers,
becoming a team, winning the race.

·6·

Windbreak: A Woman Rancher on the Northern Plains

Linda Hasselstrom

August 24   Low 78, high 98; thunderclouds marched past on the north in the morning.

George and Mike went over east, and I went to the Custer County Fair to be political. Despite all our efforts last year, the legislature passed a compact for the disposal of nuclear waste that could result in our having a huge national radioactive waste dump here. Perhaps they were aware of the mistake they made—because they did at least set up a special election at which the people will vote on whether the compact should pass.

So I spent the day running a booth at the county fair to give out information about why we must defeat the compact. The fair is held in my hometown of Hermosa, population normally four hundred; the fair swells the ranks somewhat, since everyone in the county comes.

As always when I go to the fair, I'm struck with love and a kind of nostalgia that almost overwhelm me. I grew up here; I went to grade school here; I joined a 4-H club and participated in every activity open to me at the fair—dress-making, cooking, garden exhibits. At that time, girls in the 4-H club I belonged to couldn't participate in the horse or beef cattle projects, and while I complained, it never occurred to me to campaign very hard to get the situation changed.

Now the building housing the sewing and cooking exhibits is

much quieter than the horse stalls. All the subteen and teenage girls are in the 4-H horse project, and they ride wildly around the fairgrounds, chasing boys on horseback. I see myself in many of them and when one nearly runs me down, I even growl nostalgically.

When I was fourteen, a friend and I organized a horse club drill team of 4-H members, boys and girls. We devised intricate, dangerous drill patterns performed on horseback, sometimes at a gallop, and were invited to perform at fairs all over the area for several years.

Eventually, she and I—flag-carriers—crossed flags at a gallop one day, and I received a knee injury that still plagues me. We carried our flags in front of our knees, braced on the saddle, and her horse was bigger, so when we collided my horse and I were spun half around and my left knee took the impact. I was able to stay on my horse—a matter of pride to any horse person. Unfortunately, it was my left leg, the same one Oliver damaged so badly in January. Any exertion still causes a gnawing pain, like termites at the bone.

I missed the fairs for ten or fifteen years, when I was living elsewhere. Even when we visited here at the right time, my first husband scorned them, and I was a stranger walking among people who looked familiar but whose names I had forgotten.

When I moved back to the community, the conviction began to grow in me that I *should* participate in the fair in some way. It had been such a struggle of my youth to move it to our little town, and the town had gone so far to support it—building an arena, a grandstand, a women's building, stalls for the horses—expenses the town couldn't afford, all provided through the cash, sweat, labor and donated materials of the town's men. Somehow I felt I, too, should do my part, even if only exhibiting things so there would be something for visitors to look at.

Because that's what there is to do at a fair: you walk slowly through the aisles, looking at every plate of green beans, every mayonnaise jar filled with marigolds, every calf, every child's drawing, every potholder, no matter how crudely made. You pick up the articles, if you can, and examine the stitching or the finish or the size. You discuss who is showing the item and how their children are. You pause along the way to visit with others who are doing the same thing. Everyone feels an obligation to look at everything. It's a ritual, a way of appreciating other people in the community, though you may not agree with, or like them, at other times.

At first, George nearly had fits as I fell into this routine. Gradually he began to see the people with new eyes—not exactly like my view, of course, but with some knowledge of their history and habits. The universality of the experience began to register with him, and of course as he became better known—as "that Hasselstrom girl's husband," naturally—he began to relax and enjoy himself more. Slowly he is making his own friends and acquaintances in the community.

Since yesterday was George's birthday, I invited Jim and Mavis for supper and a belated party tonight. They brought noise-makers and paper hats, and I brought out the cake I'd hidden in the freezer. He's thirty-eight, and Jim, who's already forty, regaled him with promises of how weird he can get when he reaches the magic age.

September 1   Low 54, high 85.

Something woke me at 3 a.m. yesterday, and I got up and began to wander through the house, looking out the windows. To the east, the horizon was a flickering red and gold. For a minute I just stared, before realizing it was fire, a towering wall of flames.

I called the fire number while tearing off my nightgown, and by the time I was dressed George had the pickup ready, with a tank full of water and a bundle of feed sacks. We honked as we went through my folks' yard, and I saw the bedroom light go on. We took our regular trail over east, only we threw all the gates back out of the way; behind us in the darkness we could see the lights of the neighbors' pickups and the fire trucks. When we got to my uncle Harold's pasture, we saw a lone figure silhouetted against the fire, bending as he beat at the ground— my uncle's hired man.

Our area is served by volunteer fire departments, and who is manning the trucks depends on who's available when the fire siren blows. Getting the men and trucks together takes time, so we're all volunteer fire fighters. Our standard method is to wet a gunny sack and use it to beat out the flames. When the sparks have been beaten down in one spot, you move ahead and repeat the operation. Every foot of fire is sometimes beaten out in this way if the trucks are busy somewhere else. Any flaming cow chips within five feet of the edge of the fire must be kicked well back into the burned-over zone. They hold sparks for hours, and are light enough to be blown out into the unburned grass.

The wind was blowing hard, and twice it blew flames up into my face, jumping over the spot I'd been wetting down. The roar of the wind, the crackling fire and my own hoarse breathing were all I could hear when I stopped to rest. I deliberately slowed my pace, afraid I'd pass out.

The next time I looked up, I seemed to be alone in the dark. A long tongue of flame had shot down a gully, and I could see pickup lights ahead of it, searching for a way to get to it. Figures appeared and disappeared as the flames flickered. I stayed in the same area, working back and forth along the side of the fire. Once I saw a cow chip spinning over the dry grass, throwing sparks like a pinwheel. By the time I'd caught and soaked it, I had a new trail of fire to put out.

About sunrise, I saw men gathering around a pickup about a half mile north of me. Aunt Jo, Harold's wife, was passing out cups of coffee. I joined them, and listened to fire stories for a few minutes. Several of the men came in coughing like their lungs were on fire, and then lit cigarettes. I kept following the coughs, looking for George, since his breathing is so precarious, but couldn't find him or my father. Finally Jo spotted me. "Come on. We're going to town for stuff for sandwiches."

I was too tired to argue with her. When I piled my first armload of sandwich meat on the counter at the store, the clerk peered at me and said, "For gosh sakes, I didn't recognize you. You burned your face off, honey." She slapped a package of ointment on the counter and said, "Put some of this on it. And Josephine, put that checkbook away. We'll donate this stuff. And come back if you need more."

By the time we got back several new areas of fire had spread east and south, and a slurry bomber was working back and forth over the Badlands. We picked a spot close to where the fire chiefs were parked, talking on their radios, and started making sandwiches. Soon several other women had driven up, with pots of coffee or boxes of food, and the fire fighters began to drift in as if they could smell the coffee.

One of our neighbors still had his pajama top on, stuffed into his jeans. Another man held up the wreckage of his hat; he'd come without a sack, and had beaten on the flames with the hat. My uncle Harold came in for coffee, much to Jo's relief; he'd been helping to drive his and the neighbors' cows out of the fire's path.

I stayed with the lunch crew until late in the afternoon, since I couldn't find either of our pickups, or my husband or father. I saw our nearest neighbors, as well as people I hadn't seen since I was in high school. Close friends and enemies drank coffee, stuffed sandwiches in their faces, and went back to the fire. Every now and then the wind would change, and we'd throw everything in the pickup and get it out of the way, then fight fire for awhile until the wind switched again.

At dark, the front of the fire—fifteen miles away—was under control. By that time, the reporters had been out, and the Highway Patrol had blocked a couple of ranch roads to keep spectators out. One child was missing, and officials were afraid he'd been burned. George finally appeared, black smudges on his face, and a definite wheeze in his throat. After he'd eaten we came on home, and found my father already here and my mother worried about us. George and Father had both gone ahead of the fire, to the east side, and fought over there most of the day. They were happy to report the fire didn't get to our pastures over east.

September 12   Low 76, high 93. Over east at eight this morning, heat haze already rising from the prairie.

I woke at false dawn, while the air felt slightly cool, and walked barefoot to the garden. I was sauntering along, listening to the blackbirds, when I stepped on something squishy and looked down. I was standing on a snake lying along a row of parsnips. I assumed it was a bullsnake, apologized, and walked up to the tail end—where I discovered it was a rattlesnake. It scared me so much I grabbed the hoe, and then reconsidered and just tossed him out into the trees.

We butchered the crippled heifer today since we'd have lost money on her at the sale ring. George, gritting his teeth, shot her and bled her out. He brought her up to the house swinging from the loader on the big tractor, and hoisted her to a tripod made from three tipi poles. While he skinned and gutted her, I retrieved the heart and liver, and hauled the rest out to the field for the coyotes.

Jim and Mavis, friends from Sturgis, drove down on Jim's new Harley this evening. We met them through the muzzle-loading club, and often travel to rendezvous and camp together. We visited outside, and listened to the coyotes yapping and singing as they feasted on the heifer's remains.

September 14   Low 68, high 87.

We'd planned to let the heifer hang another day or two, but yesterday was too warm so we started cutting her up. We decided to can her because canned meat is so handy and tasty for a quick meal, and with that crippled leg she may be tougher than usual.

I was prepared with jars, my big canning kettle, and newspapers spread around the dining room table where we cut her up. We discarded all the bones, and I cut the large pieces of meat into one-inch chunks and stuffed them into jars. As soon as I had a kettle full, I put them on to cook and there the bottleneck developed, because each kettle has to cook for more than an hour and a half. Meanwhile we kept filling jars. We quit cutting when we finished the front quarters. George did some chores and a little fencing, and finally went to bed while I kept cooking until almost two a.m.

October 2   Low 27, high 40. The geese and cranes are going south this morning in great dark skeins and I hear faint honkings and hootings that sound wild—even here on the plains. I lay on the porch for awhile, watching the shifting overlapping vees.

Just as I was about to go inside I noticed a meadowlark sitting on a post about to sing. Suddenly he shot into the air and seemed to explode. Another moment, and I saw a falcon like the one the cats caught, beating back into higher air, clutching the meadowlark in his claws. He struck so fast I didn't see him coming and neither did the meadowlark. A few yellow breast feathers drifted to earth. It was a harsh lesson but fitting—we saved the falcon from the cats so he could go on about his life, which happens to include killing and eating meadowlarks.

In the afternoon I saw the seven deer we watch each winter in their favorite spot, the dry dam below the house, and four antelope on the hillside; they were slow in wandering off. I love their lack of fear.

October 21   Low 42, high 59, snow melting furiously. The moon, almost full, was setting at 5:30 a.m. in the west when I got up, and false dawn started at 6:30 while I was having coffee on the porch.

This morning we repaired the stretch of fence the buffalo have been abusing over east. I enjoy fencing, partly because when

I finish I can see what I've done and it stays done for awhile—unlike cooking meals and cleaning house. We took out about twenty rotted wooden posts, and then George put in a new corner, digging the postholes deep, while I drove twenty steel posts. Then we strung four strands of new barbed wire, stapling it tight. The buffalo can jump it if they want, but they can't just walk through it anymore.

Taking a breather after putting in a post with the maul, I pictured myself in twenty years, wearing the same worn jean jacket, fixing this fence again and remembering this sunny day with George humming in the background. I felt unbearably sad for an instant.

In the afternoon we went to Lawrence's to cut wood. Resting on a log, I watched a hawk soar overhead, planing between the treetops. Lawrence said after his father died: "I wonder which swallow is my Dad."

Later I saw the flock of turkeys slipping between the trees and suddenly thought of my grandmother, how she fiercely tore the tubes from her arms and died. I had a sudden rush of joy in all the life around me, *knowing* she'd gone on in some way. When Father came to wake me at dawn to tell me she was gone, he said, "It's sunrise, and it looks like a good day to die." The force in life, he said, is so strong that it never ends; it simply goes into something else. He rarely speaks of his beliefs so I didn't question him. Did he mean it literally—burial in the earth allows us to become part of the earth and grass? Or more philosophically—as Lawrence's idea that perhaps we go on to another form? Lawrence has said he plans to be an eagle, and I've considered being an aspen.

One of the best conversations I ever had with my father was when I was about twelve and we were haying. We were lying down after lunch, under the trees in the field. He said he wondered if trees were really conscious beings, and aware of us, only living at a slower tempo than ours so we never grasp their consciousness. I've never looked at a tree in the same way since.

November 27   Low −10, high 4; no wind, about four inches of new snow.

The wind died during the night so we got the hay hooks out of the barn, loaded the ¼ ton pickup with bales of hay and went over east through snow so deep now it looks blue. By the time we got there the wind had picked up again. The normal trail was buried three or four feet deep so we wound along the ridges. We fed the cattle at the dugout after chopping through ice a foot thick.

The bales we're feeding, bought because we didn't have enough of our own, weigh from seventy to eighty-five pounds each—more than I like to lift, but I can usually use a knee to help move them, and get added leverage from the hay hook. We try to feed about ten pounds of hay to each cow, which works out to around twelve bales, a full load for the pickup.

George's back has been bothering him a little, and I felt full of energy, so he drove while I fed. By the time I'd fed the whole load I was sick of being bent over with wind whistling through my long johns, and had hay in my eyes, my nose, my crotch. My fingers were stiff and my back hurt from bending over, but I'm lucky I didn't fall off the tailgate. The cattle were hungry and they jostled me on the tailgate, long tongues swiping at stray wisps of hay. One ran beside the pickup and jerked a bale off with her teeth so I had to stop George and scatter it.

We were just leaving when we noticed two cows in the Triple Seven pasture close to our fence. They moved their cows out a month ago, so we had no choice but to go check, and sure enough they were ours. We let them in and gave them a little cake. Arrived back home at 3:00, hungry. When will I learn never to go over east without taking lunch!

❧

November 28   Low −10, high 5 above.

Back over east—the drifts are crusted over so we have to choose a route carefully or the pickup is stuck. When we got to the dugout in the school section we found two cows in it, just their heads sticking out. A drift had blown out to the midpoint of the dugout. Ice stays soft under snow. When the cows walked around the drift looking for water, they broke through.

We didn't dare walk out on the ice to get a rope around their heads and one front leg, so we finally just lassoed their heads and tied the rope to the pickup. I gunned it while George stayed outside to holler if they got tangled up or started to strangle.

The first one out was shivering so hard she could barely stand up. The minute she popped out of the dugout the water on her hide froze to ice; she wandered off and I doubt we'll see her alive again. The second one tottered up to the other cows and ate a little cake, so perhaps she'll survive. They couldn't have been in the dugout long or they'd have been dead of hypothermia.

George went down to the other pasture to get some panels so we could fence them out of the dugout, and I stayed and watched them drink one by one so I could keep them out of the drift. I noticed spatters of blood in the snow from the cows' hoofs, splitting from the pressure of walking on ice for so long. We can't do much to treat them, though when we get them in the corrals I can try to squirt on a medicated fluid that hardens and seals the hoof from moisture and manure. This is a tricky maneuver, especially on hind hoofs.

Many of the cows also have swollen knees sprained when they fell on the ice. Several have bloody heads and bleeding noses from trying to eat grass through the snow. They move like heavy old women, slowly, carefully, and when they fall they grunt and groan in pain.

We were cold and wet when we finished putting the panels in so we sat in the truck with the heater on and ate lunch, watching the cows nosing through the snow for more cake. Some of them huddled in the lee of the pickup, looking through the windows at us until we imagined accusation in their eyes.

We drove back to the ranch and told Father about the problem, suggesting that we get the cattle out of there as soon as possible because the panels we put up really won't be very effective to keep them out of the drift and the dugout. He agreed, so after we'd warmed up and dried out we went back over east, moved the cattle down to the lower pasture, and shut them out of the dugout there so they have to water at the tank. We'd hoped to be able to lead them but since they'd already been fed and they didn't want to walk against the wind, George had to walk much of the way behind them.

Neither of us could get warm tonight. We drank hot buttered rum, fed the fire, and wrapped ourselves in blankets, but we were still shivering when we went to bed. The cat and dog, as if helping, curled up between our legs.

March 3   Low 15, high 20; snowing hard and drifting all morning, with about five inches on the ground.

We shut the heifers in the barn and yearling calves in the corral so they wouldn't bunch up against a fence in the storm. When we went out to feed the calves at dark we buried our 3/4 ton pickup in a drift at the top of our hill and couldn't get it out, so we walked to the barn to feed, and then had to grope our way back along the fence because we could hardly see. How easily one could become lost.

When I checked the folks' house I found their bathroom floor covered with water and the bathtub running over. About this time of year their sewer pipes always freeze. Used the plunger to get some water running, hauled bucketsfull outside, and mopped for an hour before most of it was cleaned up.

There's a big owl hanging around the trees by the folks' house. I wonder if it's the mate of the corpse in the tree. I picture him sitting beside the dead owl, meditating perhaps.

March 4   Low 20, high 20. Sunny, with south wind.

Al came to tow our pickup out of the drift and says we lost a premature calf at the creek several days ago.

After feeding, we spent the morning collecting from the yard all the cattle we put in the Lindsay pasture two days ago. The Ugly Cow, a proficient fence-destroyer, had broken down the gate and led them all back here—again. We left her here and took the rest back to the pasture—on foot—in the afternoon.

Walking back through the yard we saw a skunk busily heading for the barn, so I followed him cautiously while George got the gun. He managed to shoot him just outside the barn instead of inside, but his memory will be with us whenever the wind's right for some time. He was fat—he's spent the winter eating cattle cake and cat food in the barn. We've known he was there by the smell and piles of his scat left contemptuously in our path.

March 5   Low 15, high 25.

After feeding at home, we headed for Lindsays, and got stuck three times. We were worn out with digging by the time we got there, and the cows paid very little attention to us, preferring the fresh grazing uncovered by last night's wind. The tank was free of ice. That's a good winter tank because the water comes into it from the bottom by pipe from the well, and the flow is sufficient to keep it ice-free except in severe weather.

This afternoon we went to Rapid City for groceries, noting some typical signs of spring: dead skunks along the highway, hitchhiker with a backpack, a couple of Airstream trailers full of tourists, and two motorcyclists.

It had been snowing lightly off and on all day but since the sun was shining we hadn't paid much attention. By the time we finished supper in town, six inches of snow had fallen and the highway was glazed with ice. We'd driven the little car instead of the pickup, and it took George nearly an hour and a half to drive the twenty-five miles home. The blizzard howled all night, keeping us both awake at different times as we worried about the cows calving.

March 6   Low 22, high 34.

The bobtail cow had a new baby calf this morning, huddled by a corral fence; it seemed healthy. Nothing else had calves, though some of the heifers look very near. Father has assured us none of them will calve until April. Feeding was a struggle with nearly a foot of new snow drifting.

We saw geese going north, and George said, "Well, we made it through another winter."

When we checked cows this morning, one of the new calves was prancing oddly in the grass. In front of him, like an audience, sat two coyotes. We shot over their heads to discourage that kind of chumminess. Spent the day feeding, checking cows and fences.

Al called to say that another calf was born at the creek and seemed to be fine. We found another new one here at dusk. He was not up yet but the cow was licking him, so he'll be all right.

March 14   Low 21, high 54; sunny, with gusty winds. The cowbirds returned.

We fed no hay today, just cake, as the cattle have plenty of grass. George made a quick trip over east with more hay for Ginger in the afternoon.

On my 6 a.m. check I found a heifer struggling to have a calf but unable to get the head out. I pulled and he slid right out, getting a mouthful of manure as his introduction to life. Come to think of it, what better preparation can he have? Everything is bound to be better from here on, and he's had a good taste of reality.

We're nearly out of frozen meat. We've been watching one yearling heifer Father said might be calfy. She's much too young to calve, and her ears and tail were frozen at birth, so she was the chosen. Today we shot, skinned and dressed her, and hung her in the yard on a tripod we made of tipi poles.

March 16   Low 21, high 56.

Three redwing blackbirds were in the trees this morning, piping a few notes, scouting for the main flock. George always says meadowlarks are the first birds back. We debate over it each year, but he had to admit he hasn't seen a meadowlark yet.

Despite the snow, it's drier and warmer than usual at this time of year, so we decided we didn't dare let the heifer hang any longer. Jim and Mavis came down to help and by evening we had two hundred pounds of meat wrapped, labeled and in the freezer. By the time we finished, we were exhausted and getting silly. The men had abandoned the meat cutting chart I'd stuck to the refrigerator, and just carved off chunks, and Mavis and I were writing labels like "teeny weeny steaks," "huge steaks," "itsy bitsy steaks."

When we finished, Mavis and I sliced the fresh liver and fried it with onions while the men scrubbed the table and floor.

March 23   Low 26, high 40; foggy, rainy, cold, with a little snow midmorning.

Redwing blackbirds are shrieking in the trees and we heard a meadowlark in the calving pasture.

We both spent much of the afternoon milking out cows with too much milk. Some are cooperative, and George can rope their heads and hold them while I slip up beside them and put in a teat valve. I'm good at putting in teat valves—a job that requires close work. I've learned to tell by the tension in the cow's back leg—the one right beside my face—exactly when the cow is going to kick at my teeth, and get out of there in time. I keep one eye on the leg and use touch to locate the swollen teat. Then the valve has to be inserted gently into the nipple. Often the teat is so sore the touch of the valve will make her kick and bawl, so I gently locate the hole, and shove the valve in fast. If I get it in the first time, I just stand back and let the milk flow. If not, the cow is mad and probably hurting and it gets a little trickier. I consider the cow trying to kick me as perfectly fair, though I may revise my opinion the day I'm too slow and one of them removes a few of my teeth.

The cats sit in a row on the steps of the barn, knowing a pail of warm milk is coming their way. One of these days we'll have a cow without enough milk, and we can put a calf on some of these cows. Lucky calf! He'll spend the summer sucking two cows and be twice as fat as his friends.

In the afternoon I transplanted some asparagus from the old bed, which is thick with grass, to the garden, and planted gladiolus and hyacinth bulbs—my annual promise to myself. Mother came out while I was working and we visited a little. She said the hole-infested pair of jeans I was wearing was disgraceful. I said I intended to mend them. She said, "Those are so far gone you'd be better off to jack up the zipper and run a new pair of jeans under it."

Life on a Hill
Maxine Kumin

"HOW'S YOUR HILL?" guests invited to dinner used to inquire.

"Fine. The sanding truck was just here," we would gloat (sometimes). Or (occasionally) when freshly plowed out, "Terrific! Much better than it is all summer." For in summer, although passable, the road turns to bone- and axle-jarring corduroy. Mufflers drop off. Gaskets loosen. Dust clouds fly about like dervishes.

More often, particularly in mud season, the answer would be equivocal.

"Depends. You have four-wheel drive? Oh, you'll make it, just come up fast, easy on the turns, and pull in to the right."

Or: "You don't? But you have three hundred pounds of grain over the rear wheels? Well, you can give it a try. Start from across the wooden bridge at the bottom so you can get a good running jump. You'll have to slow down some on that tricky little curve, but if you get past that, gun it hard up the straight part. You'll need everything you've got to make it to the top."

Some years ago, wearying of this intricate initiation of visitors, we scooped out a parking space down by the infamous "tricky little curve." Three-tenths of a mile uphill from our mailbox on the road, that bend is so nefarious that neophytes often skidded into a snowbank or wound up fender-deep in mud there. It's only another tenth of a mile uphill to the house from that elbow, though. After dinner, using the old aggie truck, a '67 Dodge Power Wagon of prodigious gifts and fearsome proportions, we pushed or pulled the hapless guests out of jams.

Actually, the top is not the top, to paraphrase Gertrude Stein. It is merely the wrist bone in this giant arm of hill. Another, broader plateau exists a little farther uphill, some fifty yards above house and barn. There, on an almost flat grassy sward, the vegetable garden flourishes. Beyond the garden, a saucer pond. And just beyond the pond, on our only truly, though briefly, level piece of earth, our riding ring.

The first settlers in this part of New England divided themselves according to economics and temperament much as they had in the Old Country. The thrifty, practiced farmers squatted along the riverbottom land and got on with their crops. The well-to-do settlers sought out the tops of hills, where admirable views were to be had, and built imposing structures out of the native pine. A hundred years ago the biggest house atop the tallest hill in any town, up and down the Merrimack River, was invariably the mill owner's house. And then the modest in-betweeners, those without resources for the land highest up or the richest bottom land, snugged homesteads into the crook of a hill, facing southeast, out of the prevailing wind. They struggled to clear the gentler peaks and valleys of their hills, as well as the occasional plateaus formed by the glaciers. Some of the homesteaders lasted, grazing cows or sheep on the thin topsoil, until World War II.

Those of us who now inhabit these hillside farms alternately bless and curse the first comers. We bless them for having the wisdom to build out of the wind. On a February day when the thermometer barely creeps up to zero and the wind-chill factor is a terrifying minus forty, our bay mares stand blissfully sunbathing in the lee of the barn. Across the road, sheltered by a fortuitous dip in the land, the heifers have folded their legs in on the snow for a midday nap.

But there's no view of the river valley below. The front of the house looks southeast across the road to the barn; the barn smiles onto a tilt-table pasture. Beyond the pasture, hills, and higher hills. The sun drops below the rim at three o'clock in winter. By four, lengthening shadows bring all the livestock back to the starting gate. Animals fed, watered, bedded down, a preprandial depression skulks in by five.

How do you build a barn on a hill? They did it putting practicality foremost, with a cavernous opening—a giant pit for the cow manure—facing downhill. Warmth coming off the pile may or may not have reached the first floor. Certainly the redolence did. Twenty years ago, we redid the barn's foundations and built stalls into the earthworks. The north and west walls are solid concrete, dungeon-damp and sure. The third wall, which follows the contour of a gentle downslope, allows for two stall windows facing south. The front, reinforced concrete below grade, stands open to morning sun or easterly drizzle. It can be closed with two mammoth sliding doors. In our innocence, we used to snug these elaborate panels shut on cold winter nights, but snow melting off the roof at sundown all too often dripped along their length and, as the temperature fell, soldered them tight by morning. If I forgot to leave the pickaxe propped outside, I frequently had to burgle my way into the barn via a stall window. A startled mare once took violent exception to my forced entry. Now we routinely leave the doors ajar. With several equines breathing inside, things are cozy enough.

No matter what ploys we resort to, however, in the spring runoff, the barn fills. First a trickle, then twelve rivulets. Then a flood. We ditch, underdrain, build ramparts of sawdust and manure, mutter annual imprecations. By May, all is habitable and forgiven. The first farmers, of course, knew all this. They kept their beasts upstairs. Their cows calved, their mares foaled in dry stalls, albeit on hard boards, probably bedded none too thickly with homegrown straw.

But in spring, time for tapping maple trees, the hill is a benevolence. Purple tubing threads its way downslope in great serpentines. We need only watch and listen to the silence as gravity does the work. No more tedious lifting and emptying of buckets. No more gently arrhythmic plinkings of sap droplets into buckets, either. Sixty trees drip their bounty into the plastic life lines. A stream of sugar water flows into the collecting vat.

Trudging uphill to check the garish lines of tubing for sags, I think, "Anything might be born in this still time, in the punky snow." Friends of ours had a slumberous bear in a hollow ash tree in their sugarbush last spring. We paid the bear a visit. It twitched and breathed and went on with its hibernation. Cubs are born, generally two to a litter, in late January or February, says the *Field Guide to American Wildlife*. I think of Jim Wright's poem in which as the bear "lay asleep, her cubs fell / Out of her hair, / And she did not know them."

In the fall, when riverbottom gardens are swathed ghostlike in sheets, drop cloths, and a season's worth of Sunday papers, our garden may have several more frost-free nights. Zucchini may wither and blacken below. Up here it is still putting out new little pencils. Still picking tomatoes and cukes and Kentucky Wonders, we have won as much as a two-week reprieve beyond the frost kill of the lowlands.

Three or four halcyon days in winter, when a new snowfall smooths the contours of our hill and cushions its sides where earlier snowbanks have hardened to icy crusts, we can ski down on cross-country skis without fear of fracture. Those same few days I long for a sleigh. Even though the slow raspings of the plow in the night are the most luxuriously welcome sounds of our hill lives, this incurable romantic wishes for a few days' respite from the world. If the plow breaks down, if Harry the operator catches the flu, if the sanding truck pops a gasket— snowbound! By sleigh I could circumnavigate the town.

When the melt begins and house and barn stand apart like Noah's ark, all of us awash on a sea of mud, I try to plan ahead, to have groceries and grain on hand for the inevitable few days when the road is all but impassable.

Farming on the slant, liming and fertilizing fourteen acres of forage fields, requires ingenuity and courage. You can do a lot of things with a walk-behind tractor, but fortunately one thing you're not likely to do is tip over on the slope. A horse-drawn spreader can also with impunity tack east and west across the hill at a sedate plod. The driver will have walked two miles per acre in intimate contact with the contours of the field. But during that week of fertilizing the fields, from the top line of those three back pastures, the view to the north is spectacular. Hilltop sitters have it on a daily basis. Here it is more precious because seldom seen: the town below like a toy set for Lionel trains, the glimpse of Kearsarge beyond, a perfect papier-mâché mountain. On the opposite ridge, the fine white farmhouses of an earlier century, well kept and gleaming as though freshly waxed.

Clearing land on the slope or simply cutting hillside trees to keep the woodlot thinned raises other difficulties. Granted, the angle can work to a woodcutter's benefit if the big oak's fall is correctly plotted. But the danger of error is enhanced, too. No margin for misstep when you must stand braced against the hill while making the second sawcut that will send forty feet of tree crashing through the forest canopy. On the other hand, bringing wood out of the lot can sometimes be a matter of a few judicious tugs and several free revolutions. No doubt the wheel was born somewhere on a primal slope.

Fencing up- and downhill is several times more arduous than running three lines of boards on the level. What the little bubble inside the carpenter's tool says may run counter to the eye of the distant beholder. Bringing those two judgments into harmony requires continual fudging of measurements and compromise of position as the hemlock lengths are hammered in place. And oh! the wrong angles at which boards are occasionally cut, the botching and mismatchings. Is the field sweeter when the fence is finished? Possibly a straightaway fence wouldn't please the eye as much.

The camaraderie of other halfway-hill people adds considerable relish to this chosen way of life. You'd be surprised how many of us there are, hidden in the pleats and folds of hills neither massive enough to have attracted the ski industry nor tame enough for paved roads and subdivisions. We have traded easy access for solitary splendor. In a sense, we live on an island, at the mercy of wind and tides, or at least of ice and mud. All of us are parts of the main, however, as John Donne pointed out. But put it in four-wheel drive before you come up to join us.

·8·

Harvest

Meridel LeSueur

IT WAS ALMOST NOON and the sun stood hot above the fields. The men would be coming in from the corn for dinner.

Ruth Winji stooped at the bean vines thinking she had not enough yet in her basket for a mess of beans. From the hour's picking of berries and beans she had leaned over in her own heat and the sun's heat driving through her until earth memory and seed memory were in her in the hot air and she was aware of all that stood in the heat around her, the trees in the bright sun, earth-rooted, swaying in sensitive darkness, the wheat like a sea in the slight wind, the cows peering from the caverns of shade of the grove behind the barns with their magic faces and curved horns. Root darkness. Tree darkness. Sun. Earth. Body. She thought: *And my body dark in the sun, root-alive, opening in the sun dark at its deep roots*, and it pained her now that she had quarrelled with her husband.

Anxiously she lifted her large fair torso looking for her young husband as he would come from the corn and wheat, swaying a little as he walked, the sun flashing up the stalk of his body, trying not to show the joy he had walking toward her. By noon she always looked to see him come back, for they had not been separated longer in the six months of their marriage. She shaded her face to see him but she could not tell him at that distance from the other two men that worked in the corn. Still she looked trying to find out what he would be doing for she grieved that a quarrel stood up between them, and now she could not tell him that they would have a child.

It was a quarrel about whether he should buy a threshing machine to harvest the ripening wheat. It wasn't that the money was her dowry money; she dreaded the machine. She knew how men came in from riding that monster all day. She had been hired out before her marriage in the three years since she had come from Bohemia and she knew the cold mindless look of them, not in a column of mounting heat as her husband came now to her, a flame from the earth, broken off as if the quick of it had taken to his very flesh.

Her heart went into a great dismay to think of him riding that machine, and she saw with what a glitter that desire sat upon him and her heart was sick. He had never had a machine and now he wanted one, and it was an encroachment like another woman or war.

She leaned over again thrusting her hand in to the warm vine foliage as the berries hung turning away from the heat upon themselves and she plucked them from the short thick stems and they fell sun-heavy in her hand. Her fingers were stained with berry juice and it had run up the naked belly of her arm and dried there.

She could not keep her mind from thinking how more and more now he looked into that catalogue at night where there were pictures shown of all the parts of a thresher. How he looked into this book all the evening without speaking a word.

Their marriage had been wonderful to her in mid-winter. Coming to his farm, snowed in together in January, and it was as if they themselves brought the spring warming, spreading it from their own bodies until it lifted and mounted from the house to the fields, until the whole earth was jutting in green.

Then she had come with him while he plowed and planted or watched him from the windows of the house as if he stood still in union with her as he strode the sunscarred earth laying it open, the seed falling in the shadows; then at evening he came from them to her, himself half young, half old in the beginnings of his body, his young brows aslant meeting above his nose, his lips full and red, the sun warming and jutting in him too as the spring advanced, and she was not loath to accept him from the fields smelling of salt sweat, and see all that he had planted ripen and grow from that wild heat into the visible world, bright and green, rising to its flower, and now a child growing unseen but certain.

Still and even now, the knowing and remembering in herself of the way of his walking or the manner of his speech, as if he were out of breath, coming partly from the newness of the language to him and partly from his eagerness to know everything, his terrible cunning to know: That was it, that was what she really feared, his new world cunning to know, that's what made the fear go up her body so she had to lift her heavy shoulders and breathe slowly looking out over the slow sheen of the turning wheat where everything seemed almost dark in the sun. Still she could not see him, only the three tiny figures of the hoeing men far afield in the corn.

Now she felt she was losing him, as if he were falling out of some soft burr, their ancient closed fertile life, being shaken from the old world tree, in ways beyond her, that she would not go.

The days in the early spring had been like great hot needles sewing them close together, in and out, binding them close, piercing through both to the marrow and binding them with the bright day and the dark night. So the earth lay and herself too, marked by the plow. The sun rose molten with intent. The sun went down and the dusk blew scented and low upon them. The light of day spun them together in utter tranquility— until he had to come saying, "What about this machine? They say that the work will be done so quick, you wouldn't believe it. They say it, Ruth. What about it? We have just enough to have it. What about it?"

And it was just as if he were about to betray her and she could say nothing, seeing that look of greed and cunning, and it was no good to argue this or that because everyone threshed his wheat with the big harvester and he would get her to peek into the catalogue and tell her how the thing mowed the wheat in terrible broad swaths and he showed her the picture of the seat where he would sit swaying sensitive in his own rich body from that iron seat and then she wouldn't look. She would turn away in fear and it came to lie heavier in her than her own planting that she bore now to the fourth month.

And he kept saying, "We could get one of those, Ruth. We could save money. We could just get one of those." With his curious way of repeating himself, beginning and ending on the same phrase. "I was over there looking at that machine in town. Pretty good, too. Yah, pretty good. I was over there looking and it was good." At those times she wouldn't know him at all, that sensual light would be gone from his young keen face, the little flicker that came up from his body gone, and he would be smiling, distracted, rubbing his palms together, as if he were falling away from her, out of the column of himself to be lost to her touch.

The salesman had even come and Winji had looked askance, speaking low so the man left quickly and she took it as a good sign.

She saw the sun topping the roof of the barn so she hurried up the lane with her berries and her beans. Then she heard a sound that made her step in fright. She saw that monster coming slowly up the road making a corrugated track. It came as if with no motion of its parts through the heat. Ruth Winji ran into the cooled house, closed the door then stood hearing that beat that was like a heart and yet monstrous. It seemed to be going straight over the house and she didn't look out until it had passed and then she saw the monstrous tracks on the road bed.

She remembered her husband had said they were demonstrating one at Olson's and had wanted her to go with him to see and she had said she would not go.

She put the beans on and sat down to wait at the window where she could first see him come up through the orchard. The sunlight made an under-darkness over the lower world so it was dark as a plum, the trees still black-tipped, a sensitive shimmer of darkness like a convulsion seemed to go over the sun or world beneath the gloom of sun so Ruth went into a swoon of heat between the bright upper sun and the painfully sensitive lower darkness.

She must have dozed because she started aware when her husband stood in the room behind her. She didn't turn from the window but knew him there in the soft heated gloom. He hadn't spoken behind her in the room and her body started alive to him like a blind antenna upreaching. He touched her shoulder coming from behind her and she saw his hands burned rosy. She thrust back against him and he still stood invisible touching her.

There was a drowsiness of noon all about them, the soft throaty cluck of the hens, the padding of the dog across the bare swept ground, the crisp whirr of a bird startled up from noon drowse winging from shadow to shadow.

She looked up, saw his face, young, dark, mounted with blood rosy beneath the burned skin, his brows winged strangely at an angle as she looked up, his full young mouth curved willfully, his eyes glinting above her like the eyes of a hawk looking at her from his narrow spare face coming down on her from above, setting his lips on hers.

"The beans," she cried.

"Never mind," he said enamored, "I turned the fire off. Never mind."

Her springing up as she had lifted his whole height to her instantly like a shaft of shadow against the bright outdoors light. Seeing the straight willful neck, plunging to the close-cropped round head, springing against his hard spare sweating body, she pinned him with her arms where the shirt was set and stuck to his strong back and felt the winging of the ribs' spare flight, spanning from her hands the hard thin breast.

At table Winji talked with the hired help about the thresher that had gone by. Ruth listened with lowered head.

"My wife here," Winji said, "doesn't want me to buy it. She wants to keep the old way, God knows why."

The other two men looked at her, the full confused woman sitting at table with them. They seemed to hardly dare lay eyes upon her.

"Well, it's a good one for getting work done," said one.

And they went on talking about threshers and their good and bad points and their makes like man enamoured until she said, "Don't talk about it please, don't speak."

"But we will," her husband said leaning towards her, his fork upraised. "And you're going down with me after this meal and see how it goes."

She did not dispute with him before the men.

After the dishes were cleared he said in the kitchen, "Listen Ruth. The thresher is just down the bend. That's the one I've been talking about. Listen Ruth. I wish you would go down there with me."

"No," she said, wiping off the dishpan carefully.

"You go down and look at it with me. I think it's the best thing we should do. Get it. Buy it. You go down, just for my sake."

"No," she said. "No, I don't want to see it. I'm afraid."

He laughed sharply, his white teeth frightening in his red mouth. "Oh, you'll think it's wonderful when you get over that. Why, it's wonderful."

"No," she said. "It's not wonderful to me."

"Think of it," he said, his eyes glistening in that way she had seen, beyond desire for her. "It will bind the sheaves after it has cut the wheat. . . ."

"What," she said, "bind the sheaves. . . ."

"Yes," he nodded and she saw that lust for knowing and what she took for cunning. "Bind the sheaves at the same time."

"At the same time," she repeated stupidly, "without going around again."

"Yes," he almost shouted, "without going around again."

"Think, how many men did it take on your father's place in the old country to harvest the wheat. . . ."

"Yes. . . . Yes, I know," she said, wringing her hands. "I used to carry a brown jug to the men full of spring water with a little meal sprinkled in it. . . ."

"You just sit on the machine and pull levers, see. Like this." He sat down and pulled levers with nothing in his hands.

"How do you know how?" she said. "You've been practicing," she cried.

"What of it," he said like a boy, as if he had got hold of something. "What if I have. Come with me, Ruth. It's your money in a way . . ."

"No, no," she said. "It's your money. Do with it as you like. It's yours. You're the master of the house, but don't make me see it. I don't want to see it. I wash my hands. I wash my hands . . ."

He stood grinning, shaking his head, chagrined a little: "But you can't wash your hands of the whole new world . . ."

But nevertheless she cried after him from the kitchen, "No. No, I wash my hands," and he went out slowly from her, bewildered.

In an hour she went with him, prevailed upon by his physical power over her. He took her hand in the road and pulled her along. Her face was partly covered by her blue sun bonnet and she hid the free hand under her apron. When they got there a clot of men gathered over the machine like black bees and she stood back. Winji joined them, hardly concealing his delight, going time and again round and round the machine. It was brand new and glinted monstrously in the light.

"Look Ruth, look," he kept saying to her, running back and pointing things out and then running back to the machine. "Look at this," he would say but she couldn't hear. She watched his face in envy and malice. The other men were laughing at her but she didn't care.

"No, no," she kept saying, half-obscured in her sun bonnet, pulling away as her husband tried to urge her to look closer at the thresher. The other men looked at her full woman's body, awed a little and thinking how the two were so newly married. They stood away from her a little sheep-faced and she stood away from them and the machine.

"Come and touch it," Winji urged.

"No, no," she cried, "I don't want to."

"Why, it won't hurt you," the men said. "Don't be afraid."

She could see her husband was a bit ashamed of her, and chagrined. "You know," he said to the men, apologizing for her, "in the old country we don't have them like this, in the old country . . ."

She saw the men patting him on the back as if he had already bought the thresher, envy showing in their eyes and he grew big from their envy, strutting around the machine, rubbing his palms together, forgetting her for a moment so she went cold with dread, then running to her to propitiate her.

"Come and touch it, isn't it splendid, look at that." She saw the big knives thrusting back movement even in their stillness, and then on driving power and the tiny manseat hidden inside, where the little living man was supposed to sit and pull the levers as her husband had been showing her. She was revolted.

But he came close to her and she was bewitched still of his body so she let herself be led straight to the giant and saw all its shining steel close to her and her husband took her hand, still stained by berries, and put it on the steel rump and it was hot as fire to the touch so she drew back nursing her hand. The men laughed and her eyes dilated holding to her husband's face but drawing away.

The men were uneasy. "Never mind, Winji," they said, "lots of our women folks takes it that way at first. My wife says her house was buried in dust the first year the thresher come." They laughed uneasily, shifting, and looking from under their brows at the woman. They turned with ease back to the machine.

She started away down the road. At the bend she turned and looked back and to her horror she saw her husband caressing the great steel body. He was dancing, a little quick dance full of desire, and with his quick living hands he was caressing the bright steel where the sun struck and flew off shining from the steel rumps into her eyes like steel splinters so she turned back sickened, but not before she saw him wave to her, a shy lifting of the hand.

She hadn't told him she was going to have a child. She thought of the child now as a weapon.

She waited while the tension went tighter between them subtly, unspoken now, with his saying now and then at breakfast, at dinner, "Have you changed? What have you against it? Is it a beast?"

She wouldn't answer, only turned against him. And then he turned against her, chagrined and lost without her, trying to win her back to his way and she wouldn't come.

She would cajole him, sitting on his lap in the evening when it was too hot to sleep. "Don't do it. Don't get it." But he knew she was playing a trick to get him. Once he got up, setting her on her own feet and walking away, and that night he didn't come in until late and didn't speak to her but went soundly to sleep.

He grew subtle against her, his summer face hot and congealed, his straight burned neck a pillar of blood against her, his brooding body hot from labor, a wall to her now that made her blind and angered.

When he came in from the cattle with the beast smell about him and milk on his shoes and the lustre of living things, she tried to pull him to her again.

At last there was enmity between them. He didn't talk any more about the machine. They sat together at table without speaking and went to bed silently in the late dusk and she thought he would never come to her again. She felt he was betraying all that and her grief was bitter against a new way, terrible in her so she didn't tell him about the child.

Then one day she went to town and came back early to be near him and go on with the fight, to bring it to come, and there she saw the salesman and Winji at the table leaning over the catalogue and figures and before they shut the book she could see the knives and parts of the machine in color. The two men looked at her guiltily. Winji got up and walked with his back to her and stood stock still at the window. The salesman left as quickly as possible and the two of them stood in the room.

"So!" she said bitterly. "You are going to get it."

"Yes!" he said and she could see the blood flush up his bared neck. "Yes, I am."

"So you don't care," she said, shaking bitterly, clenching her hands together, for she could have torn him to pieces standing there presenting his back to her. "You don't care," she said.

"I don't know what that means." Still he didn't face her. He seemed a stranger with his back turned. "It's for our good to get the machine. This is just woman's stubbornness. It will get us on. We will be powerful people in this neighborhood. . . ."

"Powerful . . ." she repeated.

"Yes," he said now, turning to her uneasily but against her.

She began to cry, not lifting her hands.

The sight of her exasperated him. "What are you crying for," he said in real anger but his face looked guilty. "What are you crying for," he shouted, raising his hand. "Stop that bellowing," he swore and struck her.

She recoiled, her face lifted wide to his. He saw her falling back, her great eyes open upon him in grief. He gave a cry and caught her falling arms, thrust her toward himself. Against her he stood straight and she began to cry from her body shaking, rent by the grief in her. He held her and for a moment seemed to know what she had been feeling but it was only for a moment.

Then it was she told him about the child.

He seemed to forget about the machine those long summer days and everything was as it had been before. She looked at him every day and it seemed that it was over. He was bound to her again and she was content.

The wheat hung heavy on the stalk.

She thought he had arranged to have the old red reaper of Olson's and hire many men and she had already spoken for two of the girls to come in and help feed since she was slower on her feet now too.

One day he came in in the early afternoon and she saw he was excited.

He prowled around the house all afternoon and she was uneasy. "Is anything the matter?" she asked him. "No," he said. But when she wasn't looking she caught him looking at her. At supper he said nervously, as if he had been preparing for it the whole afternoon:

"Tomorrow we begin." He kept looking at his coffee but he kept smiling and looking cunningly at her when she wasn't looking.

"Tomorrow?"

"Huh," he grunted.

She set down her knife and fork, unable to eat. "Well?" she said, a cold fear making her hollow.

"I've got a surprise for you," he said.

"A surprise," she said.

"Don't repeat what I say!" he suddenly shouted, threw down his spoon and left the table.

The next morning she woke sitting bolt upright and saw his place beside her empty. She ran to the window but it was just dawn and she could see nothing. She dressed and put on the coffee. Still he did not come. Suddenly she put on a sweater and went as fast as she could down the lane to the beanfield where she could see the wheat and there in the field she saw it standing new and terrible, gleaming amidst the sea of ripe wheat that crested and foamed gently to its steel prow and receded away in heavy fruition.

It was over. There it was. She couldn't say why she was so afraid but she knew it was against her and against him. It was a new way.

A bevy of men stood around. Then they saw her and Winji left them and came towards her beckoning, but she did not move towards him. He came to her.

"Don't be angry, Ruth," he said gently. "We've got to do it. We can't be behind the times, can we? Now with the child."

"No," she said. They both knew that the clot of men around the machine were half-looking their way, waiting to see what would happen.

"Isn't she a beauty," he said in his broken tongue.

"A beauty," she said.

"For God's sake, do you have to repeat after me for God's sake," he said, then beseeching, he begged of her for the first time. "You say it's all right, darling. Ruth, you say it's all right. We've got to get ahead, you know that. Now more than ever, haven't we?" he said softly, standing only a foot away, but she felt his spell.

"Yes, yes," she said in grief, "yes. . . ."

"Go on," she said. "Go on with it."

"But you come down to the fence and see me go down the field the first time," he begged.

She hated him but she went behind him, seeing his heels flicker up as he went in haste, eager to be with his new "beauty."

The mare in the pasture came up and walked near him and stood sadly with them at the fence whinnying softly as her master went down the field, letting the air tremble through her soft nostrils.

Walking away he heard the soft bleat of the mare, felt the men waiting from the machine and for a moment a kind of fear struck him through the marrow as he saw the glistening thing standing to his hand. Down his soft loins, his vulnerable breast, went a doom of fear and yet an awful pride, but he felt shaking at the bones, for leaving the moistness of sleep, the old world of close dreaming in the thick blossomed surface, and the space of mystery where the seed unfolds to the touch in the cool and thick and heavy sap, the world of close dreaming that is like a woman's hair or the breasts of men.

She saw him turn in the sun—wave to her and mount the machine.

Eight Poems from
Alvin Turner as Farmer

William Kloefkorn

1.

There is always the rock:
That, first and last, to remember.
The rock, at times at dusk the rabbit,
Robbing the garden in its own leaden way.
And I remember how once
I lost time deliberately,
Reining the team to a stop
And raising the rock high to crush it.
Underhoof it had wanted to trip
Even the full-rumped mares,
And I stood there in the furrow
With the rock raised above my head,
Powerless at last to reduce it
Or even to lose it to sight.
Yet I tried. (For in those days
I had not learned to say
There is always the rock.)
I threw it into the soft plowed ground
And dreamed that it disappeared.
How many times then it rose with the rain
I cannot say, nor can I boast
That ever its usefulness
Was fully cause for its being:
The fences failed to deplete it,
And it collared the hogs but partially.

Yet somehow I expected yesterday's blunted share
To be the last. That part which I cannot see,
I said, cannot reduce me.

2.

It is afternoon, and hot.
I split the persimmon that last Spring
I felled and trimmed and sawed.
The wood is too green yet for the best burning,
And I am probably a fool
Not to wait for colder weather.
But I want the sight of something corded.
I'll arrange the stack on the back porch,
Using the house to keep it lined.
As an anchor against this southeastern Kansas wind
It should serve better even
Than the rock.

3.

So pshaw! the hogs went loose again,
And I can't blame a woman for saying
She is sick to the death of manure.
At a time like that even the mind
Goes muddied. (But she did very well,
That woman, hip-deep in muck,
Circling those hogs like a snake hunt
Closing in. And all the while
Going to the mud on her apron
To wipe the mud off her hands.
Manure, she calls it, and I don't argue.)
At such a time
The lifting of a single thread
Unhems the world.

The price of corn is up.
Hogs are down.
The next thing you know
The government will place a tax
On prayer. All this, and more,
As we change our socks
And put on new faces for supper.

4.

The baby's cough was still in my ears
When I shot the rabbit.
Maybe that was why I found it so easy
To pull the trigger. We needed
Every peavine our plot could muster.
I don't know, maybe I
Should never have started farming.
I just don't care to see blood
On the lettuce. But the baby's cough
Was deep and going deeper,
And more than onion soup seemed necessary.
So I shot the rabbit again and again,
Sliding a deheaded stove bolt
Down the barrel to dislodge
The smoke-smeared casing. Then
In winter the blood was bright
Upon the snow as I anticipated
Spring. But the rabbit
Was always there, like the rock,
Singular as buckshot. Still,
I did what I could to save the garden,
Even long after the baby was buried.
We needed its savings for other ailments,
Other medicines. So into the seasons
I fought the rabbits,
The chamber of my .12-gauge
Like a little throat, coughing.

5.

This morning I am dizzy
With the plump brown evidence of fall.
The granary is full.
The bucket at the cistern glints its use.
The baby is solid as a tractor lug.
In the kitchen
Martha glows fuller than her cookstove's fire.
I want a dozen pancakes,
Ma'am,
A ton of sausage,
Half a crate of eggs,
Some oatmeal and a loaf of toast.
Feed me,
Woman,
Then kindly step back!
I intend to do some pretty damn fancy whistling
While I slop the hogs.

6.

Not even on the Sabbath
Can we leave the chores to heaven.
I mention this to Martha.
She tosses off a smile, not breaking stride.
It means we better hustle
Or be late for Sunday school.
Between breakfast and
The stripping of the cows
The house releases redolence.
The boys smell of yesterday's homemade haircuts,
Their talcum hovering like halos.
Martha clouds the air with stout sachet.

Into it all,
Like a bull sideboarded for market,
I stomp my barnyard boots,
Throw water to my hair and face,
Then towel it downward,
Dripping from the elbows.
The day, familiar as a necktie,
Turns like an auger in a woodknot,
And during the testimonials
I knead my chinflesh into dough,
Stanching sleep.

I sometimes fail.

Last Sunday in the center of the sermon
I tacked canvas to the hen house windows.
Three roosters, shivering, applauded,
And I looked up to see
Christ like a pea-eyed whirlwind
Sitting on a buckboard.
Are you Job? he asked.
No, I said, he lives one farm to the north.
You'll know him by the pockmarks on his face,
And by the holy stitching through his mouth.
I invited the voice to dinner,
But before I heard an answer
Its form had grown comb and feathers.

I awoke to the singing of a strange salvation
And to the shaking of weekly hands.

7.

With rope / chain / wire / terrets
I jerrybuild a halter for the rock.
It is the largest in the yard,
A nuisance rising like a single blinder
Between the house and driveway.

With double lengths of cable then
I join the rigging to a singletree
And give the mare her neck.
Breaking her knees, wide Mollie
Snaps the slack and
Lurches fetlock-deep with strain,
And splitting an obedient morning with commands
I feel the earth begin begrudgingly to move.
There is then no stopping:
The boulder, like a blunt-shared plow,
Eats out a furrow deep enough for tourists.
Across the lane the muscle-rippled mare
Gutstrains her load, until
Beyond the narrow roadway's shoulder
I scissor back the reins
And shout a halt.
One second's echo: then
The new-homed rock groans into place.
The mare, high eared, breaks wind.
And Martha, on the south-porch steps,
Is on her toes,
Clapping like a congregation,
Her face appled in sunshine,
Her stomach firm as a melon
With our first child.

Over coffee I am more than horseflesh,
And profound.
What you cannot destroy,
I say,
You pissant
To a more convenient ground.

8.

To say There is always the rock
Is not to forfeit the harvest.

Below, beside each hard place
Lies the land,
Though I remember how one summer,
Wanting rain,
I watched my topsoil disappear in wind.
I called Martha to the south porch,
To the screendoor,
And told her the future, and my plan.
When the end arrives, I said
(And it is just around the corner),
Only rock will remain.
So I told her I'd fight it no longer:
To the conqueror goes everything.
Walking out and into the dust then
I released my hat,
Intending myself to follow it
To the remotest end of oblivion.
But my bootstrings,
Pesky with sandburrs,
Snagged the treetops,
So that when the ceiling cleared
I tumbled to rest in a plowseat,
And hitched to familiar mares.
After a recent shower then
The soil turned comic and dark.
On and within it the rock chuckled,
And no longer believing in wind
I joined their joke.
Now late into each year I work the ground,
Burying seedling and seed,
Stubble and husk and leaf.
That,
And the crushed dusty felt
Of the hat.

·10·

Birth
Richard Dokey

EVERY DAY NOW the ewe was getting bigger and bigger. Billy took it food in the morning, little bunches of hay and carrot tops from the garden. The ewe grabbed the food from Billy's outstretched hand and chewed it in that quick fashion, its long, slender underjaw moving sideways. Billy patted the ewe's head. It felt odd to touch the animal's grey-white coat. The wool lay in corrugated wrinkled ropes and it was like petting the bark of one of the pine trees outside the barn, only smoother, of course. So he only patted the ewe's head and scratched its ears.

Billy sat down in the stall to watch the ewe eat. He looked at the animal's round belly. It was all belly, too much belly, as Tom Watson, the hired hand, would say. Tom Watson knew a lot about sheep and when the time came he would deliver the little lamb. And that's what Billy wanted to see. He was most eager to see that. Always before he would simply walk into one of the pastures when it was time and there would be all those little lambs stumbling and falling about. They would just be there. He had never seen one actually come out but this time he would. The ewe was having trouble. All the other ewes had dropped but this one and so his father and Tom Watson had brought it into the barn to watch and be ready. Billy had that job mainly. Tom Watson would deliver and his father would help but Billy was the watcher. And he was doing that well, better than anyone had realized, for sometimes he sneaked out at night when everybody was asleep, to watch a little. He did not carry a flashlight or even strike a match at those times because someone might have seen and then his mother would have stopped him.

So he watched in the dark of the old barn and sometimes there was moonlight in the stall.

And so the ewe just stood there, its big belly almost hiding the thin, wiry legs, and chewed the carrot tops. Always when he came the ewe would be standing. Even at night. He'd come very quietly in the dark to the stall and there would be the ewe, standing and staring out of its little yellow bubble eyes. Now the ewe stood chewing and Billy wondered if ewes could think and what they thought about and could they feel and what they felt about. Tom Watson said they couldn't feel nor think anything. Their minds were like eggshells with the insides gone. Nothing grew or happened in a ewe's head or any other animal head, Tom Watson said. And so Billy looked at the yellow bubble eyes before him and thought that must be a terrible thing, to have feelings and thoughts and know nothing about it.

Just then Billy's mother poked her head over the slats of the stall and said, "Honestly, Billy Harker, you'll be the death of me yet. You know you have chores to do. Where are my fresh eggs?"

"Yes'm," Billy said, jumping up. He knew she wasn't angry. It was just her teasing way. "I was only watching for Dad and Tom Watson."

"You think you're going to watch that little beast into life?" she asked, smiling a bit too much. Billy was Mrs. Harker's only child and she loved him more than she could say and she was always fighting it to not protect him from life.

"No, Mom," he said.

She came around the stall and stood next to him. She put a hand on his shoulder. "It is exciting, isn't it?"

"Oh, yes, Mom," he said.

"Seems to get bigger by the hour."

"It could happen anytime, Mom, just anytime."

She shook him playfully. "You get now and fetch me those eggs."

"Yes'm."

"I'll watch here a little for you."

Later that morning Billy came back to watch some more. The animal was still standing in the stall, looking vacantly out of its bubble eyes. Billy sat down in the hay. The animal usually turned its head to follow him but this time it stood simply still and quite vacant. The ewe did not blink its eyes and Billy watched how it stood there like one of those clay figures he made from the modeling set he got for Christmas. Then Billy noticed a little trembling pass along the underside of the ewe, a little shiver of movement. He looked at the ewe's eyes and the eyes were bigger and brighter, like they might burst, and the tiny trembling passed along the ewe's belly again. Billy came to his knees and bent forward. Something was happening or getting ready to happen. The ewe simply stood, quite vacant and still. Billy watched but there was nothing else. There were only the barn flies buzzing in the warm air. They landed and crept along the ewe's dirty wool rolls and their green iridescence shone under the dusty shafts of light.

Billy stood up and thought maybe he should fetch Tom Watson but the ewe lifted its head and began that sideways chewing motion with its underjaw. Billy offered the ewe some hay and the animal took it, so Billy only decided to tell Tom Watson what he had seen.

"When can you know?" he asked the hired man.

"Oh, you'll know," Tom Watson said.

"But how, Tom?"

"You'll know," the man said. "And then you come for me an' your pa. We'll get us a lamb. You'll see."

"I want to see it, Tom. I don't want to miss it."

"You'll see it," Tom Watson said. "I won't let it happen unless you're there."

"Does it hurt?"

"Does what hurt?"

"When it happens? Does it hurt the ewe?"

"No," Tom Watson said.

"Does it hurt the lamb?"

"No, it doesn't."

"But why doesn't it?" Billy asked.

"Are you writing a book?" Tom Watson joked.

"But it could hurt, couldn't it, Tom?"

"They're not people, boy. They're dumb animals. They're just animals."

"But don't they cry and bleat?"

"Sure they do."

"Well, that's hurt."

"But they don't know it, boy."

"I remember that time Prince got stepped on by that milk cow. He yelped and yowled and ran around screaming. He didn't eat for three days, Tom."

"I thought we'd have to shoot that ol' dog," the hired man said.

"But he hurt, didn't he?"

"Sure, but he didn't know it. Animals don't have minds or souls, boy. They're animals. They're just animals."

"I know," Billy said.

"All they are is animals." He patted the boy's shoulder. "Now I expect it's time for you to check again, ain't it?"

"Yessir," he said, and bolted toward the barn.

In the late afternoon Billy watched the animal some more. It stood as always, indifferent, placid and unmoving in the darkening stall. Billy sat down and watched for those tiny shivers to run along the animal's flanks but nothing happened. What am I supposed to be looking for? he wondered. Then he fed the ewe some more carrot greens and went into the big house for supper.

It was dark when he came out again. The farm was quiet in the still, warm air. Sometimes one of the cattle made that low moaning sound from the back of its throat and the sound lifted and rolled across the field toward him like a wind swirl. It was quite clear and the stars were very bright and open against the black sky. The moon would not be up for hours. Billy looked at the white stars and wondered about them.

Then he ran toward the barn. It was early yet and he hadn't gone to bed so it was all right to turn on the lights. He went to the stall and there was a cord with a bulb at the end of it. He turned the switch. A bath of yellow color flooded the stall.

The ewe was standing as always but did not turn its head to look at him. That was just like before and Billy dropped to his knees and stared at the animal's swollen belly. The ewe was shivering. All along its sides there was this shivering. Billy watched carefully. He looked at the ewe's eyes. The eyes had flattened and were withdrawn and distant. That was different, Billy thought. He hadn't seen that yet. Then the animal commenced to shake and its back legs began to tremble. Billy watched and watched. Then the ewe sighed a breathing, porous sigh and began to settle down. Its legs seemed simply to melt and it just went down and over on its side very slowly, like the last half turn on a big rubber ball.

Billy jumped to his feet and ran out of the barn. He ran straight to the bunkhouse. His heart was beating wildly when he slammed open the old screen door. Tom Watson was sitting at a wooden table playing solitaire.

"Tom!" Billy shouted.

Tom Watson rose and grabbed his hat all in one motion. "Go fetch your pa," he said.

Billy raced to the big house and his father was just sitting down to read the paper. "Dad! Dad!" he said. "It's happening! It's happening!"

"All right, Son," Billy's father said.

"Dad!"

"Did you fetch Tom?"

"He's on his way now," and he bolted from the room and ran out into the night air.

Tom Watson was already there when Billy arrived. He was kneeling beside the ewe and his hands were lost inside its body. A two foot iron bar was leaning against the wooden slats of the stall.

"It's the wrong way," Tom Watson said to himself, and just then Billy's father came up.

"What is it, Tom?" he asked.

"Wrong way," Tom Watson said.

Billy's father knelt in the hay beside the hired man and put his hands on the animal's belly.

"Feet are twisted around," Tom Watson said. "I don't know about this one."

Billy's father didn't say anything.

"I'll have to take it by the hind legs," the hired man said.

Tom Watson crept closer and his forearms disappeared into the ewe's thick body. Billy stood beside the animal's head watching. The ewe simply lay on its side. Its yellow bubble eyes still retained that vacant, withdrawn stare, as though they were looking at something inside its head. Billy leaned forward and he saw two tiny legs slide out of the animal's stomach.

"There," Tom Watson said.

The little legs were very white and the coat was matted and wet. Tom Watson worked some more and the hind quarters appeared, like a knotted, white fist.

"What do you think, Tom?" Billy's father said, holding the ewe's belly.

"She's not helping," Tom Watson said. "No strength. I'll have to pull it out."

Billy stood back a little as Tom Watson moved his hands inside the ewe's stomach. A thin smear of red became visible against the white wool of the lamb and then widened and began to flow into the wet wrinkles of its tiny body.

"I was afraid of that," Tom Watson said.

"You'll just have to pull it, Tom," Billy's father said.

Tom Watson nodded and moved his hands some more. The blood came in a little rush and Billy could see it shining on Tom Watson's arms. It was coloring the yellow hay. Some of it was on the knees of Tom Watson's pants. Billy's father looked at Billy and there was a frown on his face. He was going to say something but changed his mind.

Billy watched and watched.

"I'm just going to have to," Tom Watson said. "No other way."

"It's one of those few times all right," Billy's father said.

Tom Watson took a firm grip on the tiny lamb and leaned his weight back. Slowly the two bodies began to separate.

"I think one of the legs is still twisted," Tom Watson said. He moved his hand around inside. "Damn that blood," he said.

The red stuff shone like liquid soap on Tom Watson's arms. It was all over the hay and on Tom Watson's shirt and pants. Some of it was on Billy's father.

Billy stood back, staring. The ewe rested on its side, its eyes rolled back and empty, and then there was a wet plop and the lamb was out. It was clotted with blood and gore and Billy's father took it in his hands. It tried to lift its tiny head and the tinier legs kicked feebly.

"It's fine," Billy's father said, looking at the ewe.

Tom Watson held his hands away from his body. The hands were red and the blood dripped from them. He tried to wipe them on the hay and small bits and stalks stuck to his skin. The blood leaked out of the ewe's empty stomach.

"What do you think, Tom?" Billy's father said.

Tom Watson just shook his head. Billy's father looked at Billy.

"Go fetch an old towel from the bunkhouse," he said. "For Tom's hands."

Billy backed away.

"Go on now."

Billy turned and ran toward the barn door. But he remembered the box of rags under the work bench. He found an old one and stepped back to the stall. Billy's father was gone. He had taken the lamb out the side door to the trough to clean it. The door was open and Billy could see him.

Tom Watson was standing over the ewe. Billy could see the yellow bubble eyes, still distant and away. The ewe was breathing easily but nothing else moved. There was blood all over the hay and the blood still leaked thinly from the animal's body. It was then that Billy noticed the iron bar Tom Watson was holding.

Tom Watson stepped closer to the ewe and set himself. Billy caught his breath.

Tom Watson raised the heavy bar above his head and then swung it downward. There was a sound like no other Billy had ever heard. The animal's body seemed to jerk upward and blood spurted everywhere. Billy watched, horrified, as Tom Watson raised the iron bar and struck again. This time the sound was wet and Billy thought he would be sick. Tom Watson stood looking down at the dead ewe. He had not even realized that Billy was there.

Blood was on Tom Watson's hands. Blood was all over the ewe and all over the hay. Some was on Tom Watson's boots and some was splattered against the slats of the stall. Billy looked down. Glistening on his shirt, there between the second and third buttons, was a drop of red. It shone in the yellow light like a broken jewel.

Billy turned and ran from the barn. He tore the shirt from his body. He stood under the night, holding the shirt by one sleeve, and started to cry. Then after awhile he stopped crying and he went out behind the house where the fifty gallon incinerator drum was and he buried the shirt under the ashes.

He walked into the house.

"Billy," his mother said, "where's your shirt?"

Billy just walked past her.

"Billy, where's your shirt?"

"Outside," he said.

"Honestly, Billy, some day you'll—"

But Billy ran out of the room and up the stairs.

He went to bed. Inside his head he looked at the dead ewe. He looked at the little lamb. He did not want to see the lamb anymore. He didn't even like the little lamb. He didn't like anything. He tried to go to sleep. He wanted to go to sleep. But his eyes just kept looking at the dark.

·11·

Making Hay

Verlyn Klinkenborg

OCTOBER, IT IS SNOWING at Forty Bar Ranch in the Big Hole of Montana. Isolated squalls coast up and down the basin from the Hairpin Ranch at the southern extreme all the way north to the Pintler Wilderness. They swamp the draws on the slopes and race along the water seams between cottonwood, aspen, and willow on the valley floor. From far away the clouds seem to drag on the earth, their tops cantilevered by the wind.

Up in the timber, it has already drifted heavily. When a badger kills a ground squirrel he runs on the Twin Lakes road for easy traveling, his load in his mouth. The cattle have begun to move to lower pastures out of the heavy willows where the moose browse. On the valley bottom, Doug and M.D. are building a new bridge to replace the old plank one over the main stem of the Big Hole River. Farther downstream, well below Wisdom, the Big Hole is frozen clear across in spots.

This new bridge is no plank affair. It takes a crane, a D8 Cat, a dump truck, and a small crew from Dillon to construct because it is made from railroad flatcars, two of them, with their trucks removed. They sit on pilings over a one-lane river. The road crossing the flow here starts as a turnoff from Highway 278. It runs down among the buildings of Forty Bar Ranch, frays into a dozen tracks, skirts a triple line of massive haystacks, and peters out in a cowpath a couple haymeadows up. Follow that path carefully enough and it would take you over the Bitterroot Mountains and into Idaho.

The crane roars and shoots a black tube of smoke cloudward. Midspan, Doug does the welder's nod to flip his faceshield down, and the acetylene torch flares. The Cat, which they have had trouble starting, sputters into action along the streambed. There is no sense of urgency in this work; it is the kind of task that ranchers take on between big jobs— say, calving and haying. The gelid fringes on the fast-running river and the clattering of the aspens around Unc and Mom's place, over by the cookhouse, look and sound wintry, but there are one or two thaws still left in this autumn before the hard freeze comes. Despite the snow, Russ has time to think about building a sloping bin for the grain shed so he won't have to shovel pellets off the concrete floor into the auger. His daughter Shirley has time to knock off log-splitting and show me around. Her cousin Gary keeps the chainsaw running. There isn't *that* much time, not for young male cousins at least.

Shirley is a dental hygienist in Pocatello, home for a long weekend. She is engaged to marry a man named Joe, who does industrial work for the state of Idaho. She and Joe talk about living in Alaska, for which she has been well prepared by growing up at the Ajax and Forty Bar Ranch. Shirley is a slim woman in her early twenties with light brown hair, pretty from the outdoors and the weather, her skin a little tougher than her age. Like her father, she warms to strangers slowly but thoroughly. It is worth the wait to see her smile. Her mother, Pat, is downright adoptive in nature, her brothers, Doug and M.D., just plain shy. (Russ and Pat's younger daughter Jeanine is in nursing school at Missoula.)

The bridge crew waves (Doug waggles the torch) when we bump over the old plank structure in Shirley's red Subaru. The river, naturally, marks the low center of the valley, which is much broader than it looks from the highway cutting south along the east side. On the bridge— surrounded by the river's switchbacks, willow banks, and a web of cattle yards, haymeadows, and irrigation canals—one's visibility on the horizontal halts at about sixty yards. That is why the Petersons put their new house up by the highway: less trouble getting out in the snow, and a view from the dining room table that seems to take in most of Beaverhead County. Over coffee, you can see Homer Young, Copperhead, and Ajax Peaks. You can practically sight the tailings of the old Ajax Mine.

We don't spot Russ until we meet him at a gate. He is driving a closed-cab Case tractor and pulling a wagon with sideracks of peeled logs, full of green summer hay. Russ is a good-sized man, getting more so around the middle. He attributes his roundness to quitting smoking and Darlene the cook. He has the Peterson nose, a little on the large side, same as Unc (his uncle Melvin), and under it a black, gray-flecked moustache. He wears a flannel cowboy shirt, red suspenders, jeans, work boots, and an insulated Dillon Fertilizer cap. For a native Montanan he chews tobacco with remarkable restraint. Russ resembles his grandfather, Sam. Unc showed me a photograph taken just after the turn of the century. There sits Sam, upright and stout, on horseback in the dirt streets of Dillon. He is wearing a coat and tie.

Behind the gate Russ came through is the second reason Sam Peterson walked from Anaconda, where he worked on the smelter, into the Big Hole to homestead: hay, tons and tons of it, mounded in huge stacks. We can hear Sam's first reason mooing all around us, though the herds are hidden by fence and willow. The Forty Bar, like every other ranch in the Big Hole, is a cattle operation. Like every other ranch in the Big Hole, the Forty Bar has most of its land in haymeadow (whatever is not sagebrush, pine forest, and willow swamp) and it has seen better days.

In the Big Hole they reduce the hay/cattle relationship to its essentials: one crop—hay—and one cash source, cattle. They don't fool around with soybeans, sorghum, oats, corn, or other such nonsense, though they once made cheese here. Hay and cattle and some horses for moving the cattle down off the mountains. They do not even fuss with alfalfa here; they grow wild hay. Or rather, *they* do not grow wild hay, the valley does, as it has since long before Lewis and Clark arrived and found Indians summering their horses here in the rich native pastures along the river.

Most of the haymeadows in the Big Hole have neither been tilled nor sown in decades, but some get a touch of fertilizer (from trucks, not tractors) in October. Year after year, the soil carries timothy, redtop, bluejoint, nutgrass, a couple of fescues, creeping and meadow foxtails, clovers, and bromegrass, as well as some miscellaneous rushes and sedges (called sloughgrass locally) in the damp spots. When a midwestern steer has finished the alfalfa entrée, it needs a grain or silage course because alfalfa is high in protein and low in energy. When a Big Hole steer has finished the wild hay menu, it is done eating period until it disembarks from the semi in Minnesota or Nebraska.

During Russ's fifty-some years in the Big Hole, the hay crop has never failed, and even Unc (the twin of Russ's father, Elvin), born in 1906, cannot recall a lapse. There have been times when one rancher had to borrow a stack from another rancher, but most years they go into winter with leftovers from last winter to boot. Nineteen eighty-five has been the driest summer in Russ's memory. So the grasses can dry and the ground can firm, ranchers normally turn off the water in the irrigation ditches ten days before they mow the meadows in early August. This year the water simply disappeared two weeks before they usually divert it. Still, and to Russ's surprise, his mixed-breed herds, grazed on pasture through the hot months, are as sleek and fat as they have ever been. When we drive down the cowpaths, they bound out of our way only after we have chased them for a dozen yards. From the rear, they look like burros slung with cattle-colored panniers of grass.

Wild hay is grown in only a few high-altitude locations in the West— places like the Big Hole, at 6,200 feet above sea level, and Henry's Lake Flat, and several mountain valleys in Montana, Colorado, and Wyoming. A number of things conspire against alfalfa in these places: the wet soil, which alfalfa will not tolerate, the short growing season, the harsh winters, and the fact that winter-hardy alfalfas—those that can stand severe winters (and, as a side effect, yield less than nonhardy strains)— do not produce the bulk of hay required for the numbers of cattle these ranchers run. And then there is the question of nutritional completeness. No Big Hole rancher is about to start purchasing the quantities of silage or grain needed to supplement alfalfa. Ninety-day corn won't grow at 6,200 feet.

Partly because of these constraints, the Big Hole is a haven of traditionalism. That places it squarely at odds with the agricultural advice apparatus in this country. I talked to one member of that apparatus who began by mentioning the Big Hole's traditionalism. "It's like stepping a hundred years back in time up there," he said. "Some of those stands of grass are forty years old." The tone of his voice made it clear he found no charm in antique ranching. "They've got piss-poor irrigation practices. They turn the water on and leave it on. It's a swamp up there, the only place in the country where they farm sloughgrass." And then there are the haymaking practices themselves. "They wait till the grass has headed [produced seed] before they mow. By then, the plant has lignified—it's trying to become a tree. They get higher bulk, but nutrition goes to hell in a handbasket. So they have to feed higher volume."

This makes sense in an office, and it probably even figures on a calculator, but it does not tally in the Big Hole. The economics and technology of haying there weigh against change. Ranchers have at their feet a perennial source of nutrition that demands none of the ecological compromises of large-scale midwestern farming. Wild hay does require feeding higher volumes than alfalfa, but then the higher volumes are there for the taking. The only trick is that you have to put the hay up quickly and you have to put it up by the hundreds of tons. To do that you need special machines and you need people.

In October, the Forty Bar is almost ghostly with the hint of absent haying crews. The arrow weathervane on the log horsebarn's cupola seems to point in a direction the wind once sat and can sit no longer. The south side of the horsebarn is hung with harnesses from the days when a hundred and fifty horses grazed east of the Jackson road, nearly all of them used to pull Case or McCormick & Deering mowers or push buckrakes or draw haywagons or work the Mormon derricks or overshot stackers or beaverslides. A bear skull hangs beside the tack. Beds in the red bunkhouses are covered with newspaper and the stoves are clean of ashes, pegs free of jeans, porches of boots. Out along the fence marking the farthest perimeter of buildings, thorns grow between the floorboards of an old beaverslide hoist and poke through the perforated iron seat of an early Farmall—the kind that sold with iron-lugged wheels.

Because the past is so much present in the Big Hole, it is too easy to notice the things that have been lost with time. The things that have been saved are more important, and among those is native ingenuity. They store ingenuity in sheds and stack it along fencelines it is so abundant at the Forty Bar. To make hay in the Big Hole, you need, in the order they are used: 1. sickleblade mowers, to cut the hay; 2. siderakes, or, as they call them here, wheelrakes or greenrakes, to windrow the hay; 3. buckrakes, to push the windrows into huge piles and load the beaverslide; 4. dump or crazyrakes, to clean the corners of the field and pick up scattered hay; 5. a hoist, to raise and lower the basket on the beaverslide; 6. a beaverslide, to build the stack (more about that later); and 7. a Cat, to move the beaverslide. You also need tractors to pull the mowers and wheelrakes and crazyrakes. In winter you need hayforks to load haywagons with hay from haystacks to feed cattle. A tractor powers the hayfork and pulls the haywagon, except when diesel fuel gels in the fifty below. Then they use pitchforks and horses and haysleds, the old way.

Of all these implements, only the Cat and the tractors (and the oldest mowers) are not made in the Big Hole. The Petersons own one new Case, an older Ford, and half a dozen Farmall Cs and Ms and Hs— thirty-year-old machines that have not been seen in the Midwest, where they stay strictly current on such things, in decades. (There was even, tucked away in one small shed with the cool autumn light on its warm red paint, a Farmall B on the Forty Bar—a tiny tractor with an offset steering column—the first machine I learned how to drive.) These

Farmalls were not built in the Big Hole, but they have all been rebuilt there. When you do not have to tear up the earth, you do not need three-hundred-horse articulated four-wheel-drive tractors. An ancient C will pull a modern Big Hold wheelrake, provided you have the ingenuity to add hydraulics to the tractor. They do in Jackson.

Shirley took me through all the sheds, opening a different kind of latch at every one. Latches and gates are a subspecies of Forty Bar ingenuity. Each building Shirley and I entered had a different contraption holding the door shut. Nearly every gate we opened swung on a different kind of hinge, most fashioned from iron rings and wooden boxes. (The commonest gate latch was a horseshoe on a chain.) We walked past a homemade logsplitter where Russ and the boys shiver kindling for Russ's mom's woodstove, on which she still cooks. We cut around buckboards and green propane tanks and even, occasionally, the shank bone of a heifer and once a cow skull, still partly fleshed, that lacked a lower jaw. A dead mouse in a feed bucket bothered Shirley more than these.

One red shed held a new breed of double-sickle mower, built in Jackson. In an old log workshop we saw piles of sickle blades and a sharpening jig with an adjustable guide angle. During the mowing, sickle blades are pulled off the mowers at noon, loaded into the pickup Pat uses to carry dinners and sharp blades to the field, and brought back here, where one man sharpens all day long. (These are not serrated knives so they sharpen well.) In another shed we found four buckrakes, one of them only a season old, sleek Jackson-built machines, agricultural hot rods.

Behind the sheds rested half a dozen bright green wheelrakes (hence greenrakes), each carrying twelve huge steel wheels with forty yellow spring tines projecting outward like the sun's corona. Along one fence lay a row of thirteen-tined wooden rakes that resemble gates with teeth and bolt to the front of buckrakes. We saw three dismounted hayforks that looked like tyrannosaurus talons. Hayforks are huge steel arms with shoulder, elbow, and wrist joints that manipulate talons, which reach up and clutch a dinosaur's handful of hay from the stack and then pivot to drop it in a haywagon or feedbunk. Doug built the one mounted on the Case. Four hydraulics lines and an immense chain and sprocket maneuver it. The only thing that marks it as a homemade tool is the lack of a manufacturer's decal. As long as Doug is around, it has a lifetime warranty.

Shirley grinned as she opened one red machine shed. It sheltered a snowplane. Someone, no one remembered who, had built a closed fuselage-like shell on skis with an airplane engine and prop mounted at the rear. When winter sat deep on the Ajax, where Shirley grew up half a dozen miles from the road, they used the snowplane to reach the bus. But as Russ later told me, there were lots of ancillary snowplane sports, like impressing the womenfolk by chasing moose into the yard. They ceased to be impressed, he admitted, if you bagged one with a snow- plane's prop, as he once did by accident.

The other buildings on the floor of the Forty Bar were part domestic, part utilitarian. A white clapboard cookhouse for Darlene with a Vulcan restaurant stove, a meat locker, and a walk-in freezer (a sign inside the door says "You Are Not Locked In"), a white clapboard bunkhouse for Doug, M.D., and, temporarily, Gary, a white clapboard house set off by a low wire fence and a border of aspen for Unc and Mom. An aqua- marine corrugated-steel machine shop, a corrugated-steel calving barn with a veterinary supplies room and a dozen stalls and operating theater lights where M.D. could do Caesareans on cattle if needed. A small log shed with an iron box stove set at the back above the flume that runs through the feedlots. The stove is stoked in the winter so water keeps flowing to the cattle. (One of those basic problems: how do you water cattle when it's twenty below?) And set aside in apparent neglect, the house, a square-logged, lime-chinked, sod-roofed cabin, where Russ's father Elvin and his twin brother Melvin were born in February 1906. The cabin would fit in the living room of the main house. It looks as if they once called it a midwiving shed.

Shirley and I bump across the old plank bridge in her Subaru one last time. We are headed out to the haystacks, which have somehow migrated from the scattered haymeadows where they rose into a neat line just beyond the river. "Somehow" is one of those problems they answer in the Big Hole with hydraulics and steel. Shirley showed me a stackmover—one of three in the valley, the first built about 1967. Then she took me over to their brand-new beaverslide. Like the Peterson wheelrakes, the metal reinforcement on their beaverslide is bright green, the trademark color of Rich Shepherd, the local genius who builds these tools at his garage in Jackson. The beaverslide is the symbol of Big Hole haymaking. I have seen one or two in the Salmon River Valley and in Contact and Deeth, Nevada. But those beaverslides were built on loca- tion by Big Hole men. In the Big Hole they abound. Were it not for the

Bitterroot and Pioneer mountains and the massive stacks themselves, beaverslides would dominate the landscape.

Russ pulls up in his four-wheel-drive pickup and says, "Wanta ride up to the Ajax?" The Ajax is one of the first ranches ever built in the Big Hole, a place I had long heard about and never expected to see. I did not know that the Petersons had bought it in the forties. We stop by the elk pen for a moment, where Russ demonstrates how to call elk. He shakes a bucket with some grain pellets in it and yells "Elk! Elk! Hey Elk!" An old rancher's joke. A cow and a young bull saunter up, and Russ shakes the bull's rack through the fence, something he does every day during the rut. Then we hop in the pickup, drive past the main house, out onto 278, and cut west again on a dirt road a couple of miles north. Next thing I know we are climbing a grade and scouting the beaver swamp below us for moose.

The Farmerless Farm

Mark Kramer

SAGEBRUSH AND LIZARDS rattle and whisper behind me. I stand in the moonlight, the hot desert to my back. It's tomato harvest time, 3 A.M. The moon is nearly full and near to setting. Before me stretches the first lush tomato field to be taken this harvest. The field lies three hours northeast of Los Angeles in the middle of the bleak silvery dry-lands of California's San Joaquin Valley. Seven hundred sixty-six acres, more than a mile square of tomatoes—a shaggy vegetable green rug dappled with murky red dots, 105,708,000 ripe tomatoes lurking in the night. The field is large and absolutely level. It would take an hour and a half to walk around it. Yet, when I raise my eyes past the field to the far vaster valley floor, and to the mountains that loom further out, the harvest is lost in a big flat world.

This harvest happens nearly without people. A hundred million to-matoes grown up, irrigated, fed, sprayed, now taken, soon to be cooled, squashed, boiled, barreled and held at ready, then canned, shipped, sold, bought, and after being sold and bought a few more times, un-canned and dumped on pizza. And such is the magnitude of the vista, and the dearth of human presence that it is easy to look elsewhere and put this routine thing out of mind. But that quality—of blandness overlaying a wondrous integration of technology, finances, personnel, and business systems—seems to be just what the "future" that has befallen us has in store.

Three large tractors steam up the road toward me, headlights glaring, towing three thin latticed towers. The tractors drag the towers into place around an assembly field, then hydraulic arms raise them to vertical.

Searchlights atop the towers soon illuminate a large sandy workyard where equipment is gathering—fuel trucks, repair trucks, concession trucks, harvesters, tractor-trailers towing big open hoppers. Now small crews of Mexicans, sunburns tinted to light blue in the glare of the three searchlights, climb aboard the harvesters; shadowy drivers mount tractors and trucks. The night fills with the scent of diesel fumes and with the sounds of large engines running evenly.

The six harvesting machines drift across the gray-green tomato-leaf sea. After a time, the distant ones come to look like steamboats afloat far across a wide bay. The engine sounds are dispersed. A company foreman dashes past, tally sheets in hand. He stops nearby only long enough to deliver a one-liner. "We're knocking them out like Johnny-be-good," he says, punching the air slowly with his right fist. Then he runs off, laughing.

The nearest harvester draws steadily closer, yawing and moving in at about the speed of a slow amble, roaring as it comes. Up close, it looks like the aftermath of a collision between a grandstand and a San Francisco tramcar. It's two stories high, rolls on wheels that don't seem large enough, astraddle a wide row of jumbled and unstaked tomato vines. It is not streamlined. It resembles a Mars Lander. Gangways, catwalks, gates, conveyors, roofs and ladders are fastened on all over the lumbering rig. As it closes in, its front end snuffles up whole tomato plants as surely as a hungry pig loose in a farmer's garden. Its hind end excretes a steady stream of stems and rejects. Between the ingestion and the elimination, fourteen laborers face each other on long benches. They sit on either side of a conveyor that moves the new harvest rapidly past them. Their hands dart out and back as they sort through the red stream in front of them.

Watching them is like peering into the dining car of a passing train whose guests are absorbed in an unchanging scene. The folks aboard, though, are not dining but are working hard for low wages, culling out what is not quite fit for pizza sauce—the "greens," "molds," "mechanicals," and the odd tomato-sized clod of dirt that has gotten past the shakers and screens that have already removed tomato from vine and dumped the harvest onto the conveyor.

The absorbing nature of the work is according to plan. The workers aboard this tiny outpost of a tomato sauce factory are attempting to accomplish a chore at which they cannot possibly succeed, one designed in the near past by some anonymous practitioner of the new craft of *management*. Later in the night these tomatoes are to be delivered to a cannery. A half-full tractor-trailer runs along next to the harvester, receiving its steady flume of tomatoes. Full trucks pull away; empty ones slide in next to moving harvesters. As per cannery contract, each of the semi-trailer loads of tomatoes must contain no more than 4 percent green tomatoes, 3 percent tomatoes suffering mechanical damage from the harvester, 1 percent tomatoes that have begun to mold, and 0.5 percent clods of dirt.

"The whole idea of this thing," a harvest executive had explained earlier in the day, "is to get as many tons as you can per hour. Now, the people culling on the machines strive to sort everything that's defective. But to us, that's as bad as them picking out too little. We're getting forty to forty-seven dollars a ton for tomatoes—a bad price this year—and each truckload is fifty thousand pounds, twenty-five tons, eleven hundred bucks a load. If we're allowed seven or eight percent defective tomatoes and we don't have seven or eight percent defective tomatoes in the load, we've given away money. And what's worse, we're paying these guys to make the load too good. It's a double loss. Still, you can't say to your guys, 'Hey, leave four percent greens and one percent molds when you sort the tomatoes on that belt.' It's impossible. On most jobs you strive for perfection. They do. But you want to stop them just the right amount short of perfection—because the cannery will penalize you if your load goes over spec. So what you do is run the belt too fast, and sample the percentages in the output from each machine. If the load is too poor, we add another worker. If it's too good, we send someone home."

The workers converse as they ride the machine toward the edge of the desert. Their lips move in an exaggerated manner, but they don't shout. The few workers still needed at harvest time have learned not to fight the machine. They speak under, rather than over, the din of the harvest. They chat, and their hands stay constantly in fast motion.

Until a few years ago, it took a crew of perhaps six hundred laborers to harvest a crop this size. The six machines want about a hundred workers tonight—a hundred workers for a hundred million tomatoes, a million tomatoes per worker in the course of the month it will take to clear the field. The trucks come and go. The harvesters sweep back and forth across the field slowly. Now one stands still in midfield. A big service truck of the sort that tends jet planes bumps across the field toward it, dome light flashing. Whatever breaks can be fixed here.

After the first survey, there is nothing new to see. It will be just like this for the entire month. Like so many scenes in the new agriculture, the essence of this technological miracle is its productivity, and that is reflected in the very uneventfulness of the event. The miracle is permeated with the air of everydayness. Each detail must have persons behind it—the inventions and techniques signal insights into systems, corporate decisions, labor meetings, contracts, phone calls, handshakes, hidden skills, management guidelines. Yet it is smooth-skinned. Almost nothing anyone does here now requires manual skills or craft beyond the ability to drive and follow orders. And everyone—top to bottom—has got his orders.

The workaday mood leaves the gentleman standing next to me by the edge of the field in good humor. We'll call him Johnny Riley, and at this harvest time he is still a well-placed official on this farm. He is fiftyish and has a neatly trimmed black beard. His eyebrows and eyelashes match the beard, and his whole face, round, ruddy, and boyish, beams behind heavy black-framed glasses. He's a gladhander, a toucher, with doubleknit everything, a winning smile that demands acknowledgement, and praise to give out. It is enjoyable to talk with him.

"There are too many people out here on the job with their meters running. We can't afford trouble with tomato prices so low. If something hasn't been planned right, and it costs us extra money to get it straightened out, it's my ass," he says.

The "us" on whose behalf Johnny Riley worries is called Tejon Agricultural Partners, Inc. But there are other eligible us's who would be displeased were there to be trouble with the harvest—a host of bodies, alive and corporate, with a stake in the success of the harvest: parent companies, general partners, limited partners, associated management corporations, processors sharing contractually the risks and profits of growing this crop. Tejon Agricultural Partners, in the immediate and legal sense, owns the tomatoes.

Tejon Agricultural Partners (TAP from now on) is one of those modern bodies that exists fully, in the eyes of the shareholders, the courts and the IRS, but is an elusive creature nonetheless—not at all the sort of thing one is used to regarding as a "farmer." That linguistic awkwardness is obviously felt locally, and the word of choice used by participants to describe such entities that cause food to grow in the Central Valley is *grower*. It applies to persons and corporations interchangeably.

The tomato harvester that has been closing for some time, bearing down on our outpost by the edge of the field, now is dangerously near.

Behind the monster stretches a mile-and-a-quarter-long row of uprooted stubble, shredded leaves, piles of dirt and smashed tomatoes. Still Johnny Riley holds his ground. He has to raise his voice to make himself heard.

"I don't like to blow my own horn," he shouts, "but there are secrets to agriculture you just have to find out for yourselves. Here's one case in point. It may seem small to you at first, but profits come from doing the small things right. And one of the things I've found over the years is that a long row is better. Here's why. When you get to the end of a row, the machine"—Riley gestures up at the harvester, notices our plight, and obligingly leads me to one side. He continues, ". . . the machine here has to turn around before it can go back the other way. And that's when people get off and smoke. Long rows keep them on the job more minutes per hour. You've got less turns with long rows, and the people don't notice this. Especially at night, with lights on, row length is an important tool for people management. Three fourths of growers don't realize that. I shouldn't tell you so; it sounds like I'm patting myself on the back, but they don't."

And sure enough, as the harvester climbs off the edge of the tomato field and commences its turn on the sandy work road, the crew members descend from the catwalk, scramble to the ground and light up cigarettes. Johnny Riley nods knowingly to me, then nods again as a young fellow in a John Deere cap drives out of the moonlight in a yellow pickup to join us in the circle of floodlight the harvester has brought with it. It's as if he arrived to meet the harvester—which, it turns out, is what he did do. He is introduced as Buck Klein. Riley seems avuncular and proud as he talks about him. "I'm proud of this boy. Just a few years ago he was delivering material for a fertilizer company. Soon he was their dispatcher, then took orders. He organized the job. He came here to do pesticides, and we've been moving him up." Buck Klein keeps a neutral face for the length of this history, for which I admire him. He is of average height, sturdily built, sports a brush mustache that matches his short dark blond hair. He wears a western shirt, a belt with a huge buckle that says "Cotton" on it, and cowboy boots. He's come on business.

"We just got a truck back," he says, "all the way from the cannery at Fullerton—three hundred miles of travel and it's back with an unacceptable load. It's got twelve percent mechanical damages, so something's beating on the tomatoes. And this is the machine that's been doing it."

Johnny Riley appears to think for a moment. "We had three loads like that today. Seven, eleven and seventeen percent mechanicals. You got to take the truck back, get some workers to take out the center of the load and put in some real good tomatoes before you send it back. It ties up workers, and it ties up a truck. It's bad enough the trucks have to wait there to unload at the cannery without being sent back full."

"I'm going to go along on the harvester this trip," says Buck. "See if I can spot the trouble."

"Keep your eye on the speed," Johnny Riley says to Buck. To me he explains, "We pay a five-buck-a-load premium to the tractor driver on this machine to get him in a hurry to keep the machine on the field. Sometimes they get real hungry, and speed along a little. It lowers the quality because the machine is already set up for a certain speed. The incentive is a good management tool, but you got to watch the drivers. I took a psychology course once—as a management tool it was useful. In understanding the less educated people and why they get upset or do certain things, it's useful."

Buck eyes Johnny Riley, then walks past him to the harvester. The workers are climbing back aboard. We follow them. We look down at Johnny Riley, who is now two stories below on the ground. I cling to the starboard catwalk of the harvester. It humps off the dirt road and straddles the next unclaimed row of tomatoes. Buck rides next to me. I see Johnny Riley drive off in his car. Buck watches carefully as the first culls reach the lines of Mexican workers. Their hands flick out and back constantly. They don't look at us, and they no longer talk. Their arm motions pantomime dog paddling performed by swimmers clutching damaged tomatoes.

"It's not the tractor driver," Buck says finally. "You can see for yourself there are still too many mechanicals on the end of the belt, and they're doing everything right." He shoulders along behind the workers to the driver and shouts. The machine stops. Buck climbs down and disappears inside its innards. His cowboy boots stick out and up at an angle, all that's visible of him. When he finally wriggles back out, he says to the forewoman of the machine, "When you hit the other end of this row, stop and tell Gordon Fisher—he's the fellow with the crewcut who owns these pickers?—tell Mr. Fisher that the shaker rods here need adjusting. Understand?" The forelady nods and says, "Sí," and Buck thanks her and climbs down the ladder. We step off into the dark field. Soon the machine has left us behind. We walk back across the field toward the beginning of the row, where Buck's truck is still parked. Buck says he is beat. He's worked all day—the garlic harvest is on too. Then he went home and took his wife to Lamaze class—two months to the big day— and he napped for an hour, dozing next to his two-year-old boy.

"It's harvesting time," he explains. "Maturation goes on twenty-four hours a day. There's no overtime pay at my level—I'm management." He grins disbelievingly. "But farming work needs doing when it needs doing. You can't tell a plant, 'Stop growing, it's Sunday.' And you can't tell a bug, 'It's the Fourth of July, so stop eating the plants for the day.' " I comment to Buck that he sounds like a real farmer.

"I sort of pretend the ground's mine," he answers. "At least I know what I've put into the crops on it—I nursed these tomatoes start to finish. You talk to someone from another farm, you say, 'Over at our place . . . ,' so I guess you get to feel like it's yours. Of course I don't feel like I own it. I'd like to, but I don't have the money either. At times like this I'm pretty much in charge. Johnny Riley's probably on his way home to bed."

We walk through the tomato clutter for a while. Finally, Buck clears his throat and says, "O.K." It's as if he's decided he can go ahead and talk. "Don't get the idea it's all roses here," he continues. "Like these tomatoes. I sprayed them for worms last month—and they didn't need it. Worms are an urgent problem, and if you got them and don't spray for them, it's your butt. But we didn't really have them. I don't believe in wasting that money, if you know you don't have to. I was too young to carry weight—field got sprayed, and I had to sign the legal form as applicator, because I'm the one who took the pesticide course. I have been taught by good teachers. I was so frustrated I was ready to quit. I've seen so much money wasted on this place, things like that. Poor communications. It should be up to the field-level managers to spray or not. But I got a kid coming. After a while you just say, what the hell, I'm not going to take a reaming for sticking my neck out. You just go along with things."

As we get back to Buck's pickup truck, the two-way radio inside is squawking. Buck reaches in the window and answers it. A foreman named Les, across the night somewhere, is saying that there aren't enough trucks back now to keep up with the harvesters, and shouldn't he lay off one or two of the machines for the night?

"Where are the trucks?"

"Waiting in line at the canneries. Del Monte is about to go on strike—

there's a slowdown. Also, that trailer with the leaking hopper, the driver won't take it on the road—doesn't want to get fined."

"Have Ken make him," says Buck.

"O.K.," says the voice. Buck checks to make sure Johnny Riley has really left the scene. He can't be raised on the radio. Buck calls the field office, gets some sleepy general's number, calls on a mobile telephone, and presents his case. He mumbles into the phone for a few minutes, then is back on the radio. "Let's shut down one unit for a few hours, until more trucks show," he says. His rear is covered.

"We have budget sheets for every crop, and you better bend over if you stray very far from what it says you're going to do. It's what the management spends too much time worrying about, instead of how to make the crops better. It's all high finance. It makes sense, if you think about what they have in it. But I'll tell you something. It's expensive to farm here."

Buck points across the darkness, to the lights of the assembly yard. "Just beyond those lights there's a guy owns a piece—a section of land, and he grows tomatoes there too. A guy who works with the harvesters here, he knows tomatoes pretty well. And he says that guy has a break-even of about eighteen tons—eighteen tons of forty-dollar tomatoes pay his costs, and he's watching every row, growing better than thirty tons to the acre. Our break-even is twenty-four tons.

"Why? Because we're so much bigger. They give me more acres than I can watch that closely. They charge thirty-five or fifty bucks an acre management fee, good prices for this and that in the budget. And there is a stack of management people here, where that guy drives his own tractor while he thinks about what to do next. You can't beat him. This is not simple enough here.

"Here, they're so big, and yet they are always looking for a way to cut a dollar out of your budget. Trying to get more and more efficient. It's the workers who they see as the big expense here. They say, O.K., management is us, but maybe we can cut out some of those people on the harvesting machines. We can rent these machines from the custom harvester company for six dollars a ton bare. We got to pay the workers by the hour even when we're holding up the picking. Twenty workers to a machine, some nights, and two-ninety a worker is fifty-eight bucks for an hour of down time. You keep moving or send people home.

"Of course this will all be a thing of the past soon. There's a new machine out—Blackwelder makes it—and it's not an experimental model, I mean, it's on the job, at a hundred and four thousand dollars a shot, and it still pays. It does the same work, only better, with only two workers on it. It's faster, and there's no labor bill. It's an electronic sort. It has a blue belt, and little fingers and electric eyes, and when it spots a tomato that isn't right, the little fingers push it out of the way. You just set the amount of greens you want to be left alone, and it does that too. We're going to have two of them running later in the harvest, soon as they finish another job."

"What about the workers who have always followed the tomato harvest?" I ask.

"They're in trouble," says Buck, shaking his head. "They'll still be needed, but only toward the end of the harvest. At the beginning, most of what these cullers take away is greens. The electric eye can do that. But at the end of the harvest, most of what they take away is spoiled red, stuff that gets overripe before we pick it, and they say the machines don't do that as well. That leaves a lot of workers on welfare, or whatever they can get, hanging around waiting for the little bit we need them. They get upset about being sent away. This one guy trying to get his sister on a machine, he's been coming up to me all evening saying things about the other workers. I just ignore it, though. It's all part of the job, I guess."

·13·

Low Technology in
the Sugarbush

Noel Perrin

ONE DAY AROUND THE MIDDLE OF MARCH it begins. There's been a
good frost the night before, and today is warm and sunny. Not much
wind. Maple sap, which has been dripping very slowly from spouts for a
few days now, starts to drip fast. On the south sides of the best trees, it
might even run in a tiny trickle. A new sugar season has begun.

In Vermont that means two very different kinds of operation get under
way. Both wind up with the same products: cans of maple syrup, jars
of maple sugar, boxes of maple candy. Both are a contradiction of the
usual laws of farming, which say that you plant a crop in the spring, tend
it in the summer, and harvest it in the fall. For two hundred years
Vermonters have harvested their first cash crop even before spring has
come, even before the earliest farmer in the southernmost county in
Mississippi has a thing to sell. It may well be the one agricultural
advantage Vermont has.

The two kinds of operation are, of course, high-technology and low-
technology sugaring. They are about as different as a textile factory and
a girl with a spinning wheel. That both can thrive in the same state at the
same time is a kind of miracle.

Twenty years ago it looked as though high-technology sugaring would
take over completely. Why not? High technology generally does win. It
may be less picturesque, but it's cheaper. Take the little flocks of hens
that farmers' wives used to keep. They were charming. They still are, in
the pictures in children's books. But in the real world they have been
almost totally replaced by large, ugly, efficient battery houses, where
maybe fifty thousand hens are jammed in together, and constitute a kind

of living factory. No roosters, no chicks to peep and run about, no soil to peck. Just an assembly line for eggs. But even more economical than it is cruel. In one generation, a few hundred battery houses replaced a hundred thousand farmers' wives.

In the sugaring world, things seemed to be headed the same way. High technology duly arrived, with polyvinyl plastic in one hand and a stack of motors in the other. By all logic, the result should have been a wave of consolidations, and finally a few giant producers taking over the whole maple industry. But that hasn't happened. On the contrary, there are more people making maple syrup now than there have been for half a century. Most of them are small producers, using old-fashioned methods. It's an encouraging story.

In the beginning (and still sometimes in popular memory), sugaring was done with wooden buckets that you hung on the trees, and big iron kettles that you made the syrup in. There's such a kettle in the cellar of my house. It's thirty-two inches in diameter and weighs a hundred pounds.

After the Civil War, technology moved up a notch. By 1875 farmers hung metal buckets from their trees, and they made the syrup in evaporators which boiled maybe ten times faster than the old iron kettles. But neither of these changes made the operation less picturesque. Farm families still emptied the buckets by hand. They still hitched a team of horses to a sled when it came time to gather. And they still did the boiling over huge wood fires.

But to do all that is a very great deal of work. Say you were a farmer with a real sugarbush—that is, a large stand of hard maples bunched close together but not too close, which you trimmed and tended regularly. Say your aim was to make five or six hundred gallons of syrup each spring.

To do that, you had to go out with a hand drill and bore about twenty-five hundred tap-holes in your trees. (The rule of thumb was and still is that you can make a quart of syrup per tap in a good year.) Then you had to drive in twenty-five hundred spouts. Then hang twenty-five hundred buckets on those spouts. Then fit a specially designed lid on each, to keep the snow out.

So far, all you had done was to get ready. Once the sap started to run, serious work began. You had to go around every day or two and empty all those buckets. In the right kind of weather, they'd average a gallon of sap each, or better. So you then had to haul three or four thousand gallons of sap over to your sugarhouse. Ten or twelve tons of sloshing sap. Then you could start boiling. When you were done, many hours later, you had your first seventy-five or one hundred gallons of syrup—which you still had to put in cans. By then it was time to go gather again.

So when high technology came along, in the form of eager plastics manufacturers, there were a lot of interested producers. The new system worked like this. Now you went out with a gasoline-powered tapping drill hung around your neck. Noisy but fast. Having drilled all your holes, you linked them up with slender plastic pipe, a pale lavender kind originally developed for use in hospitals. These little pipes fed into bigger ones, and eventually a main line went right to the sugarhouse. Of course, unless your maple grove happened to be on a hillside, the sap wasn't going to flow in by itself. The system took account of that. You installed a powerful vacuum pump in the sugarhouse, and sucked the sap right out of the trees. There was some evidence you could get a little more than they really wanted to give.

You still had to do your boiling with an evaporator. (On the scale we're talking about, you'd probably use two of them in parallel, each four feet wide by fourteen feet long.) But instead of stoking it with maple trimmings, plus all the junk wood you'd gathered up around your farm, plus slabs from the nearest sawmill, you flicked a switch and your oil burner roared into life. Meanwhile, goodby to the buckets and horses and leaping fires.

Two things intervened to save traditional sugaring. One was the dramatic rise in the price of oil. Where in 1970 it took about sixty cents' worth of oil to make a gallon of maple syrup, now it takes around four dollars' worth—three gallons of oil for each gallon of syrup. The waste of fossil fuel isn't necessarily a deterrent, but the four dollars is. The big manufacturers of sugaring equipment (there are three of them, two in Vermont and one in Canada) still make oil-fired equipment, but they're not selling a whole lot of it. There has been a major shift back to wood.

The other thing is the nature of maple trees themselves. They are not a bit portable. Neither do they grow fast. Forty years is a good average from the time you plant a sugar maple until the time you can start tapping it. So while it may be easy to herd a lot of chickens into a rural ghetto, lock them in cages for life, and automate egg production, nobody is going to herd a lot of maples anywhere. You have to take them where you find them. And lots of them are to be found in small clumps, or in a row of a dozen huge old trees in front of a farmhouse, or even scattered one by one around a farm.

For maples like these, pipeline and vacuum pumps are not practical.

Buckets are actually easier. And since we're now talking about relatively small numbers, not a big sugarbush, things like power tapping drills and steam hoods and reverse osmosis are just so many unnecessary expenses. A person who is making only two or three hundred taps finds the old ways remarkably efficient. Such a producer can make his or her sixty or eighty gallons of syrup a year, sell it at the same price as the big fellows, and make the same margin of profit or better. There are hundreds and hundreds of such producers all over New England—and some in New York and Pennsylvania, too. And there are thousands more who run still smaller operations: maybe thirty taps, maybe one hundred and twenty-five. I'm one of them myself. Down here on Level Three, the equipment can be very primitive indeed. Much of it is apt to be homemade. But we, too, can sell syrup in competition with the man that has five thousand taps on pipeline. We're the exact equivalent of those farmers' wives making pin money with their little flocks of hens. Only, we still exist.

How does a small sugar operation work? Well, practically every one is different. We all have containers hanging on maple trees, and we all have some way of boiling down the sap. The rest varies. For example, I myself hang a hundred old buckets that I bought at a mountain auction in 1962, and that were probably fifty years old then. Most of my trees are along roadsides, and I gather the sap by truck. Boil it down in a small but very professional evaporator made by Grimm & Co. in Rutland. My average production is twenty-seven gallons a year, and I sell most of it by mail to out-of-staters. The rest goes on our own table.

One of my neighbors, a young wife and mother, has all spanking new buckets with shiny lids, about thirty of them. She gathers on foot, sometimes using an old sap yoke such as they used two hundred years ago. She does her boiling in a flat pan set up on concrete blocks just outside her kitchen—and dashes out about once every half hour to tend the fire. Her rate of production is very little faster than it was for the pre-Civil-War farmers. But she still makes her seven gallons a year. Most of that she puts in fancy little cans to use as Christmas presents. And each spring, between the gathering and the dashes, she gets a good deal of exercise that she professes to find more interesting than jogging.

Another nearby producer is a teenage boy. He uses around fifty one-gallon plastic milk cartons to hang on his trees. A true sap bucket holds either four or five gallons (there are two sizes), so that on the rare days you get really good sap runs, the buckets don't spill over. If there's an exceptional run on a day when Tim's at high school, either he loses sap or his mother has to gather for him. But, of course, his "buckets" cost him nothing. For boiling he has a homemade evaporator, made from a fifty-five-gallon drum. One of his uncles is a pretty good welder, and made it up for him for Christmas. Tim produces a dozen gallons a year.

Still another is a chaired professor at Dartmouth, a man nearing sixty. He has exactly seven trees in a mini-grove by his garage. Those seven are legendary for starting to run sooner than anyone else's, though, and for producing remarkable volumes of sap. Some people think there is a mystic connection between the surging oratory of Jim's lectures and the copious flow of his trees. In fact, violating the whole rational side of my nature, I think it, too. Jim makes exactly what they consume on the place: about three gallons a year.

Then there's my friend Alice, who lives one town away. Her trees are in a big hillside grove, far from any road. She and her husband couldn't gather by truck even if they wanted to, which they don't. They do it with a team of Belgian workhorses, pulling a heavy wooden sledge.

Alice loves hanging buckets (hers are even older than mine), and sometimes puts up a couple of hundred. Then, because three small children take a lot of time, and also because a team of Belgians is hard for a woman who probably doesn't weigh much over a hundred pounds to harness by herself, she has trouble keeping them emptied. Her production varies wildly. In a year when her husband can get off work enough to help her, it might be fifty gallons; another year it might be barely twenty. What runs high every year is the number of children who get a ride through the snowy woods on her sledge.

Sugaring is not one kind of activity, but many. I have no objection to the pipeline variety—I've even tried it myself—so long as it doesn't wipe out the bucket and coffee-can varieties. Because the loss would be huge.

Low technology is more than a sentimental pleasure—though God knows it's that. It is a kind of salvation for people. We live in a time when most of us, in our work, are servants of machines (and a handful, of course, are masters). In terms of the gross national product, that has worked out very nicely. In terms of the process of daily living, it has been a good deal less satisfactory. The more things there can be like sugaring, where simple and easily understood techniques can compete in the marketplace with automation, the more sense of ourselves as valuable and needed beings we will be able to keep. And that's a sense every human being and even every chicken ought to have.

·14·

The Boundary

Wendell Berry

HE CAN HEAR MARGARET at work in the kitchen. That she knows well what she is doing and takes comfort in it, one might tell from the sounds alone as her measured, quiet steps move about the room. It is all again as it has been during the almost twenty years that only the two of them have lived in the old house. Sitting in the split-hickory rocking chair on the back porch, Mat listens; he watches the smoke from his pipe drift up and out past the foliage of the plants in their hanging pots. He has finished his morning stint in the garden, and brought in a half-bushel of peas that he set down on the drainboard of the sink, telling Margaret, "There you are, ma'am." He heard with pleasure her approval, "Oh! They're nice!" and then he came out onto the shady porch to rest.

Since winter he has not felt well. Through the spring, while Nathan and Elton and the others went about the work of the fields, Mat, for the first time, confined himself to the house and barn lot and yard and garden, working a little and resting a little, finding it easier than he expected to leave the worry of the rest of it to Nathan. But slowed down as he is, he has managed to make a difference. He has made the barn his business, and it is cleaner and in better order than it has been for years. And the garden, so far, is nearly perfect, the best he can remember. By now, in the first week of June, in all its green rows abundance is straining against order. There is not a weed in it. Though he has worked every day, he has had to measure the work out in little stints, and between stints he has had to rest.

But rest, this morning, has not come to him. When he went out after breakfast he saw Nathan turning the cows and calves into the Shade

Field, so called for the woods that grows there on the slope above the stream called Shade Branch. He did not worry about it then, or while he worked through his morning jobs. But when he came out onto the porch and sat down and lit his pipe, a thought that had been on its way toward him for several hours finally reached him. He does not know how good the line fence is down Shade Branch; he would bet that Nathan, who is still rushing to get his crops out, has not looked at it. The panic of a realized neglect came upon him. It has been years since he has walked that fence himself, and he can see in his mind, as clearly as if he were there, perhaps five places where the winter spates of Shade Branch might have torn out the wire.

He sits, listening to Margaret, looking at pipe smoke, anxiously working his way down along that boundary in his mind.

"Mat," Margaret says at the screen door, "dinner's ready."

"All right," he says, though for perhaps a minute after that he does not move. And then he gets up, steps to the edge of the porch to knock out his pipe, and goes in.

When he has eaten, seeing him pick up his hat again from the chair by the door, Margaret says, "You're not going to take your nap?"

"No," he says, for he has decided to walk that length of the boundary line that runs down Shade Branch. And he has stepped beyond the feeling that he is going to do it because he should. He is going to do it because he wants to. "I got something yet I have to do."

He means to go on out the door without looking back. But he knows that she is watching him, worried about him, and he goes back to her and gives her a hug. "It's all right, my old girl," he says. He stands with his arms around her, who seems to him to have changed almost while he has held her from girl to wife to woman to mother to grandmother to great-grandmother. There in the old room where they have been together so long, ready again to leave it, he thinks, "I am an old man now."

"Don't worry," he says. "I'm feeling good."

He does feel good, for an old man, and once outside, he puts the house behind him and his journey ahead of him. At the barn he takes from its nail in the old harness room a stout stockman's cane. He does not need a cane yet, and he is proud of it, but as a concession to Margaret he has decided to carry one today.

When he lets himself out through the lot gate and into the open, past the barn and the other buildings, he can see the country lying under the sun. Nearby, on his own ridges, the crops are young and growing, the pastures are lush, a field of hay has been raked into curving windrows. Inlets of woods, in the perfect foliage of the early season, reach up the hollows between the ridges. Lower down, these various inlets join in the larger woods embayed in the little valley of Shade Branch. Beyond the ridges and hollows of the farm he can see the opening of the river valley, and beyond that the hills on the far side, blue in the distance.

He has it all before him, this place that has been his life, and how lightly and happily now he walks out again into it! It seems to him that he has cast off all restraint, left all encumbrances behind, taking only himself and his direction. He is feeling good. There has been plenty of rain, and the year is full of promise. The country looks promising. He thinks of the men he knows who are at work in it: the Coulter brothers and Nathan, Nathan's boy, Mattie, Elton Penn, and Mat's grandson, Bess's and Wheeler's boy, Andy Catlett. They are at Elton's now, he thinks, but by midafternoon they should be back here, baling the hay.

Carrying the cane over his shoulder, he crosses two fields, and then, letting himself through a third gate, turns right along the fencerow that will lead him down to Shade Branch. Soon he is walking steeply downward among the trunks of trees, and the shifting green sea of their foliage has closed over him.

He comes into the deeper shade of the older part of the woods where there is little browse and the cattle seldom come, and here he sits down at the root of an old white oak to rest. As many times before, he feels coming to him the freedom of the woods, where he has no work to do. He feels coming to him such rest as, bound to house and barn and garden for so long, he had forgot. In body, now, he is an old man, but mind and eye look out of his old body into the shifting leafy lights and shadows among the still trunks with a recognition that is without age, the return of an ageless joy. He needs the rest, for he has walked in his gladness at a faster pace than he is used to, and he is sweating. But he is in no hurry, and he sits and grows quiet among the sights and sounds of the place. The time of the most abundant blooming of the woods' flowers is past now, but the tent villages of mayapple are still perfect, there are ferns and stonecrop, and near him he can see the candle-like white flowers of black cohosh. Below him, but still out of sight, he can hear the water in Shade

Branch passing down over the rocks in a hundred little rapids and falls. When he feels the sweat beginning to dry on his face he gets up, braces himself against the gray trunk of the oak until he is steady, and stands free. The descent beckons and he yields eagerly to it, going on down into the tireless chanting of the stream.

He reaches the edge of the stream at a point where the boundary, coming down the slope facing him, turns at a right angle and follows Shade Branch in its fall toward the creek known as Willow Run. Here the fence that Mat has been following crosses the branch over the top of a rock wall that was built in the notch of the stream long before Mat was born. The water coming down, slowed by the wall, has filled the notch above it with rock and silt, and then, in freshet, leaping over it, has scooped out a shallow pool below it, where water stands most of the year. All this, given the continuous little changes of growth and wear in the woods and the stream, is as it was when Mat first knew it: the wall gray and mossy, the water, only a spout now, pouring over the wall into the little pool, covering the face of it with concentric wrinkles sliding outward.

Here, seventy-five years ago, Mat came with a fencing crew: his father, Ben, his uncle, Jack Beechum, Joe Banion, a boy then, not much older than Mat, and Joe's grandfather, Smoke, who had been a slave. And Mat remembers Jack Beechum coming down through the woods, as Mat himself has just come, carrying on his shoulder two of the long light rams they used to tamp the dirt into postholes. As he approached the pool he took a ram in each hand, holding them high, made three long approaching strides, planted the rams in the middle of the pool, and vaulted over. Mat, delighted, said, "Do it again!" And without breaking rhythm, Jack turned, made the three swinging strides, and did it again— *does* it again in Mat's memory, so clearly that Mat's presence there, so long after, fades away, and he hears their old laughter, and hears Joe Banion say, "Mistah Jack, he might nigh a *bird*!"

Forty-some years later, coming down the same way to build that same fence again, Mat and Joe Banion and Virgil, Mat's son, grown then and full of the newness of his man's strength, Mat remembered what Jack had done and told Virgil; Virgil took the two rams, made the same three strides that Jack had made, vaulted the pool, and turned back and grinned. Mat and Joe Banion laughed again, and this time Joe looked at Mat and said only "Damn."

Now a voice in Mat's mind that he did not want to hear says, "Gone.

All of them are gone." And they *are* gone. Mat is standing by the pool, and all the others are gone, and all that time has passed. And still the stream pours into the pool and the circles slide across its face.

He shrugs as a man would shake snow from his shoulders and steps away. He finds a good place to cross the branch, and picks his way carefully from rock to rock to the other side, using the cane for that and glad he brought it. Now he gives attention to the fence. Soon he comes upon signs—new wire spliced into the old, a staple newly driven into a sycamore—that tell him his fears were unfounded. Nathan has been here. For a while now Mat walks in the way he knows that Nathan went. Nathan is forty-one this year, a quiet, careful man, as attentive to Mat as Virgil might have been if Virgil had lived to return from the war. Usually, when Nathan has done such a piece of work as this, he will tell Mat so that Mat can have the satisfaction of knowing that the job is done. Sometimes, though, when he is hurried, he forgets, and Mat will think of the job and worry about it and finally go to see to it himself, almost always to find, as now, that Nathan has been there ahead of him and has done what needed to be done. Mat praises Nathan in his mind and calls him son. He has never called Nathan son aloud, to his face, for he does not wish to impose or intrude. But Nathan, who is not his son, has become his son, just as Hannah, Nathan's wife, Virgil's widow, who is not Mat's daughter, has become his daughter.

"I am blessed," he thinks. He walks in the way Nathan walked down along the fence, between the fence and the stream, seeing Nathan in his mind as clearly as if he were following close behind him, watching. He can see Nathan with axe and hammer and pliers and pail of staples and wire stretcher and coil of wire, making his way down along the fence, stopping now to chop a windfall off the wire and retighten it, stopping again to staple the fence to a young sycamore that has grown up in the line opportunely to serve as a post. Mat can imagine every move Nathan made, and in his old body, a little tired now, needing to be coaxed and instructed in the passing of obstacles, he remembers the strength of the body of a man of forty-one, unregarding of its own effort.

Now, trusting the fence to Nathan, Mat's mind turns away from it. He allows himself to drift down the course of the stream, passing through it as the water passes, drawn by gravity, bemused by its little chutes and falls. He stops beside one tiny quiet backwater and watches a family of water striders conducting their daily business, their feet dimpling the surface. He eases the end of his cane into the pool, and makes a crawfish spurt suddenly backward beneath a rock.

A water thrush moves down along the rocks of the streambed ahead of him, teetering and singing. He stops and stands to watch while a brown bird, a creeper, feeds upward in a spiral around the trunk of a big sycamore, putting its eye close to peer under the loose scales of the bark. The bird flies to the base of a tree nearer to Mat and starts upward again, earning a living, paying him no mind. He has become still as a tree, and now a hawk suddenly stands on a limb close over his head. The hawk loosens his feathers and shrugs, looking around him with his fierce eyes. And it comes to Mat that once more, by stillness, he has passed across into the wild inward presence of the place.

"Wonders," he thinks. "Little wonders of a great wonder." He feels the sweetness of time. If a man eighty years old has not seen enough, then nobody will ever see enough. Such a little piece of the world as he has before him now would be worth a man's long life, watching and listening. And then he could go two hundred feet and live again another life, listening and watching, and his eyes would never be satisfied with seeing, nor his ears filled with hearing. Whatever he saw could be seen only by looking away from something else equally worth seeing. For a second he feels and then loses some urging of the delight in a mind that could see and comprehend it all, all at once. "I could stay here a long time," he thinks. "I could stay here a long time."

He is standing at the head of a larger pool, another made by the plunging of the water over a rock wall. This one he built himself, he and Virgil, in the terribly dry summer of 1930. By the latter part of that summer, because of the shortage of both rain and money, they had little enough to do, and they had water on their minds. Mat remembered this place, where a strong vein of water opened under the roots of a huge old sycamore and flowed only a few feet before it sank uselessly among the dry stones of the streambed. "We'll make a pool," he said. He and Virgil worked several days in the August of that year, building the wall and filling in behind it so that the stream, when it ran full again, would not tear out the stones. The work there in the depth of the woods took their minds off their parched fields and comforted them. It was a kind of work that Mat loved and taught Virgil to love, requiring only the simplest tools:

a large sledgehammer, a small one, and two heavy crowbars with which they moved the big, thick rocks that were in that place. Once their tools were there, they left them until the job was done. When they came down to work they brought only a jug of water from the cistern at the barn.

"We could drink out of the spring," Virgil said.

"Of course we could," Mat said. "It's dog days now. Do you want to get sick?"

In a shady place near the creek, Virgil tilted a flagstone up against a small sycamore, wedging it between trunk and root, to make a place for the water jug. There was not much reason for that. It was a thing a boy would do, making a little domestic nook like that, so far off in the woods, but Mat shared his pleasure in it, and that was where they kept the jug.

When they finished the work and carried their tools away, they left the jug, forgot it, and did not go back to get it. Mat did not think of it again until, years later, he happened to notice the rock still leaning against the tree, which had grown over it, top and bottom, fastening the rock to itself by a kind of natural mortise. Looking under the rock, Mat found the earthen jug still there, though it had been broken by the force of the tree trunk growing against it. He left it as it was. By then Virgil was dead, and the stream, rushing over the wall they had made, had scooped out a sizable pool that had been a faithful water source in dry years.

Remembering, Mat goes to the place and looks and again finds the stone and finds the broken jug beneath it. He has never touched rock or jug, and he does not do so now. He stands, looking, thinking of his son, dead twenty years, a stranger to his daughter, now a grown woman, who never saw him, and he says aloud, "Poor fellow!" So taken is his mind by his thoughts that he does not know he is weeping until he feels his tears cool on his face.

Deliberately, he turns away. Deliberately, he gives his mind back to the day and the stream. He goes on down beside the flowing water, loitering, listening to the changes in its voice as he walks along it. He silences his mind now and lets the stream speak for him, going on, descending with it, only to prolong his deep peaceable attention to that voice that speaks always only of where it is, remembering nothing, fearing and desiring nothing.

Farther down, the woods thinning somewhat, he can see ahead of him where the Shade Branch hollow opens into the valley of Willow Run. He can see the crest of the wooded slope on the far side of the creek valley. He stops. For a minute or so his mind continues on beyond him,

charmed by the juncture he has come to. He imagines the succession of
them, openings on openings: Willow Run opening to the Kentucky
River, the Kentucky to the Ohio, the Ohio to the Mississippi, the
Mississippi to the Gulf of Mexico, the Gulf to the boundless sky. He
walks in old memory out into the river, carrying a heavy rock in each
hand, out and down, until the water closes over his head and then the
light shudders above him and disappears, and he walks in the dark cold
water, down the slant of the bottom, to the limit of breath, and then
drops his weights and cleaves upward into light and air again.

He turns around and faces the way he has come. "*Well*, old man!" he
thinks. "*Now* what are you going to do?" For he has come down a long
way, and now, looking back, he feels the whole country tilted against
him. He feels the weight of it and the hot light over it. He hears himself
say aloud, "Why, I've got to get back out of here."

But he is tired. It has been a year since he has walked even so far as he
has already come. He feels the heaviness of his body, a burden that, his
hand tells him, he has begun to try to shift off his legs and onto the cane.
He thinks of Margaret, who, he knows as well as he knows anything,
already wonders where he is and is worrying about him. Fear and
exasperation hold him for a moment, but he pushes them off; he forces
himself to be patient with himself. "Well," he says, as if joking with
Virgil, for Virgil has come back into his thoughts now as a small boy,
"going up ain't the same as coming down. It's going to be different."

It would be possible to go on down, and he considers that. He could
follow the branch on down to the Willow Run road where it passes the
Rowanberry place. That would be downhill, and if he could find Mart
Rowanberry near the house, Mart would give him a ride home. But the
creek road is little traveled these days; if he goes down there and Mart is
up on the ridge at work, which he probably is, then Mat will be farther
from home than he is now, and will have a long walk, at least as far as the
blacktop, maybe farther. Of course, he could go down there and just wait
until Mart comes to the house at quitting time. There is sense in that,
and for a moment Mat stands balanced between ways. What finally
decides him is that he is unsure what lies between him and the creek
road. If he goes down much farther he will cross the line fence onto the
Rowanberry place. He knows that he would be all right for a while,
going on down along the branch, but once in the creek bottom he would

have to make his way to the road through dense, undergrowthy thicket, made worse maybe by piles of drift left by the winter's high water. He might have trouble getting through there, he thinks, and the strangeness of that place seems to forbid him. It has begun to trouble him that no other soul on earth knows where he is. He does not want to go where he will not know where he is himself.

He chooses the difficult familiar way, and steps back into it, helping himself with the cane now. He does immediately feel the difference between coming down and going up, and he wanders this way and that across the line of his direction, searching for the easiest steps. Windfalls that he went around or stepped over thoughtlessly, coming down, now require him to stop and study and choose. He is tired. He moves by choice.

He and his father have come down the branch, looking for a heifer due to calve; they have found her and are going back. Mat is tired. He wants to be home, but he does not want to *go* home. He is hot and a scratch on his face stings with sweat. He would just as soon cry as not, and his father, walking way up ahead of him, has not even slowed down. Mat cries, "*Wait*, Papa!" And his father does turn and wait, a man taller than he looks because of the breadth of his shoulders, whom Mat would never see in a hurry and rarely see at rest. He has turned, smiling in the heavy bush of his beard, looking much as he will always look in Mat's memory of him, for Mat was born too late to know him young and he would be dead before he was old. "Come on, Mat," Ben says. "Come on, my boy." As Mat comes up to him, he reaches down with a big hand that Mat puts his hand into. "It's all right. It ain't that far." They go on up the branch then. When they come to a windfall across the branch, Ben says, "This one we go under." And when they come to another, he says, "This one we go around."

Mat, who came down late in the afternoon to fix the fence, has fixed it, and is hurrying back, past chore time, and he can hear Virgil behind him, calling to him, "Wait, Daddy!" He brought Virgil against his better judgment, because Virgil would not be persuaded not to come. "You need me," he said. "I do need you," Mat said, won over. "You're my right-hand man. Come on." But now, irritated with himself and with Virgil too, he knows that Virgil needs to be carried, but his hands are loaded with tools and he *can't* carry him. Or so he tells himself, and he walks on. He stretches the distance out between them until Virgil feels that he has been left alone in the darkening woods; he sits down on a rock and gives himself up to grief. Hearing him cry, Mat puts his tools down where he can find them in the morning, and goes back for Virgil. "Well, it's all right, old boy," he says, picking him up. "It's all right. It's all right."

He is all right, but he is sitting down on a tree trunk lying across the branch, and he has not been able to persuade himself to get up. He came up to the fallen tree, and, to his surprise, instead of stepping over it, he sat down on it. At first that seemed to him the proper thing to do. He needed to sit down. He was tired. But now a protest begins in his mind. He needs to be on his way. He ought to be home by now. He knows that Margaret has been listening for him. He knows that several times by now she has paused in her work and listened, and gone to the windows to look out. She is hulling the peas he brought her before dinner. If he were there, he would be helping her. He thinks of the two of them sitting in the kitchen, hulling peas, and talking. Such a sense of luxury has come into their talk, now that they are old and in no hurry. They talk of what they know in common and do not need to talk about, and so talk about only for pleasure.

They would talk about where everybody is today and what each one is doing. They would talk about the stock and the crops. They would talk about how nice the peas are this year, and how good the garden is.

He thought, once, that maybe they would not have a garden. There were reasons not to have one.

"We don't need a garden this year," he said to Margaret, wanting to spare her the work that would be in it for her.

"Yes," she said, wanting to spare him the loss of the garden, "of course we do!"

"Margaret, we'll go to all that work, and can all that food, and neither one of us may live to eat it."

She gave him her smile, then, the same smile she had always given him, that always seemed to him to have survived already the worst he could think of. She said, "Somebody will."

She pleased him, and the garden pleased him. After even so many years, he still needed to be bringing something to her.

His command to get up seems to prop itself against his body and stay there like a brace until finally, in its own good time and again to his surprise, his body obeys. He gets up, steps over the tree, and goes on. He keeps himself on his feet for some time now, herding himself along like a recalcitrant animal, searching for the easy steps, reconciling himself to the hard steps when there are no easy ones. He is sweating heavily. The air is hot and close, so deep in that cleft of the hill. He feels that he must stretch upward to breathe. It is as though his body has come to belong in a different element, and the mere air of that place now hardly sustains it.

He comes to the pool, the wall that he and Virgil made, and pauses there. "Now you must drink," he says. He goes to where the spring comes up among the roots of the sycamore. There is a smooth clear pool there, no bigger than his hat. He lies down to drink, and drinks, looking down into the tiny pool cupped among the roots, surrounded with stonecrop and moss. The loveliness of it holds him: the cool water in that pretty place in the shade, the great tree rising and spreading its white limbs overhead. "I am blessed," he thinks, "I could stay here." He rests where he lies, turned away from his drinking, more comfortable on the roots and rocks than he expected to be. Through the foliage he can see white clouds moving along as if mindful where they are going. A chipmunk comes in quick starts and stops across the rocks and crouches a long time not far from Mat's face, watching him, as if perhaps it would like a drink from the little pool that Mat just drank from. "Come on," Mat says to it. "There ain't any harm in me." He would like to sleep. There is a weariness beyond weariness in him that sleep would answer. He can remember a time when he could have let himself sleep in such a place, but he cannot do that now. "Get up," he says aloud. "Get up, get up."

But for a while yet he does not move. He and the chipmunk watch each other. Now and again their minds seem to wander apart, and then they look again and find each other still there. There is a sound of wings, like a sudden dash of rain, and the chipmunk tumbles off its rock and does not appear again. Mat laughs. "You'd *better* hide." And now he does get up.

He stands, his left hand propped against the trunk of the sycamore. Darkness draws across his vision and he sinks back down onto his knees, his right hand finding purchase in the cold cup of the spring. The darkness wraps closely around him for a time, and then withdraws, and he stands again. "*That* won't do," he says to Virgil. "We got to do better than that, boy." And then he sees his father too standing with Virgil on the other side of the stream. They recognize him, even though he is so much older now than when they knew him—older than either of them ever lived to be. "Well," he says, "looks like we got plenty of help." He reaches down and lets his right hand feel its way to the cane, picks it up, and straightens again. "*Yes*sir."

The world clears, steadies, and levels itself again in the light. He looks around him at the place: the wall, the pool, the spring mossy and clear in the roots of the white tree. "I am not going to come back here," he thinks. "I will never be in this place again."

Instructing his steps, he leaves. He moves with the utmost care and the utmost patience. For some time he does not think of where he is going. He is merely going up along the stream, asking first for one step and then for the next, moving by little plans that he carefully makes, and by choice. When he pauses to catch his breath or consider his way, he can feel his heart beating; at each of its beats the world seems to dilate and spring away from him.

His father and Virgil are with him, moving along up the opposite side of the branch as he moves up his side. He cannot always see them, but he knows they are there. First he does not see them, and then he sees one or the other of them appear among the trees and stand looking at him. They do not speak, though now and again he speaks to them. And then Jack Beechum, Joe Banion, and old Smoke are with them. He sees them sometimes separately, sometimes together. The dead who were here with him before are here with him again. He is not afraid. "I could stay here," he thinks. But ahead of him there is a reason he should not do that, and he goes on.

He seems to be walking in and out of his mind. Or it is time, perhaps, that he is walking in and out of. Sometimes he is with the dead as they were, and he is as he was, and all of them together are walking upward through the woods toward home. Sometimes he is alone, an old man in a later time than any of the dead have known, going the one way that he alone is going, among all the ways he has gone before, among all the ways he has never gone and will never go.

He does not remember falling. He is lying on the rocks beside the branch, and there is such disorder and discomfort in the way he is lying as he could not have intended. And so he must have fallen. He wonders if he is going to get up. After a while he does at least sit up. He shifts around so that his back can rest against the trunk of a tree. His movements cause little lurches in the world, and he waits for it to be steady. "Now you have got to stop and think," he says. And then he says, "Well, you have stopped. Now you had better think."

He does begin to think, forcing his vision and his thoughts out away from him into the place around him, his mind making little articulations of recognition. The place and his memory of it begin to speak to one another. He has come back almost to the upper wall and pool, where he first came down to the branch. When he gets there he will have a choice to make between two hard ways to go.

But his mind, having thought of those choices, now leaves him, like an undisciplined pup, and goes to the house, and goes back in time to the house the way it was when he and Margaret were still young, when Virgil was four or five years old, and Bess was eleven or twelve.

About this time in the afternoon, about this time in the year, having come to the house for something, he cannot remember what, he pushes open the kitchen door, leans his shoulder on the jamb, and looks at Margaret who stands with her back to him, icing a cake.

"Now nobody's asked for my opinion," he says, "and nobody's likely to, but if anybody ever was to, I'd say that *that* is a huggable woman."

"Don't you come near me, Mat Feltner."

"And a spirited woman."

"If you so much as lay a hand on me, I'm going to hit you with this cake."

"And a dangerous, mean woman."

"Go back to work."

"Who is, still and all, a huggable woman. Which is only my opinion. A smarter man might think different."

She turns around, laughing, and comes to get her hug. "I could never have married a smart man."

"She didn't marry *too* smart a one," he thinks. He is getting up, the effort requiring the attendance of his mind, and once he is standing he puts his mind back on his problem. That is not where it wants to be, but this time he makes it stay. If he leaves the branch and goes back up onto the ridge by the way he came down, that will require a long slanting climb up across the face of a steep slope. "And it has got steeper since I came down it," he thinks. If he goes on up Shade Branch, which would be the easiest, surest route, he will have, somehow, to get over or through the fence that crosses the branch above the wall. He does not believe that he can climb the fence. Where the fence crosses the stream it is of barbed wire, and in that place a stronger man might go through or under it. But he does not want to risk hooking his clothes on the barbs.

But now he thinks of a third possibility: the ravine that comes into Shade Branch just above him to his right hand. The dry, rocky stream-bed in the ravine would go up more gently than the slope, the rocks would afford him stairsteps of a sort for at least some of the way, and it would be the shortest way out of the woods. It would bring him out farther from home than the other ways, but he must not let that bother him. It is the most possible of the three ways, and the most important thing now, he knows, is to get up onto the open land of the ridge where he can be seen if somebody comes looking for him. Somebody will be looking for him, he hopes, for he has to admit that he is not going very fast, and once he starts up the ravine he will be going slower than ever.

For a while he kept up the belief, and then the hope, that he could make it home in a reasonable time and walk into the house as if nothing had happened.

"Where on earth have you been?" Margaret would ask.

He would go to the sink to wash up, and then he would say, drying his hands, "Oh, I went to see about the line fence down the branch, but Nathan had already fixed it."

He would sit down then to help her with the peas.

"Mat Feltner," she would say, "surely you didn't go away off down there."

But it is too late now, for something *has* happened. He has been gone too long, and is going to be gone longer.

Margaret has got up from her work and gone to the windows and looked out, and gone to the door onto the back porch and spoken his name, and walked on out to the garden gate and then to the gate to the barn lot.

He can see her and hear her calling as plainly as if he were haunting her. "Mat! Oh, Mat!"

He can hear her, and he makes his way on up the branch to the mouth of the ravine. He turns up the bed of the smaller stream. The climb is steeper here, the hard steps closer together. The ascent asks him now really to climb, and in places, where the rocks of the streambed bulge outward in a wall, he must help himself with his hands. He must stoop under and climb over the trunks of fallen trees. When he stops after each of these efforts the heavy beating of his heart keeps on. He can feel it shaking him, and darkness throbs in his eyes. His breaths come too far between and too small. Sometimes he has roots along the side of the ravine for a banister, and that helps. Sometimes the cane helps; sometimes, when he needs both hands, it is in the way. And always he is in the company of the dead.

Ahead of him the way is closed by the branchy top of a young maple, blown down in a storm, and he must climb up the side of the ravine to get around it. At the top of the climb, when the slope has gentled and he stops and his heart plunges on and his vision darkens, it seems to him that he is going to fall; he decides instead to sit down, and does. Slowly he steadies again within himself. His heart slows and his vision brightens again. He tells himself again to get up. "It ain't as far as it has been," he says to Virgil. "I'm going to be all right now. I'm going to make it."

But now his will presses against his body, as if caught within it, in bewilderment. It will not move. There was a time when his body had strength enough in it to carry him running up such a place as this, with breath left over to shout. There was a time when it had barely enough strength in it to carry it this far. There is a time when his body is too heavy for his strength. He longs to lie down. To Jack Beechum, the young man, Jack Beechum, who is watching him now, he says, "You and I were here once."

The dead come near him, and he is among them. They come and go, appear and disappear, like a flock of feeding birds. They are there and gone. He is among them, and then he is alone. To one who is not going any farther, it is a pretty place, the leaves new and perfect, a bird singing out of sight among them somewhere over his head, and the softening light slanting in long beams from the west. "I could stay here," he thinks. It is the thought of going on that turns that steep place into an agony. His own stillness pacifies it and makes it lovely. He thinks of dying, secretly, by himself, in the woods. No one now knows where he is. Perhaps it would be possible to hide and die, and never be found. It would be a clean, clear way for that business to be done, and the thought, in his weariness, comforts him, for he has feared that he might die a nuisance to Margaret and the others. He might, perhaps, hide himself in a little cave or sink hole if one were nearby, here where the dead already are, and be one of them, and enter directly into the peaceableness of this place, and turn with it through the seasons, his body grown easy in its weight.

But there is no hiding place. He would be missed and hunted for and found. He would die a nuisance, for he could not hide from all the reasons that he would be missed and worried about and hunted for. He has an appointment that must be kept, and between him and it the climb rises on above him.

He has an accounting he must come to, and it is not with the dead, for Margaret has not sat down again, but is walking. She is walking from room to room and from window to window. She has not called Bess, because she does not want Bess to drive all the way up from Hargrave, perhaps for nothing. Though she has thought about it, she has not even called Hannah, who is nearer by. She does not want to alarm anybody. But she is alarmed. She walks from room to room and from window to window, pausing to look out, and walking again. She walks with her arms tightly folded, as she has walked all her life when she has been troubled, until Mat, watching her, has imagined that he thinks as she thinks and feels as she feels, so moved by her at times that he has been startled to realize again his separateness from her.

He remembers the smile of assent that she gave him once: "Why, Mat, I thought you did. And I love you." Everything that has happened to him since has come from that—and leads to that, for it is not a moment that has ever stopped happening; he has gone toward it and aspired to it all his life, a time that he has not surpassed.

Now she is an old woman, walking in his mind in the rooms of their house. She has called no one and told no one. She is the only one who knows that she does not know where he is. The men are in the hayfield, and she is waiting for one of them or some of them to come to the barn. Or Wheeler might come by. It is the time of day when he sometimes does. She walks slowly from room to room, her arms folded tightly, and she watches the windows.

Mat, sitting in his heaviness among the trees, she does not know where, yearns for her as from beyond the grave. "Don't worry," he says. "It's going to be all right." He gets up.

And now an overmastering prayer that he did not think to pray rushes upon him out of the air and seizes him and grapples him to itself: an absolute offering of himself to his return. It is an offer, involuntary as his breath, voluntary as the new steps he has already taken up the hill, to give up his life in order to have it. The prayer does not move him beyond weariness and weakness, it moves him merely beyond all other thoughts.

He gives no more regard to death or to the dead. The dead do not appear again. Now he is walking in this world, walking in time, going home. A shadowless love moves him now, not his, but a love that he belongs to, as he belongs to the place and to the light over it. He is thinking of Margaret and of all that his plighting with her has led to. He is thinking of the membership of the fields that he has belonged to all his life, and will belong to while he breathes, and afterward. He is thinking of the living ones of that membership—at work today in the fields that the dead were at work in before them.

"I am blessed," he thinks. "I am blessed."

He is crawling now, the cane lost and forgotten. He crawls a little, and he rests a lot. The slope has gentled somewhat. The big woods has given way to thicket. He has turned away from the stream, taking the straightest way to the open slope that he can see not far above him. The cattle are up there grazing, the calves starting to play a little, now that the cool of the day is here.

When he comes out, clear of the trees, onto the grassed hillside, he seems again to have used up all his strength. "Now," he thinks, "you have got to rest." Once he has rested he will go on to the top of the ridge. Once he gets there, he can make it to the road. He crawls on up the slope a few feet to where a large walnut tree stands alone outside the woods, and sits against it so that he will have a prop for his back. He wipes his face, brushes at the dirt and litter on his knees and then subsides. Not meaning to, he sleeps.

The sun is going down when he wakes, the air cold on his damp clothes. Except for opening his eyes, he does not move. His body is still as a stone.

Now he knows what woke him. It is the murmur of an automobile engine up on the ridge—Wheeler's automobile, by the sound of it. And when it comes into sight he sees that it is Wheeler's; Wheeler is driving and Elton Penn and Nathan are with him. They are not looking for him.

They have not seen Margaret. Perhaps they did not bale the hay. Or they may have finished and got away early. But he knows that Wheeler found Nathan and Elton, wherever they were, after he shut his office and drove up from Hargrave, and they have been driving from field to field ever since, at Elton's place or at Nathan's or at Wheeler's, and now here. This is something they do, Mat knows, for he is often with them when they do it. Wheeler drives the car slowly, and they look and worry and admire and remember and plan. They have come to look at the cattle now, to see them on the new grass. They move among the cows and calves, looking and stopping. Now and then an arm reaches out of one of the car windows and points. For a long time they do not turn toward Mat. It is as though he is only part of the field, like the tree he is leaning against. He feels the strangeness of his stillness, but he does not move.

And then, still a considerable distance away, Wheeler turns the car straight toward the tree where Mat is sitting. He sees their heads go up when they see him, and he raises his right hand and gives them what, for all his eagerness, is only an ordinary little wave.

Wheeler accelerates, and the car comes tilting and rocking down the slope. Where the slope steepens, forcing the car to slow down, Mat sees Nathan leap out of it and come running toward him, Elton out too, then, coming behind him, while Wheeler is still maneuvering the car down the hill. Seeing that they are running to help him, Mat despises his stillness. He forces himself to his knees and then to his feet. He turns to face Nathan, who has almost reached him. He lets go of the tree and stands, and sees the ground rising against him like a blow. He feels himself caught strongly, steadied, and held. He hears himself say, "Papa?"

That night, when Margaret finds him wandering in the darkened house, he does not know where he is.

.2.
The Small Town

Introduction

"FOR WE MUST CONSIDER that we shall be as a city upon a hill," wrote Puritan Governor John Winthrop in 1630 of the Massachusetts Bay Colony, the archetypical small town. "The eyes of all people are upon us. . . . We must uphold a familiar commerce together in all meekness, gentleness, patience, and liberality. We must delight in each other, make others' conditions our own, rejoice together, always having before our eyes our commission [from God] and community in the work, our community as members of the same bond." Winthrop's vision of the "covenanted community" doing God's special work in the New World defined subsequent American small towns, from commercial crossroads to immigrant villages to railroad towns strung every six miles along the right-of-way of the Great Northern Railway through North Dakota and Montana. Winthrop's vision is what most people mean when they speak about "small-town mystique."

It is probably this idealized village that Americans imagine while singing of alabaster cities gleaming, undimmed by human tears. They see not New York or Los Angeles or even Chicago, but rural villages filled with all the amenities of society and none of the city's vices; friendly places, safe, peopled by warm, populist folk eager to help and be helped, slow to wrath and quick to forgive, maybe a little quaint but shrewd with an American (Yankee) wit and cunning you can't help but admire. Decent folk they are, the kind of people you'd like to go fishing with, or to a high school football game. Human enough for Halloween pranks, but not the sort to steal your bicycle or trash your car. Hard working, but hard playing as well. Friendly folks, who in a pinch stick by you every time.

The modern American suburb is in its conception not a little Boston, but a miniature Concord . . . at least to the refugees from the urban row houses and brownstones willing to gamble their futures on expensive real estate in the 'burbs. "Let not our town be large," wrote Springfield, Illinois's Vachel Lindsay, "Remembering / That little Athens was the muses's home. . . ."

Zona Gale's Friendship Village was not the first fictional articulation of the American small town as New Athens ("New Albion" in the case of Garrison Keillor's Lake Wobegon), but it was certainly one of the most compelling. Constructed decades after Mark Twain had debunked the myth of Happy Village in *The Adventures of Huckleberry Finn*, Friendship Village has endured as a stereotype of small-town America. It is a mature village, to be sure: whatever utopian visions may have shaped its founding, it has settled into religious and social orthodoxies and even a very noticeable caste system. Its inhabitants—the blood inhabitants, at least—are old and quaint, nurturing nearly to the point of busybodiness. They are precisely the kind of people who would drive Carol Kennicott of Sinclair Lewis' *Main Street* out of her college-educated mind. To Gale, however, the people and the town are motherly, quick to forgive, in essential good health, without essential sin, and warm as a Currier and Ives Thanksgiving print. Gale's Thanksgiving feast is, in fact, as symbolic as it is tasty: this town will feed you, shelter you, nourish you, take care of you.

Friendship Village is a literary creation, of course, and no town chartered as a grain collection point by railroads greedy for shipping charges, no town sprung up overnight in the gold-mining frenzy of the Black Hills or the steamboating days of the Mississippi, no town grown from a general store and a blacksmith's shop at the crossroads of two Indian trails ever, in even its most pristine moments, resembled Friendship, any more than the reality of the Massachusetts Bay Colony measured up to Winthrop's ideal city on a hill. The lie was given Friendship Village almost instantly by Edgar Lee Masters (Lewiston, Illinois, alias Spoon River), Sherwood Anderson (Clyde, Ohio, alias Winesburg), Sinclair Lewis (Sauk Centre, Minnesota, alias Gopher Prairie) and other writers of the so-called "revolt from the village." Most of these writers were Midwesterners, but as Lewis said in introducing *Main Street*, "The town is, in our tale, called 'Gopher Prairie, Minnesota.' But its Main Street is the continuation of Main Streets everywhere. The story would be the same in Ohio or Montana, in Kansas or Kentucky or Illinois, and not very differently would it be told Up York State or in the Carolina hills." Twentieth century American realists have preferred to depict the flawed version of Happy Village, the town that failed its founders' visions, the town deserted and in physical, spiritual, and moral decay. The town from which anybody who wants to amount to anything must escape, and escape early, before the village virus proves fatal.

These writers are truth-tellers born and raised in small-town, turn-of-the-century America who tired of hypocrisy and smallness of vision in their real-life villages, and revolted against falsehoods in their fictional villages. All three—but Anderson in particular—were influenced by Sigmund Freud and the new psychology, eager to write of small town sex, a subject they somehow connected with the grotesques they saw filling Main Street, U.S.A.

Anderson's collection is subtitled, as it were, "The Book of the Grotesque," and as often as not, the warping to grotesque has its roots in repressed sexuality. Alice Hindman is a case in point: at an early age she tasted (and enjoyed) the forbidden fruit in an act which, with characteristic small-town morality, she saw as cementing her and her boyfriend "together forever and ever." When Ned leaves Winesburg and does not return, Alice cannot conceive of giving to any other what belongs, somehow, to Ned, and she turns in to herself. Over the years she learns the arts of repression and denial. Ned, having escaped, forgets and grows; Alice withers to frustration, loneliness, and failed communication with a series of men, beginning with Ned and culminating in the old, metaphorically and physically deaf old man who passes that fateful fall of her twenty-seventh year. In her slow suicide she is assisted by two major social powers of the small town: business and the Methodist Church. Alice understands that she is becoming old and queer by her compulsive saving of money (and herself), and her equally compulsive attachment to inanimate objects. She knows Ned would not want her, even if he were to return. One evening when the unfulfilled desire wells within her, she determines to have an adventure in sexuality and communication. The adventure too is queer (although no stranger than the adventures of other Winesburg citizens . . . or, Anderson suggests, of the rest of us), and Alice cowers in terror before her own behavior and the town around her. Finally she turns her face to the wall and, in harsh contrast to the women of Friendship Village, resigns herself forever to the loneliness of life in Winesburg. Repression, Anderson tells us, is the price you pay for acceptance into the society of small-town America.

For most of the present century, American writers have viewed the small town as a failed dream, in the Anderson-Lewis-Masters tradition. Wright Morris's famous *Lone Tree, Nebraska* is one such failed city on a hill; William Gass's *"B," Indiana* is another. Beginning with an ironic allusion to Yeats's Byzantium ("And therefore I have sailed the seas and come / To the holy city of Byzantium," wrote Yeats in "Sailing to Byzantium"), Gass describes a different B-town entirely: "Many small Midwestern towns are nothing more than rural slums, and this community could easily become one." The houses are old and peeling. The streets are old and disintegrating. The trees have been decapitated to free telephone lines or power wires. The weather is gray. The town is gray. The people are old and gray. They are beyond caricature, they are living dead. "We are all out of luck here," Gass writes in the persona of one who is also out of luck. . . . out of love and out of luck. Out of luck precisely because out of love, and therefore ready to die. Restoration in nature? Not in the insect-infested fruit of Gass's orchard. Hope in the young? Not in the young mothers, fattish in trousers, who lounge around the speedwash smoking cigarettes. Not in the drivers of those cars which prowl up and down Main Street in the empty summer nights. Not in the weather. Not in the shops of this small town. Not in church. Not in education. Not for the confused grotesque, through whose eyes we see the unholy rural slum called "B."

In closing his study of the small town in American life, Paige Smith traced the arc from Friendship to Winesburg to "B" as an arc from the masculine to the feminine. "The town, built by the man and so often the tomb of his ambitions, was the perfect setting for the woman, who emerged in time as the indomitable forerunner of today's Mom," he wrote. The American small town became a substitute Mom, "the place where trust and love and understanding could always be found," but also—one passed puberty and began asking questions—a puritanical tyrant with no room for the father (Where are all the fathers in Mark Twain's little villages?), for the extravagant plunger or futile dreamer. Gale's village is warm and matriarchal; Gass's village is certainly a tomb of male dreams.

But Anderson's Winesburg stifles Alice Hindman and Kate Swift right along with the men, and Carol Bly, in her report from Madison, Minnesota, extends the loss of small-town sexuality to feeling in general . . . and from male to female to even children. Bly views the town as representing the values and social structures of all Middle America, especially in its refusal to consider the hard issues, its denial of anything related to "the dark side" of human nature, and its steadfast insistence on being cheerful and "nice." The town is fond of cuteness and gratuitous violence. It denies sexuality and it denies feeling. Unlike Gass's "B," Bly's Madison is not physically shabby; the decay is social (in spite of neighborly chattiness), spiritual (in spite of nearly mandatory church attendance), and moral (in spite of injunctions to politeness: "If you can't say anything nice, don't say anything at all"). Nobody in the church, nobody in the schools, nobody in small town business (the three major social forces in a small town) seems ready to admit a problem exists, let alone identify possible solutions, let alone get started with work on one solution or another. "Our countryside has inherited not Grieg, not Ibsen, not Rolvaag," she complains, "but just sitting there, cute movies, and when boredom gets bad enough, joining the Navy." At least Bly's townsmen are not physical grotesques, perhaps because grotesque cuts too close to quaint, and quaint is but another form of cute. Gale's characters are cute grotesques; Bly's Scandinavian-Americans are simply unfeeling folks, otherwise indistinguishable from you and me.

The inhabitants of Carolyn Chute's Egypt, Maine are definitely grotesque, reduced to a back, an eye, a mouth. Reduced to the most superstitious and rigid fundamentalist morality. Reduced to spare-the-rod-and-spoil-the-child, wash-the-mouth-out-with-soap discipline. Reduced to a warped, incestuous sexuality, "whether somethin' happened or not." Reduced to drunkenness and ignorance and narrow watching of the neighbors across the street through slats in the front window. Egypt is a town viewed through young eyes, and in Earlene's story is the possibility of rescue. It is underground and it is rescue by food. The children of feuding families—under threat of punishment—share their small victory for community over a chunk of blue cake in an underground bunker.

Bobbie Ann Mason's report from small-town Kentucky also highlights disintegrating relationships, although in her story the adult community struggles in more or less good faith against the deterioration. Mary Lou Skaggs is a center off which elements of the community play: the older women of a generation ahead of her, her husband and brother of her own generation, her daughter from the younger generation. She tries her best to relate to the older women although their world is not hers, and to her daughter (somewhat more successfully), although her daughter's generation is not hers, and she does not understand *Stir Crazy* or the quantum mechanics that mirror the disintegration of her own life's certainties. Nor can she successfully comprehend her brother, the wild one, who has reentered her life after these many years, or her own husband, who distances himself even as the story unfolds. Mack too tries to understand: he studies philosophy and physics and a long list of what he thinks might be college-type books, trying to keep up with his daughter. He tolerates, more or less, the rookers who invade his home periodically, driving him to television and the den. However, Mack is the hopelessly defeated male, turned finally inward to televised sports and telephone communication with the time and weather number, so he won't have to speak to anyone at the other end of the line. Like so many stories of small town life, Mason's contains little reassurance.

A commonplace of growing up in a small town is that the bright ones leave. Judy has left for college in "The Rookers," as George Willard left Winesburg, as Carol Kennicott left Gopher Prairie, as real life authors like Hamlin Garland and Mark Twain and Robert Bly and Willa Cather left their hamlets to make a mark in The World. But even a thorough-going realist like Garland finds himself returning, impelled, as Lisel Mueller once put it, "by the forked desire to break the roots and simultaneously preserve them." Despite the obvious hypocrisies of Gopher Prairie, Carol returns. From the troubled memories of Red Cloud, Nebraska, which she fled as a youth, Cather drew her most poignant fiction. Returning to Osage, Iowa, and thence to desolate Dakota, Garland found his proper material. Even Carol Bly has recently softened on the Minnesota small town.

Another Minnesotan, Garrison Keillor, also writes in a sympathetic voice of the small town. Keillor is, as I write, the most prominent spokesman for the American village which, with a typical humorist's ambiguity, he depicts as something between Friendship and Winesburg. There are hints of decay in Lake Wobegon (the empty Ford showroom), and intimations of failure (Myrtle did not make it to Minneapolis, but spent her years—like Alice Hindman—in the small town, womb-become-tomb, Lake Wobegon). There is quaintness in Wobegon that borders the grotesque, and in naming his village Wobegon, Keillor was not much more complimentary than Lewis, who named his town Gopher Prairie. But the orthodoxies and virtues are still present, and despite a good-natured humor, they are appreciated. In the first chapter of *Lake Wobegon Days*, Keillor recounts his departure from "Home," but he also recounts his return to the place he loves so well, "though he must leave ere long."

Lake Wobegon is loved in spite of, perhaps even because of, its failures. With Keillor, as with ourselves, we are never quite sure. Bill Holm is more explicit: using Minneota, Minnesota as a springboard for his long excursion into the heart and soul of this America, Holm discovers he loves his village mostly for its failures, or—more precisely—for the small lives which to an outsider would appear to be failures but are not really failures at all. Pauline Bardal and her excruciatingly laborious version of Handel's "Largo," her pathetically small life, the lifetime of possessions which don't amount to a good auction's worth of fortune— these are all you get, Holm says, and these are enough. The lad who early in his life would have defined failure as "to die in Minneota, Minnesota" returns to his village home, having concluded that "Whatever failure is, Minneota is not it. Nothing can be done about living here. Nor should it be. The heart can be filled up anywhere on earth." Holm is more elegiac than Keillor (in his eloquent contempt for this world's goods, he is perhaps the most Protestant), but in the final analysis he is more the booster, more enthusiastic in his endorsement of the small town, whatever it has become.

Dave Etter's *Alliance, Illinois* is probably the most ambitious extended treatment of the American small town in poetry since Masters' *Spoon River Anthology*. Surface analogies are easy, but Etter's real masters are more Sherwood Anderson and Vachel Lindsay, both for their optimism and wry sense of humor. Like other contemporary realists, Etter is candid in admitting the brokenness of his town, a decay of buildings and of lives. The place is old, run-down. You leave town and you return to town, and nothing has, nothing ever could have changed. Stubby Payne nurses his inadequacies and frustrations and might-have-beens at one end of the bar, while Texaco Cap and Orange Boots shoot pool and get drunk in the other corner. Fatherly advice is a string of clichés. Talk around Carl's Mainline Cafe is more petty nonsense in the manner of talk around the card table in Bobbie Ann Mason's story: "Edda's grandmother's ovary infection, a place that appeared on Thelma's arm, and the way the climate has changed." Over on B Street, Terry Reese and his wife are cracking up, locked in a blizzard and a marriage that has sunk below zero. Hotel Tall Corn is falling apart, like the people of Alliance who (in Holm's words) "have failed miserably by almost every definition our culture offers us." Still, Etter's Howard Drumgoole confides, "I sorta, kinda like it." There is a certain sweetness, a curious strength of character to the decay, and a certain certitude that comes from living in the middle of it all:

"We are living in the middle of nowhere," I said.

"Well, at least we're in the center of things," he said.

"Must you always look on the bright side," I said.

("Gretchen Naylor: Nowhere")

Neo-romantic apologists for the American small town suggest that these people have learned to accept their limitations. As Keillor put it in the Lake Wobegon town motto, "Sumus quod sumus"—we are what we are. These people have forgiven each other, and themselves, both what they are and what they are not, and that is a very great gift. Certainly there must be something fairer on the planet than what the American small town has become, but in the meantime, life there will suffice. As small-town humorist Howard Mohr would say, "Things could be lots worse!"

Frederick Busch, in "Widow Water," speaks for acceptance. "What to know about pain is how little we do to deserve it, how simple it is to give, how hard to lose," he writes. Small town life, his plumber-persona admits, can be pain . . . and there is plenty of pain in this story: the pain of a widow no longer frisky, no longer courted; the pain of young Mac, who has done nothing, really, to deserve his father's reprimands; the pain of Mac's father, a young college professor who probably doesn't make more than the boys on Buildings and Grounds, and who doesn't know a sump from a prime, a float from a ballcock. There is the pain of the dead mouse. But narrator Abe knows water and human relationships, and pain and the healing of pain. Especially he knows the virtues for which a small town is celebrated: neighborliness (although not right this minute), the small life carefully lived, social fabric well tended, the elderly well treated and the young child tutored. He knows the value of coffee, bran muffins, and blueberry jam. And good plumbing, coffee, muffins and jam will take us a long way, Busch suggests, toward the sanity and stability we all seek, the sanity and stability for which small towns are celebrated.

from *Friendship Village*
Zona Gale

TWO DAYS BEFORE THANKSGIVING the air was already filled with white turkey feathers, and I stood at a window and watched until the loneliness of my still house seemed like something pointing a mocking finger at me. When I could bear it no longer I went out in the snow, and through the soft drifts I fought my way up the Plank Road toward the village.

I had almost passed the little bundled figure before I recognized Calliope. She was walking in the middle of the road, as in Friendship we all walk in winter; and neither of us had umbrellas. I think that I distrust people who put up umbrellas on a country road in a fall of friendly flakes.

Instead of inquiring perfunctorily how I did, she greeted me with a fragment of what she had been thinking—which is always as if one were to open a door of his mind to you instead of signing you greeting from a closed window.

"I just been tellin' myself," she looked up to say without preface, "that if I could see one more good old-fashion' Thanksgivin', life'd sort o' smooth out. An' land knows, it needs some smoothin' out for me."

With this I remember that it was as if my own loneliness spoke for me. At my reply Calliope looked at me quickly—as if I, too, had opened a door.

"Sometimes Thanksgivin' *is* some like seein' the sun shine when you're feelin' rill rainy yourself," she said thoughtfully.

She held out her blue-mittened hand and let the flakes fall on it in stars and coronets.

"I wonder," she asked evenly, "if you'd help me get up a Thanksgivin' dinner for a few poor sick folks here in Friendship?"

In order to keep my self-respect, I recall that I was as ungracious as possible. I think I said that the day meant so little to me that I was willing to do anything to avoid spending it alone. A statement which seems to me now not to bristle with logic.

"That's nice of you," Calliope replied genially. Then she hesitated, looking down Daphne Street, which the Plank Road had become, toward certain white houses. There were the homes of Mis' Mayor Uppers, Mis' Holcomb-that-was-Mame-Bliss, and the Liberty sisters,—all substantial dignified houses, typical of the simple prosperity of the countryside.

"The only trouble," she added simply, "is that in Friendship I don't know of a soul rill sick, nor a soul what you might call poor."

At this I laughed, unwillingly enough. Dear Calliope! Here indeed was a drawback to her project.

"Honestly," she said reflectively, "Friendship can't seem to do anything like any other town. When the new minister come here, he give out he was goin' to do settlement work. An' his second week in the place he come to me with a reg'lar hang-dog look. 'What kind of a town is this?' he says to me, disgusted. 'They ain't nobody sick in it an' they ain't nobody poor!' I guess he could 'a' got along without the poor—most of us can. But we mostly like to hev a few sick to carry the flowers off our house plants to, an' now an' then a tumbler o' jell. An' yet I've known weeks at a time when they wasn't a soul rill flat down sick in Friendship. It's so now. An' that's hard, when you're young an' enthusiastic, like the minister."

"But where are you going to find your guests then, Calliope?" I asked curiously.

"Well," she said brightly, "I was just plannin' as you come up with me. An' I says to myself: 'God give me to live in a little bit of a place where we've all got enough to get along on, an' Thanksgivin' finds us all in health. It looks like He'd afflicted us by lettin' us hev nobody to do for.' An' then it come to me that if we was to get up the dinner,—with all the misery an' hunger they is in the world,—God in His goodness would let some of it come our way to be fed. 'In the wilderness a cedar,' you know—as Liddy Ember an' I was always tellin' each other when we kep' shop together. An' so to-day I said to myself I'd go to work an' get up the dinner an' trust there'd be eaters for it."

"Why, Calliope," I said, "Calliope!"

"I ain't got much to do with, myself," she added apologetically; "the most I've got in my sullar, I guess, is a gallon jar o' watermelon pickles. I could give that. You don't think it sounds irreverent—connectin' God with a big dinner, so?" she asked anxiously.

And, at my reply:—

"Well, then," she said briskly, "let's step in an' see a few folks that might be able to tell us of somebody to do for. Let's ask Mis' Mayor Uppers an' Mis' Holcomb-that-was-Mame-Bliss, an' the Liberty girls."

Because I was lonely and idle, and because I dreaded inexpressibly going back to my still house, I went with her. Her ways were a kind of entertainment, and I remember that I believed my leisure to be infinite.

We turned first toward the big shuttered house of Mis' Mayor Uppers, to whom, although her husband had been a year ago removed from office, discredited, and had not since been seen in Friendship, we yet gave her old proud title, as if she had been Former Lady Mayoress. For the present mayor, Authority Hubblethwaite, was, as Calliope said, "unconnect."

I watched Mis' Uppers in some curiosity while Calliope explained that she was planning a dinner for the poor and sick,—"the lame and the sick that's comfortable enough off to eat,"—and could she suggest some poor and sick to ask? Mis' Uppers was like a vinegar cruet of mine, slim and tall, with a little grotesquely puckered face for a stopper, as if the whole known world were sour.

"I'm sure," she said humbly, "it's a nice i-dea. But I declare, I'm put to it to suggest. We ain't got nobody sick nor nobody poor in Friendship, you know."

"Don't you know of anybody kind o' hard up? Or somebody that, if they ain't down sick, feels sort o' spindlin'?" Calliope asked anxiously.

Mis' Uppers thought, rocking a little and running a pin in and out of a fold of her skirt.

"No," she said at length, "I don't know a soul. I think the church'd give a good deal if a real poor family'd come here to do for. Since the Cadozas went, we ain't known which way to look for poor. Mis' Ricker gettin' her fortune so puts her beyond the wolf. An' Peleg Bemus, you can't *get* him to take anything. No, I don't know of anybody real decently poor."

"An' nobody sick?" Calliope pressed her wistfully.

"Well, there's Mis' Crawford," admitted Mis' Uppers; "she had a spell o' lumbago two weeks ago, but I see her pass the house today. Mis' Brady was laid up with toothache, too, but the *Daily* last night said she'd had it out. An' Mis' Doctor Helman did have one o' her stomach attacks this week, an' Elzabella got out her dyin' dishes an' her dyin' linen from the still-room—you know how Mis' Doctor always brings out her nice things when she's sick, so't if she should die an' the neighbours come in, it'd all be shipshape. But she got better this time an' helped put 'em back. I declare it's hard to get up anything in the charity line here."

Calliope sat smiling a little, and I knew that it was because of her secret certainty that "some o' the hunger" would come her way, to be fed.

"I can't help thinkin'," she said quietly, "that we'll find somebody. An' I tell you what: if we do, can I count on you to help some?"

Mis' Mayor Uppers flushed with quick pleasure.

"Me, Calliope?" she said. And I remembered that they had told me how the Friendship Married Ladies' Cemetery Improvement Sodality had been unable to tempt Mis' Uppers to a single meeting since the mayor ran away. "Oh, but I couldn't though," she said wistfully.

"No need to go to the table if you don't want," Calliope told her. "Just bake up somethin' for us an' bring it over. Make a couple o' your cherry pies—did you get hold of any cherries to put up this year? Well, a couple o' your cherry pies an' a batch o' your nice drop sponge cakes," she directed. "Could you?"

Mis' Mayor Uppers looked up with a kind of light in her eyes.

"Why, yes," she said, "I could, I guess. I'll bake 'em Thanksgivin' mornin'. I—I was wonderin' how I'd put in the day."

When we stepped out in the snow again, Calliope's face was shining. Sometimes now, when my faith is weak in any good thing, I remember her look that November morning. But all that I thought then was how I was being entertained that lonely day.

The dear Liberty sisters were next, Lucy and Viny and Libbie Liberty. We went to the side door,—there were houses in Friendship whose front doors we tacitly understood that we were never expected to use,— and we found the sisters down cellar, with shawls over their heads, feeding their hens through the cellar window, opening on the glassed-in coop under the porch.

In Friendship it is a point of etiquette for a morning caller never to interrupt the employment of a hostess. So we obeyed the summons of the Liberty sisters to "come right down"; and we sat on a firkin and an inverted tub while Calliope told her plan and the hens fought for delectable morsels.

"My grief!" said Libbie Liberty, tartly, "where you goin' to *get* your sick an' poor?"

Mis' Viny, balancing on the window ledge to reach for eggs, looked back at us.

"Friendship's so comfortable that way," she said, "I don' see how you can get up much of anything."

And little Miss Lucy, kneeling on the floor of the cellar to measure more feed, said without looking up:—

"You know, since mother died we ain't never done anything for holidays. No—we can't seem to want to think about Thanksgiving or Christmas or like that."

They all turned their grave lined faces toward us.

"We want to let the holidays just slip by without noticin'," Miss Viny told us. "Seems like it hurts less that way."

Libbie Liberty smiled wanly.

"Don't you know," she said, "when you hold your hand still in hot water, you don't feel how hot the water really is? But when you move around in it some, it begins to burn you. Well, when we let Thanksgiving an' Christmas alone, it ain't so bad. But when we start to move around in 'em—"

Her voice faltered and stopped.

"We miss mother terrible," Miss Lucy said simply.

Calliope put her blue mitten to her mouth, but her eyes she might not hide, and they were soft with sympathy.

"I know—I know," she said. "I remember the first Christmas after my mother died—I ached like the toothache all over me, an' I couldn't bear to open my presents. Nor the next year I couldn't either—I couldn't open my presents with any heart. But—" Calliope hesitated, "that second year," she said, "I found somethin' I could do. I saw I could fix up little things for other folks an' take some comfort in it. Like mother would of."

She was silent for a moment, looking thoughtfully at the three lonely figures in the dark cellar of their house.

"Your mother," she said abruptly, "stuffed the turkey for a year ago the last harvest home."

"Yes," they said.

"Look here," said Calliope; if I can get some poor folks together,—or even *one* poor folk, or hungry,—will you three come over to my house an' stuff the turkey? The way—I can't help thinkin' the way your mother would of, if she'd been here. An' then," Calliope went on briskly, "could you bring some fresh eggs an' make a pan o' custard over to my house? An' mebbe one o' you'd stir up a sunshine cake. You must know how to make your mother's sunshine cake?"

There was another silence in the cellar when Calliope had done, and for a minute I wondered if, after all, she had not failed, and if the bleeding of the three hearts might be so stanched. It was not self-reliant Libbie Liberty who spoke first; it was gentle Miss Lucy.

"I guess," she said, "I could, if we all do it. I know mother would of."

"Yes," Miss Viny nodded, "mother would of."

Libbie Liberty stood for a moment with compressed lips.

"It seems like not payin' respect to mother," she began; and then shook her head. "It ain't that," she said; "it's only missin' her when we begin to step around the kitchen, bakin' up for a holiday."

"I know—I know," Calliope said again. "That's why I said for you to come over in my kitchen. You come over there an' stir up the sunshine cake, too, an' bake it in my oven, so's we can hev it et hot. Will you do that?"

And after a little time they consented. If Calliope found any sick or poor, they would do that.

"We ain't gettin' many i-dees for guests," Calliope said, as we reached the street, "but we're gettin' helpers, anyway. An' some dinner, too."

Then we went to the house of Mis' Holcomb-that-was-Mame-Bliss— and called so, of course, to distinguish her from the "Other" Holcombs.

"Don't you be shocked at her," Calliope warned me, as we closed Mis' Holcomb's gate behind us; "she's dreadful diff'r'nt an' bitter since Abigail was married last month. She's got hold o' some kind of a Persian book, in a decorated cover, from the City; an' now she says your soul is like when you look in a lookin'-glass—that there ain't really nothin' there. An' that the world's some wind an' the rest water, an' they ain't no God only your own breath—oh, poor Mis' Holcomb!" said Calliope. "I guess she ain't rill balanced. But we ought to go to see her. We always consult Mis' Holcomb about everything."

Poor Mis' Holcomb-that-was-Mame-Bliss! I can see her now in her comfortable dining room, where she sat cleaning her old silver, her thin, veined hands as fragile as her grandmother's spoons.

"Of course, you don't know," she said, when Calliope had unfolded her plans, "how useless it all seems to me. What's the use—I keep sayin' to myself now'-days; what's the use? You put so much pains on somethin', an' then it goes off an' leaves you. Mebbe it dies, an' everything's all wasted. There ain't anything to tie to. It's like lookin' in a glass all the while. It's seemin',' it ain't bein'. We ain't certain o' nothin' but our breath, an' when that goes, what hev you got? What's the use o' plannin' Thanksgivin' for anybody?"

"Well, if you're hungry, it's kind o' nice to get fed up," said Calliope, crisply. "Don't you know a soul that's hungry, Mame Bliss?"

She shook her head.

"No," she said, "I don't. Nor nobody sick in body."

"Nobody sick in body," Calliope repeated absently.

"Soul-sick an' soul-hungry you can't feed up," Mis' Holcomb added.

"I donno," said Calliope, thoughtfully, "I donno but you can."

"No," Mis' Holcomb went on; "your soul's like yourself in the glass: they ain't anything there."

"I donno," Calliope said again; "some mornin's when I wake up with the sun shinin' in, I can feel my soul in me just as plain as plain."

Mis' Holcomb sighed.

"Life looks dreadful footless to me," she said.

"Well," said Calliope, "sometimes life *is* some like hearin' firecrackers go off when you don't feel up to shootin' 'em yourself. When I'm like that, I always think if I'd go out an' buy a bunch or two, an' get somebody to give me a match, I could see more sense to things. Look here, Mame Bliss; if I get hold o' any folks to give the dinner for, will you help me some?"

"Yes," Mis' Holcomb assented half-heartedly, "I'll help you. I ain't nobody much in family, now Abigail's done what she has. They's only Eppleby, an' he won't be home Thanksg'vin this year. So I ain't nothin' else to do."

"That's the *i*-dee," said Calliope, heartily; "if everything's foolish, it's just as foolish doin' nothin' as doin' somethin'. Will you bring over a kettleful o' boiled potatoes to my house Thanksgivin' noon? An' mash 'em an' whip 'em in my kitchen? I'll hev the milk to put in. You—you don't cook as much as some, do you, Mame?"

Did Calliope ask her that purposely? I am almost sure that she did. Mis' Holcomb's neck stiffened a little.

"I guess I can cook a thing or two beside mash' potatoes," she said, and thought for a minute. "How'd you like a pan o' scalloped oysters an' some baked marcaroni with plenty o' cheese?" she demanded.

"Sounds like it'd go down awful easy," admitted Calliope, smiling.

"It's just what we need to carry the dinner off full sail," she added earnestly.

"Well, I ain't nothin' else to do an' I'll make 'em," Mis' Holcomb promised. "Only it beats me who you can find to do for. If you don't get anybody, let me know before I order the oysters."

Calliope stood up, her little wrinkled face aglow; and I wondered at her confidence.

"You just go ahead an' order your oysters," she said. "That dinner's goin' to come off Thanksgivin' noon at twelve o'clock. An' you be there to help feed the hungry, Mame."

When we were on the street again, Calliope looked at me with her way of shy eagerness.

"Could you hev the dinner up to your house," she asked me, "if I do every bit o' the work?"

"Why, Calliope," I said, amazed at her persistence, "have it there, of course. But you haven't any guests yet."

She nodded at me through the falling flakes.

"You say you ain't got much to be thankful for," she said, "so I thought mebbe you'd put in the time that way. Don't you worry about folks to eat the dinner. I'll tell Mis' Holcomb an' the others to come to your house—an' I'll get the food an' the folks. Don't you worry! An' I'll bring my watermelon pickles an' a bowl o' cream for Mis' Holcomb's potatoes, an' I'll furnish the turkey—a big one. The rest of us'll get the dinner in your kitchen Thanksgivin' mornin'. My!" she said, "seems though life's smoothin' out fer me a' ready. Good-by—it's 'most noon."

She hurried up Daphne Street in the snow, and I turned toward my lonely house. But I remember that I was planning how I would make my table pretty, and how I would add a delicacy or two from the City for this strange holiday feast. And I found myself hurrying to look over certain long-disused linen and silver, and to see whether my Cloth-o'-Gold rose might be counted on to bloom by Thursday noon.

"We'll set the table for seven folks," said Calliope, "at my house on Thanksgiving morning."

"Seven!" I echoed. "But where in the world did you ever find seven, Calliope?"

"I found 'em," she answered. "I knew I could find hungry folks to do for if I tried, an' I found 'em. You'll see. I sha'n't say another word. They'll be here by twelve, sharp. Did the turkey come?"

Yes, the turkey had come, and almost as she spoke the dear Liberty sisters arrived to dress and stuff it, and to make ready the pan of custard, and to "stir up" the sunshine cake. I could guess how the pleasant bustle in my kitchen would hurt them by its holiday air, and I carried them off to see my Cloth-o'-Gold rose which had opened in the night, to the very crimson heart of it. And I told them of the seven guests whom, after all, Calliope had actually contrived to marshal to her dinner. And in the midst of our almost gay speculation on this, they went at their share of the task.

The three moved about their offices gravely at first, Libbie Liberty keeping her back to us as she worked, Miss Viny scrupulously intent on the delicate clatter of the egg-beater, Miss Lucy with eyes downcast on the sage she rolled. I noted how Calliope made little excuses to pass near each of them, with now a touch of the hand and now a pat on a shoulder, and all the while she talked briskly of ways and means and recipes, and should there be onions in the dressing or should there not be? We took a vote on this and were about to chop the onions in when Mis' Holcomb's little maid arrived at my kitchen door with a bowl of oysters which Mis' Holcomb had had left from the 'scallop, an' wouldn't we like 'em in the stuffin? Roast turkey stuffed with Oysters! I saw Libbie Liberty's eyes brighten so delightedly that I brought out a jar of seedless raisins and another of preserved cherries to add to the custard, and then a bag of sweet almonds to be blanched and split for the cake o' sunshine. Surely, one of us said, the seven guests could be preparing for their Thanksgiving dinner with no more zest than we were putting into that dinner for their sakes.

"Seven guests!" we said over and again. "Calliope, how did you do it? When everybody says there's nobody in Friendship that's either sick or poor?"

"Nobody sick, nobody poor!" Calliope exclaimed, piling a dish with watermelon pickles. "Land you might think that was the town motto. Well, the town don't know everything. Don't you ask me so many questions."

Before eleven o'clock Mis' Mayor Uppers tapped at my back door, with two deep-dish cherry pies in a basket, and a row of her delicate, feathery sponge cakes and a jar of pineapple and pie-plant preserves "to chink in." She drew a deep breath and stood looking about the kitchen.

"Throw off your things an' help, Mis' Uppers," Calliope admonished her, one hand on the cellar door. "I'm just goin' down for some sweet potatoes Mis' Holcomb sent over this morning, an' you might get 'em ready, if you will. We ain't goin' to let you off now, spite of what you've done for us."

So Mis' Mayor Uppers hung up her shawl and washed the sweet potatoes. And my Kitchen was fragrant with spices and flavourings and an odorous oven, and there was no end of savoury business to be at. I found myself glad of the interest of these others in the day and glad of the stirring in my lonely house. Even if their bustle could not lessen my own loneliness, it was pleasant, I said to myself, to see them quicken with interest; and the whole affair entertained my infinite leisure. After all, I was not required to be thankful. I merely loaned my house, cosey in its glittering drifts of turkey feathers, and the day was no more and no less to me than before, though I own that I did feel more than an amused interest in Calliope's guests. Whom, in Friendship, had she found "to do for," I detected myself speculating with real interest as in the dining room, with one and another to help me, I made ready my table. My prettiest dishes and silver, the Cloth-o'-Gold rose, and my yellow-shaded candles made little auxiliary welcomes. Whoever Calliope's guests were, we would do them honour and give them the best we had. And in the midst of all came from the City the box with my gift of hothouse fruit and a rosebud for every plate.

"Calliope!" I cried, as I went back to the kitchen, "Calliope, it's nearly twelve now. Tell us who the guests are, or we won't finish dinner!"

Calliope laughed and shook her head and opened the door for Mis' Holcomb-that-was-Mame-Bliss, who entered, followed by her little maid, both laden with good things.

"I prepared for seven," Mis' Holcomb said. "That was the word you sent me—but where you got your seven sick an' poor in Friendship beats me. I'll stay an' help for a while—but to me it all seems like so much monkey work."

We worked with a will that last half-hour, and the spirit of the kitchen came upon them all. I watched them, amused and pleased at Mis' Mayor Upper's flushed anxiety over the sweet potatoes, at Libbie Liberty furiously basting the turkey, and at Miss Lucy exclaiming with delight as she unwrapped the rosebuds from their moss. But I think that Mis' Holcomb pleased me most, for with the utensils of housewifery in her hands she seemed utterly to have forgotten that there is no use in anything at all. This was not wonderful in the presence of such a feathery cream of mashed potatoes and such aromatic coffee as she made. *There* was something to tie to. Those were real, at any rate, and beyond all seeming.

Just before twelve Calliope caught off her apron and pulled down her sleeves.

"Now," she said, "I'm going to welcome the guests. I can—can't I?" she begged me. "Everything's all ready but putting on. I won't need to come out here again; when I ring the bell on the sideboard, dish it up an' bring it in, all together—turkey ahead an' vegetables followin'. Mis' Holcomb, you help 'em, won't you? An' then you can leave if you want. Talk about an old-fashion' Thanksgivin'. My!"

"Who *has* she got?" Libbie Liberty burst out, basting the turkey. "I declare, I'm nervous as a witch, I'm so curious!"

And then the clock struck twelve, and a minute after we heard Calliope tinkle a silvery summons on the call-bell.

I remember that it was Mis' Holcomb herself—to whom nothing mattered—who rather lost her head as we served our feast, and who was about putting in dishes both her oysters and her macaroni instead of carrying in the fair, brown, smoking back pans. But at last we were ready—Mis' Holcomb at our head with the turkey, the others following with both hands filled, and I with the coffee-pot. As they gave the signal to start, something—it may have been the mystery before us, or the good things about us, or the mere look of the Thanksgiving snow on the window-sills—seemed to catch at the hearts of them all, and they laughed a little, almost joyously, those five for whom joy had seemed done, and I found myself laughing too.

So we six filed into the dining room to serve whomever Calliope had found "to do for." I wondered that I had not guessed before. There stood Calliope at the foot of the table, with its lighted candles and its Cloth-o'-Gold rose, and the other six chairs were quite vacant.

"Sit down!" Calliope cried to us, with tears and laughter in her voice. "Sit down, all six of you. Don't you see? Didn't you know? Ain't we soul-sick an' soul-hungry, all of us? An' I tell you, this is goin' to do our souls good—an' our stomachs too!"

Nobody dropped anything, even in the flood of our amazement. We managed to get our savoury burden on the table, and some way we found ourselves in the chairs—I at the head of my table where Calliope led me. And we all talked at once, exclaiming and questioning, with sudden thanksgiving in our hearts that in the world such things may be.

"I was hungry an' sick," Calliope was telling, "for an old-fashion' Thanksgivin'—or anything that'd smooth life out some. But I says to myself, 'It looks like God had afflicted us by not givin' us anybody to do for.' An' then I started out to find some poor an' some sick—an' each one o' you knows what I found. An' I ask' myself before I got home that day, 'Why not them an' me?' There's lots o' kinds o' things to do on Thanksgivin' Day. Are you ever goin' to forgive me?"

I think that we all answered at once. But what we all meant was what Mis' Holcomb-that-was-Mame-Bliss said, as she sat flushed and smiling behind the coffee-cups:—

"I declare, I feel something like I ain't felt since I don't know when!"

And Calliope nodded at her.

"I guess that's your soul, Mame Bliss," she said. "You can always feel it if you go to work an' act as if you got one. I'll take my coffee clear."

Adventure

Sherwood Anderson

ALICE HINDMAN, a woman of twenty-seven when George Willard was a mere boy, had lived in Winesburg all her life. She clerked in Winney's Dry Goods Store and lived with her mother, who had married a second husband.

Alice's step-father was a carriage painter, and given to drink. His story is an odd one. It will be worth telling some day.

At twenty-seven Alice was tall and somewhat slight. Her head was large and overshadowed her body. Her shoulders were a little stooped and her hair and eyes brown. She was very quiet but beneath a placid exterior a continual ferment went on.

When she was a girl of sixteen and before she began to work in the store, Alice had an affair with a young man. The young man, named Ned Currie, was older than Alice. He, like George Willard, was employed on the *Winesburg Eagle* and for a long time he went to see Alice almost every evening. Together the two walked under the trees through the streets of the town and talked of what they would do with their lives. Alice was then a very pretty girl and Ned Currie took her into his arms and kissed her. He became excited and said things he did not intend to say and Alice, betrayed by her desire to have something beautiful come into her rather narrow life, also grew excited. She also talked. The outer crust of her life, all of her natural diffidence and reserve, was torn away and she gave herself over to the emotions of love. When, late in the fall of her sixteenth year, Ned Currie went away to Cleveland where he hoped to get a place on a city newspaper and rise in the world, she wanted to go with him. With a trembling voice she told him what was in her mind. "I will work and you can work," she said. "I do not want to harness you to a needless expense that will prevent your making progress. Don't marry me now. We will get along without that and we can be together. Even though we live in the same house no one will say anything. In the city we will be unknown and people will pay no attention to us."

Ned Currie was puzzled by the determination and abandon of his sweetheart and was also deeply touched. He had wanted the girl to become his mistress but changed his mind. He wanted to protect and care for her. "You don't know what you're talking about," he said sharply; "you may be sure I'll let you do no such thing. As soon as I get a good job I'll come back. For the present you'll have to stay here. It's the only thing we can do."

On the evening before he left Winesburg to take up his new life in the city, Ned Currie went to call on Alice. They walked about through the streets for an hour and then got a rig from Wesley Moyer's livery and went for a drive in the country. The moon came up and they found themselves unable to talk. In his sadness the young man forgot the resolutions he had made regarding his conduct with the girl.

They got out of the buggy at a place where a long meadow ran down to the bank of Wine Creek and there in the dim light became lovers. When at midnight they returned to town they were both glad. It did not seem to them that anything that could happen in the future could blot out the wonder and beauty of the thing that had happened. "Now we will have to stick to each other, whatever happens we will have to do that," Ned Currie said as he left the girl at her father's door.

The young newspaper man did not succeed in getting a place on a Cleveland paper and went west to Chicago. For a time he was lonely and wrote to Alice almost every day. Then he was caught up by the life of the city; he began to make friends and found new interests in life. In Chicago he boarded at a house where there were several women. One of them attracted his attention and he forgot Alice in Winesburg. At the end of a year he had stopped writing letters, and only once in a long time, when he was lonely or when he went into one of the city parks and saw the moon shining on the grass as it had shone that night on the meadow by Wine Creek, did he think of her at all.

In Winesburg the girl who had been loved grew to be a woman. When she was twenty-two years old her father, who owned a harness repair shop, died suddenly. The harness maker was an old soldier, and after a few months his wife received a widow's pension. She used the first money she got to buy a loom and became a weaver of carpets, and Alice got a place in Winney's store. For a number of years nothing could have induced her to believe that Ned Currie would not in the end return to her.

She was glad to be employed because the daily round of toil in the store made the time of waiting seem less long and uninteresting. She began to save money, thinking that when she had saved two or three hundred dollars she would follow her lover to the city and try if her presence would not win back his affections.

Alice did not blame Ned Currie for what had happened in the moonlight in the field, but felt that she could never marry another man. To her the thought of giving to another what she still felt could belong only to Ned seemed monstrous. When other young men tried to attract her attention she would have nothing to do with them. "I am his wife and shall remain his wife whether he comes back or not," she whispered to herself, and for all of her willingness to support herself could not have understood the growing modern idea of a woman's owning herself and giving and taking for her own ends in life.

Alice worked in the dry goods store from eight in the morning until six at night and on three evenings a week went back to the store to stay from seven until nine. As time passed and she became more and more lonely she began to practice the devices common to lonely people. When at night she went upstairs into her own room she knelt on the floor to pray and in her prayers whispered things she wanted to say to her lover. She became attached to inanimate objects, and because it was her own, could not bear to have anyone touch the furniture of her room. The trick of saving money, begun for a purpose, was carried on after the scheme of going to the city to find Ned Currie had been given up. It became a fixed habit, and when she needed new clothes she did not get them. Sometimes on rainy afternoons in the store she got out her bank book and, letting it lie open before her, spent hours dreaming impossible dreams of saving money enough so that the interest would support both herself and her future husband.

"Ned always liked to travel about," she thought. "I'll give him the chance. Some day when we are married and I can save both his money and my own, we will be rich. Then we can travel together all over the world."

In the dry goods store weeks ran into months and months into years as Alice waited and dreamed of her lover's return. Her employer, a grey old man with false teeth and a thin grey mustache that drooped down over his mouth, was not given to conversation, and sometimes, on rainy days and in the winter when a storm raged in Main Street, long hours passed when no customers came in. Alice arranged and rearranged the stock. She stood near the front window where she could look down the deserted street and thought of the evenings when she had walked with Ned Currie and of what he had said. "We will have to stick to each other now." The words echoed and re-echoed through the mind of the maturing woman. Tears came into her eyes. Sometimes when her employer had gone out and she was alone in the store she put her head on the counter and wept. "Oh, Ned, I am waiting," she whispered over and over, and all the time the creeping fear that he would never come back grew stronger within her.

In the spring when the rains have passed and before the long hot days of summer have come, the country about Winesburg is delightful. The town lies in the midst of open fields, but beyond the fields are pleasant patches of woodlands. In the wooded places are many little cloistered nooks, quiet places where lovers go to sit on Sunday afternoons. Through the trees they look out across the fields and see farmers at work about the barns or people driving up and down on the roads. In the town bells ring and occasionally a train passes, looking like a toy thing in the distance.

For several years after Ned Currie went away Alice did not go into the wood with the other young people on Sunday, but one day after he had been gone for two or three years and when her loneliness seemed unbearable, she put on her best dress and set out. Finding a little sheltered place from which she could see the town and a long stretch of the fields, she sat down. Fear of age and ineffectuality took possession of her. She could not sit still, and arose. As she stood looking out over the land something, perhaps the thought of never ceasing life as it expresses itself in the flow of the seasons, fixed her mind on the passing years. With a shiver of dread, she realized that for her the beauty and freshness of youth had passed. For the first time she felt that she had been cheated. She did not blame Ned Currie and did not know what to blame. Sadness swept over her. Dropping to her knees, she tried to pray, but instead of prayers words of protest came to her lips. "It is not going to come to me. I will never find happiness. Why do I tell myself lies?" she cried, and an odd sense of relief came with this, her first bold attempt to face the fear that had become a part of her everyday life.

In the year when Alice Hindman became twenty-five two things happened to disturb the dull uneventfulness of her days. Her mother married Bush Milton, the carriage painter of Winesburg, and she herself became a member of the Winesburg Methodist Church. Alice joined the church because she had become frightened by the loneliness of her position in life. Her mother's second marriage had emphasized her isolation. "I am becoming old and queer. If Ned comes he will not want me. In the city where he is living men are perpetually young. There is so much going on that they do not have time to grow old," she told herself with a grim little smile, and went resolutely about the business of becoming acquainted with people. Every Thursday evening when the store had closed she went to a prayer meeting in the basement of the church and on Sunday evening attended a meeting of an organization called The Epworth League.

When Will Hurley, a middle-aged man who clerked in a drug store and who also belonged to the church, offered to walk home with her she did not protest. "Of course I will not let him make a practice of being with me, but if he comes to see me once in a long time there can be no harm in that," she told herself, still determined in her loyalty to Ned Currie.

Without realizing what was happening, Alice was trying feebly at first, but with growing determination, to get a new hold upon life. Beside the drug clerk she walked in silence, but sometimes in the darkness as they went stolidly along she put out her hand and touched softly the folds of his coat. When he left her at the gate before her mother's house she did not go indoors, but stood for a moment by the door. She wanted to call to the drug clerk, to ask him to sit with her in the darkness on the porch before the house, but was afraid he would not understand. "It is not him that I want," she told herself; "I want to avoid being so much alone. If I am not careful I will grow unaccustomed to being with people."

During the early fall of her twenty-seventh year a passionate restlessness took possession of Alice. She could not bear to be in the company of the drug clerk, and when, in the evening, he came to walk with her she sent him away. Her mind became intensely active and when, weary from the long hours of standing behind the counter in the store, she went home and crawled into bed, she could not sleep. With staring eyes she looked into the darkness. Her imagination, like a child awakened from long sleep, played about the room. Deep within her there was something that would not be cheated by phantasies and that demanded some definite answer from life.

Alice took a pillow into her arms and held it tightly against her breasts. Getting out of bed, she arranged a blanket so that in the darkness it looked like a form lying between the sheets and, kneeling beside the bed, she caressed it, whispering words over and over, like a refrain. "Why doesn't something happen? Why am I left here alone?" she muttered. Although she sometimes thought of Ned Currie, she no longer depended on him. Her desire had grown vague. She did not want Ned Currie or any other man. She wanted to be loved, to have something answer the call that was growing louder and louder within her.

And then one night when it rained Alice had an adventure. It frightened and confused her. She had come home from the store at nine and found the house empty. Bush Milton had gone off to town and her mother to the house of a neighbor. Alice went upstairs to her room and undressed in the darkness. For a moment she stood by the window hearing the rain beat against the glass and then a strange desire took possession of her. Without stopping to think of what she intended to do, she ran downstairs through the dark house and out into the rain. As she stood on the little grass plot before the house and felt the cold rain on her body a mad desire to run naked through the streets took possession of her.

She thought that the rain would have some creative and wonderful effect on her body. Not for years had she felt so full of youth and courage. She wanted to leap and run, to cry out, to find some other lonely human and embrace him. On the brick sidewalk before the house a man stumbled homeward. Alice started to run. A wild, desperate mood took possession of her. "What do I care who it is. He is alone, and I will go to him," she thought; and then without stopping to consider the possible result of her madness, called softly. "Wait!" she cried. "Don't go away. Whoever you are, you must wait."

The man on the sidewalk stopped and stood listening. He was an old man and somewhat deaf. Putting his hand to his mouth, he shouted. "What? What say?" he called.

Alice dropped to the ground and lay trembling. She was so frightened at the thought of what she had done that when the man had gone on his way she did not dare get to her feet, but crawled on hands and knees through the grass to the house. When she got to her own room she bolted the door and drew her dressing table across the doorway. Her body shook as with a chill and her hands trembled so that she had difficulty getting into her nightdress. When she got into bed she buried her face in the pillow and wept brokenheartedly. "What is the matter with me? I will do something dreadful if I am not careful," she thought, and turning her face to the wall, began trying to force herself to face bravely the fact that many people must live and die alone, even in Winesburg.

·3·

Home
Garrison Keillor

THE TOWN OF LAKE WOBEGON, Minnesota,* lies on the shore against Adams Hill, looking east across the blue-green water to the dark woods. From the south, the highway aims for the lake, bends hard left by the magnificent concrete Grecian grain silos, and eases over a leg of the hill past the SLOW CHILDREN sign, bringing the traveler in on Main Street toward the town's one traffic light, which is almost always green. A few surviving elms shade the street. Along the ragged dirt path between the asphalt and the grass, a child slowly walks to Ralph's Grocery, kicking an asphalt chunk ahead of him. It is a chunk that after four blocks he is now mesmerized by, to which he is completely dedicated. At Bunsen Motors, the sidewalk begins. A breeze off the lake brings a sweet air of mud and rotting wood, a slight fishy smell, and picks up the sweetness of old grease, a sharp whiff of gasoline, fresh tires, spring dust, and, from across the street, the faint essence of tuna hotdish at the Chatterbox Cafe. A stout figure in green coveralls disap-

---

* *"Right on this road 0.7 m. to OLD WHITE BARN, then right 1.2 m. to LAKE WOBEGON (1418 alt., 942 pop.), named for the body of water that it borders. Bleakly typical of the prairie, Lake Wobegon has its origins in the utopian vision of nineteenth-century New England Transcendentalists but now is populated mainly by Norwegians and Germans who attend LAKE WOBEGON LUTHERAN CHURCH (left at BANK .1 m.) and OUR LADY OF PERPETUAL RESPONSIBILITY CHURCH (right at CHURCH .08 m.), neither of which are remarkable. The lake itself, blue-green and brightly sparkling in the brassy summer sun and neighbored by the warm-colored marsh grasses of a wildlife-teeming slough, is the town's main attraction, though the view is spoiled somewhat by a large GRAIN ELEVATOR by the railroad track.*
  North of town .3 m. is the junction with an oiled road."
  —Minnesota, *Federal Writers' Project (2nd edition, 1939)*

pears inside. The boy kicks the chunk at the curb, once, twice, then lofts it over the curb and sidewalk across the concrete to the island of Pure Oil pumps. He jumps three times on the Bunsen bell hose, making three dings back in the dark garage. The mayor of Lake Wobegon, Clint Bunsen, peers out from the grease pit, under a black Ford pickup. His brother Clarence, wiping the showroom glass (BUNSEN MOTORS— FORD—NEW & USED—SALES & SERVICE) with an old blue shirt, knocks on the window. The showroom is empty. The boy follows the chunk a few doors north to Ralph's window, which displays a mournful cardboard pig, his body marked with the names of cuts. An old man sits on Ralph's bench, white hair as fine as spun glass poking out under his green feed cap, his grizzled chin on his skinny chest, snoozing, the afternoon sun now reaching under the faded brown canvas awning up to his belt. He is not Ralph. Ralph is the thin man in the white apron who has stepped out the back door of the store, away from the meat counter, to get a breath of fresh, meatless air. He stands on a rickety porch that looks across the lake, a stone's throw away. The beach there is stony; the sandy beach is two blocks to the north. A girl, perhaps one of his, stands on the diving dock, plugs her nose, and executes a perfect cannonball, and he hears the dull *thunsh*. A quarter-mile away, a silver boat sits off the weeds in Sunfish Bay, a man in a bright blue jacket waves his pole; the line is hooked on weeds.* The sun makes a trail of shimmering lights across the water. It would make quite a picture if you had the right lens, which nobody in this town has got.

The lake is 678.2 acres, a little more than a section, fed by cold springs and drained from the southeast by a creek, the Lake Wobegon River, which flows to the Sauk which joins the Mississippi. In 1836, an Italian count waded up the creek, towing his canoe, and camped on the lake shore, where he imagined for a moment that he was the hero who had found the true headwaters of the Mississippi. Then something about the place made him decide he was wrong. He was right, we're not the headwaters, but what made him jump to that conclusion? What has made so many others look at us and think, *It doesn't start here!*?

---

* *It is Dr. Nute, retired after forty odd years of dentistry, now free to ply the waters in the Molar II and drop a line where the fighting sunfish lie in wait. "Open wide," he says. "This may sting a little bit. Okay. Now bite down."*

The woods are red oak, maple, some spruce and pine, birch, alder, and thick brush, except where cows have been put, which is like a park. The municipal boundaries take in quite a bit of pasture and cropland, including wheat, corn, oats, and alfalfa, and also the homes of some nine hundred souls, most of them small white frame houses sitting forward on their lots and boasting large tidy vegetable gardens and modest lawns, many featuring cast-iron deer, small windmills, clothespoles and clotheslines, various plaster animals such as squirrels and lambs and small elephants, white painted rocks at the end of the driveway, a nice bed of petunias planted within a white tire, and some with a shrine in the rock garden, the Blessed Virgin standing, demure, her eyes averted, arms slightly extended, above the peonies and marigolds. In the garden behind the nunnery next door to Our Lady of Perpetual Responsibility, she stands on a brick pedestal, and her eyes meet yours with an expression of deep sympathy for the sufferings of the world, including this little town.

It is a quiet town, where much of the day you could stand in the middle of Main Street and not be in anyone's way—not forever, but for as long as a person would want to stand in the middle of a street. It's a wide street; the early Yankee promoters thought they would need it wide to handle the crush of traffic. The double white stripe is for show, as are the two parking meters. Two was all they could afford. They meant to buy more meters with the revenue, but nobody puts nickels in them because parking nearby is free. Parking is diagonal.

Merchants call it "downtown"; other people say "up town," two words, as in "I'm going up town to get me some socks."

On Main between Elm and McKinley stand four two-story brick buildings on the north side, six on the south, and the Central Building, three stories, which has sandstone blocks with carved scallops above the third-floor windows.* Buildings include the "Ingqvist Block," "Union

---

*The stone plaque on the facade fell off one hot July afternoon, the plaque that reads CENTRAL BLDG. 1913, and crashed on the sidewalk, almost hitting Bud Mueller, who had just stopped and turned to walk the other way. If he hadn't, he would have been killed. He didn't know why he had turned. "It was like something spoke to me right then," he said. Others realized then that they had been on the verge of walking by the Central Building moments before and something had spoken to them. "You know, I was thinking, 'Maybe I will go to Skoglund's and purchase a pencil,' but then something said, 'No, you wait on that,' so I didn't go. If I had gone, it would've killed me," Mr. Berge said. He was one of many whose lives had been spared by a narrow margin. The plaque broke into five pieces, which Carl Krebsbach glued together, and it was remounted on the facade with a protective mesh to keep it in place.

Block," "Security Block," "Farmers Block," and "Oleson Block," their names carved in sandstone or granite tablets set in the fancy brickwork at the top. Latticed brickwork, brickwork meant to suggest battlements, and brick towers meant to look palatial. In 1889, they hung a man from a tower for stealing. He took it rather well. They were tired of him sneaking around lifting hardware off buggies, so they tied a rope to his belt and hoisted him up where they could keep an eye on him.

Most men wear their belts low here, there being so many outstanding bellies, some big enough to have names of their own and be formally introduced. Those men don't suck them in or hide them in loose shirts; they let them hang free, they pat them, they stroke them as they stand around and talk. How could a man be so vain as to ignore this old friend who's been with him at the great moments of his life?

The buildings are quite proud in their false fronts, trying to be everything that two stories can be and a little bit more. The first stories have newer fronts of aluminum and fake marble and stucco and fiberglass stonework, meant to make them modern. A child might have cut them off a cornflakes box and fastened them with two tabs, A and B, and added the ladies leaving the Chatterbox Cafe from their tuna sandwich lunch: three old ladies with wispy white hair, in sensible black shoes and long print dresses with the waist up under the bosom, and the fourth in a deep purple pant suit and purple pumps, wearing a jet-black wig. She too is seventy but looks like a thirty-four-year-old who led a very hard life. She is Carl Krebsbach's mother, Myrtle, who, they say, enjoys two pink Daiquiris every Friday night and between the first and second hums "Tiptoe Through the Tulips" and does a turn that won her First Prize in a Knights of Columbus talent show in 1936 at the Alhambra Ballroom. It burned to the ground in 1955. "Myrtle has a natural talent, you know," people have always told her, she says. "She had a chance to go on to Minneapolis." Perhaps she is still considering the offer.

Her husband Florian pulls his '66 Chevy into a space between two pickups in front of the Clinic. To look at his car, you'd think it was 1966 now, not 1985; it's so new, especially the backseat, which looks as if nobody ever sat there unless they were gift-wrapped. He is coming to see Dr. DeHaven about stomach pains that he thinks could be cancer, which he believes he has a tendency toward. Still, though he may be dying, he takes a minute to get a clean rag out of the trunk, soak it with gasoline, lift the hood, and wipe off the engine. He says she runs cooler when she's clean, and it's better if you don't let the dirt get baked on. Nineteen years old, she has only 42,000 miles on her, as he will tell you if you admire how new she looks. "Got her in '66. Just 42,000 miles on her." It may be odd that a man should be so proud of having not gone far, but not so odd in this town. Under his Trojan Seed Corn cap pulled down tight on his head is the face of a boy, and when he talks his voice breaks, as if he hasn't talked enough to get over adolescence completely. He has lived here all his life, time hardly exists for him, and when he looks at this street and when he sees his wife, he sees them brand-new, like this car. Later, driving the four blocks home at about trolling speed, having forgotten the misery of a rectal examination, he will notice a slight arrhythmic imperfection when the car idles, which he will spend an hour happily correcting.

In school we sang

Hail to thee, Lake Wobegon, the cradle of our youth.
We shall uphold the blue and gold in honor and in truth.
Holding high our lamps, we will be thy champs, and will vanquish far
    and near
For W.H.S., the beacon of the west, the school we love so dear.

And also

We're going to fight, fight, fight for Wobegon
And be strong and resolute,
And our mighty foes will fall down in rows
When we poke 'em in the snoot! (Rah! Rah!)

But those were only for show. In our hearts, our loyalties to home have always been more modest, along the lines of the motto on the town crest—"*Sumus quod sumus*" (We are what we are)—and the annual Christmas toast of the Sons of Knute, "There's no place like home when you're not feeling well," first uttered by a long-ago Knute who missed the annual dinner dance due to a case of the trots, and even Mr. Diener's observation, "When you're around it all the time, you don't notice it so much." He said this after he tore out the wall between his living room and dining room, which he had not done before for fear that it was there for a reason. In the wall, he found the remains of a cat who had been missing for more than a year. The Dieners had not been getting full use of the dining room and had been silently blaming each other. "It's good to know that it wasn't us," he said.

In school and in church, we were called to high ideals such as truth and honor by someone perched on truth and hollering for us to come on up, but the truth was that we always fell short.* Every spring, the Thanatopsis Society sponsored a lecture in keeping with the will of the late Mrs. Bjornson, who founded the society as a *literary* society, and though they had long since evolved into a conversational society, the Thanatopsians were bound by the terms of her bequest to hire a lecturer once a year and listen. One year it was World Federalism (including a demonstration of conversational Esperanto), and then it was the benefits of a unicameral legislature, and in 1955, a man from the University came and gave us "The World of 1980" with slides of bubble-top houses, picture-phones, autogyro copter-cars, and floating factories harvesting tasty plankton from the sea. We sat and listened and clapped, but when the chairlady called for questions from the audience, what most of us wanted to know we didn't dare ask: "How much are you getting paid for this?"

Left to our own devices, we Wobegonians go straight for the small potatoes. Majestic doesn't appeal to us; we like the Grand Canyon better with Clarence and Arlene parked in front of it, smiling. We feel uneasy at momentous events.

Lake Wobegon babies are born in a hospital thirty-some miles away and held at the glass by a nurse named Betty who has worked there for three hundred years—then it's a long drive home for the new father in the small morning hours, and when he arrives, he is full of thought. His

---

* *I grew up among slow talkers, men in particular, who dropped words a few at a time like beans in a hill, and when I got to Minneapolis, where people took a Lake Wobegon comma to mean the end of the story, I couldn't speak a whole sentence in company and was considered not too bright, so I enrolled in a speech course taught by Orville Sand, the founder of reflexive relaxology, a self-hypnotic technique that enabled a person to speak up to three hundred words per minute. He believed that slow speech deprives us of a great deal of thought by slowing down the mental processes to one's word rate. He believed that the mind has unlimited powers if only a person could learn to release them and eliminate the backup caused by slow discharge. I believe that's what he said—it was hard to understand him. He'd be rattling on about relaxology one moment and then he was into photography, his father, the Baltimore Orioles, wheat germ, birth and death, central heating, the orgasm— which was satisfying for him, but which left me in the dust, so I quit, having only gotten up to about eighty-five. And after a few weeks, I was back to about ten or eleven.*

life has taken a permanent turn toward rectitude and sobriety and a decent regard for the sanctity of life; having seen his flesh in a layette he wants to talk about some deep truths he has discovered in the past few hours to his own parents, who have sat up in their pajamas, waiting for word about the baby's name and weight. Then they want to go to bed.

Lake Wobegon people die in those hospitals, unless they are quick about it, and their relations drive to sit with them. When Grandma died, she had been unconscious for three days. She was baking bread at Aunt Flo's and felt tired, then lay down for a nap and didn't wake up. An ambulance took her to the hospital. She lay asleep, so pale, so thin. It was August. We held cool washcloths to her forehead and moistened her lips with ice cubes. A nun leaned over and said in her ear, "Do you love Jesus?" We thought this might lead to something Catholic, involving incense and candles; we told her that, yes, she did love Jesus. Eight of us sat around the bed that first afternoon, taking turns holding Grandma's hand so that if she had any sensation, it would be one of love. Four more came that evening. We talked in whispers, but didn't talk much; it was hard to know what to say. "Mother always said she wanted to go in her sleep," my mother said. "She didn't want to linger." I felt that we should be saying profound things about Grandma's life and what it had meant to each of us, but I didn't know how to say that we should. My uncles were uneasy. The women saw to Grandma and wept a little now and then, a few friendly tears; the men only sat and crossed and uncrossed their legs, slowly perishing of profound truth, until they began to whisper among themselves—I heard gas mileage mentioned, and a new combine—and then they resumed their normal voices. "I wouldn't drive a Fairlane if you give it to me for nothing," Uncle Frank said. "They are nothing but grief." At the time (twenty), I thought they were crude and heartless, but now that I know myself a little better, I can forgive them for wanting to get back onto familiar ground. *Sumus quod sumus*. She was eighty-two. Her life was in all of us in the room. Nobody needed to be told that, except me, and now I've told myself.

Incorporated under the laws of Minnesota but omitted from the map due to the incompetence of surveyors, first named "New Albion" by New Englanders who thought it would become the Boston of the west, taking its ultimate name from an Indian phrase that means either "Here we are!" or "we sat all day in the rain waiting for [you]," Lake Wobegon is the seat of tiny Mist County, the "phantom county in the heart of the heartland" (Dibbley, *My Minnesota*), founded by Unitarian missionaries and Yankee promoters, then found by Norwegian Lutherans who straggled in from the west, having headed first to Lake Agassiz in what is now North Dakota, a lake that turned out to be prehistoric, and by German Catholics, who, bound for Clay County, had stopped a little short, having misread their map, but refused to admit it.

A town with few scenic wonders such as towering pines or high mountains but with some fine people of whom some are over six feet tall, its highest point is the gold ball on the flagpole atop the Norge Co-op grain elevator south of town on the Great Northern spur, from which Mr. Tollefson can see all of Mist County when he climbs up to raise the flag on national holidays, including Norwegian Independence Day, when the blue cross of Norway is flown. (No flag of Germany has appeared in public since 1917.) Next highest is the water tower, then the boulder on the hill, followed by the cross on the spire of Our Lady, then the spire of Lake Wobegon Lutheran (Christian Synod), the Central Building (three stories), the high school flagpole, the high school, the top row of bleachers at Wally ("Old Hard Hands") Bunsen Memorial Field, the First Ingqvist State Bank, Bunsen Motors, the Hjalmar Ingqvist home, etc.

I've been to the top only once, in 1958, when six of us boys broke into the Co-op one July night to take turns riding the bucket to the tiny window at the peak of the elevator. It was pitch-black in there and stifling hot, I was choking on grain dust, the motor whined and the rope groaned, and up I rode, terrified and hanging onto the bucket for dear life—it was shallow, like a wheelbarrow, and pitched back and forth so I knew I'd fall into the black and break my neck. All the way up I promised God that if He would bring me safely back to the floor, I would never touch alcohol—then suddenly I was at the window and could see faintly through the dusty glass some lights below that I knew were Lake Wobegon. The bucket swayed, I reached out for the wall to steady it, but the wall wasn't where it should have been and the bucket swung back and I fell forward in one sickening moment; out of my mouth came an animal shriek that almost tore my face off, then I felt the cable in my left hand and the bucket swung back to level, then they released the brake and the bucket fell twenty or fifty or a hundred feet before they threw the brake back on, which almost broke my back, then they cranked me down the rest of the way and lifted me out and I threw up. Nobody cared, they were all crying. Jim put his arms around me and I staggered out into the night, which smelled so good. We went to someone's house and lay on the grass, looked at the stars, and drank beer. I drank four bottles.

Right then I guess was when I loved Lake Wobegon the most, the night I didn't quite die. I turned sixteen the next week and never told my parents what a miraculous birthday it was. I looked around the table and imagined them eating this pork roast and potato salad with me gone to the graveyard, imagined the darkness in the tight box and the tufted satin quilt on my cold face, and almost burst into tears of sheer gratitude, but took another helping of pork instead. Our family always was known for its great reserve.

We climbed the water tower, of course, but spent more time on the third highest point, Adams Hill, which rose behind the school and commanded a panoramic view of town and lake from the clearing at the crest. As a small boy who listened carefully and came to his own conclusions, I assumed that the hill was where God created our first parents, the man from the dust in the hole where we built fires, the lady from his rib. They lived there for many years in a log cabin like Lincoln's and ate blueberries and sweet corn from the Tolleruds' field. Adam fished for sunnies off the point, and their kids fooled around like we did, Eve sometimes poking her head out the door and telling them to pipe down.

There was no apple tree on Adams·Hill, but that didn't weaken my faith; there were snakes. Here, above the school, God created the world.

When I was four, I told my sister about the Creation, and she laughed in my face. She was eight. She gave me a choice between going back on Scripture truth as I knew it or eating dirt, and I ate a pinch of dirt. "Chew it," she said, and I did so she could hear it crunch.

There, for years, to the peak of Paradise, we resorted every day, the old gang. Nobody said, "Let's go"; we just went. Lance was the captain. Rotting trees that lay in the clearing were our barricades, and we propped up limbs for cannons. The boulder was the command post. We sat in the weeds, decked out in commando wear—neckerchiefs and extra belts slung over our shoulders for ammo and Lance even had a canteen in a khaki cover and a khaki satchel marked *U.S.A.*—and we looked down the slope to the roofs of town, which sometimes were German landing boats pulled up on the beach, and other times were houses of despicable white settlers who had violated the Sacred Hunting Ground of us

Chippewa. We sent volleys of flaming arrows down on them and burned them to the ground many times, or we pounded the boats with tons of deadly shells, some of us dying briefly in the hot sun. "Aiiiiieeee!" we cried when it was time to die, and pitched forward, holding our throats. There were no last words. We were killed instantly.

Near the clearing was a giant tree we called the Pee Tree; a long rope hung from a lower branch, which when you swung hard on it took you out over the edge and showed you your real death. You could let go at the end of the arc and fall to the rocks and die if you wanted to.

Jim said, "It's not that far—it wouldn't kill you." He was bucking for captain. Lance said, "So jump then. I dare you." That settled it. It would kill you, all right. It would break every bone in your body, just like Richard. He was twelve and drove his dad's tractor and fell off and it ran over him and killed him. He was one boy who died when I was a boy, and the other was Paulie who drowned in the lake. Both were now in heaven with God where they were happy. It was God's will that it would happen.

"It was an accident, God didn't make it happen, God doesn't go around murdering people," Jim said. I explained that, maybe so, but God *knows* everything that will happen, He has known every single thing since time began, and everything that happens is part of God's plan.

"Does He know that I'm just about to hit you?" Jim said.

"Everything."

"What if I changed my mind at the last minute and didn't?"

"He knows everything."

Jim believed that God sort of generally watched over the world but didn't try to oversee every single detail. He said that, for example, when you're born, you could be born American *or* Chinese or Russian or African, depending. In heaven are millions of souls lined up waiting to be born, and when it's your turn, you go down the chute like a gumball to whoever put the penny in the slot. You were born to your parents because, right at that moment when they Did It, you were next in line. Two seconds later and you could have been a feeb. Or a Communist. "It's just pure luck we're Americans," he said.

When it was hot, we all lay around in the grass and talked about stuff. At least, if you were older, you could talk. Little kids had to shut up because they didn't know anything. Jim leaned on one elbow and tore off tufts of grass and threw them at my face. I told him twice to quit it. He said, "Tell God to make me quit it. It's God's plan. He knew that I was going to do it. It's not my fault." He said, "If you think God planned you, then He made a big mistake, because you're the dumbest person I know."

I was on top of him before he could blink and pounded him twice before he wriggled out and got me in an armlock and shoved my face into the dirt. Then Lance broke us up. We sat and glared at each other. We fought once more, and went home to supper.

I lived in a white house with Mother, Dad, Rudy, Phyllis, and we raised vegetables in the garden and ate certain things on the correct nights (macaroni hotdish on Thursday, liver on Friday, beans and wieners on Saturday, pot roast on Sunday) and sang as we washed dishes:

> Because God made the stars to shine,
> Because God made the ivy twine,
> Because God made the sky so blue.
> Because God made you, that's why I love you.

God created the world and ordained everything to be right and perfect, then man sinned against God's Will, but God still knew *everything*. Before the world was made, when it was only darkness and mist and waters, God was well aware of Lake Wobegon, my family, our house, and He had me all sketched out down to what size my feet would be (big), which bike I would ride (a Schwinn), and the five ears of corn I'd eat for supper that night. He had meant me to be there; it was His Will, which it was up to me to discover the rest of and obey, but the first part— being me, in Lake Wobegon—He had brought about as He had hung the stars and decided on blue for the sky.

The crisis came years later when Dad mentioned that in 1938 he and Mother had almost moved to Brooklyn Park, north of Minneapolis, but didn't because Grandpa offered them our house in Lake Wobegon, which was Aunt Becky's until she died and left it to Grandpa, and Dad got a job with the post office as a rural mail carrier. I was fourteen when I got this devastating news: that I was me and had my friends and lived in my house only on account of a pretty casual decision about real estate, otherwise I'd have been a Brooklyn Park kid where I didn't know a soul. I imagined Dad and Mother talking it over in 1938—"Oh, I don't care, it's up to you, either one is okay with me"—as my life hung in the balance. Thank goodness God was at work, I thought, because you sure couldn't trust your parents to do the right thing.

Until it became a suburb, Brooklyn Park was some of the best farmland in Minnesota, but Lake Wobegon is mostly poor sandy soil, and every spring the earth heaves up a new crop of rocks.* Piles of rock ten feet high in the corners of fields, picked by generations of us, monuments to our industry. Our ancestors chose the place, tired from their long journey, sad for having left the motherland behind, and this place reminded them of there, so they settled here, forgetting that they had left there because the land wasn't so good. So the new life turned out to be a lot like the old, except the winters are worse.

Since arriving in the New World, the good people of Lake Wobegon have been skeptical of progress. When the first automobile chugged into town, driven by the Ingqvist twins, the crowd's interest was muted, less whole-hearted than if there had been a good fire. When the first strains of music wafted from a radio, people said, "I don't know." Of course, the skeptics gave in and got one themselves. But the truth is, we still don't know.

For this reason, it's a hard place to live in from the age of fourteen on up to whenever you recover. At that age, you're no skeptic but a true believer starting with belief in yourself as a natural phenomenon never before seen on this earth and therefore incomprehensible to all the others. You believe that if God were to make you a millionaire and an idol whose views on the world were eagerly sought by millions, that it would be no more than what you deserved. This belief is not encouraged there.

Sister Brunnhilde was coaching a Krebsbach on his catechism one morning in Our Lady lunchroom and suddenly asked a question out of order. "Why did God make you?" she said sharply, as if it were an

---

* *Though unpromising for agriculture, the Lake Wobegon area is beloved among geologists for the diversity of its topography, lying within the Bowlus Moraine left by the retreat of the Western Lobe of the Superior Glacier and including the St. John's Drumlin Field of pale brown sandy till featuring numerous Precambrian rocks and pebbles that come to the surface in the spring. Certain plutonic rocks, mainly granite, appear in outcroppings, while some metamorphic minerals such as garnet and anchorite crystals have been found, but not enough to make much difference. Had the Superior Glacier moved slower twenty thousand years ago, permitting the Moorhead Glacier to race eastward with its valuable load of shale-rich soil, Lake Wobegon's history would be much brighter than it is. Adding insult to injury, geologists now point out that the town lies in a major fault zone, where deep-seated forces may one day with no warning send us running in terror from our beds.*

accusation. The boy opened his mouth, wavered, then looked at a spot on the linoleum and put his breakfast there. He ran to the lavatory, and Sister, after a moment's thought, strolled down the hall to the fifth-grade classroom. "Who wants to be a nurse when she grows up?" she asked. Six girls raised their hands, and she picked Betty Diener. "Nurses help sick people in many different ways," she told Betty as they walked to the lunchroom. "They have many different jobs to do. Now here is one of them. The mop is in the kitchen. Be sure to use plenty of Pine-Sol."

So most of Lake Wobegon's children leave, as I did, to realize themselves as finer persons than they were allowed to be at home.

When I was a child, I figured out that I was

1 person, the son of

2 parents and was the

3rd child, born

4 years after my sister and

5 years after my brother, in

1942 (four and two are 6), on the

7th day of the

8th month, and the year before

had been 9 years old and

was now 10.

To me, it spelled Destiny.

When I was twelve, I had myself crowned King of Altrusia and took the royal rubber-tipped baton and was pulled by my Altrusian people in a red wagon to the royal woods and was adored all afternoon, though it was a hot one—they didn't complain or think the honor should have gone to them. They hesitated a moment when I got in the wagon, but then I said, "Forward!" and they saw there can be only one Vincent the First and that it was me. And when I stood on the royal stump and blessed them in the sacred Altrusian tongue, "Arooaroo halama rama domino, shadrach meshach abednego," and Duane laughed, and I told him to die, he did. And when I turned and marched away, I knew they were following me.

When I was fourteen, something happened and they didn't adore me so much.

I ran a constant low fever waiting for my ride to come and take me away to something finer. I lay in bed at night, watching the red beacon on top of the water tower, a clear signal to me of the beauty and mystery of a life that waited for me far away, and thought of Housman's poem,

Loveliest of trees, the cherry now
Is hung with bloom along the bough.
It stands among the woodland ride,
Wearing white for Eastertide.
Now, of my three-score years and ten,
Twenty will not come again. . . .

and would have run away to where people would appreciate me, had I known of such a place, had I thought my parents would understand. But if I had said, "Along the woodland I must go to see the cherry hung with snow," they would have said, "Oh, no, you don't. You're going to stay right here and finish up what I told you to do three hours ago. Besides, those aren't cherry trees, those are crab apples."

Now I lie in bed in St. Paul and look at the moon, which reminds me of the one over Lake Wobegon.

I'm forty-three years old. I haven't lived there for twenty-five years. I've lived in a series of eleven apartments and three houses, most within a few miles of each other in St. Paul and Minneapolis. Every couple years the urge strikes, to pack the books and unscrew the table legs and haul off to a new site. The mail is forwarded, sometimes from a house several stops back down the line, the front of the envelope covered with addresses, but friends are lost—more all the time, it's sad to think about it. All those long conversations in vanished kitchens when for an evening we achieved a perfect understanding that, no matter what happened, we were true comrades and our affection would endure, and now our friendship is gone to pieces and I can't account for it. *Why don't I see you anymore? Did I disappoint you? Did you call me one night to say you were in trouble and hear a tone in my voice that made you say you were just fine?*

When I left Lake Wobegon, Donna Bunsen and I promised each other we'd read the same books that summer as a token of our love, which we sealed with a kiss in her basement. She wore white shorts and a blue blouse with white stars. She poured a cup of Clorox bleach in the washing machine, and then we kissed. In books, men and women "embraced passionately," but I didn't know how much passion to use, so I put my arms around her and held my lips to hers and rubbed her lovely back, under the wings. Our reading list was ten books, five picked by her and five by me, and we made a reading schedule so that, although apart, we would have the same things on our minds at the same time and would think of each other. We each picked the loftiest books we knew of, such as

Plato's *Republic*, *War and Peace*, *The Imitation of Christ*, the *Bhagavad-Gita*, *The Art of Loving*, to have great thoughts to share all summer as we read, but I didn't get far; my copy of Plato sat in my suitcase, and I fished it out only to feel guilty for letting her down so badly. I wrote her a letter about love, studded with Plato quotes picked out of Bartlett's, but didn't mail it, it was so shameless and false. She sent me two postcards from the Black Hills, and in the second she asked, "Do you still love me?" I did, but evidently not enough to read those books and become someone worthy of love, so I didn't reply. Two years later she married a guy who sold steel supermarket shelving, and they moved to San Diego. I think of her lovingly every time I use Clorox. Half a cup is enough to bring it all back.

When I left Lake Wobegon, I packed a box of books, two boxes of clothes, and two grocery sacks of miscellaneous, climbed in my 1956 Ford, and then, when my old black dog Buster came limping out from under the porch, I opened the door and boosted him into the back seat. He had arthritic hips and was almost blind, and as Dad said, it would be better to leave him die at home, but he loved to go for rides and I couldn't see making the long trip to Minneapolis alone. I had no prospects there except a spare bed in the basement of my dad's old Army buddy Bob's house. Buster was company, at least.

Bob had two dogs of his own, a bulldog named Max and a purebred Irish setter who owned the upstairs and the yard, so Buster spent his declining months on a blanket in Bob's rec room, by my bed. Bob kept telling me that Buster should be put out of his misery, but I had too much misery of my own to take care of his. Instead of shooting him, I wrote poems about him.

> Old dog, old dog, come and lay your old head
> On my knee.
> Dear God, dear God, let this poor creature go
> And live in peace.

Bob kept telling me to forget about college and he would line me up with a friend of his in the plumbers' union. "Why be so odd?" he said. "Plumbers get good money." His son Dallas was in the Air Force, stationed in Nevada, and he liked it a lot. "Why not the Air Force?" Bob asked. One day, he said, "You know what your problem is?" I said I didn't. "You don't get along with other people. You don't make an effort to get along." How could I explain the duty I felt to keep a dying dog company? A dog who had been so close to me since I was a little kid and who understood me better than anyone. I had to leave him alone when I went looking for work, and then while I was working at the Longfellow Hotel as a dishwasher, so when I got back to Bob's, I liked to give Buster some attention.

Bob remembered the war fondly and had many photographs from his days with my dad at Camp Lee and then in a linen-supply unit of the Quartermaster Corps, stationed at Governor's Island in New York City, which he showed me after supper when I was trapped at the table. "People were swell to us, they invited us into their homes, they fed us meals, they treated us like heroes," he said. "Of course, the real heroes were the guys in Europe, but it could've been us instead of them, so it was okay. You wore the uniform, people looked up to you. Those were different times. There was a lot of pride then, a lot of pride."

Clearly I was a sign of how far the country had gone downhill: an eighteen-year-old kid with no future, sleeping in the basement with a dying dog. Bob left Air Force brochures on the breakfast table, hoping I'd read them and something would click. One August morning, when a postcard arrived from the University saying I'd been accepted for fall quarter, he warned me against certain people I would find there, atheists and lefties and the sort of men who like to put their arms around young guys. "I'm not saying you have those tendencies," he said, "but it's been my experience that guys like you, who think you're better than other people, have a lot of weaknesses that you don't find out about until it's too late. I just wish you'd listen, that's all. But you're going to have to find out the hard way, I guess."

Buster died in his sleep a few days later. He was cold in the morning. I packed him in an apple crate and snuck him out to my car and buried him in the woods by the Mississippi in Lilydale, which was like the woods he had known in his youth.

I felt as bad that night as I've ever felt, I think. I lay on the army cot and stared at the joists and let the tears run off my face like rain. Bob sent his wife, Luanne, down with some supper. "Oh, for crying out loud," she said. "Why don't you grow up?"

"Okay," I said, "I will." I moved out, into a rooming house on the West Bank. I lived in a 12 x 12 room with three bunkbeds and five roommates and started school. School was okay, but I missed that old dog a lot. He was a good dog to know. He was steadfast, of course, as all dogs are, and let nothing come between us or dim his foolish affection for me. Even after his arthritis got bad, he still struggled to his feet when I came home and staggered toward me, his rear end swung halfway forward, tail waving, as he had done since I was six. I seemed to fulfill his life in some way, and even more so in his dotage than in bygone days when he could chase rabbits. He was so excited to see me, and I missed that; I certainly didn't excite anyone else.

More than his pure affection, however, I missed mine for him, which now had nowhere to go. I made the rounds of classes and did my time in the library every day, planted myself in oak chairs and turned pages, and sorely missed having someone to put my arms around, some other flesh, some hair to touch other than my own. And I missed his call to fidelity. My old black mutt reminded me of a whole long string of allegiances and loyalties, which school seemed to be trying to jiggle me free of. My humanities instructor, for example, who sounded to be from someplace east of the East, had a talent for saying "Minnesota" as if it were "moose turds," and we all snickered when he did. You don't pull that sort of crap around a dog. Dogs have a way of bringing you back to earth. Their affection shames pretense. They are guileless.

I needed Buster to be true to and thus be true by implication to much more, to the very principle of loyalty itself, which I was losing rapidly in Minneapolis. Once I saw Ronald Eichen in Gray's Drug near campus, my old classmate who twice lent me his '48 Ford now sweeping Gray's floor, and because our friendship no longer fit into my plans, I ducked down behind the paperbacks and snuck out. I was redesigning myself and didn't care to be the person he knew.

I couldn't afford to buy new clothes at Al Johnson, Men's Clothier, so I tried out a Continental accent on strange girls at Bridgeman's lunch counter: "Gud morrning. Mind eef I seat next to you? Ahh! ze greel shees! I zink I hef that and ze shicken soup. Ah, par*don*—my name ees Ramon. Ramon Day-Bwah." This puzzled most of the girls I talked to, who wondered where I was from. "Fransh? *Non*. My muthaire she vas Fransh but my fathaire come from Eetaly, so? How do you say? I am *internationale*." I explained that my fathaire wass a deeplo*mat* and we traffled efferyvhere, which didn't satisfy them either, but then my purpose was to satisfy myself and that was easy. I was *foreign*. I didn't care where I was from so long as it was someplace else.

A faint English accent was easier to manage, at least on Mondays, Wednesdays, and Fridays. My composition instructor, Mr. Staples, was

English, and an hour in the morning listening to him primed the pump and I could talk like him the rest of the day. Englishness, however, didn't free my spirit so well as being truly foreign did. Mr. Staples smelled musty, walked flat-footed, had dry thin hair, and went in for understatement to the point of blending in with his desk. European was a better deal. If I could be European, I'd be right where I wanted to be as a person.

I invented new people for the ones I knew, trying to make them more interesting. At various times, my father was a bank robber, a college professor, the President of the United States, and sometimes I imagined that we weren't really from Minnesota, we were only using it as a cover, disguising ourselves as quiet modest people until we could reveal our true identity as Italians. One day, my mother would put the wieners on the table and suddenly my father would jump up and say, "Hey! I'ma sicka this stuffa!" She'd yell, "No! No! Chonny! Please-a! The children!" But the cat was out of the bag. We weren't who we thought we were, we were The Keillorinis! *Presto! Prestone!* My father rushed to the closet and hauled out giant oil paintings of fat ladies, statues of saints, bottles of wine, and in rushed the relatives, hollering and carrying platters of spicy spaghetti, and my father would turn to me and say, "Eduardo! Eduardo, my son!" and throw his arms around me and plant big wet smackers on my cheeks. *Caramba!* Then we would dance, hands over our heads. *Aye-yi-yi-yi-yi!* Dancing, so long forbidden to us by grim theology of tight-lipped English Puritans—dancing, the language of our souls—*Mamma mia!* Now that's *amore! Viva, viva!* Do the Motorola!

I went home for Christmas and gave books for presents, Mother got *Walden*, Dad got Dostoevsky. I smoked a cigarette in my bedroom, exhaling into an electric fan in the open window. I smoked another at the Chatterbox. I wore a corduroy sportcoat with leather patches on the elbows. Mr. Thorvaldson sat down by me. "So. What is it they teach you down there?" he said. I ticked off the courses I took that fall. "No, I mean what are you learning?" he said. "Now, 'Humanities in the Modern World,' for example? What's that about?" I said, "Well, it covers a lot of ground, I don't think I could explain it in a couple of minutes." "That's okay," he said, "I got all afternoon."

I told him about work instead. My job at the Longfellow was washing dishes for the three hundred young women who lived there, who were the age of my older sister who used to jump up from dinner and clear the table as we boys sat and discussed dessert. The three hundred jumped up and shoved their trays through a hole in the wall where I, in the scullery, worked like a slave. I grabbed up plates, saucers, bowls, cups, silverware, glasses, passed them under a hot rinse, the garbage disposal grinding away, and slammed them into racks that I heaved onto the conveyor that bore them slowly, sedately, through the curtain of rubber ribbons to their bath. Clouds of steam from the dishwasher filled the room when the going got heavy. Every rack that emerged released a billow of steam, and I heaved the racks onto a steel counter to dry for a minute, then yanked the hot china and stacked it on a cloth for the servers to haul to the steam table. We had less china than customers, and since they all wanted to eat breakfast at seven o'clock, there was a pinch in the china flow about seven-fifteen, when I had to work magic and run china from trays to racks to steam table in about sixty seconds, then make a pass through the dining room grabbing up empty juice glasses because the glass pinch was next, and then the lull when I mopped up and waited for the dawdlers, and finally my own rush to nine o'clock class, American Government.

The soap powder was pungent pink stuff; it burned my nostrils when I poured it in the machine, but it made glittering white suds that smelled, as the whole scullery smelled, powerfully *clean*. The air was so hot and pure, it made me giddy to breathe it, and also the puffs of sweet food smells that wafted up from the disposal, cream and eggs and, in the evening, lime sherbet. (I saved up melted sherbet by the gallon, to dump it into the disposal fan and breathe in a burst of sugar.) I worked hard but in that steambath felt so slick and loose and graceful—it was so hot that even the hottest weeks of August, I felt cool for the rest of the day—and felt *clean:* breathed clean steam, sweated pure clean sweat, and even sang about purity as I worked—all the jazzy revival songs I knew, "Power in the Blood" and "The Old Account Was Settled Long Ago" and "O Happy Day That Fixed My Choice" and

> *Have you* come to Jesus *for the* cleansing power,
> *Are you* washed *in the* blood *of the* Lamb? (Slam. Bang.)

When Lucy of composition class, who let me have half her sandwich one day, asked me if I had a job and I told her I was a dishwasher, she made a face as if I said I worked in the sewer. She said it must be awful, and of course when I told her it was terrific, she thought I was being ironic. Composition class was local headquarters of irony; we supplied the five-county area. The more plainly I tried to say I liked dishwashing, the more ironic she thought I was, until I flipped a gob of mayo at her as a rhetorical device to show *un*subtlety and sincerity, and then she thought I was a jerk.

I didn't venture to write about dishwashing for composition and certainly not about the old home town. Mr. Staples told us to write from personal experience, of course, but he said it with a smirk, suggesting that we didn't have much, so instead I wrote the sort of dreary, clever essays I imagined I'd appreciate if I were him.

Lake Wobegon, whatever its faults, is not dreary. Back for a visit in August, I saw Wayne "Warning Track" Tommerdahl stroke the five-thousandth long fly ball of his Whippet career. "You move that fence forty feet in, and Wayne could be in the majors," said Uncle Al, seeing greatness where it had not so far appeared. Toast 'n Jelly Days was over but the Mist County Fair had begun and I paid my quarter to plunge twenty-five feet at the Hay Jump, landing in the stack a few feet from Mrs. Carl Krebsbach, who asked, "What brings you back?" A good question and one that several dogs in town had brought up since I arrived. Talking to Fr. Emil outside the Chatterbox Cafe, I made a simple mistake: pointed north in reference to Daryl Tollerud's farm where the gravel pit was, where the naked man fell out the back door of the camper when his wife popped the clutch, and of course Daryl's farm is *west*, and I corrected myself right away, but Father gave me a funny look as if to say, *Aren't you from here then?* Yes, I am. I crossed Main Street toward Ralph's and stopped, hearing a sound from childhood in the distance. The faint mutter of ancient combines. Norwegian bachelor farmers combining in their antique McCormacks, the old six-footers. New combines cut a twenty-foot swath, but those guys aren't interested in getting done sooner, it would only mean a longer wait until bedtime. I stood and listened. My eyes got blurry. Of course, thanks to hay fever, wheat has always put me in an emotional state, and then the clatter brings back memories of old days of glory in the field when I was a boy among giants. My uncle lifted me up and put me on the seat so I could ride alongside him. The harness jingled on Brownie and Pete and Queenie and Scout, and we bumped along in the racket, row by row. Now all the giants are gone; everyone's about my size or smaller. Few people could lift me up, and I don't know that I'm even interested. It's sad to be so old. I postponed it as long as I could, but when I weep at the sound of a combine, I know I'm there. A young man wouldn't have the background for it.

That uncle is dead now, one of three who went down like dominoes, of bad tickers, when they reached seventy. I know more and more people in the cemetery, including Miss Heinemann, my English teacher. She was old (my age now) when I had her. A massive lady with chalk dust on her blue wool dress, whose hair was hacked short, who ran us like a platoon, who wept when I recited the sonnet she assigned me to memorize. Each of us got one, and I was hoping for "Shall I compare thee to a summer's day?" or "Let me not to the marriage of true minds," which might be *useful* in some situations, but was given Number 73, "That time of year thou mayst in me behold," which I recited briskly, three quatrains hand over fist, and nailed on the couplet at the end. The next year I did "When in disgrace with fortune and men's eyes."

Listening to combines on a dry day that is leaning toward fall, I still remember—

> *That time of year thou mayst in me behold*
> *When yellow leaves, or none, or few, do hang*
> *Upon those boughs which shake against the cold,*
> *Bare ruined choirs where late the sweet birds sang. . . .*

Learned at sixteen in a classroom that smelled of Wildroot hair oil and Nesbitt's orange pop on my breath, it cheers me up, even "the twilight of such day/As after sunset fadeth in the west" and "the ashes of his youth."

> *This thou perceiv'st, which makes thy love more strong,*
> *To love that well which thou must leave ere long.*

•4•

Twelve Poems from
Alliance, Illinois
Dave Etter

GEORGE MAXWELL:
  County Seat

  Pushing deep into Sunflower County now,
  just minutes before sunup,
  the big semitrailer truck droning on
  in the breezy, dew-heavy darkness;
  leaving behind the cornfields,
  the red barns, the windbreak trees,
  snorting by the city limits sign
  announcing ALLIANCE, pop. 6,428,
  thumping across the railroad tracks
  of the Chicago and North Western,
  slipping past roadside produce stands
  and hamburger and milkshake drive-ins,
  bouncing and rattling again
  between the bruised bodies of billboards
  saying where to shop, eat, sleep,
  where to fill up with gas;
  LICHENWALNER'S DEPARTMENT STORE,
  CARL'S MAINLINE CAFE,
  HOTEL TALL CORN,
  BOB'S TEXACO;
  dipping toward the polluted waters
  of the sluggish Ausagaunaskee River

and the once stately section of town
where neglected Victorian houses,
with their cupolas and wide porches,
are set back on maple-shaded lawns;
remembering good and bad times,
lost faces, half-forgotten names;
and then the driver taking a last drag
from his Marlboro cigarette,
poking me in the ribs
with yellow, tobacco-stained fingers,
one letter of Jesus on each knuckle,
breaking the long silence between us
by saying over the asthmatic breathing
of the great diesel engine
that we are here, this is it,
here's that town you've been asking for;
moving slowly into the Square,
with its domed and clocked courthouse,
its bandstand and Civil War monument,
its two-story brick buildings,
lawyers and doctors above,
the town's merchants below;
stopping on Main Street
next to the Farmers National Bank,
stepping down to the curb,
thanking the driver for the lift,
grabbing a U.S. Army duffel bag,
slamming the cab door with a loud bang,
then turning around to face
ALLIANCE CHAMBER OF COMMERCE
WELCOMES YOU
TO THE HYBRID CORN CAPITAL OF AMERICA,
and thus knowing for dead certain
that I'm back in the hometown,
and that nothing has, nothing could have
really changed since I went away.

STUBBY PAYNE:
Stocking Tops

In June the syringa bushes bloom,
and I swear that I can smell oranges there.
That was your smell, Bee. I knew it well.

And I think of you today in Arne's Pub,
where all winter long you sipped Gordon's gin,
legs crossed, showing a bulge of creamy thigh
above those tantalizing stocking tops.

Green summer again. Rain. The warm earth steams.

You left town on a Burlington day coach
to visit an aunt in Prairie du Chien.
"She's full of money," you said, "and dying of cancer."

Toward the end of July,
Sunflower County cornfields turn blond.
Stiff tassels shake in the sexual sun.
There's a dust of pollen in the air.

How many bags of potato chips?
How many trips to the can?
Oh, how many quarters in the jukebox, Bee?

August heat. The girls go almost naked here.

Like some overworked Cinderella,
you always took off just before midnight
on the arm of Prince or Joe or Hal or Smith,
bound for your place above the shoe store.

Yes, I should have bedded down with you myself,
said so what if you were a bumbling barfly,
every drinking man's little honey bush.

HAMILTON RIVERS:
Noon at Carl's Mainline Cafe

Talk of septic tanks, sheep dip, soap powder.
Talk just to be talking, saying something:

"Claude says the water is more than four feet deep
in those corn bottoms south the highway bridge."

"I'm gonna sell my galvanized hay loader,
my metal detector, and my Star Wars bedspread."

"You say he's a duck decoy carver now
and you haven't seen him since last Arbor Day?"

"Joe Webb dropped dead after this evangelist fella
got him over excited and puking his guts."

"I sure guess it needs a new transmission, boy.
Why you can't even back that heap up anymore."

"He's a loud kid in Big Smith overalls.
Fergus is his name, and it fits him to a T."

"Kay don't care much for her Kenmore washing machine.
Says never again another product from Sears."

"We cleaned out all that junk in the attic.
All them boxes with your forgotten toys in them."

"Funny thing, the area code here is 312.
Yet right across my street it's 815."

"Me and Willie we used to get us free wienies
from Rukenbrod's store when we'd stop from school."

"I unwrapped it and it was waxed fruit.
Sister ain't had no sense since she gone to Tulsa."

"Leave me inform you them wienies were good.
Seems they was better tasting than cooked ones."

"If I want to talk with Mabel Anderson,
I'm required to dial for long distance."

"It wasn't junk, it wasn't junk at all.
That was my Lionel train in there, you idiot."

"Ma's got herself an old Maytag, you know.
Pa he bought a platform rocker the very same day."

"Young Fergus is a pretty fair country jock,
but he bumbles about without benefit of brains."

"You was talkin' on rusty cars what leak.
We drove up here with water sloshing in the trunk."

"Ain't it sumpthing to go to your grave like that.
And Joe he never had a girl in bed or nothin'."

"I dropped Cousin Daisy a card from Vero Beach.
It comes back stamped RETURNED TO SENDER."

"What I need is a double-oven electric range
and maybe some new oars for the rowboat."

"Well, that's our flood for this April.
That's about per usual for Sunflower County."

Damn, I wish I hadn't heard all that nonsense.
I don't even remember what the hell I ate.

STELLA LYNCH:
The Opposite Sex

You bet he was there last Saturday night,
him with all that bleached blond hair,
with his thunder and lightning shirt,
with his merry-go-round pants,
with his dude-ranch cowboy boots.
He was liquored up like a payday coal miner.
He made no effort to dance with any of us.
He was looking all over for you,
asking everybody where you was at.
"Say, where's May, where's May?" he says,
popping his gum, grinning like a fool.
If you ask me, he's a real creep.

I'd like to see him mess around after me.
I got an old man and two brothers
which are all about half crazy.
They'd pour gasoline on top of him
and melt that tail of his down to the ground.
It's guys like him what take all the fun
out of these country-western dances.
There's always at least one of his type,
always someone with a Texas-size mouth
and some refried beans for brains.
If I was you, I'd stay the hell away
from the Masonic Temple, the Dew Drop Inn,
from the Sunset Bowling Lanes,
from the corner of Sixth and Main,
and the roller rink too, if I could.
But, hey, pay no mind to me, May.
There's some of you peculiar folks
who just can't wait to take on trouble.

HOWARD DRUMGOOLE:
Hotel Tall Corn

You know, I sorta, kinda like it.

It's not very tall at all,
and the only corn about the old place
is dispensed by the night desk clerk,
who's been around since Alf Landon
stopped being presidential timber.

The beds are soft, the plumbing works.

If you miss the last bus out of town,
that's where you go to get some sleep.
One cold, gloomy December evening
I slogged through half-frozen slush
to attend a wedding reception,
held in the swankiest suite they had.

The next morning the groom was found
hanging by his farmer's red neck
in a round barn west of Rochelle.

Woody Herman's band played there once,
a real "Woodchopper's Ball."

I hope it stays alive a little while.
It's the kind of rube hotel
Sherwood Anderson would hole up in
to write about the beauty of horses,
the faded dreams of small-town girls,
and the lives of lovesick millhands.

You know, I sorta, kinda like it.

LEONARD MASSINGAIL:
Fatherly Advice

You don't know beans about girls
and you are going about half-cocked.
It will always be a wild-goose chase
until, by hook or crook,
you break the ice with her.
She'll let you cool your heels
as long as you beat about the bush.
It's no skin off my nose
if you can't cut the mustard
and act like a fish out of water.
I'm not talking through my hat
when I say you're asleep at the switch.
Getting a doll is no lead-pipe cinch,
and coming down with a case of cold feet
puts romance on the rocks.
She sure looks like the real McCoy,
so make hay while the sun shines.
Get yourself in the groove, son.
Go the whole hog, right now.
I'd sweat my good blood

to rule the roost with that chick.
Just be a chip off the old block
and you'll soon be on Easy Street.
If you're going to hem and haw,
I'm going to be madder than a wet hen.
Look, either fish or cut bait,
or you will always eat crow.
Damnit, take the bull by the horns!

CURLY VANCE:
The Pool Players

The tavern is down by the C&NW tracks,
across from Spencer Purdom's grain elevator.
The time is about eleven o'clock
on a snowbound Saturday night.
The pool table is made of northern red oak,
scarred by many railroaders' knives.
But the green felt is good
and the numbered balls run true.
The game is stripes and solids,
or "big balls" versus "little balls."
The menacing black eight-ball is left for last,
when the game is on the line.
The teams are made up of me
and Texaco Cap, from nearby Goodenowville,
shooting against Orange Boots
and that human scarecrow Sycamore Slim.
The stakes are bottles of beer,
the winners collecting after each game.
The other guys drink Pabst Blue Ribbon.
I insist on Grain Belt.
The break is won by our side,
but I can put nothing in any of the pockets.
The balls are spread all over the cloth.
Orange Boots is licking his chops.

The audience consists of two noisy drunks
wearing monogrammed bowling shirts
and a Mexican section-gang worker
who keeps saying, "No, no, don't shoot that one."
The smoke hanging over the table
is from my Washington, Missouri, corncob pipe
and Sycamore Slim's El Productos.
Texaco Cap chews Beech-Nut.
The luck runs all one way.
Sycamore Slim's tricky bank shots
are dropping balls into every pocket.
Texaco Cap is getting hot under the collar,
steaming like a baked potato.
The fight begins when I tell Orange Boots
to lay off banging the overhead light shield
with his goddamned cue stick.
Orange Boots says, "You gonna make me?"
I hit him hard on the side of the head
and Texaco Cap hits him with the nine-ball.
Then there's lots of shoving and wild swinging.
The bartender goes for the telephone.
The cops arrive in no time at all.
Sycamore Slim is last seen
running down the C&NW tracks
with four cold bottles of Pabst Blue Ribbon,
two bags of Beer Nuts, and a Slim Jim.

TERRY REESE:
　Boom Boom on B Street

It was the two feet of snow that did us in.
Man, what a blizzard that baby was.
Lois, eyes hard as icicles, kept saying
she was finished with me, kaput,
was going home to Mother, getting out for good.
"Bitch, bitch, bitch, bitch, bitch," I said,

as I had been saying for weeks and weeks,
knowing we were cracking up this winter,
what with all the snow, the goddamn snow,
piling up everywhere you'd care to look,
and that our marriage had dropped below zero.
"You can keep the dog," she said.
"I hate him more than I hate you."
What an urge I had to knock her on her can.
"But I'm taking the car," she said.
I said nothing, but got out the shotgun.
She followed me outside, without her coat or hat,
the icy wind whipping her hair about.
I tell you I must have been off my nut,
about good and ready for a rubber room.
I pumped four shells into that old Oldsmobile:
the windshield, both front tires,
then lifted up the snow-capped hood
and put a blast in the carburetor.
Lois screamed and hugged the dog.
"Not him, oh not him, too," she said.
I stumbled toward her, falling once, twice,
and we tumbled in the snowbank.
Then we cried and cried, all the frozen tears
dripping down like a bad leak in the roof.
"It's snowing again," she said at last.
"We're not going anyplace," I said.
I tossed the shotgun in the wrecked car
and kissed the dog on his runny nose.

KEVIN PRUITT:
Taking Down the Flag

We're fifth graders now,
so all of us kids are grown old enough
to take down the flag after school.
The first afternoon, I told Freddie:

"Don't let it touch the ground.
Don't let it touch the ground.
Don't let it touch the ground."
But he let it touch the ground.
Freddie let the flag touch the ground.
I told him over and over:
"Don't let it touch the ground."
But it weren't no use,
so I kicked him hard in the butt
and called him a bad word.
I don't know why they got mad on me.
It weren't me let the flag touch the ground.

NED SWIFT:
Downtown

Anything going on downtown, you ask?
You better believe it, my good friend.
The mail truck got in early
but went out late,
there's another huge pothole
right in front of the Mobil station,
the Grain Belt beer sign at Jake's
was wrecked sometime last night,
and a Funk's G-Hybrid seed salesman
and a retired pharmacist
from Prophetstown, Illinois,
were hammering out a new foreign policy
on the stone bench at the Courthouse.
But that's not all,
that's not the half of it.
Up at the Dairy Queen,
Jennifer Hornbeck told me
that she wouldn't speak to me again
unless I got rid of my shoes,
my jeans, and my T-shirt that says

IT TAKES LEATHER BALLS TO PLAY RUGBY.
Now, my question is:
Does she want me naked tonight
after the band concert in the Square?

IRA LIEBRANDT:
Failing

A failing bank in a failing town,
the president of the bank shot dead
for foreclosing on a failing farm,
the farmer, turned fugitive, not caught yet.

The slow hound sleeps away his last days
on the railroad ties of no trains.
A big old boy they call C. W.
says to me in the Harvest Moon Cafe,
"You done using that there ketchup?"

Folks sipping coffee in the back booth
talking on what used to be in town
but isn't any longer in town.

There's the bank president's daughter out there.
She strolls down the broken sidewalk,
cool and prim as a dining-car rose.
She married safe money in another town.

The jukebox snuffs out locals' local chatter.
The jukebox plays Eddy Arnold's
(ah, yes, yes) "Make the World Go Away."

C. W. puts plenty of Heinz ketchup
in his bowl of broccoli soup,
crumbles plenty of crackers on top.

"Don't tell me about no Reaganomics
and nothing about Reagan, neither."

The banker's casket is in the ground now.
Not too many friends came around.
The day is hot and dry, corn withers.
The weather has failed and failed again.

KIRBY QUACKENBUSH:
September Moon

The old houses, dusted with moonshine,
creak in the dry and dragging wind
that pokes about this town:
where potato salad and cold beans
are eaten in stuffy kitchens;
where, in tubs of tepid water,
ponytailed girls who love fast horses
slide pink soap between their thighs;
where skinny boys lift weights
in bedrooms gaudy with football stars;
where doctors read comic books
and lawyers read numbers on checks;
where sex-starved wives wait in the nude
for tipsy husbands to be bored
with beer glass and cue stick;
where children sleep like stones
and hall clocks tick and tock
and cats yowl and dogs growl,
as another hot Labor Day winds down
in the webbed and wrinkled dark;
and I, moondust on my face,
return from a long walk to the depot,
the depot of many fierce goodbyes;
and it's just this I want to say:
Luanne, my lost and lonely girl,
if you want me on this summer night,
run through the grass now and kiss me.

·5·

Lizzie, Annie, and Rosie's Rescue of Me with Blue Cake

Carolyn Chute

WE'VE GOT A RANCH HOUSE. Daddy built it. Daddy says it's called RANCH 'cause it's like houses out West which cowboys sleep in. There's a picture window in all ranch houses and if you're in one of 'em out West, you can look out and see the cattle eatin' grass on the plains and the cowboys ridin' around with lassos and tall hats. But we ain't got nuthin' like that here in Egypt, Maine. All Daddy and I got to look out at is the Beans. Daddy says the Beans are uncivilized animals. PREDA-TORS, he calls 'em.

"If it runs, a Bean will shoot it! If it falls, a Bean will eat it," Daddy says, and his lip curls. A million times Daddy says, "Earlene, don't go over on the Beans' side of the right-of-way. Not ever!"

Daddy's bedroom is pine-paneled . . . the real kind. Daddy done it all. He filled the nail holes with MIRACLE WOOD. One weekend after we was all settled in, Daddy gets up on a chair and opens a can of MIRA-CLE WOOD. He works it into the nail holes with a putty knife. He needs the chair 'cause he's probably the littlest man in Egypt, Maine.

Daddy gets a pain in his back after dinnah so we take a nap. We get under the covers and I scratch his back. Daddy says to take off my socks and shoes and overalls to keep the bed from gettin' full of dirt.

After I'm asleep the bed starts to tremble. I clutch the side of the bed and look around. Then I realize it's only Rubie Bean comin' in his loggin' truck to eat his dinnah with other Beans. Daddy's bare back is khaki-color like his carpenter's shirts. I give his shoulder blades a couple more rakes, then dribble off to sleep once more.

2

Gram pushes open the bedroom door. "What's goin' on?" Her voice is a bellow, low as a man's.

Daddy sits up quick. He rubs his face and the back of his neck. Beside the bed is a chair Daddy made. It is khaki-color like the walls and khaki-color like Daddy. And over this chair is them khaki-color carpenter's clothes, the shirt and pants, laid flat like they just been ironed. Gram's eyes look at the pants.

Gram plays the organ at church. Her fingers in her pocketbook now are able to move in many directions at once, over the readin' glasses, tappin' the comb, pressin' the change purse and plastic rain hat, as if from these objects musical refrains of WE ABIDE will come. One finger jabs at a violet hankie. Then she draws the hankie out and holds it over her nose.

I sniff at the room. I don't smell nuthin'.

"LEE!!!" Gram gasps through her hankie. "What is going on here? Can't you *tell* me?" It is warm. But Gram always wears her sweater. You never see her arms.

Gramp comes into the bedroom doorway and holds a match over his pipe. Whenever Gramp visits, he wears a white shirt. He also wears his dress-up hat. Even in church. He never takes it off in front of people . . . 'cause underneath he's PURE BALD. Daddy says he's seen it years ago . . . the head. He says it's got freckles.

On Daddy's cheeks have come brick-color dots and he gives hisself a sideways look in the vanity mirror.

"LEE! I'm talkin' to you!" Gram's deep voice rises.

Daddy says, "I'm sorry, Mumma."

Gram sniffles, wrings her hands.

I says, "Hi Gram!"

She ignores me.

"HI GRAM!!!" I say it louder.

Through the open window I hear the door of the Beans' mobile home peel open like it's a can of tuna fish. I see a BIG BEAN WOMAN come out and set a BIG BEAN BABY down to play among boxes of truck parts and a skidder wheel. The woman Bean wears black stretch pants and a long white blouse with no sleeves. Her arms are bare. The baby Bean pulls off one of its rubber boots.

Somethin' else catches my eye. It's the sun on the fender of Daddy's little khaki-color car. Inside the trunk is some of Daddy's carpenter tools and some of the birdhouses and colonial bread boxes he made for the church fair. On the bumper is Daddy's bumper sticker. It says JESUS SAVES. The sun shifts on the fender, almost blinds me, like it's God sayin' in his secret way that he approves.

But in here in Daddy's bedroom it's different. The light is queer, slantin' through Gramp's smoke. Gram covers her face with her hands now, so all I can see is her smoky blue hair wagglin'. She says through her fingers in her deep voice, "Earlene, you don't sleep here at *night*, do you?"

I says, "Yep."

The dots on Daddy's cheeks get bigger. Gramp looks across the hall at the thermostat to the oil furnace which all ranch houses got.

Daddy swings his legs out from the covers, hangs on the edge of the high bed in his underwear, with his little legs hangin' down. He says, "Mumma . . . I'm sorry. I didn't think."

Gram moans.

Daddy has said a million times that this house is a real peach . . . good leach bed . . . artesian well . . . dry cellar . . . the foundation was poured . . . lots of closet space. He went by blueprints. He says all carpenters can't read blueprints.

"Praise the Lord!" shouts Gram. She holds her clasped hands to her heart, a half-smile, a look of love. "Praise God!!" Her pocketbook is hooked over her elbow. Her arms go up and she waves them and the fingers march, stirrin' up the queer smoke overhead.

Daddy's eyes go wild. "But Mumma! It don't mean nuthin'. She's just a baby!"

"I ain't a BABY!" I scream. I drop to the floor from this high bed Daddy made, made with his lathe, hand-carved acorns on the posts, stained khaki like everything else. I don't remember him makin' the bed. Daddy says he made it before my mother went to the hospital to live. He says he and my mother used to sleep in it and she had the side he's got now.

I like my side of the bed best. I can, without takin' my head up off the pillow, look out across at the Beans' if I want. As I look out now I see a pickup truck backin' up to the Beans' barn. A BIG BEAN MAN gets out and lifts a spotted tarpaulin. It's two dead bears. I look back at Gram.

I pull Gram's sleeve. "Oh Gram . . . What's the matter?"

"Where's your *jeans!!?*" she says. "Your *jeans!!?*"

"Under the bed," I says.

"Well, *get* 'em," she says.

Daddy's cryin', workin' his shoulders. The shoulder blades open and close.

I pick up a sock.

Gram's cool bony fingers close up around my wrist. She yanks me off my feet.

Daddy stands up in his underwear and folds his arms across his chest like he's cold. But it ain't cold. He looks the littlest have ever seen him look. Gram pushes past Gramp and hauls me to my room. My bed is covered with cardboard boxes and coat hangers. She says deeply, "Start pickin' this stuff up!"

I says, "But Gram. Our nap is over. It's time to get up. Ask Daddy!"

"I ain't askin' that sick man nuthin'!" She hurls a pile of dresses I've outgrown upon the wall. I watch 'em slide down. Gram roars, "You stay in this bed for the rest of the day, maybe *two* days. And *no suppah!*"

"Gram!"

She is panting.

"GRAM . . . I'll be HUNGRY!"

"Don't sass!" She narrows her eyes. "The Lord's good meat and tatahs ain't for no dirty little girls." As she hauls the covers back, she's whimperin'. And I hear Daddy out there in the hall cryin'. He's pullin' on his pants out there . . . right in the hall. Gramp just stands there, lookin' lost under the brim of his little brown hat.

Gram takes up both my wrists and shakes them in my face. She says into my eyes, "Of course nuthin's happened!! *Of course*. I ain't sayin' somethin's *happened!*"

Daddy's in the kitchen slammin' chairs around. He made all them chairs hisself. With his lathe in the cellar.

Gram fits me into my bed, then kisses my cheek. She smells like rubber. Like rubber when it's hot. I see the lions and tigers of my bedspread reflectin' in her eyes. She says, "Are you Gram's little pixie?"

I says, "Yes."

She pulls the door shut.

3

Daddy stays out there in the kitchen a long time cryin' . . . a way long time after Gram and Gramp are gone. The water runs in the kitchen. Prob'ly Daddy's got his favorite jelly glass out of the dirty dishes and is rinsing it out. Our well, Daddy says, will never go dry. "It's a thousand feet!" he always says. Then Daddy likes to say how the Beans got the worse side of the right-of-way for water. "All ledge and clay!" In summertime you see 'em back one of them old grunty trucks to the door and they go in and out with plastic milk jugs by the dozens.

As I lay here I can still smell Gramp's pipe tobacco. It's the sweetest kind. Where Gram and Gramp live up in the village, Gram's doilies have gotten yellow from Gramp. So Gramp stopped smokin' in the house. He gets in his car with the plaid blanket on the seat and has a smoke out in the dooryard. Or he scuffs over to Beans' Variety to sit with his friends near the radiator. Gramp's got a trillion friends . . . even Beans. When he goes over to the store, he puts on his white dress-up shirt and, of course, his hat.

In the middle of the night Daddy finally comes in my room. When he puts the hall light on, my heart hits the sheet. He stands in the doorway with the hall light on his back, his hands in the pockets of his khaki pants. He stretches across my bed. He is so little his body across my ankles and feet is not much heavier than one of Gram's cotton comforters.

We sleep.

4

It's Saturday morning. All clouds. Very cold.

When Daddy's downcellah busy with his lathe, I go to the edge of our grass to get a look at the Beans. The Beans' mobile home is one of them old ones, looks like a turquoise-blue submarine. It's got blackberry bushes growin' over the windows.

I scream, "HELLO BEANS!"

About four huge heads come out of the hole. It's a hole the Bean kids and Bean babies have been workin' on for almost a year. Every day they go down the hole and they use coffee cans and a spade to make the hole bigger. The babies use spoons. Beside the hole is a pile of gingerbread-color dirt as tall as a house.

I say, "Need any help with the hole!!?"

They don't answer. One of 'em wipes its nose on its sleeve. They blink their fox-color eyes.

I mutter, "Must be the STUPIDEST hole."

The heads draw back into the hole.

A white car with one Bondo-color fender is turnin' off the paved road onto the right-of-way. It musta lost its muffler. It rumbles along, and the exhaust exploding from all sides is doughy and enormous from the cold.

The blackberry bushes quiver, scrape at the tin walls of the mobile home like claws.

The white car slowly backs into Daddy's crushed-rock driveway and a guy with yellow hair and a short cigarette looks out at me and winks. His window's rolled down and he's got his arm hangin' out in the cold air.

I scream, "NO TURNIN' IN DADDY'S DRIVEWAY!"

There's another guy in there with him. He has a sweatshirt with a pointed hood so all that shows is his huge pink cheeks and a smile. The car pulls ahead onto the right-of-way and the two guys get out.

I scream, "Daddy says KEEP OUT! You ain't ALLOWED!"

The men look at each other and chuckle. The yellow-hair guy is still smokin' his cigarette even though it's only a tiny stump.

My eyes water from the cold. My hair, very white, blows into my mouth.

The sweatshirt guy opens the back door and I see there's feet in there on the seat. The sweatshirt guy pulls on the feet.

The other guy helps. They both tug on the feet.

Out comes a big Bean, loose, very loose, like a dead cat. His arms and legs just go all over the ground. His green felt hat plops out in the dirt. About five beer bottles skid out, too, roll and clink together. The guy with the yellow hair snatches a whiskey bottle off the seat and puts it in the Bean's hand, curls his fingers around it. Both the guys laugh. "There's your baby!" one says.

They get in the car and drive away.

My heart feels like runnin'-hard shoes. I look around. No Beans come out of the mobile home. No Beans come out of the hole.

I take a step. I'm wicked glad Daddy's in the cellah with his lathe. I can picture him down there in the bluish light in his little boy-sized clothes, pickin' over his big tools with his boy-sized hand.

I take another step.

Now I'm standin' right over the Bean. He looks to me like prob'ly the biggest Bean of all. He's got one puckered-up eye, bright purple . . . a mustache big as a black hen. I cover my nose. I think he musta messed hisself. His green workshirt has yellow stitching on one pocket. I read out loud, "R-E-U-B-E-N." I squint, trying to sound out the letters.

The whiskey bottle rolls off his hand.

I says, "Wake up, Bean!"

Then some heads come out of the hole.

A noise comes from the big Bean on the ground: GLOINK! And I say, "Wowzer!" It's blood spreadin' big as a hand in the dirt.

The kid Beans are comin' fast as they can. They bring their spade and spoons, cans and a pail.

I look into the Bean man's face. I say, "YOU! Hey you! Wake up!" I scooch down and inspect the pores of his skin. His wide-open mouth. Big Bean nose. My quick hand goes out . . . touches the nose. I say, "Stop bleedin', Bean."

His good eye opens.

I jump away.

Fox-color eye.

Out of the open mouth comes a hiss. The chest heaves up. Somethin' horrible leaks out the corner of his mouth, catches in the hairs of the big mustache.

The kid Beans stand around starin' down at the green workshirt with the blood movin' out around their shoes.

I says, "Some guys brought him." I point up the road. I look among their faces for signs of panic. I say, "R-E-U-B-E-N. What's that spell?"

They look at me, breathin' through their mouths. One of 'em giggles and says, "That spells coo coo."

Another one pokes at the big Bean's shoulder with its green rubber boot. The big Bean goes "AAAARRRRR!" And his lips peel back over clenched yellow teeth.

A kid Bean with a spade says to a kid Bean with a pail, "Go get Ma off the bed. Rubie's been stabbed again."

"Go tell 'er yourself," says the kid Bean with the pail.

"No . . . you!" says the one with the spade.

"No-suh. I ain't gonna miss gettin' to see Rubie die."

I look down at the big Bean and his hand slowly drags across the dirt to his side to the torn fabric, a black place in the body, like an open mouth. And blood fills the cup of his hand.

Daddy opens the front door and hollers, "EARLENE!"

The big Bean's eye is lookin' right at me.

I says to the eye, "In heaven they got streets of gold."

Daddy screams my name again.

The big fox-color eye closes.

I say, "Oh no! He's dead!"

The kid with the spade says, "Nah! He's still breathin'."

Daddy comes off the step. "Earlene! Get away! NOW!"

I says, "Bean wake up! Don't die!"

Rubie Bean don't move. His mouth is wide open like he's died right in the middle of a big laugh. I see the blood has surrounded my left sneaker, has splashed on my white sock. I can hear the Bean kids shift in their rubber boots.

I drop down on all fours and put my ear right there on the shirt pocket where it says R-E-U-B-E-N.

"Get away from there!" Daddy almost whimpers. He's comin' fast across the grass.

The heart. A huge BOOM-BANG! almost punches at my temple through the Bean's shirt.

"Hear anything?" a Bean with a coffee can asks.

The fox-color big Bean eye opens, the teeth come together, make a deep rude raspy grunt. He says, "You kids . . . get the hell away from me, you goddam cocksuckin' little sons-a-whores!!"

'Bout then Daddy's boy-sized hands close around me.

5

I stand by the stove and Daddy gets out a new bar of LAVA soap, unwraps it. I says, "Daddy! I didn't say no swear words."

He gets one of the chairs from the suppah table and faces it in the corner where he keeps his boots. "Okay, Earlene," he says. "We're all set."

I says, "But, Daddy, soap's for swear words!" I fidget with the hem of my sweater.

His face is red. He pats the chair. I get on the chair facing the corner. I open my mouth. He sticks in the soap—hard, gritty. My mouth is almost not big enough.

He says at my back, "How many times have I told you to stay on your own side of the right-of-way?"

I take the soap out. "Daddy! I was in the middle!" I wipe my mouth with my sleeve. I sputter.

"What those Beans would do to a small girl like you would make a grown man cry," he says.

I sputter some more.

Daddy says, "Earlene, put the soap back in."

"But Daddy!"

"When I used to do what Gram told me not to do, *I* got the *strap*," Daddy says.

I narrow my eyes. I says, "But those was the olden days, Daddy."

"Spare the rod, spoil the child," Daddy says.

We hear the siren. I start to get off the chair. Daddy puts his hand on my shoulder. "Earlene, I'm serious. Listen to me."

Them rescue guys outdoor are makin' a racket, radios and everything, havin' a time gettin' Rubie Bean off the ground. He makes the wickedest snarlin' noises. But Daddy don't seem to notice. He puts his face close to mine. "If I *ever* . . ." he says slowly, "ever . . . *ever* . . . see you near them Beans again, you are gettin' the horrible-est lickin' the Lord has ever witnessed."

I says, smiling, "Daddy . . . you wouldn't really do that."

He folds his arms over his chest. "Then I'll get Gram to do it."

6

It's Thanksgiving and I help Gram set out the matchin' dishes. Every Thanksgiving is the same. Auntie Paula comes with her kids and Uncle Loren comes in his pig truck alone. You can see snow between the tree trunks goin' up the mountain overway and the gray air cracks with guns.

I says, "Gram, did you used to hit Daddy with a strap?"

Gram's sharp little fingers move over the potatoes, feelin' for bad spots. She says, "Spare the rod, spoil the child. Praise God!"

Loren keeps going out on the back steps to get some air.

Gram says, "Darn fool dresses too warm. He's got at least ten shirts on, you know."

I look out through the kitchen glass. It's raining on Uncle Loren. His arms dangle down through his legs. He smokes hard and slow.

I hum one of the songs Gram plays on the organ at church . . . the one to give thanks after they pass the plate. Uncle Loren don't go to church. Gram says Uncle Loren ain't accepted Jesus Christ as his Savior. Uncle Loren lives alone. We never visit him. We've seen the *outside* of his place about a million times. When we drive by, only his kitchen light is on. Daddy says Loren sleeps in the kitchen. Daddy says Loren's big house is cold as a barn. Uncle Loren comes back indoor and trudges into the living room where Jerry and Dennis and I are playin' the Cootie Game which Gram keeps for us kids. Uncle Loren sits on Gram's flower-print divan and he looks me in the eye.

Gram hollers from the kitchen, "Loren . . . don't go layin' your head on that lace scarf!"

Uncle Loren wears striped overalls. When I look in his eyes, I get a shiver.

Gram comes to the living room door and says that Auntie Paula made that divan scarf and that the oils off Loren's head would make it black . . . eventually.

Uncle Loren says, "Earlene . . . did you know I got ghosts in my house?"

Gram says, "He's just tryin' to scare you, Earlene. Don't listen to him."

He looks big and solid and square settin' there on the divan . . . but he's really as short as Daddy. He says, "Ghosts bust up my house all the time. They don't hurt me . . . but they keep me awake rollin' them big Blue Hubbards around and smashin' up glass. They get right under the sheets with me and run around in there under the sheets."

Jerry and Dennis watch Uncle Loren with open mouths.

Gram snorts. "He just says stuff like that so no one will visit him and discover his squalor. He *hates* people visitin' him. People, good Christian ones, upset him. He don't know Christ as his *Savior*."

Then he moves his deep pale scary eyes on me.

I look away fast.

7

After dinner, I go out to where Uncle Loren is settin' on the back step and watch him strike a match on the buckle of his overalls. It's almost dark, but there's still some shots up on the mountain.

Uncle Loren don't say nuthin', just squints his eyes as the smoke sifts up over his face.

I twirl a piece of my white hair and put it in the corner of my mouth. Loren shifts his boots on the step.

"How's the hogs?" I ask.

"Good," he says.

He smokes.

I twirl my hair.

"Uncle Loren," I says, almost in a whisper, "you ever heard this word? . . . Goddamcocksuckinlittlesonsahoowahs?"

Uncle Loren chuckles, sends his cigarette butt spinning through the rain. It hisses in the grass. "Why don't you ask your daddy, Earlene?"

I trace one of my dress-up shoes with my pointing finger. I narrow my eyes. " 'Cause . . . I got a *feelin'*."

Uncle Loren puts them pale scary eyes on me. And I shiver.

8

Across the right-of-way the Beans' black dog stands by an old rug, looking at me. "Yoo hoo!" I call through cupped hands.

Daddy's gone to Oxford to work on a bank . . . He's late gettin' home. They say the roads are greasy.

I take a step onto the Beans' side of the right-of-way. The black dog watches me, the hair on its back raised. But it don't bark.

I step over a spinach can with water froze in it, a clothespin, an Easter basket, the steerin' wheel of a car.

Out of the dog's nose its frozen breath pumps. I draw nearer to the hole with the spoons and coffee cans ringed around it. The dog charges. It gallops sideways with stiff rocking-horse legs.

I says, "You bite me and you'll regret it!!"

I look up at the closed metal door. No Beans.

The dog's eyes glow a bluish white. Its bluish tongue flutters. I say, "Beat it!" and kick a beer bottle at it.

It noses the beer bottle, picks it up in its teeth, and drops it at my feet.

"Go away! I ain't playin'." I look at the Bean windows. No faces. The dog smells my small moving feet. You ugly grimy Bean dog. You're gointa BURN IN HELL!"

There's a scalloped serving spoon at the edge of the hole. "So this is the hole," I says to myself. The dog watches me pick up a trowel. I point it at the dog. "ZEEP!" I scream. "You are instantly DEAD!" The dog blinks.

The corridor of the hole is curved. I slide down on my bottom, workin' my legs, the entrance behind me dwindling to a woolly little far-off cloud in the distance. I feel soda bottles along the way. A measuring cup. A rock drops from the ceiling and thwonks my shoulder. A spray of dirt lets go and fills my hair. I enter a big warm room. In apple crates are what feels like Barbie clothes and Barbie accessories. There's a full-sized easy chair.

"Jeezum!" I gasp. I sit in the chair. "This is real cozy."

I lean forward and feel of the dirt walls, dirt floor. My hand closes around a naked Barbie.

All of a sudden there's a thunder up there.

The warm earth lets go, feels like hundreds of butterflies on my face.

"It's GOD," I says in a choking whisper. My heart flutters.

It's Rubie Bean. The tires of his old logging rig hiss over Daddy's crushed-rock driveway. There's the ernk! of the gears.

"Uh oh!" I says to myself. "I'm trapped in this hole. I can't go up there now."

A rock from the ceiling punches my outstretched legs.

More Beans come. Three or four carloads. The mobile home door opens, closes, opens, closes. Out in their yard Bean kids big as men run over the earth's crust above me. THUMP THUMP THUMP THUMP. The soft slap of sand is on my neck. The Bean kids throw something for the black dog to catch. It sounds like a piece of tail pipe.

I hear Daddy's car.

After a while there's Daddy's voice: "Earlene! Supper!"

It's very very dark. The Beans have gone indoors.

The dog is up there at the top of the hole, sniffin' for me.

Hours and hours and hours pass. Hours of pitch black.

I says to myself in a squeak, "I am goin' ta get the strap." I turn naked Barbie over and over in my nervous fingers. I mutter, "Well . . . I just ain't *ever* gonna leave THIS HOLE."

9

There is light again at the top. The light flutters. Boots tromp. They come down waving a flashlight—Annie Bean, Lizzie Bean, Rosie Bean. They put the light in my face. "What're *you* doin' in here?" one of 'em asks.

"Nuthin'," I says. My stomach growls.

They make wet thick sniffin' sounds. Their open mouths are echoey. They fill this dirt room with their broad shoulders, broad heads. Dirt sifts down from the ceiling through the enormous light.

"You're runnin' from the law?" one of 'em asks.

"NO WAY!" I scream. My scream makes more of the ceiling fall. I think I'm gonna gag from this light in my face. Now and then I can make out a Bean nose, a sharp tooth. Then it fades into the glare.

"You're runnin' away from home?" asks one of them.

I bristle. "No! I ain't!"

"Well, how come your father's up there cryin'?"

One of 'em pushes a saucer with cake on it into the light. There is only the cake, the saucer, the hand. The cake is sky-blue. "Here!" a voice says. Their clothes rustle.

"What's *that?*" I scrunch up my nose.

"We was goin' ta eat it, but you can have it. Ain't you starved?"

I look at the cake, squinting up one eye.

"I didn't run away," I says softly.

"You prob'ly fell in here," one says.

"No-suh!" I holler.

I make out a fox-color eye which is round and hard and caked with sleepin' sand.

I take the saucer and arrange it on my knee next to Barbie. I says, "I ain't never leavin' this hole. I'm stayin' here forever . . . as long as I live."

"You like it here pretty well, huh?" one of 'em says.

I am alone. Between me and them is this wall of light. I hold the saucer with both hands, careful not to touch the cake. A bit of sand spills from the ceiling onto the cake.

The three of them giggle.

The cake is the blue of a birdless airplaneless sunless cloudless leafless sky . . . warm steaming blue. "Prob'ly POISON!" I gasp.

"No way!" one of 'em says. "It ain't. It's Betty Crocker."

·6·

In the Heart of the Heart
of the Country

William Gass

A Place

So I have sailed the seas and come . . .

to B . . .

a small town fastened to a field in Indiana. Twice there have been twelve hundred people here to answer to the census. The town is outstandingly neat and shady, and always puts its best side to the highway. On one lawn there's even a wood or plastic iron deer.

You can reach us by crossing a creek. In the spring the lawns are green, the forsythia is singing, and even the railroad that guts the town has straight bright rails which hum when the train is coming, and the train itself has a welcome horning sound.

Down the back streets the asphalt crumbles into gravel. There's Westbrook's, with the geraniums, Horsefall's, Mott's. The sidewalk shatters. Gravel dust rises like breath behind the wagons. And I am in retirement from love.

Weather

In the Midwest, around the lower Lakes, the sky in the winter is heavy and close, and it is a rare day, a day to remark on, when the sky lifts and allows the heart up. I am keeping count, and as I write this page, it is eleven days since I have seen the sun.

My House

There's a row of headless maples behind my house, cut to free the passage of electric wires. High stumps, ten feet tall, remain, and I climb these like a boy to watch the country sail away from me. They are ordinary fields, a little more uneven than they should be, since in the spring they puddle. The topsoil's thin, but only moderately stony. Corn is grown one year, soybeans another. At dusk starlings darken the single tree—a larch—which stands in the middle. When the sky moves, fields move under it. I feel, on my perch, that I've lost my years. It's as though I were living at last in my eyes, as I have always dreamed of doing, and I think then I know why I've come here: to see, and so to go out against new things—oh god how easily—like air in a breeze. It's true there are moments—foolish moments, ecstasy on a tree stump—when I'm all but gone, scattered I like to think like seed, for I'm the sort now in the fool's position of having love left over which I'd like to lose; what good is it now to me, candy ungiven after Halloween?

A Person

There are vacant lots on either side of Billy Holsclaw's house. As the weather improves, they fill with hollyhocks. From spring through fall, Billy collects coal and wood and puts the lumps and pieces in piles near his door, for keeping warm is his one work. I see him most often on mild days sitting on his doorsill in the sun. I notice he's squinting a little, which is perhaps the reason he doesn't cackle as I pass. His house is the size of a single garage, and very old. It shed its paint with its youth, and its boards are a warped and weathered gray. So is Billy. He wears a short lumpy faded black coat when it's cold, otherwise he always goes about in the same loose, grease-spotted shirt and trousers. I suspect his galluses were yellow once, when they were new.

Wires

These wires offend me. Three trees were maimed on their account, and now these wires deface the sky. They cross like a fence in front of me, enclosing the crows with the clouds. I can't reach in, but like a stick, I throw my feelings over. What is it that offends me? I am on my stump, I've built a platform there and the wires prevent my going out. The cut trees, the black wires, all the beyond birds therefore anger me. When I've wormed through a fence to reach a meadow, do I ever feel the same about the field?

The Church

The church has a steeple like the hat of a witch, and five birds, all doves, perch in its gutters.

My House

Leaves move in the windows. I cannot tell you yet how beautiful it is, what it means. But they do move. They move in the glass.

Politics

. . . for all those not in love.

I've heard Batista described as a Mason. A farmer who'd seen him in Miami made this claim. He's as nice a fellow as you'd ever want to meet. Of Castro, of course, no one speaks.

For all those not in love there's law: to rule . . . to regulate . . . to rectify. I cannot write the poetry of such proposals, the poetry of politics, though sometimes—often—always now—I am in that uneasy peace of equal powers which makes a State; then I communicate by passing papers, proclamations, orders, through my bowels. Yet I was not a State with you, nor were we both together any Indiana. A squad of Pershing Rifles at the moment, I make myself Right Face! Legislation packs the screw of my intestines. Well, king of the classroom's king of the hill. You used to waddle when you walked because my sperm between your legs was draining to a towel. Teacher, poet, folded lover—like the politician, like those drunkards, ill, or those who faucet-off while pissing heartily to preach upon the force and fullness of that stream, or pause from vomiting to praise the purity and passion of their puke—I chant, I beg, I orate, I command, I sing—

Come back to Indiana—not too late!
  (Or will you be a ranger to the end?)
Good-bye . . . Good-bye . . . oh, I shall always wait
  You, Larry, traveler—
        stranger,
          son,
            —my friend—

my little girl, my poem by heart, my self, my childhood.

But I've heard Batista described as a Mason. That dries up my pity, melts my hate. Back from the garage where I have overheard it, I slap the mended fender of my car to laugh, and listen to the metal stinging tartly in my hand.

People

Their hair in curlers and their heads wrapped in loud scarves, young mothers, fattish in trousers, lounge about in the speedwash, smoking cigarettes, eating candy, drinking pop, thumbing magazines, and screaming at their children above the whir and rumble of the machines.

At the bank a young man freshly pressed is letting himself in with a key. Along the street, delicately teetering, many grandfathers move in a dream. During the murderous heat of summer, they perch on window ledges, their feet dangling just inside the narrow shelf of shade the store has made, staring steadily into the street. Where their consciousness has gone I can't say. It's not in the eyes. Perhaps it's diffuse, all temperature and skin, like an infant's, though more mild. Near the corner there are several large overalled men employed in standing. A truck turns to be weighed on the scales at the Feed and Grain. Images drift on the drugstore window. The wind has blown the smell of cattle into town. Our eyes have been driven in like the eyes of the old men. And there's no one to have mercy on us.

Vital Data

There are two restaurants here and a tearoom. two bars. one bank, three barbers, one with a green shade with which he blinds his window. two groceries. a dealer in Fords. one drug, one hardware, and one appliance store. several that sell feed, grain, and farm equipment. an antique shop. a poolroom. a laundromat. three doctors. a dentist. a plumber. a vet. a funeral home in elegant repair the color of a buttercup. numerous beauty parlors which open and shut like night-blooming plants. a tiny dime and department store of no width but several floors. a hutch, homemade, where you can order, after lying down or squirming in, furniture that's been fashioned from bent lengths of stainless tubing, glowing plastic, metallic thread, and clear shellac. an American Legion Post and a root beer stand. little agencies for this and that: cosmetics, brushes, insurance, greeting cards and garden produce—anything— sample shoes—which do their business out of hats and satchels, over coffee cups and dissolving sugar. a factory for making paper sacks and pasteboard boxes that's lodged in an old brick building bearing the legend OPERA HOUSE, still faintly golden, on its roof. a library given by Carnegie. a post office. a school. a railroad station. fire station. lumberyard. telephone company. welding shop. garage . . . and spotted through the town from one end to the other in a line along the highway, gas stations to the number five.

Education

In 1833, Colin Goodykoontz, an itinerant preacher with a name from a fairytale, summed up the situation in one Indiana town this way:

> *Ignorance and her squalid brood. A universal dearth of intellect. Total abstinence from literature is very generally practiced. . . . There is not a scholar in grammar or geography, or a* teacher capable of instructing *in them, to my knowledge. . . . Others are supplied a few months of the year with the most antiquated & unreasonable forms of teaching reading, writing & cyphering. . . . Need I stop to remind you of the host of loathsome reptiles such a stagnant pool is fitted to breed! Croaking jealousy; bloated bigotry; coiling suspicion; wormish blindness; crocodile malice!*

Things have changed since then, but in none of the respects mentioned.

Business

One side section of street is blocked off with sawhorses. Hard, thin, bitter men in blue jeans, cowboy boots and hats, untruck a dinky carnival. The merchants are promoting themselves. There will be free rides, raucous music, parades and coneys, pop, popcorn, candy, cones, awards and drawings, with all you can endure of pinch, push, bawl, shove, shout, scream, shriek, and bellow. Children pedal past on decorated bicycles, their wheels a blur of color, streaming crinkled paper and excited dogs. A little later there's a pet show for a prize—dogs, cats, birds, sheep, ponies, goats—none of which wins. The whirlabouts whirl about. The Ferris wheel climbs dizzily into the sky as far as a tall man on tiptoe might be persuaded to reach, and the irritated operators measure the height and weight of every child with sour eyes to see if they are safe for the machines. An electrical megaphone repeatedly trumpets the names of the generous sponsors. The following day they do not allow the refuse to remain long in the street.

My House, This Place and Body

I have met with some mischance, wings withering, as Plato says obscurely, and across the breadth of Ohio, like heaven on a table, I've fallen as far as the poet, to the sixth sort of body, this house in B, in Indiana, with its blue and gray bewitching windows, holy magical insides. Great thick evergreens protect its entry. And I live *in*.

Lost in the corn rows, I remember feeling just another stalk, and thus this country takes me over in the way I occupy myself when I am well . . . completely—to the edge of both my house and body. No one notices, when they walk by, that I am brimming in the doorways. My house, this place and body, I've come in mourning to be born in. To anybody else it's pretty silly: love. Why should I feel a loss? How am I bereft? She was never mine; she was a fiction, always a golden tomgirl, barefoot, with an adolescent's slouch and a boy's taste for sports and fishing, a figure out of Twain, or worse, in Riley. Age cannot be kind.

There's little hand-in-hand here . . . not in B. No one touches except in rage. Occasionally girls will twine their arms about each other and lurch along, school out, toward home and play. I dreamed my lips would drift down your back like a skiff on a river. I'd follow a vein with the point of my finger, hold your bare feet in my naked hands.

The Same Person

Billy Holsclaw lives alone—how alone it is impossible to fathom. In the post office he talks greedily to me about the weather. His head bobs on a wild flood of words, and I take this violence to be a measure of his eagerness for speech. He badly needs a shave, coal dust has layered his face, he spits when he speaks, and his fingers pick at his tatters. He wobbles out in the wind when I leave him, a paper sack mashed in the fold of his arm, the leaves blowing past him, and our encounter drives me sadly home to poetry—where there's no answer. Billy closes his door and carries coal or wood to his fire and closes his eyes, and there's simply no way of knowing how lonely and empty he is or whether he's as vacant and barren and loveless as the rest of us are—here in the heart of the country.

Weather

For we're always out of luck here. That's just how it is—for instance in the winter. The sides of the buildings, the roofs, the limbs of the trees are gray. Streets, sidewalks, faces, feelings—they are gray. Speech is gray, and the grass where it shows. Every flank and front, each top is gray. Everything is gray: hair, eyes, window glass, the hawkers' bills and touters' posters, lips, teeth, poles and metal signs—they're gray, quite gray. Cars are gray. Boots, shoes, suits, hats, gloves are gray. Horses, sheep, and cows, cats killed in the road, squirrels in the same way, sparrows, doves, and pigeons, all are gray, everything is gray, and everyone is out of luck who lives here.

A similar haze turns the summer sky milky, and the air muffles your head and shoulders like a sweater you've got caught in. In the summer light, too, the sky darkens a moment when you open your eyes. The heat is pure distraction. Steeped in our fluids, miserable in the folds of our bodies, we can scarcely think of anything but our sticky parts. Hot cyclonic winds and storms of dust crisscross the country. In many places, given an indifferent push, the wind will still coast for miles, gathering resource and edge as it goes, cunning and force. According to the season, paper, leaves, field litter, seeds, snow, fill up the fences.

Sometimes I think the land is flat because the winds have leveled it, they blow so constantly. In any case, a gale can grow in a field of corn that's as hot as a draft from hell, and to receive it is one of the most dismaying experiences of this life, though the smart of the same wind in winter is more humiliating, and in that sense even worse. But in the spring it rains as well, and the trees fill with ice.

Place

Many small Midwestern towns are nothing more than rural slums, and this community could easily become one. Principally during the first decade of the century, though there were many earlier instances, well-to-do farmers moved to town and built fine homes to contain them in their retirement. Others desired a more social life, and so lived in, driving to their fields like storekeepers to their businesses. These houses are now dying like the bereaved who inhabit them; they are slowly losing their senses—deafness, blindness, forgetfulness, mumbling, an insecure gait, an uncontrollable trembling has overcome them. Some kind of Northern Snopes will occupy them next: large-familied, Catholic, Democratic, scrambling, vigorous, poor; and since the parents will work in larger, nearby towns, the children will be loosed upon themselves and upon the hapless neighbors much as the fabulous Khan loosed his legendary horde. These Snopes will undertake makeshift repairs with materials that other people have thrown away; paint halfway round their house, then quit; almost certainly maintain an ugly loud cantankerous dog and underfeed a pair of cats to keep the rodents down. They will collect piles of possibly useful junk in the back yard, park their cars in the front, live largely leaning over engines, give not a hoot for the land, the old community, the hallowed ways, the established clans. Weakening widow ladies have already begun to hire large rude youths from families such as these to rake and mow and tidy the grounds they will inherit.

People

In the cinders at the station boys sit smoking steadily in darkened cars, their arms bent out the windows, white shirts glowing behind the glass. Nine o'clock is the best time. They sit in a line facing the highway—two or three or four of them—idling their engines. As you walk by a machine may growl at you or a pair of headlights flare up briefly. In a moment one will pull out, spinning cinders behind it, to stalk impatiently up and down the dark streets or roar half a mile into the country before returning to its place in line and pulling up.

My House, My Cat, My Company

I must organize myself. I must, as they say, pull myself together, dump this cat from my lap, stir—yes, resolve, move, do. But do what? My will is like the rosy dustlike light in this room: soft, diffuse, and gently comforting. It lets me do . . . anything . . . nothing. My ears hear what they happen to; I eat what's put before me; my eyes see what blunders into them; my thoughts are not thoughts, they are dreams. I'm empty or I'm full . . . depending; and I cannot choose. I sink my claws in Tick's fur and scratch the bones of his back until his rear rises amorously. Mr. Tick, I murmur, I must organize myself. I must pull myself together. And Mr. Tick rolls over on his belly, all ooze.

I spill Mr. Tick when I've rubbed his stomach. Shoo. He steps away slowly, his long tail rhyming with his paws. How beautifully he moves, I think; how beautifully, like you, he commands his loving, how beautifully he accepts. So I rise and wander from room to room, up and down, gazing through most of my forty-one windows. How well this house receives its loving too. Let out like Mr. Tick, my eyes sink in the shrubbery. I am not here; I've passed the glass, passed second-story spaces, flown by branches, brilliant berries, to the ground, grass high in seed and leafage every season; and it is the same as when I passed above you in my aged, ardent body; it's, in short, a kind of love; and I am learning to restore myself, my house, my body, by paying court to gardens, cats, and running water, and with neighbors keeping company.

Mrs. Desmond is my right-hand friend; she's eighty-five. A thin white mist of hair, fine and tangled, manifests the climate of her mind. She is habitually suspicious, fretful, nervous. Burglars break in at noon. Children trespass. Even now they are shaking the pear tree, stealing rhubarb, denting lawn. Flies caught in the screens and numbed by frost awake in the heat to buzz and scrape the metal cloth and frighten her, though she is deaf to me, and consequently cannot hear them. Boards creak, the wind whistles across the chimney mouth, drafts cruise like fish through the hollow rooms. It is herself she hears, her own flesh failing, for only death will preserve her from those daily chores she climbs like stairs, and all that anxious waiting. Is it now, she wonders. No? Then: is it now? We do not converse. She visits me to talk. My task to murmur. She talks about her grandsons, her daughter who lives in Delphi, her sister or her husband—both gone—obscure friends—dead—obscurer aunts and uncles—lost—ancient neighbors, members of her church or of her clubs—passed or passing on; and in this way she brings the ends of her life together with a terrifying rush: she is a girl, a wife, a mother, widow, all at once. All at once—appalling—but I believe it; I wince in expectation of the clap. Her talk's a fence—a shade drawn, window fastened, door that's locked—for no one dies taking tea in a kitchen; and as her years compress and begin to jumble, I really believe in the brevity of life; I sweat in my wonder; death is the dog down the street, the angry gander, bedroom spider, goblin who's come to get her; and it occurs to me that in my listening posture I'm the boy who suffered the winds of my grandfather with an exactly similar politeness, that I am, right now, all my ages, out in elbows, as angular as badly stacked cards. Thus was I, when I loved you, every man I could be, youth and child—far from enough—and you, so strangely ambiguous a being, met me, heart for spade, play after play, the whole run of our suits.

Mr. Tick, you do me honor. You not only lie in my lap, but you remain alive there, coiled like a fetus. Through your deep nap, I feel you hum. You are, and are not, a machine. You are alive, alive exactly, and it means nothing to you—much to me. You are a cat—you cannot understand— you are a cat so easily. Your nature is not something you must rise to. You, not I, live in: in house, in skin, in shrubbery. Yes. I think I shall hat my head with a steeple; turn church; devour people. Mr. Tick, though, has a tail he can twitch, he need not fly his Fancy. Claws, not metrical schema, poetry his paws; while smoothing . . . smoothing . . . smoothing roughly, his tongue laps its neatness. O Mr. Tick, I know you; you are an electrical penis. Go on now, shoo. Mrs. Desmond doesn't like you. She thinks you will tangle yourself in her legs and she will fall. You murder her birds, she knows, and walk upon her roof with death in your jaws. I must gather myself together for a bound. What age is it I'm at right now, I wonder. The heart, don't they always say, keeps the true time. Mrs. Desmond is knocking. Faintly, you'd think, but she pounds. She's brought me a cucumber. I believe she believes I'm a woman. Come in, Mrs. Desmond, thank you, be my company, it looks lovely, and have tea. I'll slice it, crisp, with cream, for luncheon, each slice as thin as me.

Politics

O all ye isolate and separate powers, Sing! Sing, and sing in such a way that from a distance it will seem a harmony, a Strindberg play, a friendship ring . . . so happy—happy, happy, happy—as here we go hand in handling, up and down. Our union was a singing, though we were silent in the songs we sang like single notes are silent in a symphony. In no sense sober, we barbershopped together and never heard the discords in our music or saw ourselves as dirty, cheap, or silly. Yet cats have worn out better shoes than those thrown through our love songs at us. Hush. Be patient—prudent—politic. Still, Cleveland killed you, Mr. Crane. Were you not politic enough and fond of being beaten? Like a piece of sewage, the city shat you from its stern three hundred miles from history—beyond the loving reach of sailors. Well, I'm not a poet who puts Paris to his temple in his youth to blow himself from Idaho, or—fancy that—Missouri. My god, I said, this is my country, but must my country go so far as Terre Haute or Whiting, go so far as Gary?

When the Russians first announced the launching of their satellite, many people naturally refused to believe them. Later others were outraged that they had sent a dog around the earth. I wouldn't want to take that mutt from out that metal flying thing if he's still living when he lands, our own dog catcher said; anybody knows you shut a dog up by himself to toss around the first thing he'll be setting on to do you let him out is bite somebody.

This Midwest. A dissonance of parts and people, we are a consonance of Towns. Like a man grown fat in everything but heart, we overlabor; our outlook never really urban, never rural either, we enlarge and linger at the same time, as Alice both changed and remained in her story. You are blond. I put my hand upon your belly; feel it tremble from my trembling. We always drive large cars in my section of the country. How could you be a comfort to me now?

More Vital Data

The town is exactly fifty houses, trailers, stores, and miscellaneous buildings long, but in places no streets deep. It takes on width as you drive south, always adding to the east. Most of the dwellings are fairly spacious farm houses in the customary white, with wide wraparound porches and tall narrow windows, though there are many of the grander kind—fretted, scalloped, turreted, and decorated with clapboards set at angles or on end, with stained-glass windows at the stair landings and lots of wrought iron full of fancy curls—and a few of these look like castles in their rarer brick. Old stables serve as garages now, and the lots are large to contain them and the vegetable and flower gardens which, ultimately, widows plant and weed and then entirely disappear in. The shade is ample, the grass is good, the sky a glorious fall violet; the apple trees are heavy and red, the roads are calm and empty; corn has sifted from the chains of tractored wagons to speckle the streets with gold and with the russet fragments of the cob, and a man would be a fool who wanted, blessed with this, to live anywhere else in the world.

Education

Buses like great orange animals move through the early light to school. There the children will be taught to read and warned against Communism. By Miss Janet Jakes. That's not her name. Her name is Helen something—Scott or James. A teacher twenty years. She's now worn fine and smooth, and has a face, Wilfred says, like a mail-order ax. Her voice is hoarse, and she has a cough. For she screams abuse. The children stare, their faces blank. This is the thirteenth week. They are used to it. You will all, she shouts, you will all draw pictures of me. No. She is a Mrs.—someone's missus. And in silence they set to work while Miss Jakes jabs hairpins in her hair. Wilfred says an ax, but she has those rimless tinted glasses, graying hair, an almost dimpled chin. I must concentrate. I must stop making up things. I must give myself to life; let it mold me: that's what they say in *Wisdom's Monthly Digest* every day. Enough, enough—you've been at it long enough; and the children rise formally a row at a time to present their work to her desk. No, she wears rims; it's her chin that's dimpleless. Well, it will take more than a tablespoon of features to sweeten that face. So she grimly shuffles their sheets, examines her reflection crayoned on them. I would not dare . . . allow a child . . . to put a line around me. Though now and then she smiles like a nick in the blade, in the end these drawings depress her. I could not bear it—how can she ask?—that anyone . . . draw me. Her anger's lit. That's why she does it: flame. There go her eyes; the pink in her glasses brightens, dims. She is a pumpkin, and her rage is breathing like the candle in. No, she shouts, no—the cartoon trembling—no, John Mauck, John Stewart Mauck, this will not do. The picture flutters from her fingers. You've made me too muscular.

I work on my poetry. I remember my friends, associates, my students, by their names. Their names are Maypop, Dormouse, Upsydaisy. Their names are Gladiolus, Callow Bladder, Prince and Princess Oleo, Hieronymus, Cardinal Mummum, Mr. Fitchew, The Silken Howdah, Spot. Sometimes you're Tom Sawyer, Huckleberry Finn; it is perpetually summer; your buttocks are my pillow; we are adrift on a raft; your back is our river. Sometimes you are Major Barbara, sometimes a goddess who kills men in battle, sometimes you are soft like a shower of water; you are bread in my mouth.

I do not work on my poetry. I forget my friends, associates, my students, and their names: Gramophone, Blowgun, Pickle, Serenade . . . Marge the Barge, Arena, Uberhaupt . . . Doctor Dildoe, The Fog Machine. For I am now in B, in Indiana: out of job and out of patience, out of love and time and money, out of bread and out of body, in a temper, Mrs. Desmond, out of tea. So shut your fist up, bitch, you bag of death; go bang another door; go die, my dearie. Die, life-deaf old lady. Spill your breath. Fall over like a frozen board. Gray hair grows from the nose of your mind. You are a skull already—*memento mori*—the foreskin retracts from your teeth. Will your plastic gums last longer than your bones, and color their grinning? And is your twot still hazel-hairy, or are you bald as a ditch? . . . bitch . . . . . bitch . . . . bitch. I wanted to be famous, but you bring me age—my emptiness. Was it *that* which I thought would balloon me above the rest? Love? where are you? . . . love me. I want to rise so high, I said, that when I shit I won't miss anybody.

Business

For most people, business is poor. Nearby cities have siphoned off all but a neighborhood trade. Except for feed and grain and farm supplies, you stand a chance to sell only what one runs out to buy. Chevrolet has quit, and Frigidaire. A locker plant has left its afterimage. The lumberyard has been, so far, six months about its going. Gas stations change hands clumsily, a restaurant becomes available, a grocery closes. One day they came and knocked the cornices from the watch repair and pasted campaign posters on the windows. Torn across, by now, by boys, they urge you still to vote for half an orange beblazoned man who as a whole one failed two years ago to win at his election. Everywhere, in this manner, the past speaks, and it mostly speaks of failure. The empty stores, the old signs and dusty fixtures, the debris in alleys, the flaking paint and rusty gutters, the heavy locks and sagging boards: they say the same disagreeable things. What do the sightless windows see, I wonder, when the sun throws a passerby against them? Here a stair unfolds toward the street—dark, rickety, and treacherous—and I always feel, as I pass it, that if I just went carefully up and turned the corner at the landing, I would find myself out of the world. But I've never had the courage.

That Same Person

The weeds catch up with Billy. In pursuit of the hollyhocks, they rise in coarse clumps all around the front of his house. Billy has to stamp down a circle by his door like a dog or cat does turning round to nest up, they're so thick. What particularly troubles me is that winter will find the weeds still standing stiff and tindery to take the sparks which Billy's little mortarless chimney spouts. It's true that fires are fun here. The town whistle, which otherwise only blows for noon (and there's no noon on Sunday), signals the direction of the fire by the length and number of its blasts, the volunteer firemen rush past in their cars and trucks, houses empty their owners along the street every time like an illustration in a children's book. There are many bikes, too, and barking dogs, and sometimes—halleluiah—the fire's right here in town—a vacant lot of weeds and stubble flaming up. But I'd rather it weren't Billy or Billy's lot or house. Quite selfishly I want him to remain the way he is—counting his sticks and logs, sitting on his sill in the soft early sun—though I'm not sure what his presence means to me . . . or to anyone. Nevertheless, I keep wondering whether, given time, I might not someday find a figure in our language which would serve him faithfully, and furnish his poverty and loneliness richly out.

Wires

Where sparrows sit like fists. Doves fly the steeple. In mist the wires change perspective, rise and twist. If they led to you, I would know what they were. Thoughts passing often, like the starlings who flock these fields at evening to sleep in the trees beyond, would form a family of paths like this; they'd foot down the natural height of air to just about a bird's perch. But they do not lead to you.

> *Of whose beauty it was sung*
> *She shall make the old man young.*

They fasten me.

If I walked straight on, in my present mood, I would reach the Wabash. It's not a mood in which I'd choose to conjure you. Similes dangle like baubles from me. This time of year the river is slow and shallow, the clay banks crack in the sun, weeds surprise the sandbars. The air is moist and I am sweating. It's impossible to rhyme in this dust. Everything—sky, the cornfield, stump, wild daisies, my old clothes and pressless feelings—seem fabricated for installment purchase. Yes. Christ. I am suffering a summer Christmas; and I cannot walk under the wires. The sparrows scatter like handfuls of gravel. Really, wires are voices in thin strips. They are words wound in cables. Bars of connection.

Weather

I would rather it were the weather that was to blame for what I am and what my friends and neighbors are—we who live here in the heart of the country. Better the weather, the wind, the pale dying snow . . . the snow—why not the snow? There's never much really, not around the lower Lakes anyway, not enough to boast about, not enough to be useful. My father tells how the snow in the Dakotas would sweep to the roofs of the barns in the old days, and he and his friends could sled on the crust that would form because the snow was so fiercely driven. In Bemidji trees have been known to explode. That would be something— if the trees in Davenport or Francisville or Carbondale or Niles were to go blam some winter—blam! blam! blam! all the way down the gray, cindery, snow-sick streets.

A cold fall rain is blackening the trees or the air is like lilac and full of parachuting seeds. Who cares to live in any season but his own? Still I suspect the secret's in this snow, the secret of our sickness, if we could only diagnose it, for we are all dying like the elms in Urbana. This snow—like our skin it covers the country. Later dust will do it. Right now—snow. Mud presently. But it is snow without any laughter in it, a pale gray pudding thinly spread on stiff toast, and if that seems a strange description, it's accurate all the same. Of course soot blackens every-thing, but apart from that, we are never sufficiently cold here. The flakes as they come, alive and burning, we cannot retain, for if our tempera-tures fall, they rise promptly again, just as, in the summer, they bob about in the same feckless way. Suppose though . . . suppose they were to rise some August, climb and rise, and then hang in the hundreds like a hawk through December, what a desert we could make of ourselves—from Chicago to Cairo, from Hammond to Columbus—what beautiful Death Valleys.

Place

I would rather it were the weather. It drives us in upon ourselves—an unlucky fate. Of course there is enough to stir our wonder anywhere; there's enough to love, anywhere, if one is strong enough, if one is diligent enough, if one is perceptive, patient, kind enough—whatever it takes; and surely it's better to live in the country, to live on a prairie by a drawing of rivers, in Iowa or Illinois or Indiana, say, than in any city, in any stinking fog of human beings, in any blooming orchard of machines. It ought to be. The cities are swollen and poisonous with people. It ought to be better. Man has never been a fit environment for man—for rats, maybe, rats do nicely, or for dogs or cats and the household beetle.

And how long the street is, nowadays. These endless walls are fallen to keep back the tides of earth. Brick could be beautiful but we have covered it gradually with gray industrial vomits. Age does not make concrete genial, and asphalt is always—like America—twenty-one, un-til it breaks up in crumbs like stale cake. The brick, the asphalt, the concrete, the dancing signs and garish posters, the feed and excrement of the automobile, the litter of its inhabitants: they compose, they deco-rate, they line our streets, and there is nowhere, nowadays, our streets can't reach.

A man in the city has no natural thing by which to measure himself. His parks are potted plants. Nothing can live and remain free where he resides but the pigeon, starling, sparrow, spider, cockroach, mouse, moth, fly and weed, and he laments the existence of even these and makes his plans to poison them. The zoo? There *is* the zoo. Through its bars the city man stares at the great cats and dully sucks his ice. Living, alas, among men and their marvels, the city man supposes that his happiness depends on establishing, somehow, a special kind of harmonious accord with others. The novelists of the city, of slums and crowds, they call it love—and break their pens.

Wordsworth feared the accumulation of men in cities. He foresaw their "degrading thirst after outrageous stimulation," and some of their hunger for love. Living in a city, among so many, dwelling in the heat and tumult of incessant movement, a man's affairs are touch and go— that's all. It's not surprising that the novelists of the slums, the cities, and the crowds, should find that sex is but a scratch to ease a tickle, that we're most human when we're sitting on the john, and that the justest image of our life is in full passage through the plumbing.

> *That man, immur'd in cities, still retains*
> *His inborn inextinguishable thirst*
> *Of rural scenes, compensating his loss*
> *By supplemental shifts, the best he may.*

Come into the country, then. The air nimbly and sweetly recommends itself unto our gentle senses. Here, growling tractors tear the earth. Dust roils up behind them. Drivers sit jouncing under bright umbrellas. They wear refrigerated hats and steer by looking at the tracks they've cut behind them, their transistors blaring. Close to the land, are they? good companions to the soil? Tell me: do they live in harmony with the alternating seasons?

It's a lie of old poetry. The modern husbandman uses chemicals from cylinders and sacks, spike-ball-and-claw machines, metal sheds, and cost accounting. Nature in the old sense does not matter. It does not exist. Our farmer's only mystical attachment is to parity. And if he does not realize that cows and corn are simply different kinds of chemical engine, he cannot expect to make a go of it.

It isn't necessary to suppose our cows have feelings; our neighbor hasn't as many as he used to have either; but think of it this way a moment, you can correct for the human imputations later: how would it feel to nurse those strange tentacled calves with their rubber, glass, and metal lips, their stainless eyes?

People

Aunt Pet's still able to drive her car—a high square Ford—even though she walks with difficulty and a stout stick. She has a watery gaze, a smooth plump face despite her age, and jet black hair in a bun. She has the slowest smile of anyone I ever saw, but she hates dogs, and not very long ago cracked the back of one she cornered in her garden. To prove her vigor she will tell you this, her smile breaking gently while she raises the knob of her stick to the level of your eyes.

House, My Breath and Window

My window is a grave, and all that lies within it's dead. No snow is falling. There's no haze. It is not still, not silent. Its images are not an animal that waits, for movement is no demonstration. I have seen the sea slack, life bubble through a body without a trace, its spheres impervious as soda's. Downwound, the whore at wagtag clicks and clacks. Leaves wiggle. Grass sways. A bird chirps, pecks the ground. An auto wheel in penning circles keeps its rigid spokes. These images are stones; they are memorials. Beneath this sea lies sea: god rest it . . . rest the world beyond my window, me in front of my reflection, above this page, my shade. Death is not so still, so silent, since silence implies a falling quiet, stillness a stopping, containing, holding in; for death is time in a clock, like Mr. Tick, electric . . . like wind through a windup poet. And my blear floats out to visible against the glass, befog its country and bespill myself. The mist lifts slowly from the fields in the morning. No one now would say: the Earth throws back its covers; it is rising from sleep. Why is the feeling foolish? The image is too Greek. I used to gaze at you so wantonly your body blushed. Imagine: wonder: that my eyes could cause such flowering. Ah, my friend, your face is pale, the weather cloudy; a street has been felled through your chin, bare trees do nothing, houses take root in their rectangles, a steeple stands up in your head. You speak of loving; then give me a kiss. The pane is cold. On icy mornings the fog rises to greet me (as you always did); the barns and other buildings, rather than ghostly, seem all the more substantial for looming, as if they grew in themselves while I watched (as you always did). Oh my approach, I suppose, was like breath in a rubber monkey.

Nevertheless, on the road along the Wabash in the morning, though the trees are sometimes obscured by fog, their reflection floats serenely on the river, reasoning the banks, the sycamores in French rows. Magically, the world tips. I'm led to think that only those who grow down live (which will scarcely win me twenty-five from *Wisdom's Monthly Digest*), but I find I write that only those who live down grow; and what I write, I hold, whatever I really know. My every word's inverted, or reversed—or I am. I held you, too, that way. You were so utterly provisional, subject to my change. I could inflate your bosom with a kiss, disperse your skin with gentleness, enter your vagina from within, and make my love emerge like a fresh sex. The pane is cold. Honesty is cold, my inside lover. The sun looks, through the mist, like a plum on the tree of heaven, or a bruise on the slope of your belly. Which? The grass crawls with frost. We meet on this window, the world and I, inelegantly, swimmers of the glass; and swung wrong way round to one another, the world seems in. The world—how grand, how monumental, grave and deadly, that word is: the world, my house and poetry. All poets have their inside lovers. Wee penis does not belong to me, or any of this foggery. It is *his* property which he's thrust through what's womanly of me to set down this. These wooden houses in their squares, gray streets and fallen sidewalks, standing trees, your name I've written sentimentally across my breath into the whitening air, pale birds: they exist in me now because of him. I gazed with what intensity . . . A bush in the excitement of its roses could not have bloomed so beautifully as you did then. It was a look I'd like to give this page. For that is poetry: to bring within about, to change.

Politics

Sports, politics, and religion are the three passions of the badly educated. They are the Midwest's open sores. Ugly to see, a source of constant discontent, they sap the body's strength. Appalling quantities of money, time, and energy are wasted on them. The rural mind is narrow, passionate, and reckless on these matters. Greed, however shortsighted and direct, will not alone account for it. I have known men, for instance, who for years have voted squarely against their interests. Nor have I ever noticed that their surly Christian views prevented them from urging forward the smithereening, say, of Russia, China, Cuba, or

Korea. And they tend to back their country like they back their local team: they have a fanatical desire to win; yelling is their forte; and if things go badly, they are inclined to sack the coach. All in all, then, Birch is a good name. It stands for the bigot's stick, the wild-child-tamer's cane.

Forgetfulness—is that their object?

Oh, I was new, I thought. A fresh start: new cunt, new climate, and new country—there you were, and I was pioneer, and had no history. That language hurts me, too, my dear. You'll never hear it.

Final Vital Data

The Modern Homemakers' Demonstration Club. The Prairie Home Demonstration Club. The Night-outers' Home Demonstration Club. The IOOF, FFF, VFW, WCTU, WSCS, 4-H, 40 and 8, Psi Iota Chi, and PTA. The Boy and Girl Scouts, Rainbows, Masons, Indians and Rebekah Lodge. Also the Past Noble Grand Club of the Rebekah Lodge. As well as the Moose and the Ladies of the Moose. The Elks, the Eagles, the Jaynettes and the Eastern Star. The Women's Literary Club, the Hobby Club, the Art Club, the Sunshine Society, the Dorcas Society, the Pythian Sisters, the Pilgrim Youth Fellowship, the American Legion, the American Legion Auxiliary, the American Legion Junior Auxiliary, the Garden Club, the Bridge for Fun Club, the What-can-you-do? Club, the Get Together Club, the Coterie Club, the Worthwhile Club, the Let's Help Our Town Club, the No Name Club, the Forget-me-not Club, the Merry-go-round Club . . .

Education

Has a quarter disappeared from Paula Frosty's pocket book? Imagine the landscape of that face: no crayon could engender it; soft wax is wrong; thin wire in trifling snips might do the trick. Paula Frosty and Christopher Roger accuse the pale and splotchy Cheryl Pipes. But Miss Jakes, I *saw* her. Miss Jakes is so extremely vexed she snaps her pencil. What else is missing? I appoint you a detective, John: search her desk. Gum, candy, paper, pencils, marble, round eraser—whose? A thief. I can't watch her all the time, I'm here to teach. Poor pale fossetted Cheryl, it's determined, can't return the money because she took it home and spent it. Cindy, Janice, John, and Pete—you four who sit around her—you will be detectives this whole term to watch her. A thief. In all my time. Miss Jakes turns, unfists, and turns again. I'll handle you, she cries. To think. A thief. In all my years. Then she writes on the blackboard the name of Cheryl Pipes and beneath that the figure twenty-five with a large sign for cents. Now Cheryl, she says, this won't be taken off until you bring that money out of home, out of home straight up to here, Miss Jakes says, tapping her desk.

Which is three days.

Another Person

I was raking leaves when Uncle Halley introduced himself to me. He said his name came from the comet, and that his mother had borne him prematurely in her fright of it. I thought of Hobbes, whom fear of the Spanish Armada had hurried into birth, and so I believed Uncle Halley to honor the philosopher, though Uncle Halley is a liar, and neither the one hundred twenty-nine nor the fifty-three he ought to be. That fall the leaves had burned themselves out on the trees, the leaf lobes had curled, and now they flocked noisily down the street and were broken in the wires of my rake. Uncle Halley was himself (like Mrs. Desmond and history generally) both deaf and implacable, and he shooed me down his basement stairs to a room set aside there for stacks of newspapers reaching to the ceiling, boxes of leaflets and letters and programs, racks of photo albums, scrapbooks, bundles of rolled-up posters and maps, flags and pennants and slanting piles of dusty magazines devoted mostly to motoring and the Christian ethic. I saw a bird cage, a tray of butterflies, a bugle, a stiff straw boater, and all kinds of tassels tied to a coat tree. He still possessed and had on display the steering lever from his first car, a linen duster, driving gloves and goggles, photographs along the wall of himself, his friends, and his various machines, a shell from the first war, a record of "Ramona" nailed through its hole to a post, walking sticks and fanciful umbrellas, shoes of all sorts (his baby shoes, their counters broken, were held in sorrow beneath my nose—they had not been bronzed, but he might have them done someday before he died, he said), countless boxes of medals, pins, beads, trinkets, toys, and keys (I scarcely saw—they flowed like jewels from his palms), pictures of downtown when it was only a path by the railroad station, a brightly colored globe of the world with a dent in Poland, antique guns, belt buckles, buttons, souvenir plates and cups and saucers (I can't remember all of it—I won't), but I recall how shamefully, how rudely, how abruptly, I fled, a good story in my mouth but death in my nostrils; and how afterward I busily, righteously, burned my leaves as if I were purging the world of its years. I still wonder if this town—its life, and mine now—isn't really a record like the one of "Ramona" that I used to crank around on my grandmother's mahogany Victrola through lonely rainy days as a kid.

The First Person

Billy's like the coal he's found: spilled, mislaid, discarded. The sky's no comfort. His house and his body are dying together. His windows are boarded. And now he's reduced to his hands. I suspect he has glaucoma. At any rate he can scarcely see, and weeds his yard of rubble on his hands and knees. Perhaps he's a surgeon cleansing a wound or an ardent and tactile lover. I watch, I must say, apprehensively. Like mine-war detectors, his hands graze in circles ahead of him. Your nipples were the color of your eyes. Pebble. Snarl of paper. Length of twine. He leans down closely, picks up something silvery, holds it near his nose. Foil? cap? coin? He has within him—what, I wonder? Does he know more now because he fingers everything and has to sniff to see? It would be romantic cruelty to think so. He bends the down on your arms like a breeze. You wrote me: something is strange when we don't understand. I write in return: I think when I loved you I fell to my death.

Billy, I could read to you from Beddoes; he's your man perhaps; he held with dying, freed his blood of its arteries; and he said that there were many wretched love-ill fools like me lying alongside the last bone of their former selves, as full of spirit and speech, nonetheless, as Mrs. Desmond, Uncle Halley and the Ferris wheel, Aunt Pet, Miss Jakes, Ramona or the megaphone; yet I reverse him finally, Billy, on no evidence but braggadocio, and I declare that though my inner organs were devoured long ago, the worm which swallowed down my parts still throbs and glows like a crystal palace.

Yes, you were younger. I was Uncle Halley, the museum man and infrequent meteor. Here is my first piece of ass. They weren't so flat in those days, had more round, more juice. And over here's the sperm I've spilled, nicely jarred and clearly labeled. Look at this tape like lengths of intestine where I've stored my spew, the endless worm of words I've written, a hundred million emissions or more: oh I was quite a man right from the start; even when unconscious in my cradle, from crotch to cranium, I was erectile tissue; though mostly, after the manner approved by Plato, I had intercourse by eye. Never mind, old Holsclaw, you are blind. We pull down darkness when we go to bed; put out like Oedipus the actually offending organ, and train our touch to lies. All cats are gray, says Mr. Tick; so under cover of glaucoma you are sack gray too, and cannot be distinguished from a stallion.

I must pull myself together, get a grip, just as they say, but I feel spilled, bewildered, quite mislaid. I did not restore my house to its youth, but to its age. Hunting, you hitch through the hollyhocks. I'm inclined to say you aren't half the cripple I am, for there is nothing left of me but mouth. However, I resist the impulse. It is another lie of poetry. My organs are all there, though it's there where I fail—at the roots of my experience. Poet of the spiritual, Rilke, weren't you? yet that's what you said. Poetry, like love, is—in and out—a physical caress. I can't tolerate any more of my sophistries about spirit, mind, and breath. Body equals being, and if your weight goes down, you are the less.

Household Apples

I knew nothing about apples. Why should I? My country came in my childhood, and I dreamed of sitting among the blooms like the bees. I failed to spray the pear tree too. I doubled up under them at first, admiring the sturdy low branches I should have pruned, and later I acclaimed the blossoms. Shortly after the fruit formed there were falls— not many—apples the size of goodish stones which made me wobble on my ankles when I walked about the yard. Sometimes a piece crushed by a heel would cling on the shoe to track the house. I gathered a few and heaved them over the wires. A slingshot would have been splendid. Hard, an unattractive green, the worms had them. Before long I realized the worms had them all. Even as the apples reddened, lit their tree, they were being swallowed. The birds preferred the pears, which were small—sugar pears I think they're called—with thick skins of graying green that ripen on toward violet. So the fruit fell, and once I made some applesauce by quartering and paring hundreds; but mostly I did noth- ing, left them, until suddenly, overnight it seemed, in that ugly late September heat we often have in Indiana, my problem was upon me.

My childhood came in the country. I remember, now, the flies on our snowy luncheon table. As we cleared away they would settle, fastidiously scrub themselves and stroll to the crumbs to feed where I would kill them in crowds with a swatter. It was quite a game to catch them taking off. I struck heavily since I didn't mind a few stains; they'd wash. The swatter was a square of screen bound down in red cloth. It drove no air ahead of it to give them warning. They might have thought they'd flown headlong into a summered window. The faint pink dot where they had died did not rub out as I'd supposed, and after years of use our luncheon linen would faintly, pinkly, speckle.

The country became my childhood. Flies braided themselves on the flypaper in my grandmother's house. I can smell the bakery and the grocery and the stables and the dairy in that small Dakota town I knew as a kid; knew as I dreamed I'd know your body, as I've known nothing, before or since; knew as the flies knew, in the honest, unchaste sense: the burned house, hose-wet, which drew a mist of insects like the blue smoke of its smolder, and gangs of boys, moist-lipped, destructive as its burning. Flies have always impressed me; they are so persistently alive. Now they were coating the ground beneath my trees. Some were ordinary flies; there were the large blue-green ones; there were swarms of fruit flies too, and the red-spotted scavenger beetle; there were a few wasps, several sorts of bees and butterflies—checkers, sulphurs, monarchs, commas, question marks—and delicate dragonflies . . . but principally houseflies and horseflies and bottleflies, flies and more flies in clusters around the rotting fruit. They loved the pears. Inside, they fed. If you picked up a pear, they flew, and the pear became skin and stem. They were everywhere the fruit was: in the tree still—apples like a hive for them—or where the fruit littered the ground, squashing itself as you stepped . . . there was no help for it. The flies droned, feasting on the sweet juice. No one could go near the trees; I could not climb; so I determined at last to labor like Hercules. There were fruit baskets in the barn. Collecting them and kneeling under the branches, I began to gather remains. Deep in the strong rich smell of the fruit, I began to hum myself. The fruit caved in at the touch. Glistening red apples, my lifting disclosed, had families of beetles, flies, and bugs, devouring their rotten undersides. There were streams of flies; there were lakes and cataracts and rivers of flies, seas and oceans. The hum was heavier, higher, than the hum of the bees when they came to the blooms in the spring, though the bees were there, among the flies, ignoring me—ignoring everyone.

As my work went on and juice covered my hands and arms, they would form a sleeve, black and moving, like knotty wool. No caress could have been more indifferently complete. Still I rose fearfully, ramming my head in the branches, apples bumping against me before falling, bursting with bugs. I'd snap my hand sharply but the flies would cling to the sweet. I could toss a whole cluster into a basket from several feet. As the pear or apple lit, they would explosively rise, like monads for a moment, windowless, certainly, with respect to one another, sugar their harmony. I had to admit, though, despite my distaste, that my arm had never been more alive, oftener or more gently kissed. Those hundreds of feet were light. In washing them off, I pretended the hose was a pump. What have I missed? Childhood is a lie of poetry.

The Church

Friday night. Girls in dark skirts and white blouses sit in ranks and scream in concert. They carry funnels loosely stuffed with orange and black paper which they shake wildly, and small megaphones through which, as drilled, they direct and magnify their shouting. Their leaders, barely pubescent girls, prance and shake and whirl their skirts above their bloomers. The young men, leaping, extend their arms and race through puddles of amber light, their bodies glistening. In a lull, though it rarely occurs, you can hear the squeak of tennis shoes against the floor. Then the yelling begins again, and then continues; fathers, mothers, neighbors joining in to form a single pulsing ululation—a cry of the whole community—for in this gymnasium each body becomes the bodies beside it, pressed as they are together, thigh to thigh, and the same shudder runs through all of them, and runs toward the same release. Only the ball moves serenely through this dazzling din. Obedient to law it scarcely speaks but caroms quietly and lives at peace.

Business

It is the week of Christmas and the stores, to accommodate the rush they hope for, are remaining open in the evening. You can see snow falling in the cones of the street lamps. The roads are filling—undisturbed. Strings of red and green lights droop over the principal highway, and the water tower wears a star. The windows of the stores have been bedizened. Shamelessly they beckon. But I am alone, leaning against a pole—no . . . there is no one in sight. They're all at home, perhaps by their instruments, tuning in on their evenings, and like Ramona, tirelessly playing and replaying themselves. There's a speaker perched in the tower, and through the boughs of falling snow and over the vacant streets, it drapes the twisted and metallic strains of a tune that can barely be distinguished—yes, I believe it's one of the jolly ones, it's "Joy to the World." There's no one to hear the music but myself, and though I'm listening, I'm no longer certain. Perhaps the record's playing something else.

·7·

Letter from
the Lost Swede Towns

Carol Bly

SCOTT FITZGERALD REMARKED, somewhere toward the end of *Gatsby,* that his Middle West was the land of prep school boys' coming home at Christmas, their shouted inquiries in Chicago's Union Station, "Are you going to the Ordways'?" Fitzgerald said, very firmly, his Middle West was "not the wheat or the prairies or the lost Swede towns."

Lost Swede Towns Minnesota is where I live, and what these letters will be about. Our town of about 2,000—Madison—is 160 miles west of Minneapolis, well out of the range of Fitzgerald's readers or the Ordways' parties; out here, Groton and Exeter sound like seedcorn hybrids. This is the prairie country of the Louisiana Purchase, the endless, fainting fields, with the dusty rivers hooded by cottonwoods. As your eye sweeps this landscape you can see five or six farmers' "groves" (windbreaks around the farmhouses). At dawn and dusk the groves look like the silent, major ships of someone else's navy, standing well spaced, well out to sea.

It isn't really a country of "lost Swede towns"; the people are Norwegian and German in the main, but Fitzgerald struck true—there is a tremendous amount of loss in it:

When I came out here I thought it was just sexual loss. On my first visit, we drove in the evening. The bare bulbs were lighted in the passing farmyards. The barn lights were on for chores. I remember saying, How marvelous to think of night on this gigantic prairie—all the men and women making love in their safe houses guarded by the gloomy groves! Who wants to think of anyone making love in Los Angeles—but how great to think of it in these cozy farmhouses! The reply was: That's what *you* think!

Scandinavian-American sexual chill is a firm cliché, but what isn't so well known is that there is a restraint against *feeling in general*. There is restraint against enthusiasm ("real nice" is the adjective—not "marvelous"); there is restraint in grief ("real sober" instead of "heartbroken"); and always, always, restraint in showing your feelings, lest someone be drawn closer to you. This restraint was there with the first pioneers; the strong-minded Swiss-American writer Mari Sandoz, in describing her family's settling in Nebraska, called the newer, Scandinavian influx "mealy-mouthed." Mealy-mouthed means that when someone has stolen all four wheels off your car you say, "Oh, when I saw that car, with the wheels stripped off like that, I just thought ohhhhhhhh." "And that Vietnam War . . . well, it's just . . . well, it's just hard to know what to think!" Or "Watergate now. Well . . . it's just, well, that Watergate sure is something." If the topic is controversial, you seldom get a clear predicate to any sentence. In conversation, no predicate means the speaker has unconsciously decided not to give you that information after all.

Americans are always mourning that "the kids everywhere" have no feeling: that's another kind of phenomenon, but what you have to be clear about in Minnesota is that the Scandinavian-American doesn't feel because he doesn't *believe* in feeling. He is against it. It isn't only that he has watched too much television; his timidity and frigidity were there long before he was seduced by "The Edge of Night."

This summer *Charlotte's Web* made it to the Grand Theatre in Madison. We all flung ourselves into the movies because we'd had a drought, everyone had been anxious, and then it rained, and we celebrated. It rained well—not a rapid runoff rain that just grabs our topsoil and carries a lot of it to the Gulf of Mexico in five days, but a proper gardeners' rain, settling all night and all day, slowly crumbling the chunks near the corn stems, slowly slipping down past the thin things that are always lying around farms, spring tooth cultivators and loops of electric-fence wire flung around posts. After the movie the main street was full of Studebaker half-ton pickups collecting the farm kids, other cars gunning their engines in neutral, men in short sleeves dodging around in the light rain in the headlights. In the spooky light their arms looked black and the flesh didn't look as if it would be live and firm indefinitely. Some children who had seen the movie were crying, being hustled along by their mothers. We were all moved by the friendship of Charlotte the spider and Wilbur the pig; our ears were full of E. B. White's final comment: "It is not often that someone comes along who is a true friend and a good writer. Charlotte was both." Then, suddenly, I heard two separate mothers tell their children: "Oh, for the love of goodness, it was just a movie!" and "Okay, okay, OKAY! You don't have to feel it *that* much."

This is the real death in our countryside, this not approving of feeling. It implies a disdain for literature, of course, since literature so baldly champions feeling. Around town for a week after *Charlotte's Web* there were complaints that we had been promised "a cute movie" but the kids had cried. Actually, the producers did quite a lot to make it "a cute movie": they added 1940s songs of the "musical" kind; they removed humor, plot, and pathos; but lots of E. B. White still shone through.

I am interested in this phenomenon: the cute movie. We can all name things that happen when a whole segment of society, say, the lost Swede town part of society, fails to feel. They range from obeying murder orders at My Lai on down to Farm Bureau audiences sitting absolutely without smiles throughout a comedy routine. Addiction to meaningless entertainment (cute movies) isn't a tenth of it obviously, but it interests me because craving cute movies brings with it a craving for indifferent murder.

Nonfeeling people do not crave real death. They don't want to go out and beat up people, but they do have a very odd fascination for murders that can't possibly affect them. Movie producers know this, and since the 1960s have hiked the violence forward in the movie's playing time. No longer do you get an hour or so to empathize with Alan Ladd before someone shoots him; no longer do you know the characters before the violence enters; now you get some actor's face obliterated by shots while the credits are still being shown. This is the epitome of indifferent murder. No love, no hate, and no pity have been solicited of us. But then we didn't want any feeling solicited!

One of the various intelligent theories about the Vietnam War is that it was an unconscious replay of our murdering the American Indians. I sense another possibility: the Vietnam War was the chance of a lifetime to commit indifferent murder. Americans felt like killing where it meant nothing personally; a Southeast Asian farmer four thousand feet below one's wingtip filled the bill perfectly. It is his face that is destroyed during the movie credits.

A lingering, but unrealistic notion is that American society split its classes because of the Vietnam War, but the split, in fact, between Middle America (for our purpose here, Lost Swede Town America) and educated or enlightened America took place a long time ago. The cute movie syndrome is a good measure of it.

I first saw the cute movie syndrome in Duluth, in 1943. My gang of teenage girl friends wandered into an RAF movie. Once in, we were drawn into the Wellington's shadowy cockpit. Our faces were streaked with searchlights, and soon the prosaic girl next to me, in the perennial blue jeans and man's shirt with sleeves rolled, was replaced by my second pilot and the bomb aimer. One scene in particular affected me. Photographed from the ground, at first light of day, the crippled aircraft was flying home, over the English coastline. In the weak light everything looked ghostly and precious; the shore looked like the fine stretches between Folkestone and Dover. Then the plane sank lower and lower, over steep-pitched roofs and corbelled chimney tops. I had never thought before how fragile a village or a countryside is, how desperately close to destruction it can be, until I saw those chimney tops under the airplane. When adults talk about such feelings for one's country, we rather wish they'd got beyond facile patriotism by now. For a thirteen-year-old, however, the feeling that a country wants defending is nearly a spiritual experience.

In any case, the movie over, we clattered out and into a hot, bright bus for home. A few of the girls were annoyed we hadn't taken in a cute movie, but one voice suddenly rose over all the others: "All I can say is, if you're going to talk about the war and all that, boys are just never going to like you!"

A nice kaleidoscoping of appalling values, and the marriage of light-weight emotions to the ambitions of a sex object. If much of America has abandoned these stifling convictions, however, our lost Swede towns haven't.

Yet nobody wants to help our "Swede" to wake up. The twentieth-century way to look at the nonverbal, nonpassionate Midwesterner is to sneer. When someone asked Hemingway decades ago why he didn't write about normal Americans instead of idealists like his Robert Jordan, he replied, "Why should I write about people with broken legs?" Charles Reich's greening of America wasn't a genuine psychic revolution of affection because it was in large part merely a slap at the hardnosed classes. Reich's longhairs were johnnies come very lately onto that set: long ago, Fitzgerald saw how the Dobbs Ferry girls lifted their noses at the Lutheran syndrome; Hemingway's heroic dropouts despised wall-to-wall carpeting and nonorganic bread and the equivalent of snowmobile clubs long before the first hippy grieved because his mother wanted a blender.

The nonfeeling syndrome seems to work like this: (1) You repress the spontaneous feelings in life; (2) but spontaneous feelings are the source of enjoyment; so (3) enjoyment must be artificially applied from without (cute movies). (4) You repress your innate right to evaluate events and people, but (5) energy comes from making your own evaluations and then acting on them, so (6) therefore your natural energy must be replaced by indifferent violence.

The churches in Minnesota have had their part in vitiating the natural energy of people. Most of rural Minnesota go to church regularly, yet nearly never get a sermon on Jesus' turning the tables on the money-changers. They absolutely never get a sermon on Saul's having failed to obliterate the Amalekites so that Samuel has to cut Agag, the Amalekite king, to pieces in front of Saul, to give him an idea what the Lord had in mind; they absolutely never get a sermon on St. Stephen's being stoned while Saul, later to become St. Paul, approved. The pastors, themselves tottering around in an emotional sleepwalk, don't face the crises of their faith. They do not make themselves answer: was Hosea right in his incredible and violent hostility to women? Is Cardinal Spellman right in saying the 25th Infantry carried the cross of Christ in Vietnam? Since the pastors lack such energy—to think, and feel, and commit themselves —the people are left with no example of Christ's energy. No castle was ever well guarded by sleepwalkers, and certainly no Kingdom of the Spirit can rise up in the hearts of somnambulants.

What is crueler, however, is that it is now commercially practicable to keep our lost Swede asleep. One villain in this is the Shakespeare-in-the-Streets troupe of Minneapolis. A few years ago they took around to our towns, among them Madison, a *Hamlet* in which the characters were hashed (Hamlet appeared double: one white, one black), the plot changed into a spaced-out pas de mille choreography, and the soliloquies were done in a kind of black stomp. Having removed all the real energy of the play then, cute movie things had to be added. A dead chicken was thrown around, Polonius got kicked hard in the shins, and so on. The manager told me, "Oh we did it on purpose, because the common people [*sic*] wouldn't like it straight."

This past winter, the children's theatre group from the University of Minnesota brought to Madison a program of four Hans Christian Andersen fairy tales. They were excellent—beautiful. Still, they turned the Ugly Duckling into a kind of black-face humor piece, even done with what were ominously close to fake-black accents. They made the Ugly Duckling, in effect, a cute show. This meant that our lost Swede Minnesotan, who hadn't read the original Andersen, didn't get to hear Andersen on the injustice of early selection, the sorrow of the eccentric child, or the heartbreaking discovery of one's true element late in life.

Educated Americans spent the summer of 1973 sneering at Middle America for turning off their televisions during the Watergate hearings. It is true, in the beauty shops, the TV was turned off because of "that Watergate." But who tried sincerely to show the lady in rollers that it is strengthening, not weakening, to feel what's happening in the United States? Too many of our intellectuals have left the Swede by the roadside.

The billboard just south of Madison on U.S. 75 now reads: "Don't just sit there—Be a Navy man." If all feeling is dead, those are the choices: feeling nothing, motivated by nothing—or join an organization which specializes in indifferent killing.

Our countryside has inherited not Grieg, not Ibsen, not Rölvaag— but just sitting there, cute movies, and when boredom gets bad enough, joining the Navy.

The problem of people's not feeling is very serious, and I haven't any answers. But I think we should get onto this issue now, and we should buck each other's ideas back and forth. Selma Lägerlöf, who was emphatically a very live Swede, was right in warning that the soul cannot live on fun alone . . . it will kill. We know that now.

September 1973

·8·

Widow Water
Frederick Busch

WHAT TO KNOW ABOUT PAIN is how little we do to deserve it, how simple it is to give, how hard to lose. I'm a plumber. I dig for what's wrong. I should know. And what I think of now as I remember pain is the fat young man and his child, their staggering house, the basement filled with death and dark water, the small perfect boy on the stone cellar steps who wept, the widow's coffee gone cold.

They called on Friday to complain that the pump in their basement wouldn't work. Theirs is shallow-well country, a couple of miles from the college, a place near the fast wide river that once ran the mill that all the houses of the town depended on. The railroad came, the town grew, the large white clapboard houses spread. By the time their seedlings were in the middle growth, the mill had failed, the houses had run to blisters of rotted wood on the siding and to gaps in the black and green roofs. The old ones were nearly all dead and the railroad came twice a day, from Utica to Binghamton, to Utica from Binghamton, carrying sometimes some freight, sometimes a car of men who maintained the nearly useless track. And the new people came, took their children for walks on the river to the stone foundations of the mill. They looked at the water and went home. People now don't know the water as they should. I'm a plumber, I should know.

I told him I couldn't come on a Friday afternoon in April, when the rains were opening seams and seals and cellars all through the county. Bella was making coffee for us while I took the call, and I snapped my fingers for her to turn around. She did, all broad—not fat, though—and full of colors—red in her face, yellow in her hair going gray, the gold in her tooth, her eyes blue as pottery—and I pointed at the phone. She mouthed a mimic "Today, today, today," and I nodded, and she nodded back and poured the almost boiling water out into the instant coffee, which dissolved.

He said, "So you see, sir, we can use your help."

I said, "Yessir, sounds like a problem."

"No water, and we've got a boy who isn't toilet-trained. It gets kind of messy."

"I imagine."

"So do you think you could . . ."

"Yessir?"

"Come kind of soon?"

"Oh, I'll come kind of soon. It just won't be today."

"You're sure you couldn't . . ."

"Yessir?"

"Come today?"

"Yessir."

"Yes sir, what?"

"Yessir, I'm sure I can't come."

Bella rapped on the table with her big knuckles to tell me to come and sit. I nodded, pointed at the telephone, waited for him to try once more. He was from the college—he would try once more.

He said, "But no water—for how long? The weekend? All week?"

I heard a woman whisper in the background with the harshness of a wife making peace, and then he said, "Uh—I mean, do you know when you can come?"

I said, "When're you up?"

"Excuse me?"

"When do you wake up?"

"We'll be up. Just tell me when."

I said, "I'll be there tomorrow morning, early, if that's all right."

"I mean, how early?"

"You get up, Mr. Samuels, and you have yourself a comfortable breakfast, and I'll be there for a cup of your coffee."

He hung on the line, waiting for more. I gave him nothing more, and he said, "Thanks. I mean, we'll see you tomorrow, then. Thank you."

"Thank *you* for calling, Mr. Samuels, and I'll see you soon."

He said, "Not soon enough," and chuckled and didn't mean the laugh.

I chuckled back and meant it, because coffee was waiting, and Bella, and a quiet hour before I went back out to clear a lonely lady's pipe in a fifty-foot well. I said, "Good-bye, Mr. Samuels."

He said, "Yes," which meant he was listening to his whispering wife, not me, and then he said, "Yes, goodbye, thank you very much, see you soon."

I blew on my coffee and Bella turned the radio off—she'd been listening to it low to hear if she'd won the fur coat someone in Oneida was giving away—and we sat and ate bran muffins with her blueberry jam and talked about nothing much; we said most of it by sitting and eating too much together after so many years of coffee and preserves.

After a while she said, "A professor with a problem."

"His pump won't turn off. Somebody sold him a good big Gould brand-new when he moved in last summer, and now it won't turn off and he's mad as hell."

"Well, I can understand that. They hear that motor banging away and think it's going to explode and burn their house down. They're city people, I suppose."

"Aren't they ever. I know the house. McGregory's old place near the Keeper farm. It needs work."

"Which they wouldn't know how to do."

"Or be able to afford," I said. "He's a young one and a new professor. He wouldn't earn much more than the boys on Buildings and Grounds. I'll bill him—he won't have the money in the house or at the bank, probably—and we'll wait a couple of months."

Bella said, "We can wait."

"We will."

"What did you tell him to do?"

"I told him to unplug the pump."

"He wasn't satisfied."

"I guess I wouldn't be."

"Abe," she said, "what's it like to be young as that?"

I said, "Unhappy."

She said, "But happy, too."

"A little of that."

She bent her gray and gold head over the brown mug of dark brown coffee and picked at the richness of a moist muffin. She said, still looking down, "It's hard."

I said, "It gets easier."

She looked up and nodded, grinned her golden tooth at me, said, "Doesn't it?"

Then I spent the afternoon driving to New Hartford to the ice-cream plant for twenty-five pounds of sliced dry ice. I had them cut the ice into ten-inch-long slivers about three-quarters of an inch around, wrapped the ice in heavy brown paper, and drove it back to Brookfield and the widow's jammed drill point. It's all hard-water country here, and the crimped-pipe points they drive down for wells get sealed with calcium scales if you wait enough years, and the pressure falls, the people call, they worry about having to drill new wells and how much it will cost and when they can flush the toilets again. They worry how long they'll have to wait.

I went in the cellar door without telling her I was there, disconnected the elbow joint, went back out for the ice, and when I had carried the second bundle in, she was standing by her silent well in the damp of her basement, surrounded by furniture draped in plastic sheets, firewood stacked, cardboard boxes of web-crusted Mason jars, the growing heaps of whatever in her life she couldn't use.

She was small and white and dressed in sweaters and a thin green housecoat. She said, "Whatever do you mean to do?" Her hands were folded across her little chest, and she rubbed her gnarled throat. "Is my well dead?"

"No, ma'am. I'd like you to go upstairs while I do my small miracle here. Because I'd like you not to worry. Won't you go upstairs?"

She said, "I live alone—"

I said, "You don't have to worry."

"I don't know what to do about—this kind of thing. It gets more and more of a problem—this—all this." She waved her hand at what she lived in and then hung her hands at her sides.

I said, "You go on up and watch the television. I'm going to fix it up. I'll do a little fixing here and come back tonight and hook her up again, and you be ready to make me my after-dinner coffee when I come back. You'll have water enough to do it with."

"Just go back upstairs?" she said.

"You go on up while I make it good. And I don't want you worrying."

"All right, then," she said, "I'll go back up. I get awfully upset now.

When these—things. These—I don't know what to do anymore." She looked at me like something that was new. Then she said, "I knew your father, I think. Was he big like you?"

"You know it," I said. "Bigger. Didn't he court you one time?"

"I think everybody must have courted me one time."

"You were frisky," I said.

"Not like now," she said. Her lips were white on her white face, the flesh looked like flower petals. Pinch them and they crumble, wet dust.

"Don't you feel so good now?"

"I mean kids now."

"Oh?"

"They have a different notion of frisky now."

"Yes they do," I said. "I guess they do."

"But I don't feel so good," she said. "This. Things like this. I wish they wouldn't happen. Now. I'm very old."

I said, "It keeps on coming, doesn't it?"

"I can hear it come. When the well stopped, I thought it was a sign. When you get like me, you can hear it come."

I said, "Now listen: You go up. You wrap a blanket around you and talk on the telephone or watch the TV. Because I guarantee. You knew my father. You knew my father's word. Take mine. I guarantee."

"Well, if you're guaranteeing."

I said, "That's my girl." She was past politeness so she didn't smile or come back out of herself to say goodbye. She walked to the stairs and when she started to shuffle and haul the long way up, I turned away to the well pipe, calling, "You make sure and have my coffee ready tonight. You wait and make my after-dinner coffee, hear? There'll be water for it." I waited until she went up, and it was something of a wait. She was too tired for stairs. I thought to tell Bella that it looked like the widow hadn't long.

But when she was gone, I worked. I put my ear to the pipe and heard the sounds of hollowness, the emptiness under the earth that's not quite silence—like the whisper you hear in the long-distance wires of the telephone before the relays connect. Then I opened the brown paper packages and started forcing the lengths of dry ice down into the pipe. I carried and shoved, drove the ice first with my fingers and then with a piece of copper tube, and I filled the well pipe until nothing more would go. My fingers were red, and the smoke from dry ice misted up until I stood in an underground fog. When nothing more would fit, I capped the pipe, kicked the rest of the ice down into the sump—it steamed as if she lived above a fire, as if always her house were smoldering—and I went out, drove home.

I went by the hill roads, and near Excell's farm I turned the motor off, drifted down the dirt road in neutral, watching. The deer had come down from the high hills and they were moving carefully through the fields of last year's corn stumps, grazing like cattle at dusk, too many to count. When the truck stopped I heard the rustle as they pulled the tough silk. Then I started the motor—they jumped, stiffened, watched me for a while, went back to eating: A man could come and kill them, they had so little fear—and I drove home to Bella and a tight house, long dinner, silence for most of the meal, then talk about the children while I washed the dishes and she put them away.

And then I drove back to the house that was dark except for one lighted window. The light was yellow and not strong. I turned the engine off and coasted in. I went downstairs on the tips of my toes because, I told myself, there was a sense of silence there, and I hoped she was having some rest. I uncapped the well pipe and gases blew back, a stink of the deepest cold, and then there was a sound of climbing, of filling up, and water banged to her house again. I put the funnel and hose on the mouth of the pipe and filled my jeep can, then capped the check valve, closed the pipe that delivered the water upstairs, poured water from the jeep can through the funnel to prime the pump, switched it on, watched the pressure needle climb to thirty-eight pounds, opened the faucet to the upstairs pipes, and heard it gush.

I hurried to get the jeep can and hose and funnel and tools to the truck, and I had closed the cellar door and driven off before she made the porch to call me. I wanted to get back to Bella and tell her what a man she was married to—who could know so well the truths of ice and make a dead well live.

Saturday morning the pickup trucks were going to the dump, and the men would leave off trash and hard fill, stand at tailgates, spitting, talking, complaining, shooting at rats or nothing, firing off, picking for scrap, and I drove to see the professor and his catastrophe.

His house was tilted. It needed jacks. The asbestos siding was probably all that kept the snow out. His drainpipes were broken, and I could see the damp spots where water wasn't carried off but spilled to the roof of his small porch to eat its way in and gradually soften the house for bad winter leaks. The lawn at the side of his drive was rutted and soft, needed gravel. The barn he used for garage would have to be coated with creosote or it would rot and fall. A child's bright toys lay in his yard like litter. The cornfield behind his house went off to soft meadow and low hills, and everything was clean and growing behind where they lived; for the view they had, they might as well have owned the countryside. What they didn't own was their house.

He met me at the back steps, all puffy and breasted in his T-shirt, face in the midst of a curly black beard, dirty glasses over his eyes like a mask. He shook my hand as if I were his surgeon. He asked me to have coffee, and I told him I wouldn't now. A little boy came out, and he was beautiful: blond hair and sweetly shaped head, bright brown eyes, as red from weather as his father was pale, a sturdy body with a rounded stomach you would want to cup your hand on as if it were a breast, and teeth as white as bone. He stood behind his father and circled an arm around his father's heavy thigh, put his forehead in his father's buttocks, and then peeped out at me. He said, "Is this the fixing man? Will he fix our pump?"

Samuels put his hand behind him and squeezed the boy's head. He said, "This is the plumber, Mac." He raised his eyebrows at me and smiled, and I liked the way he loved the boy and knew how the boy embarrassed him too.

I kneeled down and said, "Hey, Mac."

The boy hid his face in his father's behind.

I said, "Mac, do you play in that sandbox over there?"

His face came out and he said, very politely, "Would you like to play with me?"

I said, "I have to look at your pump, Mac."

He nodded. He was serious now. He said, "Daddy broke it last night, and we can't fix it again."

I carried my tool pack to the cellar door—the galvanized sheeting on top of it was coming loose, several nails had gone, the weather was getting behind it and would eat the wood away—and I opened it up and started down the stone steps to the inside cellar door. They came behind me, then Samuels went ahead of me, turning on lights, scuffing through the mud and puddles on his concrete floor. The pump was on the wall to the left as I came in. The converted coal furnace in front of me leaked oil where the oilfeed came in. Stone foundation cracking that was two hundred years old, vent windows shut when they should have been opened to stop the dry rot, beams with the adze scars in them powdering almost as we watched: that was his cellar—and packing cartons and scraps of wood, broken chairs, a table with no legs. There was a stink of something very bad.

I looked at the pump, breathed out, then I looked at Mac. He breathed out too. He sounded like me. I grinned at him and he grinned back.

"We're the workers," he said. "Okay? You and me will be the workers. But Daddy can't fix anymore. Mommy said so."

Samuels said, "We'll leave him alone now, Mac."

I said, "How old is he?"

Mac said, "Six years old."

Samuels said, "Three. Almost three and a half."

"And lots of boy," I said.

Mac said, "I'm a worker."

Samuels said, "All right, Mac."

Mac said, "Can't stay here? Daddy? I'm a *work*er."

Samuels said, "Would we be in the way? I'd like to learn a little about the thing if I can."

Mac shook his head and smiled at me. He said, "What are we going to do with our Daddy?"

Samuels said, "Okay, buddy."

Mac raised his brows and shrugged his little arms.

Samuels said, "Out, Mac. Into the yard. Play in the sandbox for a while." He said, "Okay? I'll call you when we need some help."

"Sure!" Mac said.

He walked up the steps, arms slanted out to balance himself, little thighs pushing up on the steps. From outside, where we couldn't see him anymore, the boy called, "Bye and I love you," and ran away.

Samuels held his arms folded across his chest, covering his fleshy breasts. He uncrossed his arms to push his glasses up on his face when they slipped from the bridge of his flat nose. He said, "The water here— I tried to use the instruction book last night, after I talked to you. I guess I shouldn't have done that, huh?"

"Depends on what you did, Mr. Samuels." I unrolled the tool pack, got ready to work.

"I figured it wouldn't turn off on account of an air block in the pipes. The instructions mentioned that."

"Oh."

"So I unplugged the pump as you told me to, and then I drained all the water out—that's how the floor got so wet. Then it all ran into that hole over there."

"The sump."

"Oh, *that's* what a sump is. Then that motor like an outboard engine with the pipe—"

"The sump pump. The water collects in the hole and pushes the float up and the motor cuts in and pumps the water out the side of the house—over there, behind your hot-water heater."

"Oh."

"Except your sump pump isn't plugged in."

"Oh. I wondered. And I was fooling with the motor and this black ball fell off into the water."

"The float. So it wouldn't turn itself *off* if you did keep it plugged in. Don't you worry, Mr. Samuels, we'll pump her out later. Did you do anything else to the well pump?"

He pushed his glasses up and recrossed his arms. "I didn't know what else to do. I couldn't make it start again. We didn't have any water all night. There wasn't any pressure on the gauge."

"No. You have to prime it."

"Prime it?"

"I'll show you, Mr. Samuels. First, you better let me look. Right?"

"Sorry. Sorry. Do you mind if I stay here, though?" He smiled. He blushed under his whiskers. "I really have to learn something about how—this whole thing." He waved his arms around him and then covered up.

I said, "You can stay, sure. Stay."

I started to work a wrench on the heavy casing bolts, and when I'd got the motor apart from the casing, water began to run to the floor from the discharge pipe over the galvanized tank.

He said, "Should I . . ."

"Excuse me?"

"There's water coming down. Should I do anything about it?"

I said, "No, thank you. No. You just watch, thank you."

After a while the trickle slowed, and I pulled the halves apart. I took the rubber diaphragm off, put the flashlight on the motor, poked with a screwdriver, found nothing. I expected nothing. It had to be in the jet. I put the light on that and looked in and saw it, nodded, waited for him to ask.

He said, "You found it?"

"Yessir. The jet's blocked. That's what it sounded like when you called. Wouldn't let the pressure build up, so the gauge wouldn't know when to stop. It's set at forty pounds, and the block wouldn't let it up past—oh, twenty-eight or thirty, I'd say. Am I right?"

"Uh, I don't know. I don't know *anything* about these things."

I said, "When this needle hits forty, it's what you should be getting. Forty pounds of pressure per square inch. If you'd read the gauge you'd have seen it to be about thirty, I calculate. That would've told you the whole thing."

"I thought the gauge was broken."

"They generally don't break. Generally, these things work. Usually it's something simpler than machines when you can't get water up."

He pushed his glasses and covered up, said, "God, what I don't know."

I said, "It's hard to live in a house, isn't it? But you'll learn."

"Jesus, I hope so. I don't know. I hope so. We never lived in a house before."

"What'd you live in? Apartment houses?"

"Yeah—where you call the janitor downstairs and he comes up while you're at work and you never see him. Like magic. It's just all better by the time you get home."

"Well, we'll get this better for you."

He frowned and nodded very seriously. "I'll bet you will," he said. It was a gift he gave me, a bribe.

I said, "So why don't you go on up and ask the missus for about three inches of aluminum foil. Would you do that? And a coat hanger, if you don't mind."

"Coat hanger?"

"Yessir. If you don't mind."

He walked across the floor to the wooden steps that went upstairs above the furnace; he tried to hide the sway and bounce of his body in the way that he walked, the boy coming down the outside concrete steps as the father went up the inside ones. "Do you need any help?" the boy said.

I said, "Mac, you old helper. Hello."

"Do you need any help?"

"I had a boy like you."

"A little bit big, like me?"

"Little bit big. Except now he's almost a daddy too."

He said, "Is he *your* daddy now?"

I said, "Not yet."

"Not yet?"

"Not for a while."

"Oh. Well, then what happened to him?"

"He just got big. He grew up."

"Does he go to the college?"

"He's bigger than that, even."

Mac smiled and showed his hand, fingers held together. "*That* big? *So* big?"

"Bigger," I said.

Mac said, "That's a big boy you have."

Samuels handed me the foil and coat hanger. I rolled the foil around a cigar until it was a cylinder, and I stuck it in the well side of the nozzle. I opened the hanger and straightened her out.

Mac said, "What's he doing, Daddy?"

Samuels said, "I don't know. I don't know, Mac. Why don't you go outside? I don't know."

I said, "Mr. Samuels, I wonder if you would hold that foil firmly in there and cup your hand under it while I give her a shove."

He held. Mac watched him. I pushed at the other side of the jet, felt it, pushed again, and it rolled down the aluminum foil to his palm: a flat wet pebble half the size of the nail on his little finger. He said, "That's it? That's all it is? This is what ruined my life for two days?"

I said, "That's all it ever takes, Mr. Samuels. It came up with the water—you have to have gravel where there's water—and it lodged in the jet, kept the pressure from building up. If it happens again, I'll put a screen in at the check valve. May never happen again. If it does, we'll know what to do, won't we?"

Samuels said, "I wonder when I'll ever know what to do around here."

I said, "You'll learn."

I fastened the halves of the pump together, then went out for my jeep can, still half full from the widow's house. I came back in and I unscrewed the pipe plug at the top of the pump and poured the water in, put the plug back on, connected the pump to the switch.

Mac jumped, then stood still, holding to his father's leg.

The pump chirred, caught on the water from the widow's well, drew, and we all watched the pressure climb to forty, heard the motor cut out, heard the water climb in the copper pipes to the rest of the house as I opened the valve.

I was putting away tools when I heard Samuels say, "Now keep away from there!" I heard the *whack* of his hand on Mac's flesh, and heard the weeping start, in the back of the boy's throat, and then the wail. Samuels said, "That's *filthy* in there—Christ knows what you've dragged up. And I *told* you not to mess with things you don't know anything about. Dammit!"

Mac wailed louder. I watched his face clench and grow red, ugly. He put his left sleeve in his mouth and chewed on it, backed away to the stone steps, fumbled with his feet and stepped backwards up one step. "But *Dad*-dy," he said. "But *Dad*-dy." Then he stood on the steps and chewed his sleeve and cried.

Samuels said, "God, look at that."

I said, "There's that smell you've been smelling, Mr. Samuels. Mouse. He must've fallen into the sump and starved to death and rotted there. That's what you've been smelling."

"God. Mac—go up and wash your hands. Mac! Go upstairs and wash your hands. I mean *now!*"

The small brown lump of paws and tail and teeth, its stomach swollen, the rest looking almost dissolved, lay in its puddle on the floor beside the sump. The stink of its death was everywhere. The pump cut in and built the pressure up again. Mac stood on the cellar steps and cried. His father pushed his glasses up and looked at the corpse of the rotted mouse and hugged his arms around himself and looked at his son. I walked past Samuels, turned away from the weeping boy, and pushed up at the lever that the float, if he had left it there, would have released on the sump pump. Nothing happened, and I stayed where I was, waiting, until I remembered to plug the sump pump in. I pushed the lever again, its motor started, the filthy reeking water dropped, the wide black rubber pipe it passed through on the ceiling swung like something alive as all that dying passed along it and out.

I picked the mouse up by its tail after the pump had stopped and Samuels, waiting for my approval, watching my face, had pulled out the plug. I carried my tools under my arm and the jeep can in my hand. I nodded to Samuels and he was going to speak, then didn't, just nodded back. I walked past Mac on the steps, not crying anymore, but wet-faced and stunned. I bent down as I passed him. I whispered, "What shall we do with your Daddy?" and went on, not smiling.

I walked to the truck in their unkempt drive that went to the barn that would fall. I carried the corpse. I thought to get home to Bella and say how sorry I was for the sorrow I'd made and couldn't take back. I spun the dripping mouse by its tail and flung it beyond the barn into Keeper's field of corn stumps. It rose and sank from the air and was gone. I had primed the earth. It didn't need the prime.

•9•

The Rookers

Bobbie Ann Mason

MARY LOU SKAGGS RUNS ERRANDS for her husband. She hauls lumber, delivers bookshelves, even makes a special trip to town just to exchange flathead screws. Mack will occasionally go out to measure people's kitchens for the cabinets and countertops he makes, but he gets uncomfortable if he has to be away long. And the highway makes him nervous. Increasingly, he stays at home, working in his shop in the basement. They live on a main road between two small Kentucky towns, and the shop sign has been torn down by teenagers so many times that Mack has given up trying to keep it repaired. Mary Lou feels that Mack never charges enough for his work, but she has always helped out—keeping the books, canning and sewing, as well as periodically working for H & R Block—and they have managed to send their youngest child to college. The two older daughters are married, with homes nearby, but Judy is a freshman at Murray State. After she left, Mack became so involved with some experimental woodworking projects that Mary Lou thought he had almost failed to notice that the children had all gone.

For some neighbors, Mack made a dinette booth out of a church pew salvaged from an abandoned country church. The sanding took days. "I'm sanding off layers of hypocrisy," Mack said.

"You sound like that guy that used to stand out on the corner and yell when church let out on Sunday," said Mary Lou. " 'Here come the hyps,' he'd say."

"Who was that?"

"Oh, just some guy in town. That was years ago. He led a crusade against fluoride too."

"Fluoride's O.K. It hardens the teeth."

For their twenty-fifth anniversary, Mack made Mary Lou a round card table from scrap pine, with an old sprocket from a bulldozer as a base. It was connected to the table with a length of lead pipe. "It didn't cost a thing," Mack said. "Just imagination."

The tabletop, a mosaic of wood scraps, was like a crazy quilt, Mary Lou thought. It was heavily varnished with polyurethane, making a slick surface. Mack had spray-painted the sprocket black.

"Do you like it?" he asked.

"Sure."

"No, you don't. I can tell you don't."

"It's real pretty."

"It's not something you would buy in a store," Mack said apologetically.

Mary Lou had never seen a table like it. Automatically, she counted the oddly shaped pieces Mack had fit together for the top. Twenty-one. It seemed that Mack was trying to put together the years of their marriage into a convincing whole and this was as far as he got. Mary Lou is concerned about Mack. He seems embarrassed that they are alone in the house now for the first time in years. When Judy fails to come home on weekends, he paces around restlessly. He has even started reading books and magazines, as if he can somehow keep up with Judy and her studies. Lately he has become obsessed with the weather. He likes to compare the weather with the predictions in the *Old Farmer's Almanac*. He likes it when the *Almanac* is wrong. Anyone else would be rooting for the *Almanac* to be right.

When the women Mary Lou plays Rook with come over, Mack stays in the den watching TV, hardly emerging to say hello. Thelma Crandall, Clausie Dowdy, and Edda Griffin—the Rookers, Mary Lou calls them—are all much older than Mary Lou, and they are all widows. Mack and Mary Lou married young, and even though they have three grown daughters, they are only in their late forties. Mack says it is unhealthy for her to socialize with senior citizens, but Mary Lou doesn't believe him. It does her good to have some friends.

Mary Lou shows off the new card table when the women arrive one evening. They all come in separate cars, not trusting each other's driving.

"It's set on a bulldozer sprocket," Mary Lou explains.

"How did Mack come up with such an idea?" asks Clausie, admiring the table.

Thelma, the oldest of the group, is reluctant to sit at the table, for fear she will catch her foot in one of the holes at the base.

"Couldn't you cover up the bottom of that table with a rug or something?" asks Edda. "We might catch our feet."

Mary Lou finds an old afghan and drapes it around the bulldozer sprocket, tamping it down carefully in the holes. She gets along with old people, and she feels exhilarated when she is playing cards with her friends. "They tickle me," she told Mack once. "Old people are liable to say anything." Mack said old people gave him the creeps, the way they talked about diseases.

Mary Lou keeps a list of whose turn it is to deal, because they often lose track. When they deal the cards on the new table, the cards shoot across the slick surface. This evening they discuss curtain material, Edda's granddaughter's ovary infection, a place that appeared on Thelma's arm, and the way the climate has changed. All three of the widows live in nice houses in town. When Mary Lou goes to their houses to play Rook, she is impressed by their shag rugs, their matching sets of furniture, their neat kitchens. Their walls are filled with pictures of grandchildren and great-grandchildren. Mary Lou's pictures are scattered around in drawers, and her kitchen is always a mess.

"They're beating the socks off of us," Mary Lou tells Mack when he watches the game for a moment. Mary Lou is teamed up with Thelma. "I had the bird—that was the only trump I had."

"I haven't had it a time," says Clausie, a peppy little woman with a trim figure.

"I put thirty in the widow and they caught it," Thelma tells Mack.

"The rook's a sign of bad luck," Mack says. "A rook ain't nothing but a crow."

When he returns to the football game he is watching on TV, Edda says with a laugh, "Did y'all hear what Erma Bombeck said? She said any man who watches more than a hundred and sixty-eight football games in one year ought to be declared legally dead."

They all laugh in little bursts and spasms, but Mary Lou says defensively, "Mack doesn't watch that much football. He just watches it because it's on. Usually he has his nose stuck in a book."

"I used to read," says Clausie. "But I got out of the habit."

Later, Mary Lou complains to Mack about his behavior. "You could at least be friendly," she says.

"I like to see you playing cards," says Mack.

"You're changing the subject."

"You light up and you look so pretty."

"I'll say one thing for those old gals. They get out and *go*. They don't hide under a bushel. Like some people I know."

"I don't hide under a bushel."

"You think they're just a bunch of silly old widow women."

"You look beautiful when you're having a good time," says Mack, goosing her and making her jump.

"They're not that old, though," says Mary Lou. "They don't act it. Edda's a great-grandmother, but she's just as spry! She goes to Paducah driving that little Bobcat like she owned the road. And Clausie hasn't got a brain in her head. She's just like a kid—"

But now Mack is absorbed in something on TV, a pudding commercial. Mary Lou has tried to be patient with Mack, thinking that he will grow out of his current phase. Sooner or later, she and Mack will have to face growing older together. Mack says that having a daughter in college makes him feel he has missed something, but Mary Lou has tried to make him see that they could still enjoy life. Before she began playing regularly with the Rookers, she had several ideas for doing things together, now that they were no longer tied down with a family. She suggested bowling, camping, a trip to Opryland. But Mack said he'd rather improve his mind. He has been reading *Shōgun*. He made excuses about the traffic. They had a chance to go on a free weekend to the Paradise Valley Estates, a resort development in the Ozarks. There was no obligation. All they had to do was hear a talk and watch some slides. But Mack hated the idea and said there was a catch. Mack made Mary Lou feel she was pressuring him, and she decided not to bring up these topics for a while. She would wait for him to come out of his shell. But she was disappointed about the free weekend. The resort had swimming, nature trails, horseback riding, golf, fishing, and pontoon boat rentals. The bathrooms had whirlpools.

When the telephone rings at five o'clock one morning, Mary Lou is certain there must be bad news from Judy. As she runs to the kitchen to answer the telephone, her mind runs through dope, suicide, dorm fires. The man on the phone has a loud voice that blares out at her. He makes her guess who he is. He turns out to be Ed Williams, her long-lost brother. Mary Lou is speechless, having concluded several years ago that he must be dead. Ed had gone to Texas for his health, traveling with a woman with a dark complexion and pierced ears. Now he tells Mary Lou he is married to that woman, named Linda, and they are living in California with her two children from a former marriage.

"What do you look like?" asks Mary Lou.

"I'm a beanpole. I have to bend over to make a shadow."

Mary Lou says, "I'm old and fat and ugly. Mack would whip me to hear that. I'm not really, but after nine years, you'd know the difference. It's been nine years, Ed Williams. I could kill you for doing us like that."

"I just finished building me a house, but I don't have a thing I want to put in it except a washer and dryer."

"All the girls are gone. Judy's in college—first one to go. We're proud. She says she's going to make a doctor. Betty and Janie are married, with younguns."

"I've got me a camper and a pickup and a retirement lot," Ed says. "What's Mack up to?"

"Oh, he's so lonesome with all the girls gone that he's acting peculiar."

Disturbed and excited, Mary Lou burns the bacon while she's telling Mack about the call. Mack seems surprised that Ed is still with the same woman.

"How did she get him wrapped around her little finger? Ed would never even stay in one place long enough to get a crop out."

Mary Lou shoves Mack's plate in front of him. "I thought to my *soul* he was dead. When he went out there, he looked terrible. He thought he had TB. But it was just like him not to write or call or say boo."

"Ed always was wild. I bet he was drunk."

Mary Lou sits down to eat. Cautiously, she says, "He wants us to come out and see him."

"Why can't he come here?"

"He's got a family now. He's tied down."

Mack flips through the *Old Farmer's Almanac* as he eats.

Mary Lou says, "We could go out there. We're not tied down."

Mack fastens his finger on a page. "What if Judy wanted to come home? She'd have to stay here by herself."

"You beat all I've ever seen, Mack." Mary Lou smears jelly on her toast and eats a bite. She says, "Ed said he just got to thinking how he wanted to hear from home. He said Christmas was coming up and—you want to know something, Mack? Ed was on my mind all one day last week. And then he calls, just like that. I must have had a premonition. What does the *Farmer's Almanac* say to that?"

Mack points to a weather chart. "It says here we're due for a mild winter—no snow hardly a-tall. But I don't believe it. I believe we're going to have snow before Christmas."

Mack sounds so serious. He sounds like the President delivering a somber message on the economy. Mary Lou doesn't know what to think.

The next evening at Clausie's house, the Rookers are elated over Mary Lou's news, but she doesn't go into details about her brother's bad reputation.

"It sounded just like him," she says. "His voice was just as *clear*."

Clausie urges Mary Lou to persuade Mack to go to California.

"Oh, we could never afford it," says Mary Lou. "I'm afraid to even bring it up."

"It's awful far," says Thelma. "My oldest girl's daughter went out in May of seventy-three. She left the day school was out."

"Did he say what he was doing?" Edda asks Mary Lou.

"He said he just built him a house and didn't have anything he wanted to put in it but a washer and dryer. Mack's making fun of me for carrying on so, but he never liked Ed anyway. Ed was always a little wild."

For refreshments, Clausie has made lemon chiffon cake and boiled custard. Mary Lou loves being at Clausie's. Her house is like her chiffon cakes, all soft surfaces and pleasant colors, and she has a new factory-waxed Congoleum floor in her kitchen, patterned after a brick wall.

When Clausie clears away the dishes, she pats Mary Lou's hand and says, "Well, maybe your brother will come back home, if you all can't go out. Sounds like his mind's on his family now."

"You and Mack need to go more," says Edda.

"You ought to get Mack out square-dancing!" says Clausie, who belongs to a square-dancing club.

Mary Lou has to laugh, that idea is so farfetched.

"My fiftieth wedding anniversary would have been day before yesterday," says Thelma, whose husband had died the year before.

"It's too bad Otis couldn't have lived just a little longer," says Clausie sympathetically.

"He bought us eight grave plots. Otis wanted me and him to have plenty of room."

The widows compare prices of caskets.

"Law, I wouldn't want to be cremated the way some of them are doing now," says Edda. "To save space."

"Me neither," says Clausie with a whoop. "Did y'all see one of them Russians on television while back? At his funeral there was this horse and buggy pulling the body, and instead of a casket there was this little-bitty vase propped up there. It was real odd looking."

"The very idea!" cries Edda. "Keeping somebody in a vase on the mantel. Somebody might use it for a ashtray."

Clausie and Edda and Thelma are all laughing. Mary Lou shuffles the cards distractedly, the way Mack flips through the *Old Farmer's Almanac*, as if some wisdom might rub off.

"Come on, y'all, let's play," she says.

But the women cannot settle down and concentrate on the game yet. They are still laughing, overflowing with good humor. Mary Lou shuffles the cards endlessly, as though she can never get them exactly right.

Mack hardly watches TV anymore, except when the Rookers are there. He sits in his armchair reading. He belongs to a book club. Since Judy went away to college, he has read *Shōgun*, *Rage of Angels*, *The Clowns of God*, and *The Covenant*. He reads parts of *Cosmos*, which Mary Lou brought him from the library. He does not believe anything he has read in *Cosmos*. It was not on TV in their part of the country. Now he is struggling along with *The Encyclopedia of Philosophy*. When he reads that, his face is set in a painful frown.

Mary Lou delivers a gun cabinet to a young couple in a trailer park. How they can afford a gun cabinet, she has no idea. She picks up some sandpaper for Mack. Mack will never make a list. He sends her to town for one or two things at a time. At home, he apologizes for not going on the errand himself. He is rubbing a piece of wood with a rag.

"Look at this," he says excitedly, showing Mary Lou a sketch of some shelves. "I decided what I want to make Judy for Christmas, for a surprise."

The sketch is an intricate design with small compartments.

"Judy called while you were gone," Mack says. "After I talked to her, I got an inspiration. I'm making her this for her dorm room. It's going to have a place here for her turntable, and slots for records. It's called a home entertainment center."

"It's pretty. What did Judy call for?"

"She's coming home tomorrow. Her roommate quit school, and Judy's coming home early to study for her exams next week."

"What happened to her roommate?"

"She wouldn't say. She must be in some kind of trouble, though."

"Is Judy all right?"

"Yeah. After she called, I just got to thinking that I wanted to do something nice for her." Mack is fitting sandpaper onto his sander, using a screwdriver to roll it in. Suddenly he says, "You wouldn't go off and leave me, would you?"

"What makes you say that?"

Mack sets down the sander and takes her by the shoulders, then holds her close to him. He smells like turpentine. "You're always wanting to run around," he says. "You might get ideas."

"Don't worry," says Mary Lou. "I wouldn't think of leaving you." She can't help adding sarcastically, "You'd starve."

"You might go off to find Ed."

"Well, not in that pickup anyway," she says. "The brakes are bad."

When he releases her, he looks happy. He turns on the sander and runs it across the piece of wood, moving with the grain. When he turns off the sander and begins rubbing away the fine dust with a tack rag, Mary Lou says, "People were always jealous of Ed. The only reason he ever got in trouble was that people picked on him because he carried so much money around with him. People heard he had money, and when he'd pull into town in that rig he drove, the police would think up some excuse to run him in. People were just jealous. Everything he touched turned to money."

The way Mack is rubbing the board with the tack rag makes Mary Lou think of Aladdin and his lamp. He rubs and rubs, nodding when she speaks.

Judy drives a little Chevette she bought with money she earned working at the Burger Chef. She arrives at suppertime the next day with a pizza and a tote bag of books. Mary Lou serves green beans, corn, and slaw with the pizza. She and Mack hover over their daughter. At their insistence, Judy tries to explain what happened to her roommate.

"Stephanie had a crush on this Western Civ professor and she made it into a big thing. Now her boyfriend is giving her a real hard time. He accused her of running around with the teacher, but she didn't. Now he's mad at her, and she just took off to straighten out her head."

"Did she go back home to her mama and daddy?" Mary Lou asks.

Judy shakes her head no, and her hair flies around like a dust mop being shaken. Mary Lou almost expects things to fly out. Judy's hair is curly and flyaway. She has put something on it. Judy is wearing a seashell on a chain around her neck.

"This pizza's cold," says Judy. She won't touch the green beans.

Mack says, "I don't see why she won't stay and finish her tests at least. Now she'll have to pay for a whole extra semester."

"Well, I hope she don't go off the deep end like her mama," says Mary Lou. Judy once told them that Stephanie's mother had had several nervous breakdowns.

"Her daddy don't eat meat a-tall?" asks Mack.

"No. He's a vegetarian."

"And he don't get sick?"

Judy shakes her head again.

After supper, Judy dumps out the contents of her tote bag on the love seat. She has a math book, a science book, something called *A Rhetoric for the Eighties*, and a heavy psychology book. She sits cross-legged on the love seat, explaining quantum mechanics to Mary Lou and Mack. She calls her teacher Bob.

Judy says, "It's not that weird. It's just the study of elementary particles—the littlest things in the world, smaller than atoms. There's some things called photons that disappear if you look for them. Nobody can find them."

"How do they know they're there, then?" asks Mack skeptically.

"Where do they go?" Mary Lou asks.

The seashell bounces between Judy's breasts as she talks excitedly, moving her arms like a cheerleader. She is wearing a plaid flannel shirt with the cuffs rolled back. She says, "If you try to separate them, they disappear. They don't even *exist* except in a group. Bob says this is one of the most *important* discoveries in the history of the world. He says it just *explodes* all the old ideas about physics."

Bob is not the same teacher Stephanie had the crush on. That teacher's name is Tom. Mary Lou has this much straight. Mack is pacing the floor, the way he does sometimes when Judy doesn't come home on the weekend.

"I thought it was philosophy you were taking," he says.

"No, physics."

"Mack's been reading up on philosophy," says Mary Lou. "He thought you were taking philosophy."

"It's similar," Judy says. "In quantum mechanics, there's no final answer. Anything you look at might have a dozen different meanings. Bob says the new physics is discovering what the Eastern mystics have known all along."

Mary Lou is confused. "If these things don't exist, then how do they know about them?"

"They know about them when they're in bunches." Judy begins writing in her notebook. She looks up and says, "Quantum mechanics is like a statistical study of group behavior."

Abruptly, Mack goes to the basement. Mary Lou picks up her sewing and begins watching *Real People* on TV. She can hear the signs of her husband's existence: the sound of the drill from the shop, then his saw. A spurt of swearing.

The next evening, Judy talks Mary Lou into going to a movie, but Mack says he has work to do. He is busy with the home entertainment center he is building for Judy. Mary Lou is embarrassed to be going to an R-rated movie, but Judy laughs at her. Judy drives her Chevette, and they stop to pick up Clausie, whom Mary Lou has invited.

"Clausie changes with the times," Mary Lou tells her daughter apologetically. "You ought to see the way she gets out and goes. She even square-dances."

Clausie insists on climbing in the back seat because she is small. "I wore pants 'cause I knew y'all would," she says. "I don't wear them when I come to your house, Mary Lou, because I just don't feel right wearing pants around a man."

"I haven't worn a dress since 1980," says Judy.

"This show is going to curl our ears," Mary Lou tells Clausie.

"Oh, Mom," Judy says.

"Is it a dirty movie?" Clausie asks eagerly.

"It's R-rated," says Mary Lou.

"Well, I say live and learn," says Clausie, laughing. "Thelma and Edda would have a fit if they knew what we was up to."

"Mack wouldn't go," says Mary Lou. "He doesn't like to be in the middle of a bunch of women—especially if they're going to say dirty-birds."

"Everybody says those words," says Judy. "They don't mean anything."

The movie is *Stir Crazy*. Mary Lou has to hold her side, she laughs so hard. When the actors cuss, she sinks in her seat, clutching Judy's arm. Judy doesn't even flinch. As she watches the movie, which drags in places, Mary Lou now and then thinks about how her family has scattered. If you break up a group, the individuals could disappear out of existence. She has the unsettling thought that what is happening with Mack is that he is disappearing like that, disconnected from everybody, the way Ed did. On the screen, Gene Wilder is on a mechanical bull, spinning around and around, raising his arm in triumph.

Later, after they drop off Clausie and are driving home, Judy turns on the car radio. Mary Lou is still chuckling over the movie, but Judy seems depressed. She has hardly mentioned her roommate, so Mary Lou asks, "Where'd Stephanie go then, if she didn't go home?"

Judy turns the radio down. "She went to her sister's, in Nashville. Her brother-in-law's a record promoter and they've got this big place with a swimming pool and horses and stuff."

"Well, maybe she can make up with her boyfriend when she cools off."

"I don't think so." Judy turns right at the high school and heads down the highway. She says, "She wants to break up with him, but he won't leave her alone, so she just took off."

Mary Lou sighs. "This day and time, people just do what they please. They just hit the road. Like those guys in the show. And like Ed."

"Stephanie's afraid of Jeff, though, afraid of what he might do."

"What?"

"Oh, I don't know. Just something crazy." Judy turns up the volume of the radio, saying, "Here's a song for you, Mom. It's a dirty song. 'The Horizontal Bop'—get it?"

Mary Lou listens for a moment. "I don't get it," she says, fearing something as abstruse as the photons. In the song, the singer says repeatedly, "Everybody wants to do the Horizontal Bop."

"Oh, I get it," Mary Lou says with a sudden laugh. "I don't dare tell my Rookers about that." A moment later, she says, "But they wouldn't get it. It's the word 'bop.' They probably never heard the word 'bop.' "

Mary Lou feels a little pleased with herself. Bop. Bebop. She's not so old. Her daughter is not so far away. For a brief moment, Mary Lou feels that rush of joy that children experience when they whirl around happily, unconscious of time.

When Mary Lou's friends come to play Rook the following evening, they are curious about Judy's roommate, but Judy won't divulge much. She is curled on the love seat, studying math. Mary Lou explains to the Rookers, "Stephanie comes from a kind of disturbed family. Her mother's had a bunch of nervous breakdowns and her daddy's a vegetarian." Mack has the TV too loud, and it almost seems that the Incredible Hulk is in on the card game. Mary Lou gets Mack to turn down the sound. Later, he turns the TV off and picks up Judy's physics book. As the game goes on, he periodically goes to the telephone and dials the time-and-temperature number. The temperature is dropping, he reports. It is already down to twenty-four. He is hoping for snow, but the Rookers worry about the weather, fearful of driving back in the freezing night air.

When Clausie tells about *Stir Crazy*, Mary Lou tries to describe the scene that cracked her up—Richard Pryor and Gene Wilder dressed up in elaborate feathered costumes. They were supposed to be woodpeckers.

Clausie says, "*I* liked to died when the jailer woke 'em up in the morning, and they was both of 'em trying to use the commode at the same time."

The Rookers keep getting mixed up, missing plays. Thelma plays the wrong color.

"What did you do that for?" asks Edda, her partner tonight. "Trumps is green."

Thelma says, "I'm so bumfuzzled I can't think. I don't know when I've ever listened to such foolishness. Peckerwoods and niggers and a dirty show."

Mary Lou has been thinking of commenting on a new disease she has heard of, in which a person is afflicted by uncontrollable twitching and compulsive swearing, but she realizes that's a bad idea. She jumps up, saying, "Let's stop for refreshments, y'all. I made coconut cake with seven-minute icing."

Mary Lou serves the cake on her good plates, and everyone comments on how moist it is. After finishing her cake and iced tea, Thelma suddenly insists on leaving because of the weather. She says her feet are cold. Mary Lou offers to turn up the heat, but Thelma already has her coat on. She whips out her flashlight and heads for the door. Thelma's Buick sounds like a cement mixer. As they hear it backing out of the driveway, Clausie says, in a confidential tone, "She's mad because we saw that dirty show. The weather, my eye."

"She's real religious," says Edda.

"Well, golly-Bill, I'm as Christian as the next one!" cries Mary Lou. "Them words don't mean anything against religion. I bet Mack just got her stirred up about the temperature."

"Thelma's real old-timey," says Clausie. "She don't have any idea some of the things kids do nowadays."

"Times has changed, that's for sure," says Mary Lou.

Edda says, "Otis spoiled her. He carried her around on a pillow."

Mary Lou takes Mack some cake on a paper plate. He is still reading the physics book.

"We went set," Mary Lou says. "I had the Rook last hand, but it didn't do me any good."

"Thelma fixed your little red wagon, didn't she?" Mack says with a satisfied grin.

"It was your fault, getting her all worked up about the cold. Why don't you play with us—and take Thelma's place?"

"I'm busy studying. I think I've found a mistake in this book." He takes a large bite of cake. "Your coconut is my favorite," he says.

"I'll give you my recipe," Mary Lou snaps, wheeling away.

To Mary Lou's surprise, Judy offers to take Thelma's place and finish the card game. Mary Lou apologizes to her daughter for taking her away from her books, but Judy says she needs a break. Judy wins several hands, trumping with a flourish and grabbing the cards gleefully. Mary Lou is relieved. After Clausie and Edda leave, she feels excited and talkative. She finds herself telling Judy more about Ed, trying to make Judy remember her uncle. Mary Lou finds a box of photographs and shows Judy a picture of him. In the snapshot, he is standing in front of his tractor-trailer truck, holding a can of Hudepohl.

Mary Lou says, "He used to drive these long hauls, and when he'd come back through here, the police would try and pick him up. They heard he had money."

Mack joins Judy on the love seat. He shuffles silently through the pictures, and Mary Lou talks rapidly. "They'd follow him around, just waiting for him to cross that line, to start something. One time he and his first wife, Pauline, went to the show and when they got out they stuck him with a parking ticket. All because he had a record."

Judy and Mack are looking at the pictures together. Mack is studying a picture of himself with Judy, a bald-headed baby clutching a rattle.

"How did he get a record?" asks Judy.

"Wrecks."

"D.W.I.?" asks Judy knowingly. "Driving while intoxicated?"

Mary Lou nods. "Wrecks. A man got killed in one."

"Did they charge him?" Judy asks with sudden eagerness.

"No. It wasn't his fault," Mary Lou says quickly.

"You take after Ed," Mack tells Judy. "You kind of favor him around the eyes."

"He said he was a beanpole," says Mary Lou. "He said he had to bend over to make a shadow. He never had a ounce of fat on his bones."

Judy looks closely at her uncle's picture again, as though trying to memorize it for an exam.

"Wow," she says. "Far out."

Mack, shuffling some of the snapshots into a ragged stack, says to Judy in a plaintive tone, "Your mother wants to leave us and go out to California."

"I never said that," says Mary Lou. "When did I say that?"

Judy is not listening. She is in the kitchen, searching the refrigerator. "Don't we have any Cokes?" she asks.

"No. We drunk the last one at supper," says Mary Lou, confused.

Judy puts on her jacket. "I'll run out and get some."

"It's freezing out there," says Mack anxiously.

"They're high at the Convenient," Mary Lou calls as Judy goes out the door. "But I guess that's the only place open this late."

Mary Lou sees Mack looking at her as though he is blaming her for Judy's leaving. "What are you looking at me in that tone of voice for?" she demands. "You're always making fun of me. I feel like an old stringling cat."

"Why, I didn't mean to," says Mack, pretending innocence.

"She's gone. Furthermore, she's *grown* and she can go out in the middle of the night if she wants to. She can go to South *America* if she wants to."

Mary Lou puts the cover on the cake stand and runs water in the sink over the cake plates. Before she can say more, Mack has lifted the telephone and is dialing the time-and-temperature number again. He listens, while his mouth drops open, as if in disbelief.

"The temperature's going down a degree every hour," he says in a whisper. "It's down to twenty-one."

Mary Lou suddenly realizes that Mack calls the temperature number because he is afraid to talk on the telephone, and by listening to a recording, he doesn't have to reply. It's his way of pretending that he's involved. He wants it to snow so he won't have to go outside. He is afraid of what might happen. But it occurs to her that what he must really be afraid of is women. Then Mary Lou feels so sick and heavy with her power over him that she wants to cry. She sees the way her husband is standing there, in a frozen pose. Mack looks as though he could stand there all night with the telephone receiver against his ear.

·10·

The Music of Failure: Variations on an Idea

Bill Holm

Prelude, the Theme for the Variations

The ground bass is failure; America is the key signature; Pauline Bardal is the lyrical tune that sings at the center; Minneota, Minnesota is the staff on which the tunes are written; poverty, loneliness, alcoholism, greed, disease, insanity, war, and spiritual and political emptiness are the tempo markings; Walt Whitman and this sentence from the *Bhagavad-Gita* are the directions for expression:

> *Die, and you win heaven. Conquer, and you enjoy the earth. Stand up now . . . and resolve to fight. Realize that pleasure and pain, gain and loss, victory and defeat, are all one and the same: then go into battle. Do this and you cannot commit any sin.*

This true subject, the melody that counterpoints everything but is never heard, like Elgar's secret theme for the *"Enigma Variations,"* is my own life, and yours, and how they flow together to make the life of a community, and then a country, and then a world.

Another idea from Walt Whitman that no one wants to hear.

At fifteen, I could define failure fast: to die in Minneota, Minnesota. Substitute any small town in Pennsylvania, or Nebraska, or Bulgaria, and the definition held. To be an American meant to move, rise out of a mean life, make yourself new. Hadn't my own grandfathers transcended Iceland, learned at least some English, and died with a quarter section free and clear? No, I would die a famous author, a distinguished and respected professor at an old university, surrounded by beautiful women, witty talk, fine whiskey, Mozart. There were times, at fifteen, when I would have settled for central heat and less Jello, but I kept my mental eye on the "big picture."

Later, teaching Walt Whitman in school, I noticed that my students did not respond with fervor to the lines,

> *With music strong I come, with my cornets and my drums,*
> *I play not marches for accepted victors only, I play marches for*
>   *conquer'd and slain persons.*
>
> *Have you heard that it was good to gain the day?*
> *I also say it is good to fall, battles are lost in the same spirit in which*
>   *they are won.*
>
> *I beat and pound for the dead,*
> *I blow through my embouchures my loudest and gayest for them.*
>
> *Vivas to those who have fail'd!*
> *And to those war-vessels sunk in the sea!*
> *And to those themselves who sank in the sea!*
> *And to all generals that lost engagements, and all overcome heroes!*
> *And to the numberless unknown heroes equal to the greatest heroes*
>   *known!*

I left Minneota at the beginning of America's only lost war. While I traveled, got educated, married, divorced, and worldly, the national process of losing went on: a president or two shot, an economy collapsed, a man whom every mother in America warned every child against accepting rides or candy from, was in the flesh overwhelmingly elected president, and then drummed into luxurious disgrace for doing the very things those mothers warned against. The water underneath America turned out to be poisoned. Cities like Denver, Los Angeles, Chicago were invisible under air that necessitated warning notices in the newspaper. A rumor flourished that the Arabs bought the entire Crazy Mountains in Montana. Oil gurgled onto gulls' backs north of San Francisco. The war finally ended in disgrace, the Secretary of State mired as deep in lies as Iago. America, the realized dream of the eighteenth century European Enlightenment, seemed to have sunk into playing out a Shakespearean tragedy, or perhaps a black comedy.

Yet as history brought us failure, it brought us no wisdom. The country wanted as little as my students to hear those lines from *Leaves of Grass*. It was not "good to fall," not good to be "sunk in the sea," not good to be among the "numberless unknown heroes." We elected, in fact, a famous actor to whom failure was incomprehensible as history itself, a man who responded to visible failure around him by ignoring it and cracking hollow jokes.

In the meantime, I aged from twenty to forty, found myself for all practical purposes a failure, and settled almost contentedly back into the same rural town which I tried so fiercely to escape. I could not help noticing that personal and professional failure were not my private bailiwick. I knew almost no one still on their first marriage, friends, too, were short of money and doing work that at twenty they would have thought demeaning or tedious, children were not such an unpremeditated joy as maiden aunts led us to expect, and for the precocious middle aged, health and physical beauty had begun to fail. It looked, as the old cliché had it, as if we were going to die after all, and the procedure would not be quite so character-building as the *Reader's Digest* and the Lutheran minister implied.

Heard from inside, the music of failure sounded not the loudest, gayest marches for cornets and drums, but a melancholy cello, strings slowly loosening, melody growing flaccid, receding toward silence. The country closed its ears against the tune; citizens denied that they had ever heard it. "Tomorrow," they said, but this was only another way of saying "yesterday," which did not exist quite as they imagined it. This continual denial gave a hollow, whining quality to conversations. Discussions of politics, work, or marriage sounded like a buzzsaw speaking English.

The first settlers of America imagined paradise, God's city made visible on earth. Grand rhetoric for a pregnancy, it was, like all births, bloodier and messier than anyone imagined at the moment of conception. English Puritans who came to build a just and godly order began by trying to exterminate Indian tribes. They tried to revise the English class system of rich landowners and poor yeomen by sharing a common bounty, but this lasted only until somebody realized that true profit lay in landowning, here as in England. The same settlers who declared with

Proudhon that "property is theft" wound up working as real estate agents. Old European habits of success died hard.

Hypocrisy is not unusual in human history; it is the order of the day. What has always been unusual in the United States is the high-toned rhetoric that accompanied our behavior, our fine honing of the art of sweeping contradictions under the rug with our eternal blank optimism. But if we examined, without sentimentality, the failures and contradictions of our own history, it would damage beyond repair the power of that public rhetoric, would remove the arch-brick from the structure of the false self we have built for ourselves, in Minneota as elsewhere.

I labored under the weight of that rhetoric as a boy, and when I am tired now, I labor under it still. It is the language of football, a successful high school life, earnest striving and deliberate ignoring, money, false cheerfulness, mumbling about weather. Its music is composed by the radio, commercials for helpful banks and deodorants breathing out at you between stanzas. In cities now, ghetto blasters play it at you in the street; you are serenaded by tiny orchestras hidden in elevators or in rafters above discount stores. It is the music of tomorrow and tomorrow and tomorrow. It is not what Whitman had in mind by beating and pounding for the dead. True dead, unlike false dead, hear what we sing to them. . . .

Pauline Bardal at the piano.

I first heard a piano in the backroom of Peterson's farmhouse, three miles east of my father's place. An only child, too young and disinterested to do any real work, I was left indoors while my father was out giving Wilbur a hand with some chore, probably splitting a half-pint to make the job more pleasant. Wilbur was a bachelor, but kept his aged father, Steve, and a sort of combination housekeeper and nurse, Pauline Bardal, to look after both of them. Pauline was born in 1895 to the first generation of Icelandic immigrants in western Minnesota. When I knew her in the late 40's or early 50's, she must have been nearing 60. Age is relative to children, so I did not think of her as being particularly old. She was simply Pauline, and would remain that way until she died 30 years later.

She was almost six feet tall, without a bit of fat on her, and this made her bones visible, particularly in the hands, joints moving with large gestures as if each finger had reasoning power of its own. Her leanness was partly genetic, but partly also the result of continual work. In the cities she would have been called a domestic, though her duties at Peterson's and elsewhere always involved nursing the infirm and dying. In Minneota's more informal class labeling, she was simply Pauline.

After finishing her duties with bread, chickens, or tending to old Steve, Pauline retired to the den for a half hour of music. I was invited to listen and always delighted by the prospect. She sat herself on the bench, arranging her bones with great dignity and formality. Music was not a trifling matter even if your hands were fresh from flour bin or hen house. Pauline did not play light music; though she was conventionally religious in a Lutheran sort of way, I knew, even as a child, that music was her true spiritual exercise. She always played slowly, and I suppose, badly, but it made no difference. She transported both herself and me by the simple act of playing. Her favorite pieces were Handel's "Largo" from *Xerxes*, and a piano arrangement of the finale of Bach's *St. Matthew Passion*: "In Deepest Grief." She had never learned true fingering, and got most of her musical experience at an old pump organ that she played for church services. She did not so much strike the keys as slide with painstaking slowness from one to the next, leaving sufficient time for the manual rearrangement of the bones in her hands. This gave all her performances a certain halting dignity, even if sometimes questionable accuracy. It was always said around Minneota that her most moving performances were at funerals, where enormously slow tempos seemed appropriate. She played the sad Bach as a postlude while mourners filed past the open coffin for the last time.

But Pauline at the keyboard was not a lugubrious spirit. Watching that joy on her bony face as her fingers slid over the yellowed keyboard of the old upright, it became clear to me even as a child that neither her nor my true life came from kneading bread or candling eggs or fluffing pillows in a sick bed, but happened in the presence of those noises, badly as they might be made by your own hands. They lived in the inner lines of that Bach, so difficult to manage cleanly with work-stiffened fingers. You felt Bach's grandeur moving under you at whatever speed. The Handel "Largo," though it has become something of a joke for sophisticated listeners through its endless bad piano transcriptions is, in fact, a glorious piece, one of the great gifts from Europe. Even on farms in rural Minnesota, you deserve the extraordinary joy of hearing it for the first time, as if composed in your presence, only for you. I heard it that way, under Pauline's hands. The Minneapolis Symphony playing Beethoven's

Ninth in the living room could not have been so moving or wonderful as that "Largo" in Peterson's back room.

Pauline, in American terms, was a great failure: always poor, never married, living in a shabby small house when not installed in others' backrooms, worked as a domestic servant, formally uneducated, English spoken with the odd inflections of those who learn it as a second language, gawky and not physically beautiful, a badly trained musician whose performances would have caused laughter in the cities. She owned nothing valuable, traveled little, and died alone, the last of her family. If there were love affairs, no one will now know anything about them, and everyone involved is surely dead. Probably she died a virgin, the second most terrible fate, after dying broke, that can befall an American.

But, as the scripture bids, "Let us now praise famous men," and I mean to praise not merely Pauline, but her whole failed family, and through them the music of failure in America.

The history of a failed immigrant.

Minneota is a community born out of failure about 1880. By that I mean that no one ever arrived in Minneota after being a success elsewhere. It is an immigrant town, settled by European refuse, first those starved out of Ireland, then Norway, Iceland, Sweden, Holland, Belgium. Given the harshness of western Minnesota's climate and landscape, people did not come to retire or loaf. They came to farm, and had they been successful at it in the old world, would not have uprooted their families, thrown away culture and language, and braved mosquitos and blizzards for mere pleasure. Minneota is, of course, a paradigm for the settling of the whole country. We are a nation of failures who have done all right and been lucky. Perhaps it is some ancient dark fear of repeating our own grandfathers' lives that makes us reluctant to acknowledge failure in national or private life.

Pauline's father, Frithgeir, came in 1880 in the third wave of nationalities to Minneota: the Icelanders. He likely read one of the pamphlets circulated by the American government in all Scandinavian countries, describing free and fertile land available on the Great Plains for farmers of sturdy, sufficiently Caucasian stock. The United States was always particular about the race of its failures. The pamphlet probably mentioned glowingly the bountiful harvests, rich topsoil, good drainage and pasturage, cheap rail transport, and healthful bracing climate. Frithgeir Joakimsson, who took his new last name, Bardal, from his home valley in north Iceland, arrived in 1880, found most of the best land gone, and picked perhaps the hilliest, stoniest, barest though loveliest farm acreage in that part of western Minnesota.

He was 37 years old, single, and, in all likelihood, knew not a word of English when he came. Pauline, when she was old, disposed of her family's books to good homes, and gave me her father's first English grammar and phrase book that she said he used on the boat. It was in Danish, English, and Icelandic, well-worn though intact. Pauline clearly treasured it. Leafing through it now, I imagine rough farmer's hands, something like Pauline's, holding the book on an open deck in mid-Atlantic, sea wind rustling the pages under his thumb—*"Hvar er vegurinn vestur till Minneota?"*

For the first five years, Frithgeir farmed alone. Probably he raised sheep and hay, the only things an Icelandic farmer knew. In 1886, at age 43, he married Guthlaug Jonsdottir, a new immigrant whose family came from the wildest, most remote fjord in east Iceland, Borgarfjord, ringed with blood-red liparite mountains and precipitous scree slopes. Already 35 then, she was pregnant five times between 1887 and 1895 when Pauline, the last daughter, was born. One son, Pall, died an infant in 1889. Four out of five children alive was a lucky percentage then. But Frithgeir's luck did not hold for long in the new world. I give his obituary in its entirety, as I found it on a yellow, brittle page of the *Minneota Mascot* for Friday, September 8, 1899:

> *Last Saturday, while F.J. Bardal was mowing hay on his farm in Lincoln Co., the horses made a sudden start, jerking the mower which happened at that time to be on the slope of a hill, so that Mr. Bardal fell from his machine. His leg was caught in a wheel and he was dragged that way for a while until the horses stopped. The leg was broken above the knee and other injuries were sustained. Mr. Bardal managed to get on the mower and drive home. Dr. Thordason was sent for. He hurried out, set the bone and did all that could be done for the unfortunate man. But the injuries proved to be so serious that Mr. Bardal died last Monday morning. The funeral took place last Wednesday from the new Icelandic church in Lincoln County, Rev. B.B. Jonsson officiating.*

F. Bardal was born January 13, 1843 in Bardardal
Thingeyarsysla, Iceland and came to this country in 1880 and settled
on his farm in Lincoln County. He leaves a wife, three children and a
stepdaughter.
   Mr. Bardal was a much liked man in the community, an active
member in his church, and a general favorite among his neighbors.

Done in by his own farm. He had found the only lovely hills in a flat country, but they killed him; his widow (who knew at best minimal English) was left with four children between 9 and 12 years old, and the poorest farm in the county. Nineteen years in the new world.

The further history of three children, all failed.

Perhaps a few genealogical books in Icelandic libraries, or some distant relatives might provide a bit more history of the Bardals, but not much . . . and this is after a single century in the most information-rich country on earth! It is amazing to me sometimes how little basis we have as humans on which to remember Pericles, Augustine, Charlemagne, or for that matter, Abraham Lincoln.

Four children reached adulthood. One married and left Minneota. Guthlaug, the widow, remained on the farm till she lost it in 1937, another victim of the Great Depression. She was then a very old lady and, as local report had it, not entirely in her right mind. She died in 1943, bedridden in her little house, 92 years old, 57 years in America.

There were three Bardals left when I was a boy: Gunnar, the oldest brother, gaunt, melancholy, silent; Rose, the middle sister, not quite right in the head, with a sideways cast to her eye, as if she saw the world from a different angle than normal people, mouth half smiling, but the unsmiling half colored by something dark and unknown; finally, Pauline, their custodian, housekeeper, surrogate mother and father. The three trooped every Sunday morning to the old wood frame Icelandic church a block from their small house, and ascended the creaky choir loft stairs. Pauline played for services every other Sunday, and sang when she did not play.

The choir at St. Paul's Lutheran consisted of perhaps ten to fifteen elderly Icelandic ladies, mostly unmarried and immensely dignified. They formed the foundation of singing. Only three men joined them:

Gunnar, a thin cavernous bass, another equally thin but raspier baritone, and me, a small fat boy of 11 or 12 who sang soprano or tenor, depending on his semi-changed voice. I was generally the single member of St. Paul's choir under seventy.

I sat by Gunnar who seemed always contemplating some indefinable sadness about which nothing could be done. His voice sounded octaves below everyday life, as if it came from a well bottom. He wore a brown, itchy, wool suit, decades out of style.

Crazy Rose sat close to Pauline. After Rose's death, when I was a teenager, I heard stories of her madness, her religious mania, wandering off to preach in Icelandic in the cornfields, but as a little boy, she seemed only Rose to me, and within the range of possible normality for adults. Children judge each other harshly, but don't make nice distinctions among the grown. Sane or mad, pillar or rake, drunk or sober, adults seem merely themselves, distinguished more by age than by variations of habit, character or physiognomy.

Rose looked like a bird ordered to continue eating despite an interesting ruckus going on in the next nest. She pecked toward the floor a few times, not paying much attention to the kernels at her feet, then raised her beak to glance furtively around, the half smile breaking on her lips, as if what she saw was almost funny. Her face was small and thin, eyes pale and watery, almost without irises.

Rose died in 1956, in her sixties, of an embolism. Whatever was frail in the architecture of her cerebral arteries collapsed at last. Gunnar died in 1961 at 74. I sang at both their funerals, and though I have no recollection of what the hymns might have been, they were surely sad and heavy-footed, perhaps *"Come Ye Disconsolate"* or the Icelandic hymn *"Just as the Flower Withers,"* or *"Abide With Me."* Hymn singing seemed one kind of preparation for the last great mysterious failure—the funeral, when the saddest and noblest of church tunes could be done with their proper gravity.

Pauline, now alone in her little house with all the family bric-a-brac piled around her, had no one to attend to, and a social security check to keep her from having to attend others for money. Yet her habits were too strong, and having worked for 50 or 60 years, she could not stop. Now she dispensed munificence like a queen. She cared for the dying and the horribly ill with no fuss, as if she were born to it. She was a one-woman hospice movement.

She once fried steaks in a farmers' night club out in the country, an odd job for a teetotaler, and for this she was probably paid a pittance. My mother tended the bar, and the two of them often drove out together. I saw them at work once; in the middle of loud country music and boisterous drinking, they tended these rough farmers, not like hired help, but like indulgent great aunts looking benevolently after children having a good time. Pauline owned an old Ford which she drove with enthusiasm. Well into her eighties she took friends on vacation and shopping trips, and made lunch runs for the senior citizens. Speaking of people sometimes 10 or 20 years her junior, she said, "They're getting old, you know, and it's hard for them to get around." Pauline's gifts to me included not only music. She tended both my parents at their death beds, and when my mother, a week before she died, lost her second language, English, and spoke to me only in her first, Icelandic, which I did not understand, Pauline translated. The gifts of the unschooled are often those we did not know we would need—the right words, the right music.

Eternal though she seemed to me, age caught her. The end began with the trembling hands of Parkinson's disease, a cruel irony for a woman who took her delight in playing music, however badly. After Gunnar and Rose died, she had a bit more money, and made room in the old house by turning the spare bedrooms into storerooms. She bought a used church organ, a monster from the 40's that crowded her tiny living room with speakers, pedal boards, and a gigantic brown console. The organ seemed larger and heavier than the house itself, as if even a tornado couldn't have budged it off the worn carpet. I once asked what she was playing; she looked at me sadly: "See these hands, how shaky? I can't even keep them on the keys anymore. They just shake off . . ." Soon after this she went into the nursing home, and died not long after, still peeved with the universe, I think, for taking music away from her at the end. I don't even know who was there to tend her bedside at the last. Probably she had had enough of that, and wanted to be alone. Indeed, the solitariness of her whole life prepared her for it. This was 1981, 101 years after her father left Thingeyarsysla for a new life. She had lived in America 86 years.

Music for an old pump organ.

Pauline was buried among the Bardals in the graveyard next to the Icelandic country church in Lincoln County. In 1922, Pauline picked out the congregation's new reed organ, and played it for services there for almost 40 years, until the church, a victim of rural urbanization and of Icelanders who refused to reproduce or stay on the farm, closed its doors for lack of business. While a few miles to the west, the Poles sensibly planted their Catholic Church in a hollow protected from the wind, the Icelanders defied Minnesota by building on a rise in the only ridge of hills on that flat prairie. On even a calm day at that wind-swept knoll, the church windows rattled, shingles flapped, and the black granite gravestones seemed to wobble.

Pauline and I drove out to that church a few years before her death. She carried a shopping bag full of flowers and rat poison. She had a key for the back door of the church and we went up through the minister's dressing room into the sanctuary. The room, carpentered in good oak, was furnished only with chairs, pews, organ, pulpit, and the simple altar crowned by a wood cross; no statues, paintings, bric-a-brac—nothing but that wood, goldened by afternoon light from the pale yellow windows. Wind seemed to come up from inside the church, whooshing over the fine dust that covered everything. "Nobody's cleaned it since last year. It's a shame," Pauline muttered, then went to work. First, she arranged her long legs on the organ bench, carefully folding them between two wooden knee guards below the keyboard. Thus constricted, she pumped, and while checking the stops with one hand, slid over the keys with the other, playing the chords from Handel's "Largo." "The mice have not eaten the bellows," she announced with satisfaction, then launched into an old hymn with both hands. We played for each other for a while, Pauline marveling at my clean fingering. She knew, I think, that she had some responsibility for my love of playing, and was proud of herself, and of me, but it was not the sort of thing Icelanders discussed openly with each other. Skill could be remarked on, but the heart was private, and disliked language.

When we finished, she swept up the old poison in a newspaper, opened her yellow skull-and-crossboned boxes, and laid down a fresh lunch for any rodents who might presume to make a meal of God's own organ bellows. Even though the church would never likely be opened, nor the organ publicly played there again, such things ought to be attended to for their own sake. Who knew? Perhaps the dead a few feet away liked an occasional sad tune, and didn't fancy the idea of rats interfering with their music?

Pauline locked the church carefully, looking back at it with a sort of melancholy nostalgia. She proceeded to the graveyard with the rest of the contents of her shopping bag, and there performed her next errand. She swept off the graves, then put a flower or two on all of them. The row read:

Pall	Fridgeir	Gudlaug
7/25–8/2 '89	1843–1899	1851–1943
Rose		Gunnar
1890–1956		1887–1961

"And I will be between Rose and Gunnar," she said, "in not too long."

Indeed, within a few years the row was full; six dead in the graveyard of a dead church, no progeny, no empire following them, only the dry wind of a new world which promised them and all of us so much.

Pack rat houses, and what they tell.

The opening of the Bardal house was not greeted with amazement and that is, in itself, amazing. Traditionally in Minneota, as in villages all across the world, pack rats, generally unmarried, die in houses stuffed to the ceiling with moldy newspapers, rusted coffee cans full of money, and an over-population of bored cats.

The first astonishing fact about the house was the sheer amount inside it. Though tiny, it held the combined goods for a family of six who threw nothing away. It was neither dirty, nor disorderly. The piles had been dusted, and the narrow crevices between them vacuumed and scrubbed, but within some mounds, nothing had moved for 40 years. Papers were stacked neatly in order, probably put there the week they arrived, from 1937 onward. The Bardals were schooled historically and genetically by a thousand years of Icelandic poverty of the meanest, most abject variety. They moved to a poor farm in the poorest county of Minnesota, and when the Depression reduced penury to catastrophe, moved into a poor, small house in Minneota. While their storage space shrank, their goods expanded, and the double beds became single beds after the floor space filled up to the bedsprings. They were a family on whom nothing was lost, not even the useless doo-dads that arrived from answering every "free special offer" ad for over a half century.

They accumulated no cans full of bank notes, no hidden treasure, nothing of any genuine monetary value; the Bardals were, in that regard truly poor. But not poor in mind and spirit! They owned books in three or four languages: Plato, Homer, Bjornsson in Norwegian, Snorri Sturlasson in Icelandic, Whitman, Darwin, Dickens, Ingersoll, Elbert Hubbard, piles of scores by Handel, Bach, Mozart, George Beverly Shea and Bjorgvin Gudmundsson, old cylinders of Caruso, Galla-Curci, Schumann-Heink, John McCormack, cheap books reproducing paintings and sculpture from great European museums, organ, piano, violin, trumpet, manuals for gardening, cooking and home remedies, the best magazines of political commentary and art criticism next to *Capper's Farmer*, the *Minneota Mascot*, and the *Plain Truth*, dictionaries and grammars in three or four languages, books of scientific marvels, Richard Burton's travel adventures, old text books for speech and mathematics, Bibles and hymn books in every Scandinavian language, *Faust*, *The Reader's Digest*, and "*Sweet Hour of Prayer.*" That tiny house was a space ship stocked to leave the planet after collecting the best we have done for each other for the last 4,000 years of human consciousness. And none of it worth ten cents in the real world of free enterprise! The executors might as well have torched the house, thus saving the labor of sorting it, giving mementos to friends and peddling the rest at a garage sale on a sweltering summer afternoon. What one realized with genuine astonishment was that the Bardals piled this extraordinary junk not only inside their cramped house; that house was a metaphor for their interior life which they stocked with the greatest beauty and intelligence they understood. They read the books, played the instruments, carried the contents of that house in their heads, and took it off with them at last into their neat row in the Lincoln County graveyard.

But not entirely. . . . Anyone who carries a whole civilization around inside gives it to everyone they meet in conversations and public acts. Pauline gave me music; Gunnar, the model of a man who read and thought; literally, he gave me a first edition of Arthur Waley, Epictetus and the *Heimskringla*; and Rose, in her odd way, her crazed longing for God. Not one of them had so much as a high school diploma. They gave what teachers hired for it so often fail to give. . . .

A coda: the still small voice of Minneota.

This has been a long incoherent journey toward this idea. The reader must perhaps exercise "good will" and remember that the whole culture, perhaps the whole weight of western civilization, is against it. The

English language even denies it, as one tries to bulldoze a word from one definition to another. And yet, I know it's true. What proof have I offered? The life of Pauline Bardal and her family, a poor tiny country on the edge of the arctic, a half dozen books, experience, some music, finally only a feeling . . . not much. Yet in every artery in my body, and in yours too, that music of failure plays—continually. It sounds like Bach to me, and you must make up your mind what it sounds like to you.

Should you not hear it where you are now, let me remind you that it plays in Minneota, Minnesota daily, under the water tower, or deep inside the grain elevator bins. You do not need the price of a bus ticket to arrive here, since it is where you are now, wherever that is. You must simply decide to be here, and then you will be.

Always remember, though, that it is a real place in both senses of that word, though not much of a place in American terms. It will never make it on television, though it has ground, water, sky, weather, all the ingredients of placeness. It has pianos, clarinets, and songs too, though it wants violins, and the wind that blows over it comes from Prague and Nairobi and Auckland and brings part of them to live in it. Its humans are often tedious, but sometimes astonishing, here as elsewhere, and the endless weather talk once had a piece of poetry under it. The Bardals lived here, still do in a way, under stones with their names, but in air, too, that comes into the house when you take off the storm windows in spring. I live here now, and plan to always, wherever I am.

Whatever failure is, Minneota is not it. Nothing can be done about living here. Nor should it be. The heart can be filled up anywhere on earth.

.3.
The Wilderness

Introduction

"THE GREAT FACT WAS THE LAND ITSELF, which seemed to overwhelm the little beginnings of human society that struggled in its sombre wastes," wrote Willa Cather of the Great Divide in *O Pioneers!* "It was from facing this vast hardness that the boy's mouth had become so bitter; because he felt that men were too weak to make any mark here, that the land wanted to be let alone, to preserve its own fierce strength, its peculiar, savage kind of beauty, its uninterrupted mournfulness."

Immigrants to America came, most of them, out of stable, structured, pieced and plotted landscapes with history reaching back one or two millennia, and social orders that stretched to feudal hierarchies. They came to a landscape of nothing. America was an enormous country, rich in beauty and resources, and—once its native inhabitants had been reduced (through all varieties of Christian theology) to a status not higher than that of bison and beaver—it was a wilderness there for the taking. For perhaps the last time in his history, as F. Scott Fitzgerald remarks in closing *The Great Gatsby*, mankind came face to face with something commensurate to his capacity for wonder.

This great American immensity was at once both an opportunity and a threat. To Europeans hungry for land and wealth, the promise of infinite resources of timber and fur for logging and trapping, of 160 acres free for homesteading, of a farm of one's own up York state or in the Carolina hills—these were opportunities never to be expected again, best seized immediately. But who came to the New World mentally prepared for such amplitudes? How could Old World experience prepare one to conceptualize this vast, seemingly endless expanse? How turn a man's mind from wonder to the business of founding a kingdom, a woman's mind from terror to the work of developing a culture? How structure the infinite?

Wilderness has been, for much of America's history, the most prominent feature of its national life. The problems and possibilities of structuring space have obsessed Americans for generations. American writers too have devoted much thought to the idea of wilderness . . . at least American writers of the eighteenth and nineteenth centuries. (Is it mere coincidence, Wallace Stegner wonders, that our national literature turned from hope to bitterness almost precisely at the moment when the frontier closed and a genuine American wilderness experience ceased, for all practical purposes, forever?) As civilization swept east to west across the continent, then back to fill in white spots on the map of the Upper Midwest, some geographies ranged ahead, others behind, in conceptualizing space. Yet it is possible to identify distinct stages in American wilderness thought and writing.

First, of course, is the terror of struggle for survival in the wilderness. Pilgrim diaries resound with this terror as do the adventure stories of explorers, trappers, frontiersmen, and pioneers. In O.E. Rolvaag's classic *Giants in the Earth*, terror drove Beret insane. The captivity narratives popular in late nineteenth-century America belong to the genre of adventure stories drawn from this moment in our national experience with wilderness; so too does James Dickey's *Deliverance* (although the Indians have been replaced by hillbillies). Dickey's narrator finds the wilderness environment a place of "unbelievable violence and brutality," indifferent and inhospitable to human intruders. A single, bedrock goal plants itself firmly in his mind:

"Pure survival," I said.

"This is what it comes to," he said. "I told you."

"Yes, you told me."

At some point, however, the American Unknown becomes relatively known; the Indians and wolves are largely exterminated; food, shelter, sleep and warmth are taken for granted. True, prairie fires still claim lives in ranching areas of the Dakotas and Montana; true, blizzards kill a dozen Minnesotans each year; true, flash floods threaten established settlements in Kentucky and western Pennsylvania—yet, the wilderness is not what it once was, and the major losses are mostly commercial: crops, livestock, property, income. Man's struggle against this newer, tamer Nature becomes a contest not for survival, but for success. The wilderness has yielded life; will it yield riches? If so, what riches at what price? Americans find themselves in a protracted struggle to wring wealth and comfort from the rural environment for minimal labor and loss of soul.

A profound change in perception of the wilderness takes place at this point. Initially, writers like Cather saw only the vastness, a land strange and inhospitable. Wrote Stephen Long of western Nebraska in 1821, "I do not hesitate in giving the opinion, that it is almost wholly unfit for civilization." Of the same land, however, Cather could write in *O Pioneers!* "The Land did it. It had its little joke. It pretended to be poor because nobody knew how to work it right; and then, all at once, it worked itself." Hamlin Garland would write in *A Son of the Middle Border*, the prairie "needed only to be tickled with a hoe to laugh into harvest." Paul Engle would write in *Always the Land*, "Nowhere in the world was there so much nourishment in every acre for so great an area." Suddenly the farmers were wealthy, and the ranch hands become fossil-fuel cowboys, Montana Banana-Belt cowboys—makin' out fine, even if they do seem a little light on character, a little short in the jeans. The new Eskimo leaders plan tribal futures based on the recommendations of San Francisco-based investment consultants.

The third phase of American wilderness experience begins here, at the point when some spirit is perceived as having gone out of the wilderness and thus out of our collective lives. This phase is nostalgia. Late in *O Pioneers!*, after the Divide has been pieced and fenced, Alexandra Bergson's friend Carl Linstrum (the boy with the bitter mouth) returns for a visit. He confides, "I even think I liked the old country better. This is all very splendid in its way, but there was something about this country when it was a wild old beast that has haunted me all these years. Now, when I come back to all this milk and honey, I feel like the old German song, 'Wo bist du, wo bist du, mein geliebtest Land?'—Do you ever feel like that, I wonder?"

Paradoxically, man never admires the more savage aspects of nature until he is comparatively safe from them, and he no sooner builds cities as a haven from wilderness than he begins plotting his escape to the countryside, nostalgic for all the wilderness has to offer: simplicity, isolation, the space in which to grow big and free. The thrill of struggling for success seems so infinitely smaller than that of a struggle for survival; the human combatant has lost soul, Nature has lost spirit. Today, some nostalgic Americans tag yuppie condominium developments "Wolf Creek" or "Eden Prairie." Other Americans set out in search of small fragments of wilderness for seasons of stripping down to essentials, muscle-building, and fronting—as Henry Thoreau put it— only the bare essentials of life. Families move further west, individuals retreat to a farm or purchase a cabin on a lake, vacations are spent not in New York City or Disneyland, but back-packing in the Boundary Waters.

The final phase is militant preservation, even reconstruction. At the least, we attempt to stop by any means necessary further transformation of wilderness into human habitat. We place strong limitations on the use of wilderness. We try to recreate the very prairies we have so recently destroyed. Militant preservationists, for example, would heartily second Ed Abbey's proposed restrictions on wilderness areas: "No more cars in the national parks. Let people walk. Or ride horses, bicycles, mules, wild pigs. . . ." No more damming rivers to create recreational or industrially useful lakes. No more condos on the shores of Lake Superior. If possible, replant prairies, reforest forests. The Bureau of Reclamation, John McPhee tells us, credits David Brower (Friends of the Earth) with singlehandedly preventing construction of two major dams in the Grand Canyon and another on the Green River. Brower claims that all he wants is two percent of the country as wilderness . . . less than is under concrete. He is not fooling around.

Our perception of Nature changes as we move along the arc of this paradigm. Initially Nature is a dangerous, although beautiful, antagonist. This nature Truman Everts saw during his ordeal in Yellowstone, and it is the Nature Fanny Kelley witnessed in her 1872 book, *My Captivity Among the Sioux Indians:*

> *The scenery through which we had passed was wildly grand; it now became serenely beautiful, and to a lover of nature, with a mind free from fear and anxiety, the whole picture would have been a dream of delight.*

Nature may be anthropomorphized, as Rolvaag personified the Great Plains ("The Great Plain Drinks the Blood of Christian Men and Is Satisfied"), as Ann Zwinger personifies the streams of Constant Friendship. Or Nature may be reduced to just another fact of life, to be manipulated as one would any of the other "ins and outs of agribusiness" (Greg Keeler). Nature may be a woman in distress in search of deliverance, although most preservationists do not necessarily view Nature as in distress. Paul Gruchow is fond of warning audiences that "social systems which have not been in harmony with the natural system, which have demanded more of it than it could deliver without undue stress, or that have taken from it more than they returned, have not, historically, survived for any great length of time." Environmentalists warn us that in the long run Nature will prevail. Writing in *Newsweek* (July 24, 1989), Greg Easterbrook pointed out, "The environment is damned near indestructible. It has survived ice ages, bombardments of cosmic radiation, fluctuations of the sun, reversals of the seasons caused by shifts in the planetary axis, collisions of comets and meteors bearing far more force than man's doomsday arsenals and the lightless 'nuclear winters' that followed these impacts. Though mischievous, human assaults are pinpricks compared with forces of the magnitude nature is accustomed to resisting. One aspect of the environment is genuinely delicate, though. Namely, the set of conditions favorable to human beings."

The selections of American writing which follow reflect various views of the wilderness. Some are tales of adventure and survival: man against the forces of nature. Truman Everts' chronicle of thirty-seven days of peril, published first in *Scribner's Magazine* in 1871, is characteristic. Everts confronts an impressive array of natural enemies: cold, exposure, forest fire, hunger, wild animals, even—looming threateningly in the background—Sioux Indians. He admits the essential loveliness of his surroundings, and hopes one day after the park has been opened to what Abbey would call "industrial tourism" to revisit "scenes fraught for me with such thrilling interest." Despite random thoughts on the supernatural (provoked by hallucinations mentioned also by Thoreau) and the requisite thanks to God, Everts' tale is a struggle for survival, as exciting as Jack London's "To Build a Fire" or Stephen Crane's "The Open Boat" or Fred Manfred's remarkable retelling of the Hugh Glass story, *Lord Grizzly*.

Some of the stories which follow recount the day-to-day lives of persons living in what remains of the American wilderness: Sue Hubbell tending her bees in the wilds of Missouri, John Anttonen minding the school in Barrow, Alaska, and Clifford Stelly trapping nutrias and muskrats in the bayous of Louisiana. Their stories contain elements of adventure, but they focus for the most part on economics, on the business of getting on with life at the edge of wilderness. Beauty is understated. Adventure is muted or lost. Philosophy takes a back seat to getting a new universal joint for the pick-up truck or preparing furs for the market. Two of the three have reached what environmentalists would consider a healthy equilibrium between human society and nature, taking about as much as they give, achieving a symbiotic relationship with their environment. Christopher Hallowell invites us to side with Stelly against the animal-lovers who object to leg traps, against the "harvesting" of muskrats and nutrias. The report from Barrow, however, is straight exploitation. ("M-I-L-K them for all they're worth, and screw the rest," I hear Greg Keeler singing. ". . . Have not, historically, survived for any great length of time," I hear Paul Gruchow warning.) Whether Alaskan oil is necessary in the long run or not (David Brower would argue it is not), the work at Barrow is inexorable, wringing wealth from a now somewhat-neutralized wilderness.

The speculative nature journal has a long and variegated tradition in American literature. Thoreau did not invent the form in *Walden* or in his journals, but he defined it in a way no subsequent American writer could ignore. Because the journal balances the "I" of the narrator with the objective facts of the world around him, because it nicely combines the specific and the general, because environmentalist organizations like the Sierra Club have grown so strong in twentieth-century America, the naturalist's journal has become almost a cottage industry for naturalists and writers. Thoreau's formula, with variation, is still the standard: use a mixture of book learning and naturalist observations—preference given, always, to observation over book learning—as the foundation for speculation on larger elements of life: time, God, man, the universe. "What I have observed of the pond is no less true in ethics. It is the law of average," wrote Thoreau. Set the mixture into a cycle (more often than not a cycle of months or of seasons). Add sketches or drawings if you like. Print many copies and hit the lecture circuit.

The popularity of this form owes much to the notion, shared by many Americans, that wilderness is somehow necessary, and that in leaving the wilderness we have somehow lost an important part of ourselves. "In wildness," Thoreau wrote, "is the preservation of the world." (This line titled one of the Sierra Club's early coffee table pictures-with-text books.) Writes Wallace Stegner, echoing Thoreau, "An American, insofar as he is new and different at all, is a civilized man who has renewed himself in the wild." Both are restating an argument developed early in the nineteenth century by Americans attempting to justify American life against perceived (or real) European cultural superiority. What, in

1840, could American culture throw against German philosophy, Italian art, British literature, French culture . . . the whole weight of civilization which immigrants had, of necessity, left behind on the shores of the Old World? What except the only thing it had in abundance: wildness? The argument proved a masterstroke, for the American became the very embodiment of that renewal which Rousseau and other Romantic philosophers claimed would be worked on decrepit urban poor by a season in the wilderness. Man is renewed not by honing his intellect by book study, but by sharpening the senses and strengthening the muscles as far away from books as possible (although books keep popping up in the remotest wilderness cabins, including Thoreau's cabin at Walden Pond). American philosophers pole-vaulted themselves onto the cutting edge of civilization itself: what others thought, the American had done. "One does not need universities and libraries," Gary Snyder quotes the sutra of Hui Neg as saying; one needs to be alive to what is about. And what more conducive a place to awaken than in the wilderness, where distractions fall away on every side and the senses are sharpened by renewed and intensive use? (The most popular recent expression of wilderness as the tonic for whatever ails you is Ken Kesey's *One Flew Over the Cuckoo's Nest*, in the wilderness call to Chief Broom and the rehabilitation worked by one fishing trip on that bunch of loonies from the nuthouse.)

The contrast between civilization and wilderness is one hallmark of the philosophical wilderness essay . . . or, in Gary Snyder's case, poem. There are others. Isolation, for example, an absolute terror to Everts, becomes in Thoreau's eyes one of the great blessings of wilderness. "The gift of the gods," Thoreau proclaimed it. "A reintegration of the world," Norbert Blei (echoing Thoreau) called it. In one of her letters from the country, Carol Bly claimed that the value of a winter blizzard was the period of enforced isolation it provided—the chance to investigate, with the encouragement of the season, one's private thoughts.

But a season in the wilderness is more than just a chance to think; it is an invitation to see and hear again, as if for the first time. In a classic example of less becoming more, the sensory deprivation caused by removing urban and suburban distractions refines each of the senses, until a great wealth of very precise detail invariably marks the writing of those who spend time alone in the wilderness—details of plant and animal behavior, of climate and weather patterns, of the language of pigs and the sounds of snow, of specific birdlore, gnawed fragments of grass stems, snails, mayfly nymphs, leeches, planariums. The richness of wilderness is either very large scale or very small scale (it defies traditional visual esthetics, resisting composition into tidy framed pictures). In details, Thoreauvean naturalists discover, lives God. Or science. Get out of your car and walk. Better yet, crawl, advises Abbey. Then you may begin to understand.

Interestingly, careful observation seems to nudge observers in two directions. One is a delight in detail so rich that the details begin to break, like light in an Impressionist painting, into millions of tiny dots, so that the picture becomes less, rather than more focused (until, of course, the points reintegrate at a distance). We are, almost, where we began. The second direction is generalization, for the underlying assumption behind close observation of natural phenomena is always, in Gruchow's words, "If I could explain the sound of a footstep upon the snow or come to know the underlying principles that govern the meandering of the snow along a fenceline, I should then be attuned in a new way to the largely unheard and mysterious music of the universe."

Aldo Leopold's classic *A Sand County Almanac* (1948) nudged writers of nature journals a little further than *Walden* in the direction of details, although Leopold, like Thoreau, used the minutiae of wilderness life as a springboard for philosophy. Annie Dillard, too, integrates natural phenomena into a system of ideas. The works of recent journalists like John Janovy (*Keith County Journal* and *Back in Keith County*), Ronald Rood (*Who Wakes the Groundhog?*), Barry Lopez (*Arctic Dreams*), and Ann Zwinger concentrate ever more specifically on anecdote and detail, freeing whole galaxies of biological life and discovering some of the millions of as yet undescribed species of fauna and flora with which the wilderness teems.

The preservationist theme sounded by Thoreau is by now commonplace in our culture. John McPhee's account of the classic confrontation between David Brower and geologist Charles Park is somewhat unusual in that the developer gets at least a few good licks, and the fight is as equal in the telling as it is in real life. In most written accounts of this battle, preservationists get all the good lines, from Keeler's satiric songs to Abbey's encounter with the visitor from Cleveland:

> "Nice for pictures but my God I'm glad I don't have to live here."
> "I'm glad too, sir. We're in perfect agreement. You wouldn't want to live here, and I wouldn't want to live in Cleveland."

("Take a jet back to Cleveland and dream," sings Keeler.)
Initially part of Nature and a worshiper of Nature gods, then split

from Nature by Judaic-Christian theology and the philosophy of the Enlightenment to govern over nature, man now becomes again a part of the interrelatedness of things, a part of wilderness. Gruchow recalls his reasons for wanting to trap a mink: "I could in a sense partake of his wildness." He also recalls his remorse at succeeding, because he has trapped, in effect, his own wild self. Realizing the kinship of man and wild animal, Gruchow desisted forever from trapping. Preserving wilderness to preserve a part of our human selves becomes more than a pleasant Romantic thought, although hard-core preservationists (and reconstructionists) are generally held to be dreamer-obstructionists who might better spend their time contributing realistic schemes for integrating social and natural spheres than in dreaming of returning to old mythologies. The herds of white Buffalo are not going to return from the clouds above the Medicine Bow Mountains; to think they will is mere story-telling and fantasy, most of us would argue. However, by preserving and tending the small wilderness remaining in our landscape and our souls, we may reach the equivalent of such a return, that reintegration of man and nature which was broken in the nineteenth, or the sixteenth, or the fourteenth, or the first century A.D.

That wilderness may be the wastelands of Wyoming, the wooded shores of a lake a few miles outside of Concord, Massachusetts, a national wildlife refuge, a small pond in Wisconsin. It could, in theory at least, be a park in Chicago or Los Angeles. The birds and small rodents, and even an occasional deer are, after all, everywhere. Gruchow reports having seen a mink in Minneapolis or St. Paul. On a small scale, at least, the planet remains filled with pockets unmonkeyed with by human beings—wildness is surprisingly insistent. All that is essential is an opportunity for close observation of life that is non-human, a sense of solitude, and some interaction with forces beyond our direct control. In these terms, wilderness—and an opportunity for wonder and awe—is within reach of most of us, even in late twentieth-century America.

·1·

Solitude

Henry Thoreau

THIS IS A DELICIOUS EVENING, when the whole body is one sense, and imbibes delight through every pore. I go and come with a strange liberty in Nature, a part of herself. As I walk along the stony shore of the pond in my shirt sleeves, though it is cool as well as cloudy and windy, and I see nothing special to attract me, all the elements are unusually congenial to me. The bullfrogs trump to usher in the night, and the note of the whippoorwill is borne on the rippling wind from over the water. Sympathy with the fluttering alder and poplar leaves almost takes away my breath; yet, like the lake, my serenity is rippled but not ruffled. These small waves raised by the evening wind are as remote from storm as the smooth reflecting surface. Though it is now dark, the wind still blows and roars in the wood, the waves still dash, and some creatures lull the rest with their notes. The repose is never complete. The wildest animals do not repose, but seek their prey now; the fox, and skunk, and rabbit, now roam the fields and woods without fear. They are Nature's watchmen—links which connect the days of animated life.

When I return to my house I find that visitors have been there and left their cards, either a bunch of flowers, or a wreath of evergreen, or a name in pencil on a yellow walnut leaf or a chip. They who come rarely to the woods take some little piece of the forest into their hands to play with by the way, which they leave, either intentionally or accidentally. One has peeled a willow wand, woven it into a ring, and dropped it on my table. I could always tell if visitors had called in my absence, either by the bended twigs or grass, or the print of their shoes, and generally of what sex or age or quality they were by some slight trace left, as a flower dropped, or a bunch of grass plucked and thrown away, even as far off as the railroad, half a mile distant, or by the lingering odor of a cigar or pipe. Nay, I was frequently notified of the passage of a traveler along the highway sixty rods off by the scent of his pipe.

There is commonly sufficient space about us. Our horizon is never quite at our elbows. The thick wood is not just at our door, nor the pond, but somewhat is always clearing, familiar and worn by us, appropriated and fenced in some way, and reclaimed from Nature. For what reason have I this vast range and circuit, some square miles of unfrequented forest, for my privacy, abandoned to me by men? My nearest neighbor is a mile distant, and no house is visible from any place but the hilltops within half a mile of my own. I have my horizon bounded by woods all to myself; a distant view of the railroad where it touches the pond on the one hand, and of the fence which skirts the woodland road on the other. But for the most part it is as solitary where I live as on the prairies. It is as much Asia or Africa as New England. I have, as it were, my own sun and moon and stars, and a little world all to myself. At night there was never a traveler passed my house, or knocked at my door, more than if I were the first or last man; unless it were in the spring, when at long intervals some came from the village to fish for pouts—they plainly fished much more in the Walden Pond of their own natures, and baited their hooks with darkness—but they soon retreated, usually with light baskets, and left "the world to darkness and to me," and the black kernel of the night was never profaned by any human neighborhood. I believe that men are generally still a little afraid of the dark, though the witches are all hung, and Christianity and candles have been introduced.

Yet I experienced sometimes that the most sweet and tender, the most innocent and encouraging society may be found in any natural object, even for the poor misanthrope and most melancholy man. There can be no very black melancholy to him who lives in the midst of Nature and has his senses still. There was never yet such a storm but it was Aeolian music to a healthy and innocent ear. Nothing can rightly compel a simple and brave man to a vulgar sadness. While I enjoy the friendship of the seasons I trust that nothing can make life a burden to me. The gentle rain which waters my beans and keeps me in the house today is not drear and melancholy, but good for me too. Though it prevents my hoeing them, it is of far more worth than my hoeing. If it should continue so long as to cause the seeds to rot in the ground and destroy the potatoes in the lowlands, it would still be good for the grass on the uplands, and, being good for the grass, it would be good for me. Sometimes, when I compare myself with other men, it seems as if I were more favored by the gods than they, beyond any deserts that I am conscious of; as if I had a warrant and surety at their hands which my fellows have not, and were especially guided and guarded. I do not flatter myself, but if it be possible they flatter me. I have never felt lonesome, or in the least oppressed by a sense of solitude, but once, and that was a few weeks after I came to the woods, when, for an hour, I doubted if the near neighborhood of man was not essential to a serene and healthy life. To be alone was something unpleasant. But I was at the same time conscious of a slight insanity in my mood, and seemed to foresee my recovery. In the midst of a gentle rain while these thoughts prevailed, I was suddenly sensible of such sweet and beneficent society in Nature, in the very pattering of the drops, and in every sound and sight around my house, an infinite and unaccountable friendliness all at once like an atmosphere sustaining me, as made the fancied advantages of human neighborhood insignificant, and I have never thought of them since. Every little pine needle expanded and swelled with sympathy and befriended me. I was so distinctly made aware of the presence of something kindred to me, even in scenes which we are accustomed to call wild and dreary, and also that the nearest of blood to me and humanest was not a person nor a villager, that I thought no place could ever be strange to me again.

> "*Mourning untimely consumes the sad;*
> *Few are their days in the land of the living,*
> *Beautiful daughter of Toscar.*"

Some of my pleasantest hours were during the long rainstorms in the spring or fall, which confined me to the house for the afternoon as well as the forenoon, soothed by their ceaseless roar and pelting; when an early twilight ushered in a long evening in which many thoughts had time to take root and unfold themselves. In those driving northeast rains which tried the village houses so, when the maids stood ready with mop and pail in front entries to keep the deluge out, I sat behind my door in my little house, which was all entry, and thoroughly enjoyed its protection. In one heavy thundershower the lightning struck a large pitch pine across the pond, making a very conspicuous and perfectly regular spiral groove from top to bottom, an inch or more deep, and four or five inches wide, as you would groove a walking-stick. I passed it again the other day, and was struck with awe on looking up and beholding that mark, now more distinct than ever, where a terrific and resistless bolt came down out of the harmless sky eight years ago. Men frequently say to me, "I should think you would feel lonesome down there, and want to be nearer to folks, rainy and snowy days and nights especially." I am tempted to reply to such, This whole earth which we inhabit is but a point in space. How far apart, think you, dwell the two most distant inhabitants of yonder star, the breadth of whose disk cannot be appreciated by our instruments? Why should I feel lonely? is not our planet in the Milky Way? This which you put seems to me not to be the most important question. What sort of space is that which separates a man from his fellows and makes him solitary? I have found that no exertion of the legs can bring two minds much nearer to one another. What do we want most to dwell near to? Not to many men surely, the depot, the post-office, the barroom, the meeting-house, the school-house, the grocery, Beacon Hill, or the Five Points, where men most congregate, but to the perennial source of our life, whence in all our experience we have found that to issue, as the willow stands near the water and sends out its roots in that direction. This will vary with different natures, but this is the place where a wise man will dig his cellar. . . . I one evening overtook one of my townsmen, who has accumulated what is called "a handsome property"—though I never got a *fair* view of it—on the Walden road, driving a pair of cattle to market, who inquired of me how I could bring my mind to give up so many of the comforts of life. I answered that I was very sure I liked it passably well; I was not joking. And so I went home to my bed, and left him to pick his way through the darkness and the mud to Brighton—or Brighttown—which place he would reach some time in the morning.

Any prospect of awakening or coming to life to a dead man makes indifferent all times and places. The place where that may occur is always the same, and indescribably pleasant to all our senses. For the most part we allow only outlying and transient circumstances to make our occasions. They are, in fact, the cause of our distraction. Nearest to all things is that power which fashions their being. *Next* to us the grandest laws are continually being executed. *Next* to us is not the workman whom we have hired, with whom we love so well to talk, but the workman whose work we are.

"How vast and profound is the influence of the subtile powers of Heaven and of Earth!

"We seek to perceive them, and we do not see them; we seek to hear them, and we do not hear them; identified with the substance of things, they cannot be separated from them.

"They cause that in all the universe men purify and sanctify their hearts, and clothe themselves in their holiday garments to offer sacrifices and oblations to their ancestors. It is an ocean of subtile intelligences. They are everywhere, above us, on our left, on our right; they environ us on all sides."

We are the subjects of an experiment which is not a little interesting to me. Can we not do without the society of our gossips a little while under these circumstances, have our own thoughts to cheer us? Confucius says truly, "Virtue does not remain as an abandoned orphan; it must of necessity have neighbors."

With thinking we may be beside ourselves in a same sense. By a conscious effort of the mind we can stand aloof from actions and their consequences; and all things, good and bad, go by us like a torrent. We are not wholly involved in Nature. I may be either the driftwood in the stream, or Indra in the sky looking down on it. I *may* be affected by a theatrical exhibition; on the other hand, I *may not* be affected by an actual event which appears to concern me much more. I only know myself as a human entity; the scene, so to speak, of thoughts and affections; and am sensible of a certain doubleness by which I can stand as remote from myself as from another. However intense my experience, I am conscious of the presence and criticism of a part of me, which, as it were, is not a part of me, but spectator, sharing no experience, but taking note of it; and that is no more I than it is you. When the play, it may be the tragedy, of life is over, the spectator goes his way. It was a kind of fiction, a work of the imagination only, so far as he was concerned. This doubleness may easily make us poor neighbors and friends sometimes.

I find it wholesome to be alone the greater part of the time. To be in company, even with the best, is soon wearisome and dissipating. I love to be alone. I never found the companion that was so companionable as solitude. We are for the most part more lonely when we go abroad among men than when we stay in our chambers. A man thinking or working is always alone, let him be where he will. Solitude is not measured by the miles of space that intervene between a man and his fellows. The really diligent student in one of the crowded hives of Cambridge College is as solitary as a dervish in the desert. The farmer can work alone in the field or the woods all day, hoeing or chopping, and not feel lonesome, because he is employed; but when he comes home at night he cannot sit down in a room alone, at the mercy of his thoughts, but must be where he can "see the folks," and recreate, and as he thinks remunerate, himself for his day's solitude; and hence he wonders how the student can sit alone in the house all night and most of the day without ennui and "the blues"; but he does not realize that the student, though in the house, is still at work in *his* field, and chopping in *his* woods, as the farmer in his, and in turn seeks the same recreation and society that the latter does, though it may be a more condensed form of it.

Society is commonly too cheap. We meet at very short intervals, not having had time to acquire any new value for each other. We meet at meals three times a day, and give each other a new taste of that old musty cheese that we are. We have had to agree on a certain set of rules, called etiquette and politeness, to make this frequent meeting tolerable and that we need not come to open war. We meet at the post-office, and at the sociable, and about the fireside every night; we live thick and are in each other's way, and stumble over one another, and I think that we thus lose some respect for one another. Certainly less frequency would suffice for all important and hearty communications. Consider the girls in a factory—never alone, hardly in their dreams. It would be better if there were but one inhabitant to a square mile, as where I live. The value of a man is not in his skin, that we should touch him.

I have heard of a man lost in the woods and dying of famine and exhaustion at the foot of a tree, whose loneliness was relieved by the grotesque visions with which, owing to bodily weakness, his diseased imagination surrounded him, and which he believed to be real. So also, owing to bodily and mental health and strength, we may be continually cheered by a like but more normal and natural society, and come to know that we are never alone.

I have a great deal of company in my house; especially in the morning, when nobody calls. Let me suggest a few comparisons, that someone may convey an idea of my situation. I am no more lonely than the loon in the pond that laughs so loud, or than Walden Pond itself. What company has that lonely lake, I pray? And yet it has not the blue devils, but the blue angels in it, in the azure tint of its waters. The sun is alone, except in thick weather, when there sometimes appear to be two, but one is a mock sun. God is alone—but the devil, he is far from being alone; he sees a great deal of company; he is legion. I am no more lonely than a single mullein or dandelion in a pasture, or a bean leaf, or sorrel, or a horsefly, or a bumblebee. I am no more lonely than the Mill Brook, or a weather-cock, or the North Star, or the south wind, or an April shower, or a January thaw, or the first spider in a new house.

I have occasional visits in the long winter evenings, when the snow falls fast and the wind howls in the wood, from an old settler and original proprietor, who is reported to have dug Walden Pond, and stoned it, and fringed it with pine woods; who tells me stories of old time and of new eternity; and between us we manage to pass a cheerful evening with social mirth and pleasant views of things, even without apples or cider—a most wise and humorous friend, whom I love much, who keeps himself more secret than ever did Goffe or Whalley; and though he is thought to be dead, none can show where he is buried. An elderly dame, too, dwells in my neighborhood, invisible to most persons, in whose odorous herb garden I love to stroll sometimes, gathering simples and listening to her fables; for she has a genius of unequaled fertility, and her memory runs back farther than mythology, and she can tell me the original of every fable, and on what fact every one is founded, for the incidents occurred when she was young. A ruddy and lusty old dame, who delights in all weathers and seasons, and is likely to outlive all her children yet.

The indescribable innocence and beneficence of Nature—of sun and wind and rain, of summer and winter—such health, such cheer, they afford forever! and such sympathy have they ever with our race, that all Nature would be affected, and the sun's brightness fade, and the winds would sigh humanely, and the clouds rain tears, and the woods shed their leaves and put on mourning in midsummer, if any man should ever for a just cause grieve. Shall I not have intelligence with the earth? Am I not partly leaves and vegetable mould myself?

What is the pill which will keep us well, serene, contented? Not my or thy great-grandfather's, but our great-grandmother Nature's universal, vegetable, botanic medicines, by which she has kept herself young always, outlived so many old Parrs in her day, and fed her health with their decaying fatness. For my panacea, instead of one of those quack vials of a mixture dipped from Acheron and the Dead Sea, which come out of those long shallow black-schooner-looking wagons which we sometimes see made to carry bottles, let me have a draught of undiluted morning air. Morning air! If men will not drink of this at the foun-tainhead of the day, why, then, we must even bottle up some and sell it in the shops, for the benefit of those who have lost their subscription ticket to morning time in this world. But remember, it will not keep quite till noonday even in the coolest cellar, but drive out the stopples long ere that and follow westward the steps of Aurora. I am no worshiper of Hygeia, who was the daughter of that old herb-doctor Aesculapius, and who is represented on monuments holding a serpent in one hand, and in the other a cup out of which the serpent sometimes drinks; but rather of Hebe, cupbearer to Jupiter, who was the daughter of Juno and wild lettuce, and who had the power of restoring gods and men to the vigor of youth. She was probably the only thoroughly sound-conditioned, healthy, and robust young lady that ever walked the globe, and wherever she came it was spring.

·2·

Thirty-Seven Days of Peril

Truman C. Everts

ON THE DAY THAT I FOUND MYSELF separated from the company, and for several days previous, our course had been impeded by the dense growth of the pine forest, and occasional large tracts of fallen timber, frequently rendering our progress almost impossible. Whenever we came to one of these immense windfalls, each man engaged in the pursuit of a passage through it, and it was while thus employed, and with the idea that I had found one, that I strayed out of sight and hearing of my comrades. We had a toilsome day. It was quite late in the afternoon. As separations like this had frequently occurred, it gave me no alarm, and I rode on, fully confident of soon rejoining the company, or of finding their camp. I came up with the pack-horse, which Mr. Langford afterwards recovered, and tried to drive him along, but failing to do so, and my eyesight being defective, I spurred forward, intending to return with assistance from the party. This incident tended to accelerate my speed. I rode on in the direction which I supposed had been taken, until darkness overtook me in the dense forest. This was disagreeable enough, but caused me no alarm. I had no doubt of being with the party at breakfast the next morning. I selected a spot for comfortable repose, picketed my horse, built a fire, and went to sleep.

The next morning I rose at early dawn, saddled and mounted my horse, and took my course in the supposed direction of the camp. Our ride of the previous day had been up a peninsula jutting into the lake, for the shore of which I started, with the expectation of finding my friends camped on the beach. The forest was quite dark, and the trees so thick, that it was only by a slow process I could get through them at all. In searching for the trail I became somewhat confused. The falling foliage of the pines had obliterated every trace of travel. I was obliged frequently to dismount, and examine the ground for the faintest indications. Coming to an opening, from which I could see several vistas, I dismounted for the purpose of selecting one leading in the direction I had chosen, and leaving my horse unhitched, as had always been my custom, walked a few rods into the forest. While surveying the ground my horse took fright, and I turned around in time to see him disappearing at full speed among the trees. That was the last I ever saw of him. It was yet quite dark. My blankets, gun, pistols, fishing tackle, matches—everything, except the clothing on my person, a couple of knives, and a small opera-glass were attached to the saddle.

I did not yet realize the possibility of a permanent separation from the company. Instead of following up the pursuit of their camp, I engaged in an effort to recover my horse. Half a day's search convinced me of its impracticability. I wrote and posted in an open space several notices, which, if my friends should chance to see, would inform them of my condition and the route I had taken, and then struck out into the forest in the supposed direction of their camp. As the day wore on without any discovery, alarm took the place of anxiety at the prospect of another night alone in the wilderness, and this time without food or fire. But even this dismal foreboding was cheered by the hope that I should soon rejoin my companions, who would laugh at my adventure, and incorporate it as a thrilling episode into the journal of our trip. The bright side of a misfortune, as I found by experience, even under the worst possible circumstances, always presents some features of encouragement. When I began to realize that my condition was one of actual peril, I banished from my mind all fear of an unfavorable result. Seating myself on a log, I recalled every foot of the way I had traveled since the separation from my friends, and the most probable opinion I could form of their whereabouts was, that they had, by a course but little different from mine, passed by the spot where I had posted the notices, learned of my disaster, and were waiting for me to rejoin them there, or searching for me in that vicinity. A night must be spent amid the prostrate trunks before my return could be accomplished. At no time during my period of exile did I experience so much mental suffering from the cravings of hunger as when, exhausted with this long day of fruitless search, I resigned myself to a couch of pine foliage in the pitchy darkness of a thicket of small trees. Naturally timid in the night, I fully realized the exposure of my condition. I peered upward through the darkness, but all was blackness and gloom. The wind sighed mournfully through the pines. The forest seemed alive with the screeching of night birds, the angry barking of coyotes, and the prolonged, dismal howl of the gray wolf. These sounds, familiar by their constant occurrence throughout the journey, were now full of terror, and drove slumber from my eye-lids. Above all this, however, was the hope that I should be restored to my comrades the next day.

Early the next morning I rose unrefreshed, and pursued my weary way over the prostrate trunks. It was noon when I reached the spot where my notices were posted. No one had been there. My disappointment was almost overwhelming. For the first time, I realized that I was lost. Then came a crushing sense of destitution. No food, no fire; no means to procure either; alone in an unexplored wilderness, one hundred and fifty miles from the nearest human abode, surrounded by wild beasts, and famishing with hunger. It was no time for despondency. A moment afterwards I felt how calamity can elevate the mind, in the formation of the resolution "not to perish in that wilderness."

The hope of finding the party still controlled my plans. I thought, by traversing the peninsula centrally, I would be enabled to strike the shore of the lake in advance of their camp, and near the point of departure for the Madison. Acting upon this impression, I rose from a sleepless couch, and pursued my way through the timber-entangled forest. A feeling of weakness took the place of hunger. Conscious of the need of food, I felt no cravings. Occasionally, while scrambling over logs and through thickets, a sense of faintness and exhaustion would come over me, but I would suppress it with the audible expression, "This won't do; I *must* find my company." Despondency would sometimes strive with resolution for the mastery of my thoughts. I would think of home—of my daughter—and of the possible chance of starvation, or death in some more terrible form; but as often as these gloomy forebodings came, I would strive to banish them with reflections better adapted to my immediate necessities. I recollect at this time discussing the question, whether there was not implanted by Providence in every man a principle of self-preservation equal to any emergency which did not destroy his reason. I decided this question affirmatively a thousand times afterwards in my wanderings, and I record this experience here, that any person who reads it, should he ever find himself in like circumstances, may not despair. There is life in the thought. It will revive hope, allay hunger, renew energy, encourage perseverance, and, as I have proved in my own case, bring a man out of difficulty, when nothing else can avail.

It was mid-day when I emerged from the forest into an open space at the foot of the peninsula. A broad lake of beautiful curvature, with magnificent surroundings, lay before me, glittering in the sunbeams. It was full twelve miles in circumference. A wide belt of sand formed the margin which I was approaching, directly opposite to which, rising seemingly from the very depths of the water, towered the loftiest peak of a range of mountains apparently interminable. The ascending vapor from innumerable hot springs, and the sparkling jet of a single geyser, added the feature of novelty to one of the grandest landscapes I ever beheld. Nor was the life of the scene less noticeable than its other attractions. Large flocks of swans and other water-fowl were sporting on the quiet surface of the lake; otters in great numbers performed the most amusing aquatic evolutions; mink and beaver swam around unscared, in most grotesque confusion. Deer, elk, and mountain sheep stared at me, manifesting more surprise than fear at my presence among them. The adjacent forest was vocal with the songs of birds, chief of which were the chattering notes of a species of mockingbird, whose imitative efforts afforded abundant merriment. Seen under favorable circumstances, this assemblage of grandeur, beauty, and novelty would have been transporting; but, jaded with travel, famishing with hunger, and distressed with anxiety, I was in no humor for ecstasy. My tastes were subdued and chastened by the perils which environed me. I longed for food, friends, and protection. Associated with my thoughts, however, was the wish that some of my friends of peculiar tastes could enjoy this display of secluded magnificence, now, probably, for the first time beheld by mortal eyes. . . .

During the first two days, the fear of meeting with Indians gave me considerable anxiety; but, when conscious of being lost, there was nothing I so much desired as to fall in with a lodge of Bannacks or Crows. Having nothing to tempt their cupidity, they would do me no personal harm, and, with the promise of reward, would probably minister to my wants and aid my deliverance. Imagine my delight, while gazing upon the animated expanse of water, at seeing sail out from a distant point a large canoe containing a single oarsman. It was rapidly approaching the shore where I was seated. With hurried steps I paced the beach to meet it, all my energies stimulated by the assurance it gave of food, safety, and restoration to friends. As I drew near to it, it turned towards the shore, and oh! bitter disappointment, the object which my eager fancy had transformed into an angel of relief stalked from the water, an enormous pelican, flapped its dragon-wings as if in mockery of my sorrow, and flew to a solitary point farther up the lake. This little incident quite unmanned me. The transition from joy to grief brought with it a terrible consciousness of the horrors of my condition. But night was fast approaching, and darkness would come with it. While looking for a spot where I might repose in safety, my attention was attracted to a small green plant of so lively a hue as to form a striking contrast with the deep pine foliage. For closer examination I pulled it up by the root, which was long and tapering, not unlike a radish. It was a thistle. I tasted it; it was palatable and nutritious. My appetite craved it, and the first meal in four days was made on thistle-roots. Eureka! I had found food. No optical illusion deceived me this time; I could subsist until I rejoined my companions. Glorious counterpoise to the wretchedness of the preceding half-hour!

Overjoyed at this discovery, with hunger allayed, I stretched myself under a tree, upon the foliage which had partially filled a space between contiguous trunks, and fell asleep. How long I slept I know not; but suddenly I was roused by a loud, shrill scream, like that of a human being in distress, poured, seemingly, into the very portals of my ear. There was no mistaking that fearful voice. I had been deceived by and answered it a dozen times while threading the forest, with the belief that it was a friendly signal. It was the screech of a mountain lion, so alarmingly near as to cause every nerve to thrill with terror. To yell in return, seize with convulsive grasp the limbs of the friendly tree, and swing myself into it, was the work of a moment. Scrambling hurriedly from limb to limb, I was soon as near the top as safety would permit. The savage beast was snuffing and growling below, apparently on the very spot I had just abandoned. I answered every growl with a responsive scream. Terrified at the delay and pawing of the beast, I increased my voice to its utmost volume, broke branches from the limbs, and, in the impotency of fright, madly hurled them at the spot whence the continued howlings proceeded.

Failing to alarm the animal, which now began to make the circuit of the tree, as if to select a spot for springing into it, I shook, with a strength increased by terror, the slender trunk until every limb rustled with the motion. All in vain. The terrible creature pursued his walk around the tree, lashing the ground with his tail, and prolonging his howlings almost to a roar. It was too dark to see, but the movements of the lion kept me apprised of its position. Whenever I heard it on one side of the tree I speedily changed to the opposite—an exercise which, in my weakened state, I could only have performed under the impulse of terror. I would alternately sweat and thrill with horror at the thought of being torn to pieces and devoured by this formidable monster. All my attempts to frighten it seemed unavailing. Disheartened at its persistency, and expecting every moment it would take the deadly leap, I tried to collect my thoughts, and prepare for the fatal encounter which I knew must result. Just at this moment it occurred to me that I would try silence. Clasping the trunk of the tree with both arms, I sat perfectly still. The lion, at this time ranging round, occasionally snuffing and pausing, and all the while filling the forest with the echo of his howlings, suddenly imitated my example. This silence was more terrible, if possible, than the clatter and crash of his movements through the brushwood, for now I did not know from what direction to expect his attack. Moments passed with me like hours. After a lapse of time which I cannot estimate, the beast gave a spring into the thicket and ran screaming into the forest. My deliverance was effected.

Had strength permitted, I should have retained my perch till daylight, but with the consciousness of escape from the jaws of the ferocious brute came a sense of overpowering weakness which almost palsied me, and made my descent from the tree both difficult and dangerous. Incredible as it may seem, I lay down in my old bed, and was soon lost in a slumber so profound that I did not awake until after daylight. The experience of the night seemed like a terrible dream; but the broken limbs which in the agony of consternation I had thrown from the tree, and the rifts made in the fallen foliage by my visitant in his circumambulations, were too convincing evidences of its reality. I could not dwell upon my exposure and escape without shuddering, and reflecting that probably like perils would often occur under less fortunate circumstances, and with a more fatal issue. I wondered what fate was in reserve for me—whether I would ultimately sink from exhaustion and perish of starvation, or become the prey of some of the ferocious animals that roamed these vast fastnesses. My thoughts then turned to the loved ones at home. They could never know my fate, and would indulge a thousand conjectures concerning it, not the least distressing of which would be that I had been captured by a band of hostile Sioux, and tortured to death at the stake.

I was roused from this train of reflections by a marked change in the atmosphere. One of those dreary storms of mingled snow and rain, common to these high latitudes, set in. My clothing, which had been much torn, exposed my person to its "pitiless peltings." An easterly wind, rising to a gale, admonished me that it would be furious and of long duration. None of the discouragements I had met with dissipated the hope of rejoining my friends; but foreseeing the delay, now unavoidable, I knew that my escape from the wilderness must be accomplished, if at all, by my own unaided exertions. This thought was terribly afflicting, and brought before me, in vivid array, all the dreadful realities of my condition. I could see no ray of hope. In this condition of mind I could find no better shelter than the spreading branches of a spruce tree, under which, covered with earth and boughs, I lay during the two succeeding days; the storm, meanwhile, raging with unabated violence. While thus exposed, and suffering from cold and hunger, a little benumbed bird, not larger than a snow-bird, hopped within my reach. I instantly seized and killed it, and, plucking its feathers, ate it raw. It was a delicious meal for a half-starved man.

Taking advantage of a lull in the elements, on the morning of the third day I rose early and started in the direction of a large group of hot springs which were steaming under the shadow of Mount Everts. The distance I traveled could not have been less than ten miles. Long before I reached the wonderful cluster of natural caldrons, the storm had recommenced. Chilled through, with my clothing thoroughly saturated, I lay down under a tree upon the heated incrustation until completely warmed. My heels and the sides of my feet were frozen. As soon as warmth had permeated my system, and I had quieted my appetite with a few thistle-roots, I took a survey of my surroundings, and selected a spot between two springs sufficiently asunder to afford heat at my head and feet. On this spot I built a bower of pine branches, spread its incrusted surface with fallen foliage and small boughs, and stowed myself away to await the close of the storm. Thistles were abundant, and I had fed upon them long enough to realize that they would, for a while at least, sustain life. In convenient proximity to my abode was a small, round, boiling spring, which I called my dinner-pot, and in which, from time to time, I cooked my roots. . . .

Nothing gave me more concern than the want of fire. I recalled everything I had ever read or heard of the means by which fire could be produced; but none of them were within my reach. An escape without it was simply impossible. It was indispensable as a protection against night attacks from wild beasts. Exposure to another storm like the one just over would destroy my life, as this one would have done, but for the warmth derived from the springs. As I lay in my bower anxiously awaiting the disappearance of the snow, which had fallen to the depth of a foot or more, and impressed with the belief that for want of fire I should be obliged to remain among the springs, it occurred to me that I would erect some sort of monument, which might, at some future day, inform a casual visitor of the circumstances under which I had perished. A gleam of sunshine lit up the bosom of the lake, and with it the thought flashed upon my mind that I could, with a lens from my opera-glasses, get fire from Heaven. Oh, happy, life-renewing thought! Instantly subjecting it to the test of experiment, when I saw the smoke curl from the bit of dry wood in my fingers, I felt, if the whole world were offered me for it, I would cast it all aside before parting with that little spark. I was now the happy possessor of food and fire. These would carry me through. All thoughts of failure were instantly abandoned. Though the food was barely adequate to my necessities—a fact too painfully attested by my attenuated body—I had forgotten the cravings of hunger, and had the means of producing fire. I said to myself, "I will not despair."

My stay at the springs was prolonged several days by an accident that befell me on the third night after my arrival there. An unlucky movement while asleep broke the crust on which I reposed, and the hot steam, pouring upon my hip, scalded it severely before I could escape. This new affliction, added to my frost-bitten feet, already festering, was the cause of frequent delay and unceasing pain through all my wanderings. After obtaining fire, I set to work making preparations for as early departure as my condition would permit. I had lost both knives since parting from the company, but I now made a convenient substitute by sharpening the tongue of a buckle which I cut from my vest. With this I cut the legs and counters from my boots, making of them a passable pair of slippers, which I fastened to my feet as firmly as I could with strips of bark. With the ravelings of a linen handkerchief, aided by the magic buckle-tongue, I mended my clothing. Of the same material I made a fish-line, which, on finding a piece of red tape in one of my pockets better suited to the purpose, I abandoned as a "bad job." I made of a pin that I found in my coat a fish-hook, and, by sewing up the bottoms of my boot-legs, constructed a very good pair of pouches to carry my food in, fastening them to my belt by the straps.

Thus accoutered, on the morning of the eighth day after my arrival at the springs I bade them a final farewell, and started on my course directly across that portion of the neck of the peninsula between me and the southeast arm of Yellowstone Lake. It was a beautiful morning. The sun shone bright and warm, and there was a freshness in the atmosphere truly exhilarating. As I wandered musingly along, the consciousness of being alone, and of having surrendered all hope of finding my friends, returned upon me with crushing power. I felt, too, that those friends, by the necessities of their condition, had been compelled to abandon all efforts for my recovery, The thought was full of bitterness and sorrow. I tried to realize what their conjectures were concerning my disappearance; but could derive no consolation from the long and dismal train of circumstances they suggested. Weakened by a long fast, and the unsatisfying nature of the only food I could procure, I know that from this time onward to the day of my rescue, my mind, though unimpaired in those perceptions needful to self-preservation, was in a condition to receive impressions akin to insanity. I was constantly traveling in dreamland, and indulging in strange reveries such as I had never before known. I seemed to possess a sort of duality of being, which, while constantly reminding me of the necessities of my condition, fed my imagination with vagaries of the most extravagant character. Nevertheless, I was perfectly conscious of the tendency of these morbid influences, and often tried to shake them off, but they would ever return with increased force, and I finally reasoned myself into the belief that their indulgence, as it afforded me pleasure, could work no harm while it did not interfere with my plans for deliverance. Thus I lived in a world of ideal happiness, and in a world of positive suffering at the same time.

A change in the wind and an overcast sky, accompanied by cold, brought with them a need of warmth. I drew out my lens and touchwood, but alas! there was no sun. I sat down on a log to await his friendly appearance. Hours passed; he did not come. Night, cold, freezing night, set in, and found me exposed to all its terrors. A bleak hillside sparsely covered with pines afforded poor accommodations for a half-clad, famishing man. I could only keep from freezing by the most active exertion in walking, rubbing, and striking my benumbed feet and hands against the logs. It seemed the longest, most terrible night of my life, and glad was I when the approaching dawn enabled me to commence retracing my steps to Bessie Lake. I arrived there at noon, built my first fire on the beach, and remained by it, recuperating, for the succeeding two days. . . .

Filling my pouches with thistle-roots, I took a parting survey of the little solitude that had afforded me food and fire the preceding ten days, and with something of that melancholy feeling experienced by one who leaves his home to grapple with untried adventures, started for the nearest point on Yellowstone Lake. All that day I traveled over timberheaps, amid tree-tops, and through thickets. At noon I took the precaution to obtain fire. With a brand which I kept alive by frequent blowing, and constant waving to and fro, at a late hour in the afternoon, faint and exhausted, I kindled a fire for the night on the only vacant spot I could find amid a dense wilderness of pines. The deep gloom of the forest, in the spectral light which revealed on all sides of me a compact and unending growth of trunks, and an impervious canopy of somber foliage; the shrieking of night-birds; the supernaturally human scream of the mountain lion; the prolonged howl of the wolf, made me insensible to all other forms of suffering.

The burn on my hip was so inflamed that I could only sleep in a sitting posture. Seated with my back against a tree, the smoke from the fire almost enveloping me in its suffocating folds, I vainly tried, amid the din and uproar of this horrible serenade, to woo the drowsy god. My imagination was instinct with terror. At one moment it seemed as if, in the density of a thicket, I could see the blazing eyes of a formidable forest monster fixed upon me, preparatory to a deadly leap; at another I fancied that I heard the swift approach of a pack of yelping wolves through the distant brushwood, which in a few moments would tear me limb from limb. Whenever, by fatigue and weakness, my terrors yielded to drowsiness; the least noise roused me to a sense of the hideousness of my condition. Once, in a fitful slumber, I fell forward into the fire, and inflicted a wretched burn on my hand. Oh! with what agony I longed for day!

A bright and glorious morning succeeded the dismal night, and brought with it the conviction that I had been the victim of uncontrollable nervous excitement. I resolved henceforth to banish it altogether; and, in much better spirits than I anticipated, resumed my journey towards the lake. Another day of unceasing toil among the treetops and thickets overtook me, near sunset, standing upon a lofty headland jutting into the lake, and commanding a magnificent prospect of the mountains and valley over an immense area. In front of me, at a distance of fifty miles away, in the clear blue of the horizon, rose the arrowy peaks of the three Tetons. On the right, and apparently in close proximity to the eminence I occupied, rolled the picturesque range of the Madison, scarred with clefts, ravines, gorges, and cañons, each of which glittered in the sunlight or deepened in shadow as the fitful rays of the descending luminary glanced along their varied rocky irregularities. Above where I stood were the lofty domes of Mounts Langford and Doane, marking the limits of that wonderful barrier which had so long defied human power in its efforts to subdue it. Rising seemingly from the promontory which favored my vision was the familiar summit of Mount Everts, at the base of which I had dwelt so long, and which still seemed to hold me within its friendly shadow. All the vast country within this grand enclosure of mountains and lake, scarred and seamed with the grotesque ridges, rocky escarpments, undulating hillocks, and miniature lakes, and steaming with hot springs, produced by the volcanic forces of a former era, lay spread out before me like a vast panorama.

I doubt if distress and suffering can ever entirely obliterate all sense of natural grandeur and magnificence. Lost in the wonder and admiration inspired by this vast world of beauties, I nearly forgot to improve the few moments of remaining sunshine to obtain fire. With a lighted brand in my hand, I effected a most difficult and arduous descent of the abrupt and stony headland to the beach of the lake. The sand was soft and yielding. I kindled a fire, and removing the stiffened slippers from my feet, attached them to my belt, and wandered barefoot along the sandy shore to gather wood for the night. The dry, warm sand was most grateful to my lacerated and festering feet, and for a long time after my wood-pile was supplied, I sat with them uncovered. At length, conscious of the need of every possible protection from the freezing night atmosphere, I sought my belt for the slippers, and one was missing. In gathering the wood it had become detached, and was lost. Darkness was closing over the landscape, when, sorely disheartened with the thought of passing the night with one foot exposed to a freezing temperature, I commenced a search for the missing slipper. I knew I could not travel a day without it. Fearful that it had dropped into the lake, and been carried by some recurrent wave beyond recovery, my search for an hour among fallen trees and bushes, up the hill-side and along the beach, in darkness and with flaming brands, at one moment crawling on hands and feet into a brush-heap, another was filled with anxiety and dismay. Success at length rewarded my perseverance, and no language can describe the joy with which I drew the cause of so much distress from beneath the limb that, as I passed, had torn it from my belt. With a feeling of great relief, I now sat down in the sand, my back to a log, and listened to the dash and roar of the waves. It was a wild lullaby, but had no terrors for a worn-out man. I never passed a night of more refreshing sleep. When I awoke my fire was extinguished save a few embers, which I soon fanned into a cheerful flame. I ate breakfast with some relish, and started along the beach in pursuit of a camp, believing that if successful I should find directions what to do, and food to sustain me. The search which I was making lay in the direction of my pre-arranged route to the Madison Mountains, which I intended to approach at their lowest point of altitude.

Buoyed by the hope of finding food and counsel, and another night of undisturbed repose in the sand, I resumed my journey along the shore, and at noon found the camp last occupied by my friends on the lake. I struck their trail in the sand some time before I came to it. A thorough search for food in the ground and trees revealed nothing, and no notice to apprise me of their movements could be seen. A dinner-fork, which afterwards proved to be of infinite service in digging roots, and a yeast-powder can, which would hold half a pint, and which I converted into a drinking-cup and dinner-pot, were the only evidences that the spot had ever been visited by civilized man. "Oh!" thought I, "why did they forget to leave me food!" it never occurring to me that they might have cached it, as I have since learned they did, in several spots nearer the place of my separation from them. I left the camp in deep dejection, with the purpose of following the trail of the party to the Madison. Carefully inspecting the faint traces left of their course of travel, I became satisfied that from some cause they had made a retrograde movement from this camp, and departed from the lake at a point farther down stream. Taking this as an indication that there were obstructions above, I commenced retracing my steps along the beach. An hour of sunshine in the afternoon enabled me to procure fire, which, in the usual manner, I carried to my camping-place. There I built a fire, and to protect myself from the wind, which was blowing violently, lashing the lake into foam, I made a bower of pine and fell asleep. How long I slept I know not, but I was aroused by the snapping and cracking of the burning foliage, to find my shelter and the adjacent forest in a broad sheet of flame. My left hand was badly burned, and my hair singed closer than a barber would have trimmed it, while making my escape from the semicircle of burning trees. Among the disasters of this fire, there was none I felt more seriously than the loss of my buckle-tongue knife, my pin fish-hook, and tape fish-line.

The grandeur of the burning forest surpasses description. An immense sheet of flame, following to their tops the lofty trees of an almost impenetrable pine forest, leaping madly from top to top, and sending thousands of forked tongues a hundred feet or more athwart the midnight darkness, lighting up with lurid gloom and glare the surrounding scenery of lake and mountains, fills the beholder with mingled feelings of awe and astonishment. I never before saw anything so terribly beautiful. It was marvelous to witness the flash-like rapidity with which the flames would mount the loftiest trees. The roaring, cracking, crashing, and snapping of falling limbs and burning foliage was deafening. On, on, on traveled the destructive element, until it seemed as if the whole forest was enveloped in flame. Afar up the wood-crowned hill, the overtopping trees shot forth pinnacles and walls and streamers of arrowy fire. The entire hill-side was an ocean of glowing and surging fiery billows. Favored by the gale, the conflagration spread with lightning swiftness over an illimitable extent of country, filling the atmosphere with driving clouds of suffocating fume, and leaving a broad and blackened trail of spectral trunks shorn of limbs and foliage, smoking and burning, to mark the immense sweep of its devastation.

Resolved to search for a trail no longer, when daylight came I selected for a landmark the lowest notch in the Madison Range. Carefully surveying the jagged and broken surface over which I must travel to reach it, I left the lake and pushed into the midst of its intricacies. All the day, until nearly sunset, I struggled over rugged hills, through windfalls, thickets, and matted forests, with the rock-ribbed beacon constantly in view. As I advanced it receded, as if in mockery of my toil. Night overtook me with my journey half accomplished. The precaution of obtaining fire gave me warmth and sleep, and long before daylight I was on my way. The hope of finding an easy pass into the valley of the Madison inspired me with fresh courage and determination; but long before I arrived at the base of the range, I scanned hopelessly its insurmountable difficulties. It presented to my eager vision an endless succession of inaccessible peaks and precipices, rising thousands of feet sheer and bare above the plain. No friendly gorge or gully or cañon invited such an effort as I could make to scale this rocky barrier. Oh for the faith that could remove mountains! How soon should this colossal fabric open at my approach! What a feeling of helpless despair came over me with the conviction that the journey of the last two days had been in vain! I seated myself on a rock, upon the summit of a commanding hill, and cast my eyes along the only route which now seemed tenable—down the Yellowstone. How many dreary miles of forest and mountain filled the terrible panorama! I thought that before accepting this discouraging alternative I would spend a day in search for a pass. Twenty miles at most would take me into the Madison Valley, and thirty more restore me to friends who had abundance. Supposing that I should find plenty of thistles, I had left the lake with a small supply, and that was entirely spent. I looked in vain for them where I then was.

While I was thus considering whether to remain and search for a passage or return to the Yellowstone, I experienced one of those strange hallucinations which many of my friends have misnamed insanity, but which to me was Providence. An old clerical friend, for whose character and counsel I had always cherished peculiar regard, in some unaccountable manner seemed to be standing before me, charged with advice which would relieve my perplexity. I seemed to hear him say, as if in a voice and with the manner of authority:—

"Go back immediately, as rapidly as your strength will permit. There is no food here, and the idea of scaling these rocks is madness."

"Doctor," I rejoined, "the distance is too great. I cannot live to travel it."

"Say not so. Your life depends upon the effort. Return at once. Start now, lest your resolution falter. Travel as fast and as far as possible—it is your only chance."

"Doctor, I am rejoiced to meet you in this hour of distress, but doubt the wisdom of your counsel. I am within seventy miles of Virginia. Just over these rocks, a few miles away, I shall find friends. My shoes are nearly worn out, my clothes are in tatters, and my strength is almost overcome. As a last trial, it seems to me I can but attempt to scale this mountain or perish in the effort, if God so wills."

"Don't think of it. Your power of endurance will carry you through. I will accompany you. Put your trust in Heaven. Help yourself and God will help you."

Overcome by these and other persuasions, and delighted with the idea of having a traveling companion, I plodded my way over the route I had come, intending at a certain point to change it so as to strike the river at the foot of the lake. Stopping after a few miles of travel, I had no difficulty in procuring fire, and passed a comfortable night. When I resumed my journey the next day the sun was just rising. Whenever I was disposed, as was often the case, to question the wisdom of the change of routes, my old friend appeared to be near with words of encouragement, but his reticence on other subjects both surprised and annoyed me. I was impressed at times, during the entire journey, with the belief that my return was a fatal error, and if my deliverance had failed should have perished with that conviction. Early this day I deflected from my old route and took my course for the foot of the lake, with the hope, by constant travel, to reach it the next day. The distance was greater than I anticipated. Nothing is more deceptive than distance in these high latitudes. At the close of each of the two succeeding days, my point of destination was seemingly as far from me as at the moment I took leave of the Madison Range, and when, cold and hungry, on the afternoon of the fourth day, I gathered the first food I had eaten in nearly five days, and lay down by my fire near the debouchure of the river, I had nearly abandoned all hope of escape. . . .

I lost all sense of time. Days and nights came and went, and were numbered only by the growing consciousness that I was gradually starving. I felt no hunger, did not eat to appease appetite, but to renew strength. I experienced but little pain. The gaping sores on my feet, the severe burn on my hip, the festering crevices at the joints of my fingers, all terrible in appearance, had ceased to give me the least concern. The roots which supplied my food had suspended the digestive power of the stomach, and their fibres were packed in it in a matted, compact mass.

Not so with my hours of slumber. They were visited by the most luxurious dreams. I would apparently visit the most gorgeously decorated restaurants of New York and Washington; sit down to immense tables spread with the most appetizing viands; partake of the richest oyster stews and plumpest pies; engage myself in the labor and preparation of curious dishes, and with them fill range upon range of elegantly furnished tables until they fairly groaned beneath the accumulated dainties prepared by my own hands. Frequently the entire night would seem to have been spent in getting up a sumptuous dinner. I would realize the fatigue of roasting, boiling, baking, and fabricating the choicest dishes known to the modern *cuisine*, and in my disturbed slumbers would enjoy with epicurean relish the food thus furnished even to repletion. Alas! there was more luxury than life in these somnolent vagaries.

It was a cold, gloomy day when I arrived in the vicinity of the falls. The sky was overcast and the snow-capped peaks rose chilly and bleak through the biting atmosphere. The moaning of the wind through the pines, mingling with the sullen roar of the falls, was strangely in unison with my own saddened feelings. I had no heart to gaze upon a scene which a few weeks before had inspired me with rapture and awe. One moment of sunshine was of more value to me than all the marvels amid which I was famishing. But the sun had hid his face and denied me all hope of obtaining fire. The only alternative was to seek shelter in a thicket. I penetrated the forest a long distance before finding one that suited me. Breaking and crowding my way into its very midst, I cleared a spot large enough to recline upon, interlaced the surrounding brushwood, gathered the fallen foliage into a bed, and lay down with a prayer for sleep and forgetfulness. Alas! neither came. The coldness increased through the night. Constant friction with my hands and unceasing beating with my legs and feet saved me from freezing. It was the most terrible night of my journey, and when, with the early dawn, I pulled myself into a standing posture, it was to realize that my right arm was partially paralyzed, and my limbs so stiffened with cold as to be almost immovable. Fearing lest paralysis should suddenly seize upon the entire system, I literally dragged myself through the forest to the river. Seated near the verge of the great cañon below the falls, I anxiously awaited the appearance of the sun. That great luminary never looked so beautiful as when, a few moments afterwards, he emerged from the clouds and exposed his glowing beams to the concentrated powers of my lens. I kindled a mighty flame, fed it with every dry stick and broken tree-top I could find, and without motion, and almost without sense, remained beside it several hours. The great falls of the Yellowstone were roaring within three hundred yards, and the awful cañon yawned almost at my feet; but they had lost all charm for me. In fact, I regarded them as enemies which had lured me to destruction, and felt a sullen satisfaction in morbid indifference.

My old friend and adviser, whose presence I had felt more than seen the last few days, now forsook me altogether. But I was not alone. By some process which I was too weak to solve, my arms, legs, and stomach were transformed into so many traveling companions. Often for hours I would plod along conversing with these imaginary friends. Each had his peculiar wants which he expected me to supply. The stomach was importunate in his demand for a change of diet—complained incessantly of the roots I fed him, their present effect and more remote consequences. I would try to silence him with promises, beg of him to wait a few days, and when this failed of the quiet I desired, I would seek to intimidate him by declaring, as a sure result of negligence, our inability to reach home alive. All to no purpose—he tormented me with his fretful humors through the entire journey. The others would generally concur with him in these fancied altercations. The legs implored me for rest, and the arms complained that I gave them too much to do. Troublesome as they were, it was a pleasure to realize their presence. I worked for them, too, with right good will, doing many things for their seeming comfort which, had I felt myself alone, would have remained undone. They appeared to be perfectly helpless of themselves; would do nothing for me or for each other. I often wondered, while they ate and slept so much, that they did not aid in gathering wood and kindling fires. As a counterpoise to their own inertia, whenever they discovered languor in me on necessary occasions, they were not wanting in words of encouragement and cheer. I recall as I write an instance where, by prompt and timely interposition, the representative of the stomach saved me from a death of dreadful agony. One day I came to a small stream issuing from a spring of mild temperature on the hillside, swarming with minnows. I caught some with my hands and ate them raw. To my taste they were delicious. But the stomach refused them, accused me of attempting to poison him, and would not be reconciled until I had emptied my pouch of the few fish I had put there for future use. Those that I ate made me very sick. Poisoned by the mineral in the water, had I glutted my appetite with them as I intended, I should doubtless have died in the wilderness, in excruciating torment. . . .

At many of the streams on my route I spent hours in endeavoring to catch trout, with a hook fashioned from the rim of my broken spectacles, but in no instance with success. The tackle was defective. The country was full of game in great variety. I saw large herds of deer, elk, antelope, occasionally a bear, and many smaller animals. Numerous flocks of ducks, geese, swans, and pelicans inhabited the lakes and rivers. But with no means of killing them, their presence was a perpetual aggravation. At all the camps of our company I stopped and recalled many pleasant incidents associated with them.

One afternoon, when approaching "Tower Falls," I came upon a large hollow tree, which, from the numerous tracks surrounding it, and the matted foliage in the cavity, I recognized as the den of a bear. It was a most inviting couch. Gathering a needful supply of wood and brush, I lighted a circle of piles around the tree, crawled into the nest, and passed a night of unbroken slumber. I rose the next morning to find that during the night the fires had communicated with the adjacent forest, and burned a large space in all directions, doubtless intimidating the rightful proprietor of the nest, and saving me from another midnight adventure. . . .

Soon after leaving "Tower Falls," I entered the open country. Pine forests and windfalls were changed for sage brush and desolation, with occasional tracts of stinted verdure, barren hillsides, exhibiting here and there an isolated clump of dwarf trees, and ravines filled with the rocky *débris* of adjacent mountains. My first camp on this part of the route, for the convenience of getting wood, was made near the summit of a range of towering foot-hills. Towards morning a storm of wind and snow nearly extinguished my fire. I became very cold; the storm was still raging when I arose, and the ground white with snow. I was perfectly bewildered, and had lost my course of travel. No visible object, seen through the almost blinding storm, reassured me, and there was no alternative but to find the river and take my direction from its current. Fortunately, after a few hours of stumbling and scrambling among rocks and over crests, I came to the precipitous side of the cañon through which it ran, and with much labor, both of hands and feet, descended it to the margin. I drank copiously of its pure waters, and sat beside it for a long time, waiting for the storm to abate, so that I could procure fire. The day wore on, without any prospect of a termination to the storm. Chilled through, my tattered clothing saturated, I saw before me a night of horrors unless I returned to my fire. The scramble up the side of the rocky cañon, in many places nearly perpendicular, was the hardest work of my journey. Often while clinging to the jutting rocks with hands and feet, to reach a shelving projection, my grasp would unclose and I would slide many feet down the sharp declivity. It was night when, sore from the bruises I had received, I reached my fire; the storm, still raging, had nearly extinguished it. I found a few embers in the ashes, and with much difficulty kindled a flame. Here, on this bleak mountain side, as well as I now remember, I must have passed two nights beside the fire, in the storm. Many times during each night I crawled to the little clump of trees to gather wood, and brush, and the broken limbs of fallen tree-tops. All the sleep I obtained was snatched from the intervals which divided these labors. It was so harassed with frightful dreams as to afford little rest. I remember, before I left this camp, stripping up my sleeves to look at my shrunken arms. Flesh and blood had apparently left them. The skin clung to the bones like wet parchment. A child's hand could have clasped them from wrist to shoulder. "Yet," thought I, "it is death to remain; I cannot perish in this wilderness."

Taking counsel of this early formed resolution, I hobbled on my course through the snow, which was rapidly disappearing before the rays of the warm sun. Well knowing that I should find no thistles in the open country, I had filled my pouches with them before leaving the forest. My supply was running low, and there were yet several days of heavy mountain travel between me and Boteler's ranch. With the most careful economy, it could last but two or three days longer. I saw the necessity of placing myself and imaginary companions upon allowance. The conflict which ensued with the stomach, when I announced this resolution, required great firmness to carry through. I tried wheedling and coaxing and promising; failing in these, I threatened to part company with a comrade so unreasonable, and he made no further complaint.

Two or three days before I was found, while ascending a steep hill, I fell from exhaustion into the sage brush, without the power to rise. Unbuckling my belt, as was my custom, I soon fell asleep. I have no idea of the time I slept, but upon awaking I fastened my belt, scrambled to my feet, and pursued my journey. As night drew on I selected a camping-place, gathered wood into a heap, and felt for my lens to procure fire. It was gone. If the earth had yawned to swallow me I would not have been more terrified. The only chance for life was lost. The last hope had fled. I seemed to feel the grim messenger who had been so long pursuing me knocking at the portals of my heart as I lay down by the side of the wood-pile, and covered myself with limbs and sage brush, with the dreadful conviction that my struggle for life was over, and that I should rise no more. The floodgates of misery seemed now to be opened, and it rushed in living tide upon my soul. With the rapidity of lightning, I ran over every event of my life. Thoughts doubled and trebled upon me, until I saw, as if in vision, the entire past of my existence. It was all before me, as if painted with a sunbeam, and all seemingly faded like the phantoms of a vivid dream.

As calmness returned, reason resumed her empire. Fortunately, the weather was comfortable. I summoned all the powers of my memory, thought over every foot of the day's travel, and concluded that the glass must have become detached from my belt while sleeping. Five long miles over the hills must be retraced to regain it. There was no alternative, and before daylight I had staggered over half the distance. I found the lens on the spot where I had slept. No incident of my journey brought with it more of joy and relief.

Returning to the camp of the previous night, I lighted the pile I had prepared, and lay down for a night of rest. It was very cold, and towards morning commenced snowing. With difficulty I kept the fire alive. Sleep was impossible. When daylight came, I was impressed with the idea that I must go on despite the storm. A flash—momentary but vivid—came over me, that I should be saved. Snatching a lighted brand, I started through the storm. In the afternoon the storm abated and the sun shone at intervals. Coming to a small clump of trees, I set to work to prepare a camp. I laid the brand down which I had preserved with so much care, to pick up a few dry sticks with which to feed it, until I could collect wood for a camp-fire, and in the few minutes thus employed it expired. I sought to revive it, but every spark was gone. Clouds obscured the sun, now near the horizon, and the prospect of another night of exposure without fire became fearfully imminent. I sat down with my lens and the last remaining piece of touchwood I possessed to catch a gleam of sunshine, feeling that my life depended on it. In a few moments the cloud passed, and with trembling hands I presented the little disk to the face of the glowing luminary. Quivering with excitement lest a sudden cloud should interpose, a moment passed before I could hold the lens steadily enough to concentrate a burning focus. At length it came. The little thread of smoke curled gracefully upwards from the Heaven-lighted spark, which, a few moments afterwards, diffused with warmth and comfort my desolate lodgings.

I resumed my journey the next morning, with the belief that I should make no more fires with my lens. I must save a brand, or perish. The day was raw and gusty; an east wind, charged with storm, penetrated my nerves with irritating keenness. After walking a few miles the storm came on, and a coldness unlike any other I had ever felt seized me. It entered all my bones. I attempted to build a fire, but could not make it burn. Seizing a brand, I stumbled blindly on, stopping within the shadow of every rock and clump to renew energy for a final conflict for life. A solemn conviction that death was near, that at each pause I made my limbs would refuse further service, and that I should sink helpless and dying in my path, overwhelmed me with terror. Amid all this tumult of the mind, I felt that I had done all that man could do. I knew that in two or three days more I could effect my deliverance, and I derived no little satisfaction from the thought that, as I was now in the broad trail, my remains would be found, and my friends relieved of doubt as to my fate. Once only the thought flashed across my mind that I should be saved, and I seemed to hear a whispered command to "Struggle on." Groping along the side of a hill, I became suddenly sensible of a sharp reflection, as of burnished steel. Looking up, through half-closed eyes, two rough but kindly faces met my gaze.

"Are you Mr. Everts?"

"Yes. All that is left of him."

"We have come for you."

"Who sent you?"

"Judge Lawrence and other friends."

"God bless him, and them, and you! I am saved!" and with these words, powerless of further effort, I fell forward into the arms of my preservers, in a state of unconsciousness. I was saved. On the very brink of the river which divides the known from the unknown, strong arms snatched me from the final plunge, and kind ministrations wooed me back to life.

Baronet and Prichette, my two preservers, by the usual appliances, soon restored me to consciousness, made a camp upon the spot, and while one went to Fort Ellis, a distance of seventy miles, to return with remedies to restore digestion and an ambulance to convey me to that post, the other sat by my side, and with all the care, sympathy, and solicitude of a brother, ministered to my frequent necessities. In two days I was sufficiently recovered in strength to be moved twenty miles down the trail to the cabin of some miners who were prospecting in that vicinity. From these men I received every possible attention which their humane and generous natures could devise. A good bed was provided, game was killed to make broth, and the best stores of their larder placed at my command. For four days, at a time when every day's labor was invaluable in their pursuit, they abandoned their work to aid in my restoration. Owing to the protracted inaction of the system, and the long period which must transpire before Prichette's return with remedies, my friends had serious doubts of my recovery.

The night after my arrival at the cabin, while suffering the most excruciating agony, and thinking that I had only been saved to die among friends, a loud knock was heard at the cabin door. An old man in mountain costume entered—a hunter, whose life was spent among the mountains. He was on his way to find a brother. He listened to the story of my sufferings, and tears rapidly coursed each other down his rough, weather-beaten face. But when he was told of my present necessity, brightening in a moment, he exclaimed:

"Why, Lord bless you, if that is all, I have the very remedy you need. In two hours' time all shall be well with you."

He left the cabin, returning in a moment with a sack filled with the fat of a bear which he had killed a few hours before. From this he rendered out a pint measure of oil. I drank the whole of it. It proved to be the needed remedy, and the next day, freed from pain, with appetite and digestion re-established, I felt that good food and plenty of it were only necessary for an early recovery.

In a day or two I took leave of my kind friends, with a feeling of regret at parting, and of gratitude for their kindness as enduring as life. Meeting the carriage on my way, I proceeded to Boseman, where I remained among old friends, who gave me every attention until my health was sufficiently restored to allow me to return to my home at Helena.

My heartfelt thanks are due to the members of the Expedition, all of whom devoted seven, and some of them twelve days to the search for me before they left Yellowstone Lake; and to Judge Lawrence, of Helena, and the friends who co-operated with him in the offer of reward which sent Baronet and Prichette to my rescue.

My narrative is finished. In the course of events the time is not far distant when the wonders of the Yellowstone will be made accessible to all lovers of sublimity, grandeur, and novelty in natural scenery, and its majestic waters become the abode of civilization and refinement; and when that arrives, I hope, in happier mood and under more auspicious circumstances, to revisit scenes fraught for me with such thrilling interest; to ramble along the glowing beach of Bessie Lake; to sit down amid the hot springs under the shadow of Mount Everts; to thread unscared the mazy forests, retrace the dreary journey to the Madison Range, and with enraptured fancy gaze upon the mingled glories and terrors of the great falls and marvelous cañon, and to enjoy, in happy contrast with the trials they recall, their power to delight, elevate, and overwhelm the mind with wondrous and majestic beauty.

·3·

The Streams

Ann Zwinger

THERE ARE TWO SOUNDS that will forever remind me of Constant Friendship. One is the intermittent rhythm of wind through the pines and aspen, sometimes sibilant, sometimes sonorous. The other sound is the persistent perpetual purling of the streams. Even in the depths of winter, under a foot of snow, I can hear the quiet murmuring. The wind may or may not blow, the sun may or may not shine, but the streams speak as long as there is water.

Some years the streams thin to a trickle in August and September. Some springs their waters scour the banks with the impetus of melting mountain snows. But always the water goes down: down to the lake, down to far meadows, down to other streams and rivers, down to the sea, a continuum against which birdsong is lute and wind is recorder.

Each of the streams has its own personality. The south stream is clear and bright, flowing purposefully to the lake. The north stream is devious and often hidden, seeming to flow along because it has nothing better to do. The runoff stream below the dam is usually full and chortling, larking through protected grassy banks to the lower limits of the land.

I often walk the length of the south stream as it crosses our land, a pleasant walk in woods stocked with wildflowers. The stream enters the land just a few feet from the southwest corner and runs diagonally across the aspen grove to the lake, dropping about thirty feet on the way. It is a swift clean-flowing stream, wetting the soil along the edges of its banks, but never stagnating. Its banks are grassed to the edge and high enough above the stream to be stable on one side or the other. The stream's flow, except in the desperate days of drought, is continuous and consistent. But even when the weather is dry, the bottom flickers with running water.

Most of the time the chatter of the stream describes the obstacles it must pass on its way from above to below. The current makes riffles, twinkling around boulders and trapped logs. Its sounds tell of a different world for plants and animals than the stiller waters of the lake. The south stream is cooler than the lake because it is continuously flowing, preventing the accumulation of heat soaked up from the sun. The lake is open to the sun; the stream is shaded for almost its entire length. Its current mixes the water, maintaining a constant temperature throughout. When I plant watercress in the stream each spring, my hands get cold so fast that I can only do a few sprigs at a time and eventually resort to using an iced-tea spoon to keep my hands from numbing.

The lake is dependent upon the spring freshets to recharge its water with oxygen. The stream is permanent, whereas the lake is temporary. As long as there is water, the stream will run downhill, for it was there before the lake and it will be there after.

I could walk down the middle of the stream, were I so courageous, and never step on a plant other than the watercress I have planted. The south stream has few of the aquatic plants which form the basis of the lake's food chains. No skeins of algae thread its surface. No water striders hyphenate the stream from bank to bank. A jar of water from it looks empty and absolutely clear. I set it beside a jar of lake water which is slightly cloudy and pale brown and animated with all kinds of movement. The stream water looks sterile. It contains none of the miniature shamrock clusters of duckweed, no bobbing water fleas or darting ostracods. The current of the stream is too swift for the plankton of the lake.

But the occupants are there. Every mossy stick I pick up is well attended. Stonefly larvae and snails lurk inside the moss's protection. Clinging tightly to stones are flat planarian worms and tan-pink leeches. From every rock crevice tiny antennae sample the stream, well anchored against springtime rushes which can clean out the banks. If I hold a fine mesh screen from bank to bank downstream and Jane does some vigorous gravel-stirring and rock-turning upstream, an amazing number of surprised and undone inhabitants are snared, bucketing down into the screen.

One day in February, when it was much too cold to work outdoors, I brought indoors a plastic bag full of moss from the streamside. On the side of the bag, imprisoned in a tiny drop of water, no more than an eighth of an inch across, was a stonefly nymph. It was pushing and poking at the edges of the drop in an irritable way, imprisoned by the surface tension. A larger nymph appeared in the moss itself. The nymphs are almost impossible to find unless they venture out on their own, for they are the same dark brown as the dead sticks and debris in the stream, and can slither into hiding in a second. They are active even in winter when the temperature is zero and the stream is running ice water, and any sensible creature should be hibernating or sitting feet up in front of a warm Franklin stove.

Stonefly larvae are never found in stagnant or polluted waters with a low oxygen content, or where the water is still. Since swift current provides good aeration, the nymphs seek shelter along the bank or flatten themselves out on rocks, clinging by the double claws on each foot. In this bottom sixteenth inch of the stream the current is perceptibly less. The nymphs feed mainly on the detritus swept along the stream bottom or caught in the moss and liverworts of the stream border; as they grow larger, they also eat other smaller nymphs.

Another wriggling body likely to turn up in my collecting bag is that of a mayfly nymph, easily recognized by the seven pairs of gills extending from the abdomen and looking like fourteen small paddles. A long period of feeding and growth is necessary to store enough energy for molting and reproduction, since mayflies do not feed as adults and they may remain nymphs for several years.

The mayfly's three long cerci—tail-like projections that stream out behind like a train—act as balancers. (Stonefly larvae have two.) Mayfly larvae swim little, however, preferring to lurk in the dark corners of the stream bed. They survive because of their agility and high reproductive rate, for they are sought out for supper by the larger nymphs of the stream. Mayfly larvae themselves are primary consumers, living on tiny particles of vegetation.

Nymphs of another mayfly species live in the silt, burrowing to eat the riches of the diatom ooze. They have only a few single abdominal gills; the remainder are reduced in number and are tucked under a protecting flap on the back. The last pair of gills is transformed into a peplum-like cover which protects the functioning gills; a fringe of hairs on the cover interlocks to sift out the silt and prevent gill damage.

Mayflies are the only insects to molt again after reaching adult form. They live only long enough to mate and for the female to lay eggs. Ephemeroptera, the order of mayflies, is derived from the Greek *ephemeros*, meaning lasting but a day and from which our word "ephemeral" comes. The females swarm in lacy clouds, always against the light where they can be easily seen by the males. After mating, the female quickly lays her fertilized eggs near or in the water where the young will be properly housed and fed. Then she flies toward the lights, to which she never was attracted as a photo-negative nymph. We find dozens dead on the ground around the night lanterns, their short lives ended in a swift singe of wings.

Lake life fills the collecting jars; stream life has to be looked for. I find that I have to examine a stream rock for some time before my eye can discover a planarian worm. Its flat ribbon-like body adheres so closely to the rock that only a glint of water shows movement. The current flows over and around it as if it were indeed part of the rock.

A planarian in the slide dish is an animated ribbon, folding back on itself, winding and unwinding, spiraling through the water. Thousands of cilia, or tiny hairs, pulsing in succession, give planarians their flowing gliding movement which would be the envy of any water ballet team. Two slight points, called auricles, differentiate head from tail and give direction to the planarian's gyrations. To feed, it swings out a pharynx tube from its underside through which it sucks up films of algae. Planarians are also carnivorous, and a good way to catch them is to dangle a piece of fresh liver in the water.

Planarians reproduce by simple division and through eggs. Cut a planarian in half in either direction, and each portion grows what it lacks. Even more intriguing, some researchers suggest that the new side takes advantage of the "intelligence" of the older side and learns more quickly than a totally new all-of-one-piece planarian.

Leeches, in spite of their bad reputation, are quite delicate and as sinuously beautiful as the planarians. A pale pink-beige, they are segmented and the segments are further creased with deep wrinkles. They can expand like an accordion, stretching until their bodies are almost translucent. They can make themselves flat and are able to paste their bodies to stones or to slither into a crevice. Our leeches, although bloodsuckers, are not especially fond of humans and feed on the smaller animals of the stream.

When they feed, they insert the same kind of noncoagulating substance into the wound that a mosquito does. It is said that if one waits until a leech finishes feeding there will be no itching from the bite. I have found no one who can verify this and have chosen not to experiment myself.

·4·

Winter

Paul Gruchow

1

IN JANUARY CAME THE STING of hard winter, of polar winds, of driven snow, of sunshine without warmth.

The little winter birds—the chickadees, the juncos, the nuthatches—gathered at the backyard feeders and ate and shivered. They survived the handicaps of the weather and of their own tiny bodies by, among other strategies, eating and shivering. The birds that survived would shiver until the first warm day of spring.

The squirrels, so inconspicuous in summer, perched on the limbs of bald trees, their tails draped forward over their backs. The crows had given up calling to each other in the mornings and the evenings.

I sat one winter night in a town café listening to a farmer talk about the surprisingly complex language of pigs. The farmer said that simply from the sound of a pig, one could with experience tell its age, its approximate weight, and what had prompted it to cry out, whether it was being stepped on, or denied mother's milk, or whatever. He and his wife, the farmer said, had once occupied themselves during a long drive in cataloging the number of pig expressions they knew, and they had made a list of fifty before their journey had come to an end.

I am not a raiser of pigs. I cannot tell one pig noise from another. But I am a walker, and it occurred to me that it can be said in the same sense that the snow speaks. With proper attention, one can learn to tell the temperature of the air, the depth of snowfall on the ground, and the condition of the weather in the preceding week from the sound of snow underfoot.

By sound of foot against snow, one can tell the powdery snows of early winter from the wet snows of late winter, and both of them from the denser, harder snows of high winter.

One can tell the crunch of snow against foot on a day of more than 20°F from the squeak of snow on a day of 0°, and both from the hollow moan of the snow on a subzero day. One can distinguish by the sound of it the thin snow of open places from the drifted snow of sheltered places.

The deep snow of the first of January does not sound at all like the crusted snow after the thaw of early February. The Objibwe, in fact, named the months for the differences between the two: first there was the Moon of the Deep Snow and then the Moon of the Crusted Snow.

Are the sounds of the snow based on differences in crystalline structure? I have never seen this worked out anywhere. Snow crystals, with sometimes six, sometimes three, sometimes five sides, form in hexagonal plates at temperatures from 28°F to freezing; in needles from 24° to 27°; in hollow prismatic columns from 19° to 23°; in another kind of hexagonal plate from 11° to 18°; in fernlike stars from 4° to 10°; in plates again from −13° to 3°; and again in hollow prismatic columns at temperatures below −13°.

There is some principle of physics at work in the music of snow underfoot, just as there is a mathematical principle to explain why snow drifts at a fenceline in a scalloped pattern of elongated ovals rather than in the straight line of the fence. It does so for the same reason that a river meanders rather than advances in a straight line. I cannot explain the mathematics involved any more than I can articulate the structural underpinnings of the music of snow underfoot.

If I could explain the sound of a footstep upon the snow or come to know the underlying principles that govern the meandering of the snow along a fenceline, I should then be attuned in a new way to the largely unheard and mysterious music of the universe. It has often been said, and I shall argue the case myself, that the only remark of nature is its silence, but that is not because the world around us has nothing to say. It is because we come unequipped with ears to hear.

I am as unequipped as the next person. I listen in the dead of winter to the song the snow sings, and strain as I might, I cannot make it out. I listen to the coyotes howling in the nights and to the crows cawing in the mornings and to the wind washing in the leaves of the cottonwoods in the evenings, and I know that I have not really heard anything of it except the mystery in it. But the mystery has captivated me, and under the spell of it, I have meandered, like the drifts of snow, across the wide prairies.

2

The winter sky is the plain and homely sister of the skies, the sad-sack one, the ash sky, all gray and featureless, pale in the morning, pale at noon, pale at night. The winter sunrises are late and boringly pastel, and the sunsets are early and boringly pastel.

The earth in winter stares blankly back at the cold and featureless sky, does nothing to enhance or mimic it. Even the stars in winter do not seem to sparkle as they do at other times of the year.

I was driving through Minneapolis one winter night with my five-year-old daughter. She looked out of her window and spied the moon. "Oh!" she exclaimed. "That's why we haven't been having a moon at home. It's been up here in Minneapolis!"

She stared at the moon in silence for a long time. "The moon looks so sad in winter," she said. She stared up at the moon a while longer. "No wonder it's so sad," she said at last. "It doesn't even have any stars to keep it company."

The winter sky does, however, have its moments. They are the moments at dusk or at dawn when the angle of the light is exactly right to catch the crystalline haze in the air. Then the sun can be seen to be crowned with a halo or bracketed by sun dogs, and sometimes these dogs are as brilliantly multicolored as the rainbows that follow the summer rains. Or the sun seems just at the moment of setting to take the shape of a Roman cross, belled at the bottom and luminescent. It is on such nights that the lights of the little prairie towns stretch up into the sky like searchlights. Every settlement seems surrounded then by its private show of Northern Lights.

And there are the dawns and the dusks when the snow is falling, when the lights in the villages take on a fat and gauzy glow, when the whole prairie world, although dark, seems somehow aglow, when the sky above the storm becomes the particular pale pink of a prairie rose in bloom. When the winter sky puts on that face, the only possible response is to keep silent, as before any many-splendored thing.

3

It was a bright, mild, sparkling morning in early February. There was scarcely a breeze. There had been a snowfall six days earlier. The road to the quarry showed the tracks of the rabbits that had run there, but there was no sign of the humans who flocked to the place at any other time of year. Even in its prettiest dress, winter attracts scant notice.

Birds were singing everywhere in the thicket of trees at the base of the cliff. Half a dozen chickadees smartly capped in black jockeyed for places on the limbs of an oak tree. A crow passed overhead.

Beneath the trees, there was a place among the talus where the passing animals had traveled so frequently on one kind of business or another that a smooth, firm path had been worn in the snow.

On a little ledge in the face of the cliff rested the frozen carcass of a spider, one of thousands of casualties of the season in that place.

Atop the cliff, the isolated blond tufts of buffalo grass stood in the cracks of red rocks, each tuft bundled in white snow. The bunches of dried blue grama grass, a survivor in the harshest and driest of places, nodded their long eyelashes.

Where the high prairie had been burned in the fall before, the landscape was black and barren, but where the grasses still stood, the landscape was covered with a soft, loose blanket of snow. It was one of the services that the dense sod performed for all the plants on the prairie: to catch and save the precious snow to feed the burst of new growth in the spring.

There were fewer footprints on high than in the valley below: signs of deer, of a fox, of a rabbit, of a mouse, of a shrew perhaps pregnant by now, and they were widely scattered.

No birds sang. The grasses did not rustle. There was no buzzing of insects. And no croaking of frogs at the stock ponds. Even the farm implements were silent.

In the summer, everything in this place seemed to quiver with the continuous wavering of a thousand songs and sounds. But on this day, the quavering had stopped, and a clear, bright calm had descended and had covered everything with its sweet peace.

4

The blue light of the full moon, the Moon of the Crusted Snow, was already beginning to wane.

Talcot Lake. Midafternoon. The glare of sun on snow was blinding. It was necessary to make a shade with your hands to see into the distance.

In the open, the snow was packed hard enough to hold the weight of a human. In some spots, it was so hard that the hooves of the passing deer had not completely penetrated it. But in the woods, the snow was soft and deep, and walking was nearly impossible except on the numerous paths the deer had made in their extensive yard. Everywhere there were icy ruts where deer had bedded down and melted the snow with the warmth of their bodies.

I stood in the shadow of an uprooted tree at the edge of the lake and watched and listened.

Beyond the tall plumes of the *Phragmites*, there seemed at first to be no life. Then one deer stepped out onto the lake, and two, then deer were apparent everywhere, standing along the lakeshore, among the cattail rushes, on the hillsides, in the fields and woods beyond the lake. The lake seemed suddenly to be as alive with the motion of deer as an anthill is with the business of ants on a hot day in August. Then I became aware of a spot of brown at midlake. I realized I was seeing a red fox and that the fox was stalking some invisible quarry.

The deer in the farther distance were, like me, at a standstill. They were gathered in groups, their ears up, their heads high, watching the hunt of the fox too. The fox seemed oblivious to the spectacle it was creating.

It stole forward. Forward a little more. Suddenly, a pair of ducks, the objects of the fox's quest, took to the air with a clamor and headed north to a quieter place. Their quacks grew fainter and fainter.

The fox pursued them for a few yards, stopped, looked sheepish, turned, and loped easily across the lake, passed through the crowds of onlooking deer, and disappeared around a bend in the shoreline.

Now a second fox appeared, a second watcher in the wings. It soon turned and ran away too.

The deer began to move again. They came in a steady stream out of the woods and onto the surface of the lake. There seemed to be no end to them.

I thought of the profusion of life that had once teemed upon the prairies: great herds of bison, pronghorn antelopes by the millions, clouds of locusts that blackened the skies, waterfowl in spring and fall settling on hundreds of sloughs by the tens of thousands.

A few of the deer moved around a bed of reeds, passed the dam, and came to within a hundred yards of me. The small doe leading the way was frisky. She seemed to leap for the pleasure of leaping, prancing rather than running. She danced her way across the ice. Then she spied me. She stopped short. She assessed the potential for danger, decided to move ahead. When she did, the frisk had gone out of her step. She ran swiftly in high, bounding leaps.

I watched as she sailed into the cattails. Her white tail was up all the way. It waved back and forth like a flag of truce after the rest of her body had disappeared from view.

5

It has been to places like Rush Lake that I have repaired in every season of the year from the time when I was a young boy. I have been afflicted with wanderlust for as long as I can remember. It is the characteristic hunger of isolation.

I was born at mid-century. My parents, who were poor and rural, had never amounted to anything, and never would, and never expected to. They were rather glad for the inconsequence of their lives. They got up with the sun and retired with it. Their routines were dictated by the seasons. In summer they tended; in fall they harvested; in winter they repaired; in spring they planted. It had always been so; so it would always be.

The farmstead we occupied was on a hilltop overlooking a marshy river bottom that stretched from horizon to horizon. It was half a mile from any road and an eternity from any connection with the rest of the culture. There were no books there; there was no music; there was no television; for a long time, no telephone. Only on the rarest of occasions—a time or two a year—was there a social visitor other than the pastor. There was no conversation in that house.

The highest event of the year was the night in October when the tomcat who ruled the territory came. He came every October without fail. Like the pastor, the cat was always offered something to eat. In the cat's case, it was always a tin pie plate of goat's milk into which a thick slice or two of dense homemade bread had been crumbled. He was an enormous yellow cat with eyes the size of a horned owl's. Eventually all the other barn cats in the neighborhood came to look just like him. Nobody knew how many generations of kittens he had sired. He loved his goat's milk and his chunks of soggy bread. His purr filled the farmstead kitchen. He loved to be petted. After he had been fed, he spent an hour or more circling the little room, holding his tail high, arching his back, rubbing himself against our ankles. It was a kind of prenuptial dance. Then he would beg to be let out into the night, and it would be October again before he would return. We always stood in the doorway and watched him disappear across the yard.

One October, the cat didn't come back. Nobody ever saw him again. After that, there was a new degree of silence in our household.

I knew even as a young boy that I would not bear the silence. I ran away for the first time at eighteen months of age. I got a mile and a half. I was on a bridgetop mesmerized by the music of the water running into the drainage ditch below when the gasman found me and carried me home. I was soundly spanked. But there was no keeping me.

I was six or seven when I stopped wandering along the roads and started taking the back way to the wildernesses, to the fencerows, to the meadows, to the marshes, to the river.

I took a liking to bones, made a collection of them in the hayloft. I believed in ghosts, heard them in the night, saw their faces in the bald moonlit trunks of cottonwoods. It was the ghostliness in the bones that attracted me. I was indiscriminate about them. The pincers of crayfish were as satisfying to me as the femurs of cows.

There were mudholes in the meadows where cattle ran and these sometimes entrapped cows. The femurs, even the skulls, of cattle were available for the taking. I knew a place where there was a whole skeleton, picked clean by scavengers, lying white as a ghost and half-immersed in the muck. I visited it often as a boy and hoped to catch in the eerie silence of the place even something so compromised as the half-wild spirit of the creature who had died there.

Perhaps I did catch something of this spirit. My habit of collecting bones came to an end. I took up the trapping of the furbearers that lived in the river bottom. I learned to catch muskrats, skunks, and weasels. I subscribed to *Fur, Fish & Game*. I dreamed of living someday in a cabin in the Adirondacks. In these dreams, I was always alone, it was always winter, and I was always out on my snowshoes tending one of my traplines. It was an evergreen world, silent and unsullied.

I was not after the pelts, nor the money I got from selling them. I had to be nagged to skin the creatures I caught and to see to stretching the pelts and scraping and drying them. Once I had caught a creature, I was through with it.

I was after a share of the wildness in the creatures I was pursuing. I wanted the thrill of thinking like something wild, of guessing where I would be if I were, say, a weasel, of imagining the things that might then rouse my curiosity, of thinking just where I would step. I wanted to be able to read the landscape in the way that a weasel does, to share its habit of seeing, to assume its language. I was like a blind man imagining sight or a deaf man hearing. I yearned for that leap of imagination that would send me off into the unimaginable wildness.

The day came when I thought I might match wits against a mink, the smartest, the most elusive of the wild creatures I knew. I had spent years by now watching the life in my valley, but the mink was a creature of the night, and I had never chanced even to catch a glimpse of one. Nevertheless, I knew they existed, and I knew where. The signs of them, which I had learned to read, were all around.

My father showed me how to set a trap on a slide so that when I caught my mink, it would be quickly drowned. He showed me the basic principles of positioning a trap for a mink: how to follow the trail of the mink along a streambank, what sort of obstruction would force it down into the water, where it would be likely to move when it was so diverted, how to construct an artificial diversion, how to conceal a trap without demobilizing it, how to use a bit of musk oil as a come-on and where to apply it in relation to the trap. I followed my father's instructions and felt myself drawn nearer to the wildness I sought. I imagined that I was an Indian boy long ago and that the instruction I was getting was ultimately in the art of survival. I wished to need to know how to survive, as boys once did.

I set my traps and tended them. When they failed to produce, I made adjustments. Once or twice I found a sprung trap, and these gave me encouragement. But the mink remained elusive.

A new season came, and I set out my lines again. Every trap was aimed at a mink. I could not be bothered with such mundane matters as catching mere muskrats. I did catch two or three of them quite by accident that season, however. No mink.

One day near the end of the season, there was warning of a blizzard. My father told me to pull in my traps while I still could, but I ignored the advice. Before I could make a last check of them, the snow started to fall so heavily and the winds began to drive it so fiercely that there could be no thought of going down into the valley. The snow fell all that day and the next, and the wind blew for two nights and three days before there was peace again.

Midway through my rounds the next spring, at a set that had been sprung the preceding fall, I found a trap out of place. I yanked its stake up, and when I began to pull on its chain, I realized there was more than a trap at the other end of it. The little stream was swollen with the debris of the spring flood, and it was nasty business to get the catch untangled and up into the air. When the trap finally drew up, I saw that I had a mink on the end of it, a fine buck mink in a splendid dark winter coat. It was somewhat the worse for wear, having spent its winter in ice and its spring being bumped and scraped about in the muck of the melt, but it was still quite a prize.

I was wild with excitement. But when I unsnared it, I saw that my slide had not worked properly. The mink had not drowned right away. It had very nearly gnawed its leg through before death had come. I understood that the creature had been caught as that storm had come up. It had been intent upon finding shelter and a bit less wary than usual. It had made a desperate attempt to free itself, had nearly succeeded, and only the fact of the storm had finally done it in.

I took the mink home, skinned it, fleshed it, stretched it, hung it up to dry. The carcass I gave to the barn cats, which chewed it down to bones before the night was out. And then I took myself away to a private place and faced the sadness that had swollen up inside me. I did not understand it then or ever. The best I could make of it was that I was feeling a kind of shame for having taken advantage of the mink I had so admired. I could in a sense partake of its wildness; with enough patience and study I could make out its ways and deliver it into my own hands; I could learn the language of the wild mink. But the consequence was, and always would be, some kind of destruction.

From that day on, I put a distance between myself and the mink. I never again tried to trap it or any other creature. It was, I suppose, something of a denial of my own nature. Perhaps this was in itself a step back toward wildness.

After that it seemed as though I was always happening upon a mink somewhere. I saw mink many times even in daylight, always fleetingly. I would be passing around the shore of a lake or approaching the edge of a marsh or sitting in a tree somewhere, watching the spectacle all about, when out of the corner of my eye I would catch the dark blur of motion. A mink under these circumstances had a serpentine look: low, furtive, fast-moving. It had always the manner of a creature just escaping from the scene of the crime. A time or two, I had even seen a mink crossing a highway in broad daylight, and once I had seen one on a city street in midafternoon, crouched down and running like hell from a bank robbery or whatever.

One springtime years later, I went down to the dam in Blue Mounds State Park to watch the annual migration of the carp. In the springtime, like the fabled salmon of the Northwest, the carp in the park's lower pond try to make their way up a tiny stream, over a dam, and into the upper pond. The height of the dam is six or eight feet above spring water level; it is an overwhelming barrier to a leaping carp. I have never seen one make it.

The length of the odds is nothing to discourage a carp. Time and time again, one will use the strength of its tail to throw itself up into the air. Generally, it will land upon the jagged rocks somewhere forward of the position from which it started. It will come down with a slap, and then either it will be washed back into the pool it started from, or it will be in a position to heave itself up into the air again and try its luck at another advance upon the waterfall. The efforts of an hour might bring it at last to the base of the concrete dam, where it will try again and again to leap up into the pond until, in tiredness or miscalculation, it makes a jump that causes it to fall out of range of the highest holding pool. Then it will slide and bang down into the stream again, from which it will mount a new assault on the pond.

I was there at the edge of the uppermost pond, altogether caught up in the ordeal of the carp, when I became aware, as one does by some sixth sense, that I was not alone. The tension of the second presence was palpable. I tried to see where the creature was, taking care not to make any grand or jagged movement that would alarm it. But I could see nothing.

A minute or two passed. A small carp almost at my feet made a feeble assault on the mountainous dam, failed, fell with a splash back into the pool. Momentarily stunned from the fall, it was taking a few seconds to get its sense of direction again. That hesitation proved fatal: a dark creature lunged forward, snared the fish in its claws, secured it behind the head in its jaws, and disappeared into the thicket of rushes at the edge of the holding pool. The whole action took a few seconds. It was like the brief shadow of a cloud passing.

I turned quickly, looked down the bank of the stream. In two spots where it was exposed, I saw the mink emerge with the fish in its mouth and disappear again into the young green vegetation. In a minute it was gone, forever out of sight. I spent a long time trying to trace it, to get another glimpse of it, to discover where it had gone with the fish, but the search came to nothing. It was as futile an effort as the one the vulnerable carp was making at the foot of the dam. Water fell over the dam and crashed down upon the rocks with a roar and ran off in the mysterious direction of the mink.

That was all there was to it. But the experience stayed with me. For at least those couple of minutes one springtime afternoon, the mink and I had stood side by side on the bank of that little stream, both fishing after the same object, in our unique ways. In that evanescence, we had been— however briefly, however tangentially—soul mates.

Now it was high winter on Rush Lake, and I was wandering again. The landscape was as clean and spare as any the prairie winter offers: signs of a mouse, here and there the tracks of a pheasant, at a few of the muskrat houses on the lake open breathing holes indicating residents, a pair of cottontail rabbits in the shelter of the shore, a shrike shouting from a treetop, a pair of chickadees, in the distance the calling of a crow. The wind had piled the snow in waves and scalloped them to look like the beached and empty shells of sea creatures. The waves of the lake itself had been caught and frozen in midair. Here not only sound but motion had been suspended.

And then, at midlake, the creature presented itself again. I had stopped at one of the largest muskrat houses to look for signs of occupancy. In the fresh snow around the rather large air hole, I saw the footprints of a mink. The mink had not entered the house. It had merely paused there to investigate; then it had urinated at the edge of the hole, dropped its scat, and gone on its way. The snow on the surface of the lake was older and harder-packed. In a few feet, the trail of the mink disappeared. The droppings on the house were full of muskrat hair.

I wandered until dusk, drinking in the sharpness, the cleanness of the winter air. When the sun set, it was almost colorless, as understated as everything else in winter, except for the wind.

I came out upon the road again and climbed a little knoll toward the highway. The light was falling rapidly. The cars passing on the highway were already operating with headlights. And then in the shadows ahead I saw the mink. It may have been the one I had seen signs of earlier. The mink turned, stared at me for a long, deliberate second, disappeared.

It was for all the world like a wink.

·5·

Seeing

Annie Dillard

WHEN I WAS SIX OR SEVEN YEARS OLD, growing up in Pittsburgh, I used to take a precious penny of my own and hide it for someone else to find. It was a curious compulsion; sadly, I've never been seized by it since. For some reason I always "hid" the penny along the same stretch of sidewalk up the street. I would cradle it at the roots of a sycamore, say, or in a hole left by a chipped-off piece of sidewalk. Then I would take a piece of chalk, and, starting at either end of the block, draw huge arrows leading up to the penny from both directions. After I learned to write I labeled the arrows: SURPRISE AHEAD or MONEY THIS WAY. I was greatly excited, during all this arrow-drawing, at the thought of the first lucky passer-by who would receive in this way, regardless of merit, a free gift from the universe. But I never lurked about. I would go straight home and not give the matter another thought, until, some months later, I would be gripped again by the impulse to hide another penny.

It is still the first week in January, and I've got great plans. I've been thinking about seeing. There are lots of things to see, unwrapped gifts and free surprises. The world is fairly studded and strewn with pennies cast broadside from a generous hand. But—and this is the point—who gets excited by a mere penny? If you follow one arrow, if you crouch motionless on a bank to watch a tremulous ripple thrill on the water and are rewarded by the sight of a muskrat kit paddling from its den, will you count that sight a chip of copper only, and go your rueful way? It is dire poverty indeed when a man is so malnourished and fatigued that he won't stoop to pick up a penny. But if you cultivate a healthy poverty and simplicity, so that finding a penny will literally make your day, then, since the world is in fact planted in pennies, you have with your poverty bought a lifetime of days. It is that simple. What you see is what you get.

I used to be able to see flying insects in the air. I'd look ahead and see, not the row of hemlocks across the road, but the air in front of it. My eyes would focus along that column of air, picking out flying insects. But I lost interest, I guess, for I dropped the habit. Now I can see birds. Probably some people can look at the grass at their feet and discover all the crawling creatures. I would like to know grasses and sedges—and care. Then my least journey into the world would be a field trip, a series of happy recognitions. Thoreau, in an expansive mood, exulted, "What a rich book might be made about buds, including, perhaps, sprouts!" It would be nice to think so. I cherish mental images I have of three perfectly happy people. One collects stones. Another—an Englishman, say—watches clouds. The third lives on a coast and collects drops of seawater which he examines microscopically and mounts. But I don't see what the specialist sees, and so I cut myself off, not only from the total picture, but from the various forms of happiness.

Unfortunately, nature is very much a now-you-see-it, now-you-don't affair. A fish flashes, then dissolves in the water before my eyes like so much salt. Deer apparently ascend bodily into heaven; the brightest oriole fades into leaves. These disappearances stun me into stillness and concentration; they say of nature that it conceals with a grand nonchalance, and they say of vision that it is a deliberate gift, the revelation of a dancer who for my eyes only flings away her seven veils. For nature does reveal as well as conceal: now-you-don't-see-it, now-you-do. For a week last September migrating red-winged blackbirds were feeding heavily down by the creek at the back of the house. One day I went out to investigate the racket; I walked up to a tree, an Osage orange, and a hundred birds flew away. They simply materialized out of the tree. I saw a tree, then a whisk of color, then a tree again. I walked closer and another hundred blackbirds took flight. Not a branch, not a twig budged: the birds were apparently weightless as well as invisible. Or, it was as if the leaves of the Osage orange had been freed from a spell in the form of red-winged blackbirds; they flew from the tree, caught my eye in the sky, and vanished. When I looked again at the tree the leaves had reassembled as if nothing had happened. Finally I walked directly to the trunk of the tree and a final hundred, the real diehards, appeared, spread, and vanished. How could so many hide in the tree without my seeing them? The Osage orange, unruffled, looked just as it had looked from the house, when three hundred red-winged blackbirds cried from its crown. I looked downstream where they flew, and they were gone. Searching, I couldn't spot one. I wandered downstream to force them to play their hand, but they'd crossed the creek and scattered. One show to a customer. These appearances catch at my throat; they are the free gifts, the bright coppers at the roots of trees.

It's all a matter of keeping my eyes open. Nature is like one of those line drawings of a tree that are puzzles for children: Can you find hidden in the leaves a duck, a house, a boy, a bucket, a zebra, and a boot? Specialists can find the most incredibly well-hidden things. A book I read when I was young recommended an easy way to find caterpillars to rear: you simply find some fresh caterpillar droppings, look up, and there's your caterpillar. More recently an author advised me to set my mind at ease about those piles of cut stems on the ground in grassy fields. Field mice make them; they cut the grass down by degrees to reach the seeds at the head. It seems that when the grass is tightly packed, as in a field of ripe grain, the blade won't topple at a single cut through the stem; instead, the cut stem simply drops vertically, held in the crush of grain. The mouse severs the bottom again and again, the stem keeps dropping an inch at a time, and finally the head is low enough for the mouse to reach the seeds. Meanwhile, the mouse is positively littering the field with its little piles of cut stems into which, presumably, the author of the book is constantly stumbling.

If I can't see these minutiae, I still try to keep my eyes open. I'm always on the lookout for antlion traps in sandy soil, monarch pupae near milkweed, skipper larvae in locust leaves. These things are utterly common, and I've not seen one. I bang on hollow trees near water, but so far no flying squirrels have appeared. In flat country I watch every sunset in hopes of seeing the green ray. The green ray is a seldom-seen streak of light that rises from the sun like a spurting fountain at the moment of sunset; it throbs into the sky for two seconds and disappears. One more reason to keep my eyes open. A photography professor at the University of Florida just happened to see a bird die in midflight; it jerked, died, dropped, and smashed on the ground. I squint at the wind because I read Stewart Edward White: "I have always maintained that if you looked closely enough you could *see* the wind—the dim, hardly-made-out, fine débris fleeing high in the air." White was an excellent observer, and devoted an entire chapter of *The Mountains* to the subject of seeing deer: "As soon as you can forget the naturally obvious and construct an artificial obvious, then you too will see deer."

But the artificial obvious is hard to see. My eyes account for less than one percent of the weight of my head; I'm bony and dense; I see what I expect. I once spent a full three minutes looking at a bullfrog that was so unexpectedly large I couldn't see it even though a dozen enthusiastic campers were shouting directions. Finally I asked, "What color am I looking for?" and a fellow said, "Green." When at last I picked out the frog, I saw what painters are up against: the thing wasn't green at all, but the color of wet hickory bark.

The lover can see, and the knowledgeable. I visited an aunt and uncle at a quarter-horse ranch in Cody, Wyoming. I couldn't do much of anything useful, but I could, I thought, draw. So, as we all sat around the kitchen table after supper, I produced a sheet of paper and drew a horse. "That's one lame horse," my aunt volunteered. The rest of the family joined in: "Only place to saddle that one is his neck"; "Looks like we better shoot the poor thing, on account of those terrible growths." Meekly, I slid the pencil and paper down the table. Everyone in that family, including my three young cousins, could draw a horse. Beautifully. When the paper came back it looked as though five shining, real quarter horses had been corraled by mistake with a papier-mâché moose; the real horses seemed to gaze at the monster with a steady, puzzled air. I stay away from horses now, but I can do a creditable goldfish. The point is that I just don't know what the lover knows. I just can't see the artificial obvious that those in the know construct. The herpetologist asks the native, "Are there snakes in that ravine?" "Nosir." And the herpetologist comes home with yessir, three bags full. Are there butterflies on that mountain? Are the bluets in bloom, are there arrowheads here, or fossil shells in the shale?

Peeping through my keyhole I see within the range of only about thirty percent of the light that comes from the sun; the rest is infrared and some little ultraviolet, perfectly apparent to many animals, but invisible to me. A nightmare network of ganglia, charged and firing without my knowledge, cuts and splices what I do see, editing it for my brain. Donald E. Carr points out that the sense impressions of one-celled animals are *not* edited for the brain: "This is philosophically interesting in a rather mournful way, since it means that only the simplest animals perceive the universe as it is."

A fog that won't burn away drifts and flows across my field of vision. When you see fog move against a backdrop of deep pines, you don't see the fog itself, but streaks of clearness floating across the air in dark shreds. So I see only tatters of clearness through a pervading obscurity. I can't distinguish the fog from the overcast sky; I can't be sure if the light is direct or reflected. Everywhere darkness and the presence of the unseen appalls. We estimate now that only one atom dances alone in every cubic meter of intergalactic space. I blink and squint. What planet or power yanks Halley's Comet out of orbit? We haven't seen that force yet; it's a question of distance, density, and the pallor of reflected light. We rock, cradled in the swaddling band of darkness. Even the simple darkness of night whispers suggestions to the mind. Last summer, in August, I stayed at the creek too late.

Where Tinker Creek flows under the sycamore log bridge to the tear-shaped island, it is slow and shallow, fringed thinly in cattail marsh. At this spot an astonishing bloom of life supports vast breeding populations of insects, fish, reptiles, birds, and mammals. On windless summer evenings I stalk along the creek bank or straddle the sycamore log in absolute stillness, watching for muskrats. The night I stayed too late I was hunched on the log staring spellbound at spreading, reflected stains of lilac on the water. A cloud in the sky suddenly lighted as if turned on by a switch; its reflection just as suddenly materialized on the water upstream, flat and floating, so that I couldn't see the creek bottom, or life in the water under the cloud. Downstream, away from the cloud on the water, water turtles smooth as beans were gliding down with the current in a series of easy, weightless push-offs, as men bound on the moon. I didn't know whether to trace the progress of one turtle I was sure of, risking sticking my face in one of the bridge's spider webs made invisible by the gathering dark, or take a chance on seeing the carp, or scan the mudbank in hope of seeing a muskrat, or follow the last of the swallows who caught at my heart and trailed it after them like streamers as they appeared from directly below, under the log, flying upstream with their tails forked, so fast.

But shadows spread, and deepened, and stayed. After thousands of years we're still strangers to darkness, fearful aliens in an enemy camp with our arms crossed over our chests. I stirred. A land turtle on the bank, startled, hissed the air from its lungs and withdrew into its shell.

An uneasy pink here, an unfathomable blue there, gave great suggestion of lurking beings. Things were going on. I couldn't see whether that sere rustle I heard was a distant rattlesnake, slit-eyed, or a nearby sparrow kicking in the dry flood debris slung at the foot of a willow. Tremendous action roiled the water everywhere I looked, big action, inexplicable. A tremor welled up beside a gaping muskrat burrow in the bank and I caught my breath, but no muskrat appeared. The ripples continued to fan upstream with a steady, powerful thrust. Night was knitting over my face an eyeless mask, and I still sat transfixed. A distant airplane, a delta wing out of nightmare, made a gliding shadow on the creek's bottom that looked like a stingray cruising upstream. At once a black fin slit the pink cloud on the water, shearing it in two. The two halves merged together and seemed to dissolve before my eyes. Darkness pooled in the cleft of the creek and rose, as water collects in a well. Untamed, dreaming lights flickered over the sky. I saw hints of hulking underwater shadows, two pale splashes out of the water, and round ripples rolling close together from a blackened center.

At last I stared upstream where only the deepest violet remained of the cloud, a cloud so high its underbelly still glowed feeble color reflected from a hidden sky lighted in turn by a sun halfway to China. And out of that violet, a sudden enormous black body arced over the water. I saw only a cylindrical sleekness. Head and tail, if there was a head and tail, were both submerged in cloud. I saw only one ebony fling, a headlong dive to darkness; then the waters closed, and the lights went out.

I walked home in a shivering daze, up hill and down. Later I lay openmouthed in bed, my arms flung wide at my sides to steady the whirling darkness. At this latitude I'm spinning 836 miles an hour round the earth's axis; I often fancy I feel my sweeping fall as a breakneck arc like the dive of dolphins, and the hollow rushing of wind raises hair on my neck and the side of my face. In orbit around the sun I'm moving 64,800 miles an hour. The solar system as a whole, like a merry-go-round unhinged, spins, bobs, and blinks at the speed of 43,200 miles an hour along a course set east of Hercules. Someone has piped, and we are dancing a tarantella until the sweat pours. I open my eyes and I see dark, muscled forms curl out of water, with flapping gills and flattened eyes. I close my eyes and I see stars, deep stars giving way to deeper stars, deeper stars bowing to deepest stars at the crown of an infinite cone.

"Still," wrote van Gogh in a letter, "a great deal of light falls on everything." If we are blinded by darkness, we are also blinded by light. When too much light falls on everything, a special terror results. Peter Freuchen describes the notorious kayak sickness to which Greenland Eskimos are prone. "The Greenland fjords are peculiar for the spells of completely quiet weather, when there is not enough wind to blow out a match and the water is like a sheet of glass. The kayak hunter must sit in his boat without stirring a finger so as not to scare the shy seals away. . . . The sun, low in the sky, sends a glare into his eyes, and the landscape around moves into the realm of the unreal. The reflex from the mirror-like water hypnotizes him, he seems to be unable to move, and all of a sudden it is as if he were floating in a bottomless void, sinking, sinking, and sinking. . . . Horror-stricken, he tries to stir, to cry out, but he cannot, he is completely paralyzed, he just falls and falls." Some hunters are especially cursed with this panic, and bring ruin and sometimes starvation to their families.

Sometimes here in Virginia at sunset low clouds on the southern or northern horizon are completely invisible in the lighted sky. I only know one is there because I can see its reflection in still water. The first time I discovered this mystery I looked from cloud to no-cloud in bewilderment, checking my bearings over and over, thinking maybe the ark of the covenant was just passing by south of Dead Man Mountain. Only much later did I read the explanation: polarized light from the sky is very much weakened by reflection, but the light in clouds isn't polarized. So invisible clouds pass among visible clouds, till all slide over the mountains; so a greater light extinguishes a lesser as though it didn't exist.

In the great meteor shower of August, the Perseid, I wail all day for the shooting stars I miss. They're out there showering down, committing hara-kiri in a flame of fatal attraction, and hissing perhaps at last into the ocean. But at dawn what looks like a blue dome clamps down over me like a lid on a pot. The stars and planets could smash and I'd never know. Only a piece of ashen moon occasionally climbs up or down the inside of the dome, and our local star without surcease explodes on our heads. We have really only that one light, one source for all power, and yet we must turn away from it by universal decree. Nobody here on the planet seems aware of this strange, powerful taboo, that we all walk about carefully averting our faces, this way and that, lest our eyes be blasted forever.

Darkness appalls and light dazzles; the scrap of visible light that doesn't hurt my eyes hurts my brain. What I see sets me swaying. Size and distance and the sudden swelling of meanings confuse me, bowl me over. I straddle the sycamore log bridge over Tinker Creek in the summer. I look at the lighted creek bottom: snail tracks tunnel the mud in quavering curves. A crayfish jerks, but by the time I absorb what has happened, he's gone in a billowing smokescreen of silt. I look at the water: minnows and shiners. If I'm thinking minnows, a carp will fill my brain till I scream. I look at the water's surface: skaters, bubbles, and leaves sliding down. Suddenly, my own face, reflected, startles me witless. Those snails have been tracking my face! Finally, with a shuddering wrench of the will, I see clouds, cirrus clouds. I'm dizzy, I fall in. This looking business is risky.

Once I stood on a humped rock on nearby Purgatory Mountain, watching through binoculars the great autumn hawk migration below, until I discovered that I was in danger of joining the hawks on a vertical migration of my own. I was used to binoculars, but not, apparently, to balancing on humped rocks while looking through them. I staggered. Everything advanced and receded by turns; the world was full of unexplained foreshortenings and depths. A distant huge tan object, a hawk the size of an elephant, turned out to be the browned bough of a nearby loblolly pine. I followed a sharp-shinned hawk against a featureless sky, rotating my head unawares as it flew, and when I lowered the glass a glimpse of my own looming shoulder sent me staggering. What prevents the men on Palomar from falling, voiceless and blinded, from their tiny, vaulted chairs?

I reel in confusion; I don't understand what I see. With the naked eye I can see two million light-years to the Andromeda galaxy. Often I slop some creek water in a jar and when I get home I dump it in a white china bowl. After the silt settles I return and see tracings of minute snails on the bottom, a planarian or two winding round the rim of water, roundworms shimmying frantically, and finally, when my eyes have adjusted to these dimensions, amoebae. At first the amoebae look like muscae volitantes, those curled moving spots you seem to see in your eyes when you stare at a distant wall. Then I see the amoebae as drops of water congealed, bluish, translucent, like chips of sky in the bowl. At length I choose one individual and give myself over to its idea of an evening. I see it dribble a grainy foot before it on its wet, unfathomable way. Do its unedited sense impressions include the fierce focus of my eyes? Shall I take it outside and show it Andromeda, and blow its little endoplasm? I stir the water with a finger, in case it's running out of oxygen. Maybe I should get a tropical aquarium with motorized bubblers and lights, and keep this one for a pet. Yes, it would tell its fissioned descendants, the universe is two feet by five, and if you listen closely you can hear the buzzing music of the spheres.

Oh, it's mysterious lamplit evenings, here in the galaxy, one after the other. It's one of those nights when I wander from window to window, looking for a sign. But I can't see. Terror and a beauty insoluble are a ribband of blue woven into the fringes of garments of things both great and small. No culture explains, no bivouac offers real haven or rest. But it could be that we are not seeing something. Galileo thought comets were an optical illusion. This is fertile ground: since we are certain that they're not, we can look at what our scientists have been saying with fresh hope. What if there are *really* gleaming, castellated cities hung upside-down over the desert sand? What limpid lakes and cool date palms have our caravans always passed untried? Until, one by one, by the blindest of leaps, we light on the road to these places, we must stumble in darkness and hunger. I turn from the window. I'm blind as a bat, sensing only from every direction the echo of my own thin cries.

I chanced on a wonderful book by Marius von Senden, called *Space and Sight*. When Western surgeons discovered how to perform safe cataract operations, they ranged across Europe and America operating on dozens of men and women of all ages who had been blinded by cataracts since birth. Von Senden collected accounts of such cases; the histories are fascinating. Many doctors had tested their patients' sense perceptions and ideas of space both before and after the operations. The vast majority of patients, of both sexes and all ages, had, in von Senden's opinion, no idea of space whatsoever. Form, distance, and size were so many meaningless syllables. A patient "had no idea of depth, confusing it with roundness." Before the operation a doctor would give a blind patient a cube and a sphere; the patient would tongue it or feel it with his hands, and name it correctly. After the operation the doctor would show the same objects to the patient without letting him touch them; now he had no clue whatsoever what he was seeing. One patient called lemonade "square" because it pricked on his tongue as a square shape pricked on the touch of his hands. Of another postoperative patient, the doctor writes, "I have found in her no notion of size, for example, not even within the narrow limits which she might have encompassed with the aid of touch. Thus when I asked her to show me how big her mother was, she did not stretch out her hands, but set her two index-fingers a few inches apart." Other doctors reported their patients' own statements to similar effect. "The room he was in . . . he knew to be but part of the house, yet he could not conceive that the whole house could look bigger"; "Those who are blind from birth . . . have no real conception of height or distance. A house that is a mile away is thought of as nearby, but requiring the taking of a lot of steps. . . . The elevator that whizzes him up and down gives no more sense of vertical distance than does the train of horizontal."

For the newly sighted, vision is pure sensation unencumbered by meaning: "The girl went through the experience that we all go through and forget, the moment we are born. She saw, but it did not mean anything but a lot of different kinds of brightness." Again, "I asked the patient what he could see; he answered that he saw an extensive field of light, in which everything appeared dull, confused, and in motion. He could not distinguish objects." Another patient saw "nothing but a confusion of forms and colours." When a newly sighted girl saw photographs and paintings, she asked, " 'Why do they put those dark marks all over them?' 'Those aren't dark marks,' her mother explained, 'those are shadows. That is one of the ways the eye knows that things have shape. If it were not for shadows many things would look flat.' 'Well, that's how things do look,' Joan answered. 'Everything looks flat with dark patches.' "

But it is the patients' concepts of space that are most revealing. One patient, according to his doctor, "practiced his vision in a strange fashion; thus he takes off one of his boots, throws it some way off in front of him, and then attempts to gauge the distance at which it lies; he takes a few steps towards the boot and tries to grasp it; on failing to reach it, he moves on a step or two and gropes for the boot until he finally gets hold of it." "But even at this stage, after three weeks' experience of seeing," von Senden goes on, " 'space,' as he conceives it, ends with visual space, i.e. with colour-patches that happen to bound his view. He does not yet have the notion that a larger object (a chair) can mask a smaller one (a dog), or that the latter can still be present even though it is not directly seen."

In general the newly sighted see the world as a dazzle of color-patches. They are pleased by the sensation of color, and learn quickly to name the colors, but the rest of seeing is tormentingly difficult. Soon after his operation a patient "generally bumps into one of these colour-patches and observes them to be substantial, since they resist him as tactual objects do. In walking about it also strikes him—or can if he pays attention—that he is continually passing in between the colours he sees, that he can go past a visual object, that a part of it then steadily disappears from view; and that in spite of this, however he twists and turns—whether entering the room from the door, for example, or returning back to it—he always has a visual space in front of him. Thus he gradually comes to realize that there is also a space behind him, which he does not see."

The mental effort involved in these reasonings proves overwhelming for many patients. It oppresses them to realize, if they ever do at all, the tremendous size of the world, which they had previously conceived of as something touchingly manageable. It oppresses them to realize that they have been visible to people all along, perhaps unattractively so, without their knowledge or consent. A disheartening number of them refuse to use their new vision, continuing to go over objects with their tongues, and lapsing into apathy and despair. "The child can see, but will not make use of his sight. Only when pressed can he with difficulty be brought to look at objects in his neighbourhood; but more than a foot away it is impossible to bestir him to the necessary effort." Of a twenty-one-year-old girl, the doctor relates, "Her unfortunate father, who had hoped for so much from this operation, wrote that his daughter carefully shuts her eyes whenever she wishes to go about the house, especially when she comes to a staircase, and that she is never happier or more at ease than when, by closing her eyelids, she relapses into her former state of total blindness." A fifteen-year-old boy, who was also in love with a girl at the asylum for the blind, finally blurted out, "No, really, I can't stand it any more; I want to be sent back to the asylum again. If things aren't altered, I'll tear my eyes out."

Some do learn to see, especially the young ones. But it changes their lives. One doctor comments on "the rapid and complete loss of that striking and wonderful serenity which is characteristic only of those who have never yet seen." A blind man who learns to see is ashamed of his old habits. He dresses up, grooms himself, and tries to make a good impression. While he was blind he was indifferent to objects unless they were edible; now, "a sifting of values sets in . . . his thoughts and wishes are mightily stirred and some few of the patients are thereby led into dissimulation, envy, theft and fraud."

On the other hand, many newly sighted people speak well of the

world, and teach us how dull is our own vision. To one patient, a human
hand, unrecognized, is "something bright and then holes." Shown a
bunch of grapes, a boy calls out, "It is dark, blue and shiny. . . . It isn't
smooth, it has bumps and hollows." A little girl visits a garden. "She is
greatly astonished, and can scarcely be persuaded to answer, stands
speechless in front of the tree, which she only names on taking hold of it,
and then as 'the tree with the lights in it.' " Some delight in their sight
and give themselves over to the visual world. Of a patient just after her
bandages were removed, her doctor writes, "The first things to attract
her attention were her own hands; she looked at them very closely,
moved them repeatedly to and fro, bent and stretched the fingers, and
seemed greatly astonished at the sight." One girl was eager to tell her
blind friend that "men do not really look like trees at all," and astounded
to discover that her every visitor had an utterly different face. Finally, a
twenty-two-old girl was dazzled by the world's brightness and kept her
eyes shut for two weeks. When at the end of that time she opened her
eyes again, she did not recognize any objects, but, "the more she now
directed her gaze upon everything about her, the more it could be seen
how an expression of gratification and astonishment overspread her
features; she repeatedly exclaimed: 'Oh God! How beautiful!' "

I saw color-patches for weeks after I read this wonderful book. It was
summer; the peaches were ripe in the valley orchards. When I woke in
the morning, color-patches wrapped round my eyes, intricately, leaving
not one unfilled spot. All day long I walked among shifting color-patches
that parted before me like the Red Sea and closed again in silence, transfigured, wherever I looked back. Some patches swelled and loomed,
while others vanished utterly, and dark marks flitted at random over the
whole dazzling sweep. But I couldn't sustain the illusion of flatness. I've
been around for too long. Form is condemned to an eternal danse
macabre with meaning: I couldn't unpeach the peaches. Nor can I
remember ever having seen without understanding; the color-patches of
infancy are lost. My brain then must have been smooth as any balloon.
I'm told I reached for the moon; many babies do. But the color-patches
of infancy swelled as meaning filled them; they arrayed themselves in
solemn ranks down distance which unrolled and stretched before me like
a plain. The moon rocketed away. I live now in a world of shadows that
shape and distance color, a world where space makes a kind of terrible

sense. What gnosticism is this, and what physics? The fluttering patch I saw in my nursery window—silver and green and shape-shifting blue—is gone; a row of Lombardy poplars takes its place, mute, across the distant lawn. That humming oblong creature pale as light that stole along the walls of my room at night, stretching exhilaratingly around the corners, is gone, too, gone the night I ate of the bittersweet fruit, put two and two together and puckered forever my brain. Martin Buber tells this tale: "Rabbi Mendel once boasted to his teacher Rabbi Elimelekh that evenings he saw the angel who rolls away the light before the darkness, and mornings the angel who rolls away the darkness before the light. 'Yes,' said Rabbi Elimelekh, 'in my youth I saw that too. Later on you don't see these things any more.'"

Why didn't someone hand those newly sighted people paints and brushes from the start, when they still didn't know what anything was? Then maybe we all could see color-patches too, the world unraveled from reason, Eden before Adam gave names. The scales would drop from my eyes; I'd see trees like men walking; I'd run down the road against all orders, hallooing and leaping.

Seeing is of course very much a matter of verbalization. Unless I call my attention to what passes before my eyes, I simply won't see it. It is, as Ruskin says, "not merely unnoticed, but in the full, clear sense of the word, unseen." My eyes alone can't solve analogy tests using figures, the ones which show, with increasing elaborations, a big square, then a small square in a big square, then a big triangle, and expect me to find a small triangle in a big triangle. I have to say the words, describe what I'm seeing. If Tinker Mountain erupted, I'd be likely to notice. But if I want to notice the lesser cataclysms of valley life, I have to maintain in my head a running description of the present. It's not that I'm observant; it's just that I talk too much. Otherwise, especially in a strange place, I'll never know what's happening. Like a blind man at the ball game, I need a radio.

When I see this way I analyze and pry. I hurl over logs and roll away stones; I study the bank a square foot at a time, probing and tilting my head. Some days when a mist covers the mountains, when the muskrats won't show and the microscope's mirror shatters, I want to climb up the blank blue dome as a man would storm the inside of a circus tent, wildly, dangling, and with a steel knife claw a rent in the top, peep, and, if I must, fall.

But there is another kind of seeing that involves a letting go. When I see this way I sway transfixed and emptied. The difference between the two ways of seeing is the difference between walking with and without a camera. When I walk with a camera I walk from shot to shot, reading the light on a calibrated meter. When I walk without a camera, my own shutter opens, and the moment's light prints on my own silver gut. When I see this second way I am above all an unscrupulous observer.

It was sunny one evening last summer at Tinker Creek; the sun was low in the sky, upstream. I was sitting on the sycamore log bridge with the sunset at my back, watching the shiners the size of minnows who were feeding over the muddy sand in skittery schools. Again and again, one fish, then another, turned for a split second across the current and flash! the sun shot out from its silver side. I couldn't watch for it. It was always just happening somewhere else, and it drew my vision just as it disappeared: flash, like a sudden dazzle of the thinnest blade, a sparking over a dun and olive ground at chance intervals from every direction. Then I noticed white specks, some sort of pale petals, small, floating from under my feet on the creek's surface, very slow and steady. So I blurred my eyes and gazed towards the brim of my hat and saw a new world. I saw the pale white circles roll up, roll up, like the world's turning, mute and perfect, and I saw the linear flashes, gleaming silver, like stars being born at random down a rolling scroll of time. Something broke and something opened. I filled up like a new wineskin. I breathed an air like light; I saw a light like water. I was the lip of a fountain the creek filled forever; I was ether, the leaf in the zephyr; I was flesh-flake, feather, bone.

When I see this way I see truly. As Thoreau says, I return to my senses. I am the man who watches the baseball game in silence in an empty stadium. I see the game purely; I'm abstracted and dazed. When it's all over and the white-suited players lope off the green field to their shadowed dugouts, I leap to my feet; I cheer and cheer.

But I can't go out and try to see this way. I'll fail, I'll go mad. All I can do is try to gag the commentator, to hush the noise of useless interior babble that keeps me from seeing just as surely as a newspaper dangled before my eyes. The effort is really a discipline requiring a lifetime of dedicated struggle; it marks the literature of saints and monks of every order East and West, under every rule and no rule, discalced and shod. The world's spiritual geniuses seem to discover universally that the mind's muddy river, this ceaseless flow of trivia and trash, cannot be dammed, and that trying to dam it is a waste of effort that might lead to madness. Instead you must allow the muddy river to flow unheeded in the dim channels of consciousness; you raise your sights; you look along it, mildly, acknowledging its presence without interest and gazing beyond it into the realm of the real where subjects and objects act and rest purely, without utterance. "Launch into the deep," says Jacques Ellul, "and you shall see."

The secret of seeing is, then, the pearl of great price. If I thought he could teach me to find it and keep it forever I would stagger barefoot across a hundred deserts after any lunatic at all. But although the pearl may be found, it may not be sought. The literature of illumination reveals this above all: although it comes to those who wait for it, it is always, even to the most practiced and adept, a gift and a total surprise. I return from one walk knowing where the killdeer nests in the field by the creek and the hour the laurel blooms. I return from the same walk a day later scarcely knowing my own name. Litanies hum in my ears; my tongue flaps in my mouth Ailinon, alleluia! I cannot cause light; the most I can do is try to put myself in the path of its beam. It is possible, in deep space, to sail on solar wind. Light, be it particle or wave, has force: you rig a giant sail and go. The secret of seeing is to sail on solar wind. Hone and spread your spirit till you yourself are a sail, whetted, translucent, broadside to the merest puff.

When her doctor took her bandages off and led her into the garden, the girl who was no longer blind saw "the tree with the lights in it." It was for this tree I searched through the peach orchards of summer, in the forests of fall and down winter and spring for years. Then one day I was walking along Tinker Creek thinking of nothing at all and I saw the tree with the lights in it. I saw the backyard cedar where the mourning doves roost charged and transfigured, each cell buzzing with flame. I stood on the grass with the lights in it, grass that was wholly fire, utterly focused and utterly dreamed. It was less like seeing than like being for the first time seen, knocked breathless by a powerful glance. The flood of fire abated, but I'm still spending the power. Gradually the lights went out in the cedar, the colors died, the cells unflamed and disappeared. I was still ringing. I had been my whole life a bell, and never knew it until at that moment I was lifted and struck. I have since only very rarely seen the tree with the lights in it. The vision comes and goes, mostly goes, but I live for it, for the moment when the mountains open and a new light roars in spate through the crack, and the mountains slam.

·6·

Water
Edward Abbey

"THIS WOULD BE GOOD COUNTRY," a tourist says to me, "if only you had some water."

He's from Cleveland, Ohio.

"If we had water here," I reply, "this country would not be what it is. It would be like Ohio, wet and humid and hydrological, all covered with cabbage farms and golf courses. Instead of this lovely barren desert we would have only another blooming garden state, like New Jersey. You see what I mean?"

"If you had more water more people could live here."

"Yes sir. And where then would people go when they wanted to see something besides people?"

"I see what you mean. Still, I wouldn't want to live here. So dry and desolate. Nice for pictures but my God I'm glad I don't have to live here."

"I'm glad too, sir. We're in perfect agreement. You wouldn't want to live here, I wouldn't want to live in Cleveland. We're both satisfied with the arrangement as it is. Why change it?"

"Agreed."

We shake hands and the tourist from Ohio goes away pleased, as I am pleased, each of us thinking he has taught the other something new.

The air is so dry here I can hardly shave in the mornings. The water and soap dry on my face as I reach for the razor: aridity. It is the driest season of a dry country. In the afternoons of July and August we may get thundershowers but an hour after the storms pass the surface of the desert is again bone dry.

It seldom rains. The geography books credit this part of Utah with an annual precipitation of five to nine inches but that is merely a statistical average. Low enough, to be sure. And in fact the rainfall and snowfall vary widely from year to year and from place to place even within the Arches region. When a cloud bursts open above the Devil's Garden the sun is blazing down on my ramada. And wherever it rains in this land of unclothed rock the runoff is rapid down cliff and dome through the canyons to the Colorado.

Sometimes it rains and still fails to moisten the desert—the falling water evaporates halfway down between cloud and earth. Then you see curtains of blue rain dangling out of reach in the sky while the living things wither below for want of water. Torture by tantalizing, hope without fulfillment. And the clouds disperse and dissipate into nothingness.

Streambeds are usually dry. The dry wash, dry gulch, *arroyo seco*. Only after a storm do they carry water and then but briefly—a few minutes, a couple of hours. The spring-fed perennial stream is a rarity. In this area we have only two of them, Salt Creek and Onion Creek, the first too salty to drink and the second laced with arsenic and sulfur.

Permanent springs or waterholes are likewise few and far between though not so rare as the streams. They are secret places deep in the canyons, known only to the deer and the coyotes and the dragonflies and a few others. Water rises slowly from these springs and flows in little rills over bare rock, over and under sand, into miniature fens of wire grass, rushes, willow and tamarisk. The water does not flow very far before disappearing into the air and under the ground. The flow may reappear farther down the canyon, surfacing briefly for a second time, a third time, diminishing in force until it vanishes completely and for good.

Another type of spring may be found on canyon walls where water seeps out between horizontal formations through cracks thinner than paper to support small hanging gardens of orchids, monkeyflower, maidenhair fern, and ivy. In most of these places the water is so sparingly measured that it never reaches the canyon floor at all but is taken up entirely by the thirsty plant life and transformed into living tissue.

Long enough in the desert a man like other animals can learn to smell water. Can learn, at least, the smell of things associated with water—the unique and heartening odor of the cottonwood tree, for example, which in the canyonlands is the tree of life. In this wilderness of naked rock burnt to auburn or buff or red by ancient fires there is no vision more pleasing to the eyes and more gratifying to the heart than the translucent acid green (bright gold in autumn) of this venerable tree. It signifies water, and not only water but also shade, in a country where shelter from the sun is sometimes almost as precious as water.

Signifies water, which may or may not be on the surface, visible and available. If you have what is called a survival problem and try to dig for this water during the heat of the day the effort may cost you more in sweat than you will find to drink. A bad deal. Better to wait for nightfall when the cottonwoods and other plants along the streambed will release some of the water which they have absorbed during the day, perhaps enough to allow a potable trickle to rise to the surface of the sand. If the water still does not appear you may then wish to attempt to dig for it. Or you might do better by marching farther up the canyon. Sooner or later you should find a spring or at least a little seep on the canyon wall. On the other hand you could possibly find no water at all, anywhere. The desert is a land of surprises, some of them terrible surprises. Terrible as derived from terror.

When out for a walk carry water; not less than a gallon a day per person.

More surprises. In places you will find clear-flowing streams, such as Salt Creek near Turnbow Cabin, where the water looks beautifully drinkable but tastes like brine.

You might think, beginning to die of thirst, that any water however salty would be better than none at all. Not true. Small doses will not keep you going or alive and a deep drink will force your body to expend water in getting rid of the excess salt. This results in a net loss of bodily moisture and a hastening of the process of dehydration. Dehydration first enervates, then prostrates, then kills.

Nor is blood, your own or a companion's, any adequate substitute for water; blood is too salty. The same is true of urine.

If it's your truck or car which has failed you, you'd be advised to tap the radiator, unless it's full of Prestone. If this resource is not available and water cannot be found in the rocks or under the sand and you find yourself too tired and discouraged to go on, crawl into the shade and wait for help to find you. If no one is looking for you write your will in the sand and let the wind carry your last words and signature east to the borders of Colorado and south to the pillars of Monument Valley— someday, never fear, your bare elegant bones will be discovered and wondered and marveled at.

A great thirst is a great joy when quenched in time. On my first walk down into Havasupai Canyon, which is a branch of the Grand Canyon, never mind exactly where, I took with me only a quart of water, thinking that would be enough for a mere fourteen-mile downhill hike on a warm day in August. At Topocoba on the rim of the canyon the temperature was a tolerable ninety-six degrees but it rose about one degree for each mile on and downward. Like a fool I rationed my water, drank frugally, and could have died of the heatstroke. When late in the afternoon I finally stumbled—sun-dazed, blear-eyed, parched as an old bacon rind—upon that blue stream which flows like a miraculous mirage down the floor of the canyon I was too exhausted to pause and drink soberly from the bank. Dreamily, deliriously, I waded into the waist-deep water and fell on my face. Like a sponge I soaked up moisture through every pore, letting the current bear me along beneath a canopy of overhanging willow trees. I had no fear of drowning in the water—I intended to drink it all.

In the Needles country high above the inaccessible Colorado River there is a small spring hidden at the heart of a maze of fearfully arid grabens and crevasses. A very small spring: the water oozes from the grasp of moss to fall one drop at a time, one drop per second, over a lip of stone. One afternoon in June I squatted there for an hour—two hours? three?—filling my canteen. No other water within miles, the local gnat population fought me for every drop. To keep them out of the canteen I had to place a handkerchief over the opening as I filled it. Then they attacked my eyes, drawn irresistibly by the liquid shine of the human eyeball. Embittered little bastards. Never have I tasted better water.

Other springs, more surprises. Northeast of Moab in a region of gargoyles and hobgoblins, a landscape left over from the late Jurassic, is a peculiar little waterhold named Onion Spring. A few wild onions grow in the vicinity but more striking, in season, is the golden princess plume, an indicator of selenium, a mild poison often found in association with uranium, a poison not so mild. Approaching the spring you notice a sulfurous stink in the air though the water itself, neither warm nor cold, looks clear and drinkable.

Unlike most desert waterholes you will find around Onion Spring few traces of animal life. Nobody comes to drink. The reason is the very good one that the water of Onion Spring contains not only sulfur, and perhaps selenium, but also arsenic. When I was there I looked at the water and smelled it and ran my hands through it and after a while, since the sampling of desert water is in my line, I tasted it, carefully, and spat it out. Afterwards I rinsed my mouth with water from my canteen.

This poison spring is quite clear. The water is sterile, lifeless. There are no bugs, which in itself is a warning sign, in case the smell were not sufficient. When in doubt about drinking from an unknown spring look for life. If the water is scummed with algae, crawling with worms, grubs, larvae, spiders and liver flukes, be reassured, drink hearty, you'll get nothing worse than dysentery. But if it appears innocent and pure, beware. Onion Spring wears such a deceitful guise. Out of a tangle of poison-tolerant weeds the water drips into a basin of mud and sand, flows from there over sandstone and carries its potent solutions into the otherwise harmless waters of the creek.

There are a number of springs similar to this one in the American desert. Badwater pool in Death Valley, for example. And a few others in the canyonlands, usually in or below the Moenkopi and Shinarump formations—mudstone and shales. The prospector Vernon Pick found a poison spring at the source of the well-named Dirty Devil River, when he was searching for uranium over in the San Rafael Swell a few years ago. At the time he needed water; he *had* to have water; and in order to get a decent drink he made something like a colander out of his canteen, punching it full of nail holes, filling it with charcoal from his campfire and straining the water through the charcoal. How much this purified the water he had no means of measuring but he drank it anyway and although it made him sick he survived, and is still alive today to tell about it.

There are rumors that when dying of the thirst you can save your soul *and* body by extracting water from the barrel cactus. This is a dubious proposition and I don't know anyone who has made the experiment. It might be possible in the Sonoran desert where the barrel cactus grows tall as a man and fat as a keg of beer. In Utah, however, its nearest relative stands no more than a foot high and bristles with needles curved like fishhooks. To get even close to this devilish vegetable you need leather gloves and a machete. Slice off the top and you find inside not water but only the green pulpy core of the living plant. Carving the core into manageable chunks you might be able to wring a few drops of bitter liquid into your cup. The labor and the exasperation will make you sweat, will cost you dearly.

When you reach this point you are doomed. Far better to have stayed at home with the TV and a case of beer. If the happy thought arrives too late, crawl into the shade and contemplate the lonely sky. See those big black scrawny wings far above, waiting? Comfort yourself with the reflection that within a few hours, if all goes as planned, your human flesh will be working its way through the gizzard of a buzzard, your essence transfigured into the fierce greedy eyes and unimaginable consciousness of a turkey vulture. Whereupon you, too, will soar on motionless wings high over the ruck and rack of human suffering. For most of us a promotion in grade, for some the realization of an ideal.

In July and August on the high desert the thunderstorms come. Mornings begin clear and dazzling bright, the sky as blue as the Virgin's cloak, unflawed by a trace of cloud in all that emptiness bounded on the north by the Book Cliffs, on the east by Grand Mesa and the La Sal Mountains, on the south by the Blue Mountains and on the west by the dragon-tooth reef of the San Rafael. By noon, however, clouds begin to form over the mountains, coming it seems out of nowhere, out of nothing, a special creation.

The clouds multiply and merge, cumuli-nimbi piling up like whipped cream, like mashed potatoes, like sea foam, building upon one another into a second mountain range greater in magnitude than the terrestrial range below.

The massive forms jostle and grate, ions collide, and the sound of thunder is heard over the sun-drenched land. More clouds emerge from empty sky, anvil-headed giants with glints of lightning in their depths. An armada assembles and advances, floating on a plane of air that makes it appear, from below, as a fleet of ships must look to the fish in the sea.

At my observation point on a sandstone monolith the sun is blazing down as intensely as ever, the air crackling with dry heat. But the storm clouds continue to spread, gradually taking over more and more of the sky, and as they approach the battle breaks out.

Lightning streaks like gunfire through the clouds, volleys of thunder shake the air. A smell of ozone. While the clouds exchange their bolts with one another no rain falls, but now they begin bombarding the buttes and pinnacles below. Forks of lightning—illuminated nerves— join heaven and earth.

The wind is rising. For anyone with sense enough to get out of the rain now is the time to seek shelter. A lash of lightning flickers over Wilson Mesa, scorching the brush, splitting a pine tree. Northeast over the Yellowcat area rain is already sweeping down, falling not vertically but in a graceful curve, like a beaded curtain drawn lightly across the desert.

Between the rain and the mountains, among the tumbled masses of vapor, floats a segment of a rainbow—sunlight divided. But where I stand the storm is only beginning.

Above me the clouds roll in, unfurling and smoking billows in malignant violet, dense as wool. Most of the sky is lidded over but the sun remains clear halfway down the west, shining in under the storm. Overhead the clouds thicken, then crack and split with a roar like that of cannonballs tumbling down a marble staircase; their bellies open—too late to run now—and the rain comes down.

Comes down: not softly not gently, with no quality of mercy but like heavy water in buckets, raindrops like pellets splattering on the rock, knocking the berries off the junipers, plastering my shirt to my back, drumming on my hat like hailstones and running in a waterfall off the brim.

The pinnacles, arches, balanced rocks, fins and elephantbacks of sandstone, glazed with water but still in sunlight, gleam like old gray silver and everything appears transfixed in the strange wild unholy light of the moment. The light that never was.

For five minutes the deluge continues under the barrage of thunder and lightning, then trails off quickly, diminishing to a shower, to a sprinkling, to nothing at all. The clouds move off and rumble for a while in the distance. A fresh golden light breaks through and now in the east, over the turrets and domes, stands the rainbow sign, a double rainbow with one foot in the canyon of the Colorado and the other far north in Salt Wash. Beyond the rainbow and framed within it I can see jags of lightning still playing in the stormy sky over Castle Valley.

The afternoon sun falls lower; above the mountains and the ragged black clouds hangs the new moon, pale fragment of what is to come; in another hour, at sundown, Venus too will be there, planet of love, to glow bright as chromium down on the western sky. The desert storm is over and through the pure sweet pellucid air the cliff swallows and the nighthawks plunge and swerve, making cries of hunger and warning and—who knows?—maybe of exultation.

Stranger than the storms, though not so grand and symphonic, are the flash floods that follow them, bursting with little warning out of the hills and canyons, sometimes an hour or more after the rain has stopped.

I have stood in the middle of a broad sandy wash with not a trickle of moisture to be seen anywhere, sunlight pouring down on me and on the flies and ants and lizards, the sky above perfectly clear, listening to a queer vibration in the air and in the ground under my feet—like a freight train coming down the grade, very fast—and looked up to see a wall of water tumble around a bend and surge toward me.

A wall of water. A poor image. For the flash flood of the desert poorly resembles water. It looks rather like a loose pudding or a thick dense soup, thick as gravy, dense with mud and sand, lathered with scuds of bloody froth, loaded on its crest with a tangle of weeds and shrubs and small trees ripped from their roots.

Surprised by delight, I stood there in the heat, the bright sun, the quiet afternoon, and watched the monster roll and roar toward me. It advanced in crescent shape with a sort of forelip about a foot high streaming in front, making hissing sucking noises like a giant amoeba, nosing to the right and nosing to the left as if on the spoor of something good to eat. Red as tomato soup or blood it came down on me about as fast as a man could run. I moved aside and watched it go by.

A flick of lightning to the north
where dun clouds grumble—
while here in the middle of the wash
black beetles tumble
and horned toads fumble
over sand as dry as bone
and hard-baked mud and glaring stone.

Nothing here suggests disaster
for the ants' shrewd play;
their busy commerce for tomorrow
shows no care for today;
but a mile away
and rolling closer in a scum of mud
comes the hissing lapping blind mouth of the flood.

Through the tamarisk whine the flies
in pure fat units of conceit
as if the sun and the afternoon
and blood and the smells and the heat
and something to eat
would be available forever, never die
beyond the fixed imagination of a fly.

The flood comes, crawls thickly by, roaring
with self-applause, a brown
spongy smothering liquid avalanche:
great ant-civilizations drown,
worlds go down,
trees go under, the mud bank breaks
and deep down underneath the bedrock shakes.

A few hours later the bulk of the flood was past and gone. The flow dwindled to a trickle over bars of quicksand. New swarms of insect life would soon come to recover the provinces of those swept away. Nothing had changed but the personnel, a normal turnover, and the contours of the watercourse, that not much.

Now we've mentioned quicksand. What is quicksand anyway? First of all, quicksand is *not* as many think a queer kind of sand which has the hideous power to draw men and animals down and down into a bottomless pit. There can be no quicksand without water. The scene of the sand-drowned camel boy in the movie *Lawrence of Arabia* is pure fakery. The truth about quicksand is that it is simply a combination of sand and water in which the upward force of the water is sufficient to neutralize the frictional strength of the particles of sand. The greater the force and saturation, the less weight the sand can bear.

Ordinarily it is possible for a man to walk across quicksand, if he keeps moving. But if he stops, funny things begin to happen. The surface of the quicksand, which may look as firm as the wet sand on an ocean beach, begins to liquefy beneath his feet. He finds himself sinking slowly into a jelly-like substance, soft and quivering, which clasps itself around his ankles with the suction power of any viscous fluid. Pulling out one foot, the other foot necessarily goes down deeper, and if a man waits too long, or cannot reach something solid beyond the quicksand, he may soon find himself trapped. The depth to which he finally sinks depends upon the depth and the fluidity of the quicksand, upon the nature of his efforts to extricate himself, and upon the ratio of body weight to volume of quicksand. Unless a man is extremely talented, he cannot work himself in more than waist-deep. The quicksand will not *pull* him down. But it will not let him go either. Therefore the conclusion is that while quicksand cannot drown its captive, it could possibly starve him to death. Whatever finally happens, the immediate effects are always interesting.

My friend Newcomb, for instance. He has only one good leg, had an accident with the other, can't hike very well in rough country, tends to lag behind. We were exploring a deep dungeon-like defile off Glen Canyon one time (before the dam). The defile turned and twisted like a snake under overhanging and interlocking walls so high, so close, that for most of the way I could not see the sky. The floor of this cleft was irregular, wet, sandy, in places rather soupy, and I was soon far ahead and out of sight of Newcomb.

Finally I came to a place in the canyon so narrow and dark and wet and ghastly that I had no heart to go farther. Retracing my steps I heard, now and then, a faint and mournful wail, not human, which seemed to come from abysmal depths far back in the bowels of the plateau, from the underworld, from subterranean passageways better left forever unseen and unknown. I hurried on, the cries faded away. I was glad to be getting out of there. Then they came again, louder and as it seemed from all sides, out of the rock itself, surrounding me. A terrifying caterwauling it was, multiplied and amplified by echoes piled on echoes, overlapping and reinforcing one another. I looked back to see what was hunting me but there was only the naked canyon in the dim, bluish light that filtered down from far above. I thought of the Minotaur. Then I thought of Newcomb and began to run.

It wasn't bad. He was in only a little above the knees and sinking very slowly. As soon as he saw me he stopped hollering and relit his pipe. Help, he said, simply and quietly.

What was all the bellowing about? I wanted to know. I'm sorry, he said, but it's a horrible way to die. Get out of that mud, I said, and let's get out of here. It ain't just mud, he said. I don't care what it is, get out of there; you look like an idiot. I'm sinking, he said.

And he was. The stuff was now halfway up his thighs.

Don't you ever read any books? I said. Don't you have sense enough to know that when you get in quicksand you have to lie down flat? Why? he asked. So you'll live longer, I explained. Face down or face up? he asked next.

That stumped me. I couldn't remember the answer to that one. You wait here, I said, while I go back to Albuquerque and get the book.

He looked down for a moment. Still sinking, he said; please help?

I stepped as close to him as I could without getting bogged down myself but our extended hands did not quite meet. Lean forward, I said. I am, he said. All the way, I said; fall forward.

He did that and then I could reach him. He gripped my wrist and I gripped his and with a slow steady pull I got him out of there. The quicksand gurgled a little and made funny, gasping noises, reluctant to let him go, but when he was free the holes filled up at once, the liquid sand oozing into place, and everything looked as it had before, smooth and sleek and innocent as the surface of a pudding. It was in fact the same pool of quicksand that I had walked over myself only about an hour earlier.

Quicksand is more of a menace to cattle and horses, with their greater weight and smaller feet, than it is to men, and the four-legged beasts generally avoid it when they can. Sometimes, however, they are forced to cross quicksand to reach water, or are driven across, and then the cattleman may have an unpleasant chore on his hands. Motor vehicles, of course, cannot negotiate quicksand; even a four-wheel-drive jeep will bog down as hopelessly as anything else.

Although I hesitate to deprive quicksand of its sinister glamour I must confess that I have not yet heard of a case where a machine, an animal or a man has actually sunk *completely* out of sight in the stuff. But it may have happened; it may be happening to somebody at this very moment. I sometimes regret that I was unable to perform a satisfactory experiment with my friend Newcomb when the chance presented itself; such opportunities come but rarely. But I needed him; he was among other things a good camp cook.

After the storms pass and the flash floods have dumped their loads of silt into the Colorado, leaving the streambeds as arid as they were before, it is still possible to find rainwater in the desert. All over the slickrock country there are natural cisterns or potholes, tubs, tanks and basins sculptured in the soft sandstone by the erosive force of weathering, wind and sand. Many of them serve as little catchment basins during rain and a few may contain water for days or even weeks after a storm, the length of time depending on the shape and depth of the hole and the consequent rate of evaporation.

Often far from any spring, these temporary pools attract doves, ravens and other birds, and deer and coyotes; you, too, if you know where to look or find one by luck, can slake your thirst and fill your water gourd. Such pools may be found in what seem like the most improbable places: out on the desolate White Rim below Grandview Point, for example, or on top of the elephant-back dome above the Double Arch. At Toroweap in Grand Canyon I found a deep tank of clear sweet water almost over my head, countersunk in the summit of a sandstone bluff which over-hung my campsite by a hundred feet. A week after rain there was still enough water there to fill my needs; hard to reach, it was well worth the effort. The Bedouin know what I mean.

The rain-filled potholes, set in naked rock, are usually devoid of visible plant life but not of animal life. In addition to the inevitable microscopic creatures there may be certain amphibians like the spade-foot toad. This little animal lives through dry spells in a state of estiva-tion under the dried-up sediment in the bottom of a hole. When the rain comes, if it comes, he emerges from the mud singing madly in his fashion, mates with the handiest female and fills the pool with a swarm of tadpoles, most of them doomed to a most ephemeral existence. But a few survive, mature, become real toads, and when the pool dries up they dig into the sediment as their parents did before, making burrows which they seal with mucus in order to preserve that moisture necessary to life. There they wait, day after day, week after week, in patient spadefoot torpor, perhaps listening—we can imagine—for the sound of raindrops pattering at last on the earthen crust above their heads. If it comes in time the glorious cycle is repeated; if not, this particular colony of *Bufonidae* is reduced eventually to dust, a burden on the wind.

Rain and puddles bring out other amphibia, even in the desert. It's a strange, stirring, but not uncommon thing to come on a pool at night, after an evening of thunder and lightning and a bit of rainfall, and see the frogs clinging to the edge of their impermanent pond, bodies immersed in water but heads out, all croaking away in tricky counterpoint. They are windbags: with each croak the pouch under the frog's chin swells like a bubble, then collapses.

Why do they sing? What do they have to sing about? Somewhat apart from one another, separated by roughly equal distances, facing outward from the water, they clank and croak all through the night with tireless perseverance. To human ears their music has a bleak, dismal, tragic quality, dirgelike rather than jubilant. It may nevertheless be the case that these small beings are singing not only to claim their stake in the pond, not only to attract a mate, but also out of spontaneous love and joy, a contrapuntal choral celebration of the coolness and wetness after weeks of desert fire, for love of their own existence, however brief it may be, and for joy in the common life.

Has joy any survival value in the operations of evolution? I suspect that it does; I suspect that the morose and fearful are doomed to quick extinction. Where there is no joy there can be no courage; and without courage all other virtues are useless. Therefore the frogs, the toads, keep on singing even though we know, if they don't, that the sound of their uproar must surely be luring all the snakes and ringtail cats and kit foxes and coyotes and great horned owls toward the scene of their happiness.

What then? A few of the little amphibians will continue their metamorphosis by way of the nerves and tissues of one of the higher animals, in which process the joy of one becomes the contentment of the second. Nothing is lost, except an individual consciousness here and there, a trivial perhaps even illusory phenomenon. The rest survive, mate, multiply, burrow, estivate, dream, and rise again. The rains will come, the potholes shall be filled. Again. And again. And again.

More secure are those who live in and around the desert's few perennial waterholes, those magical hidden springs that are scattered so austerely through the barren vastness of the canyon country. Of these only a rare few are too hot or too briny or too poisonous to support life—the great majority of them swarm with living things. Here you will see the rushes and willows and cottonwoods, and four-winged dragonflies in green, blue, scarlet and gold, and schools of minnows in the water, moving from sunlight to shadow and back again. At night the mammals come—deer, bobcat, cougar, coyote, fox, jackrabbit, bighorn sheep, wild horse and feral burro—each in his turn and in unvarying order under the declaration of a truce. They come to drink, not to kill or be killed.

Finally, in this discussion of water in the desert, I should make note of a distinctive human contribution, one which has become a part of the Southwestern landscape no less typical than the giant cactus, the juniper growing out of solid rock or the red walls of a Navajo canyon. I refer to the tiny oasis formed by the drilled well, its windmill and storage tank. The windmill with its skeleton tower and creaking vanes is an object of beauty as significant in its way as the cottonwood tree, and the open tank at its foot, big enough to swim in, is a thing of joy to man and beast, no less worthy of praise than the desert spring.

Water, water, water. . . . There is no shortage of water in the desert but exactly the right amount, a perfect ratio of water to rock, of water to sand, insuring that wide, free, open, generous spacing among plants and animals, homes and towns and cities, which makes the arid West so different from any other part of the nation. There is no lack of water here, unless you try to establish a city where no city should be.

The Developers, of course—the politicians, businessmen, bankers, administrators, engineers—they see it somewhat otherwise and complain most bitterly and interminably of a desperate water shortage, especially in the Southwest. They propose schemes of inspiring proportions for diverting water by the damful from the Columbia River, or even from the Yukon River, and channeling it overland down into Utah, Colorado, Arizona and New Mexico.

What for? "In anticipation of future needs, in order to provide for the continued industrial and population growth of the Southwest." And in such an answer we see that it's only the old numbers game again, the monomania of small and very simple minds in the grip of an obsession. They cannot see that growth for the sake of growth is a cancerous madness, that Phoenix and Albuquerque will not be better cities to live in when their populations are doubled again and again. They would never understand that an economic system which can only expand or expire must be false to all that is human.

So much by way of futile digression: the pattern is fixed and protest alone will not halt the iron glacier moving upon us.

No matter, it's of slight importance. Time and the winds will sooner or later bury the Seven Cities of Cibola, Phoenix, Tucson, Albuquerque, all of them, under dunes of glowing sand, over which blue-eyed Navajo bedouin will herd their sheep and horses, following the river in winter, the mountains in summer, and sometimes striking off across the desert toward the red canyons of Utah where great waterfalls plunge over silt-filled, ancient, mysterious dams.

Only the boldest among them, seeking visions, will camp for long in the strange country of the standing rock, far out where the spadefoot toads bellow madly in the moonlight on the edge of doomed rainpools, where the arsenic-selenium spring waits for the thirst-crazed wanderer, where the thunderstorms blast the pinnacles and cliffs, where the rust-brown floods roll down the barren washes, and where the community of the quiet deer walk at evening up glens of sandstone through tamarisk and sage toward the hidden springs of sweet, cool, still, clear, unfailing water.

·7·

Lookout's Journal

Gary Snyder

Crater Mountain

22 *June 52*   Marblemount Ranger Station
Skagit District, Mt. Baker National Forest

Hitchhiked here, long valley of the Skagit. Old cars parked in the weeds, little houses in fields of bracken. A few cows, in stumpland.

Ate at the "parkway café" real lemon in the pie
        "—why don't you get a jukebox in here"
        "—the man said we weren't important enough"

28 June

                    Blackie Burns:
"28 years ago you could find a good place to fish.
GREEDY & SELFISH   **NO RESPECT FOR THE
    LAND**
            tin cans, beer bottles, dirty dishes
            a shit within a foot of the bed
one sonuvabitch out of fifty
fishguts in the creek

the door left open for the bear.
If you're takin forestry fellas keep away
from the recreation side of it:
first couple months you see the women you say
     'there's a cute little number'
the next three months it's only another woman
after that you see one coming out of the can
     & wonder if she's just shit on the floor

ought to use pit toilets"

Granite creek Guard station   *9 July*

  the boulder in the creek never moves
     the water is always falling
   together!

A ramshackle little cabin built by Frank Beebe the miner.
Two days walk to here from roadhead.
     arts of the Japanese: moon-watching
                insect-hearing
Reading the sutra of Hui Nêng.

  one does not need universities and libraries
  one needs to be alive to what is about

saying "I don't care"

11 July

cut fresh rhubarb by the bank
the creek is going down
last night caught a trout
today climbed to the summit of Crater Mountain and back
high and barren: flowers I don't recognize
ptarmigan and chicks, feigning the broken wing.

Baxter: "Men are funny, once I loved a girl
so bad it hurt, but I drove her away. She was
throwing herself at me—and four months later she
married another fellow."

A doe in the trail, unafraid.
A strange man walking south
A boy from Marblemount with buckteeth, learning machine shop.

Crater Mountain Elevation: 8049 feet *23 July*

Really wretched weather for three days now—wind, hail, sleet,
snow; the FM transmitter is broken / rather the receiver is /
what can be done?

 Even here, cold foggy rocky place, there's life—4 ptarmigan
by the A-frame, cony by the trail to the snowbank.

 hit my head on the lamp,
 the shutters fall, the radio quits,
 the kerosene stove won't stop, the wood stove
 won't start, my fingers are too numb to write.

& this is mid-July. At least I have energy enough to read
science-fiction. One has to go to bed fully clothed.

The stove burning wet wood—windows misted over giving the
blank white light of shoji. Outside wind blows, no visibility.
I'm filthy with no prospect of cleaning up. (Must learn
yoga-system of Patanjali—)

Crater Shan   *28 July* .

Down for a new radio, to Ross Lake, and back up. Three days walking. Strange how unmoved this place leaves one; neither articulate or worshipful; rather the pressing need to look within and adjust the mechanism of perception.

A dead sharp-shinned hawk, blown by the wind against the lookout. Fierce compact little bird with a square head.

—If one wished to write poetry of nature, where an audience? Must come from the very conflict of an attempt to articulate the vision   poetry & nature in our time.

> (reject the human; but the tension of
> human events, brutal and tragic, against
> a non-human background? like Jeffers?)

Pair of eagles soaring over Devil's Creek canyon

31 July

This morning:

> floating face down in the water bucket
> a drowned mouse.

"Were it not for Kuan Chung, we should be wearing our hair unbound and our clothes buttoning on the left side"

> A man should stir himself with poetry
> Stand firm in ritual
> Complete himself in music
> lun yü

Comparing the panoramic Lookout View photo dated 8 August
1935: with the present view. Same snowpatches; same shapes.
Year after year; snow piling up and melting.

> "By God" quod he, "for pleynly, at a word
> Thy drasty ryming is not worth a tord."

Crater Shan   *3 August*

How pleasant to squat in the sun
Jockstrap & zoris

form—leaving things out at the right spot
ellipse, is emptiness
>   these ice-scoured valleys
>   swarming with plants
>   "I am the Queen Bee!
>   Follow Me!"

Or having a wife and baby,
   living close to the ocean, with skills for
   gathering food.

QUEBEC DELTA 04 BLACK

Higgins to Pugh (over)
      "the wind comes out of the east
      or northeast,

> the chimney smokes all over the room.
> the wind comes out of the west;
> the fire burns clean."

Higgins L.O. reads the news:
> "flying saucer with a revolving black band
> drouth in the south.

Are other worlds watching us?"
The rock alive,   not barren.
> flowers   lichen   pinus albicaulis   chipmunks

mice   even grass.

—first I turn on the radio
—then make tea & eat breakfast
—study Chinese until eleven

—make lunch, go chop snow to melt for water,
read Chaucer in the early afternoon.

> "Is this real
> Is this real
> This life I am living?"
> > —Tlingit or Haida song

"Hidden Lake to Sourdough"
—"This is Sourdough"
—"Whatcha doing over there?"
—"Readin some old magazines
        they had over here."

6 August

Clouds above and below, but I can see Kulshan, Mt. Terror,
Shuksan; they blow over the ridge between here and
Three-fingered Jack, fill up the valleys. The Buckner Boston
Peak ridge is clear.

What happens all winter; the wind driving snow; clouds—
wind, and mountains—repeating
    this is what always happens here,

and the photograph of a young female torso hung in the lookout
window, in the foreground. Natural against natural, beauty.

        two butterflies
      a chilly clump of mountain
          flowers.

zazen   non-life.   An art: mountain-watching.

    leaning in the doorway whistling
        a chipmunk popped out
           listening

9 August

Sourdough: Jack, do you know if a fly is an electrical
   conductor? (over)
Desolation: A fly? Are you still trying to electrocute flies? (over)
Sourdough: Yeah   I can make em twitch a little. I got five
   number six batteries on it (over)
Desolation: I don't know, Shubert, keep trying. Desolation
   clear.

10 August

First wrote a haiku and painted a haiga for it; then repaired
the Om Mani Padme Hum prayer flag, then constructed a stone
platform, then shaved down a shake and painted a zenga on it,
then studied the lesson:

      a butterfly
         scared up from its flower

caught by the wind and swept over the cliffs
                              SCREE
Vaux Swifts: in great numbers, flying before the storm,
arcing so close that the sharp wing-whistle is heard.

                         "The śrāvaka
disciplined in Tao, enlightened, but on the wrong path."
summer,
              on the west slopes creek beds are brushy
              north-faces of ridges, steep and
                   covered late with snow

         slides and old burns on dry hills.

(In San Francisco: I live on the Montgomery Street drainage
—at the top of a long scree slope just below a cliff.)

sitting in the sun in the doorway
picking my teeth with a broomstraw
listening to the buzz of the flies.

12 August

         A visit all day, to the sheep camp, across the
glacier and into Devil's park. A tent under a clump of Alpine
fir; horses, sheep in the meadow.

                   take up solitary occupations.

Horses stand patiently, rump to the wind.
              —gave me one of his last two cigars.

Designs, under the shut lids, glowing in sun

         (experience! that drug.)
Then the poor lonely lookouts, radioing forth and back.

After a long day's travel, reached the ridge,
followed a deer trail down
        to five small lakes.
in this yuga, the moral imperative is to COMMUNICATE.
Making tea.

fewer the artifacts, less the words,
        slowly the life of it
a knack for non-attachment.

Sourdough radioing to the smoke-chaser crew

"you're practically there
you gotta go up the cliff
you gotta cross the rock slide
look for a big blaze on a big tree
       [two climbers killed by lightning
        on Mt. Stuart]
"are you on the timber stand
or are you on the side of the cliff?
Say, Bluebell, where are you?
A patch of salmonberry and tag-alder to the right"
        —must take a look.

Cratershan   *15 August*

   When the mind is exhausted of images, it invents its own.

    orange juice is what she asked for
      bright chrome restaurant, 2 a.m.
    the rest of us drinking coffee
    but the man brought orange pop.   haw!

late at night, the eyes tired, the teapot empty, the tobacco damp.

Almost had it last night: *no identity*. One thinks, "I emerged
from some general, non-differentiated thing, I return to it." One
has in reality never left it; there is no return.
        my language fades.   Images of erosion.

"That which includes all change never changes; without change
time is meaningless; without time, space is destroyed. Thus we
arrive at the void."

"If a Bodhisattva retains the thought of an ego, a person, a
being, or a soul, he is no more a Bodhisattva."

> You be Bosatsu,
> I'll be the taxi-driver
> Driving you home.

The curious multi-stratified metamorphic rock. Blue and white,
clouds reaching out. To survive a winter here learn to browse
and live in holes in the rocks under snow.
Sabi: One does not have a great deal to give. That which one
does give has been polished and perfected into a spontaneous
emptiness; sterility made creative, it has no pretensions, and
encompasses everything.

Zen view, o.k.?

21 August

   Oiling and stowing the tools.   (artifact / tools: now there's
a topic.)
When a storm blows in, covering the south wall with rain and
blotting out the mountains. Ridges look new in every light. Still
discovering new conformations——every cony has an ancestry
but the rocks were just here.
   Structure in the lithosphere / cycles of change in rock / only
the smallest percentage sanded and powdered and mixed with
life-derived elements.
Is chemical reaction a type of perception??—Running through
all things   motion and reacting, object against object / there is
more than enough time for all things to happen: swallowing
its own tail.

Diablo Dam   *24 August*

Back down off Crater in a snowstorm, after closing up the
lookout. With Baxter from Granite Creek all the way to the
dam for more supplies. Clouds on the rocks; rain falls and
falls. Tomorrow we shall fill the packs with food and return to
Granite Creek.

In San Francisco: *September 13.*

Boys on bicycles in the asphalt playground wheeling and circling
aimlessly like playful gulls or swallows. Smell of a fresh
parked-car.

·8·

Marsh Family
Christopher Hallowell

THE LITTLE SHED AND WHARF hanging over the water were just visible halfway down the canal. At the sound of the boat, Clifford Stelly came onto the wharf to watch its approach. In one hand he held a bedraggled pelt, which he began lashing back and forth with a rhythmic motion, so that droplets of water showed as a fine mist about his short white brush of hair. Now he tossed the skin into a bucket that overflowed with others like it. As he stood waiting, he rested one hand on his waist and the other against his thigh, tilting over ever so slightly, one arm supporting his barrel-like torso. His hands were the most massive I had ever seen.

After I had climbed onto the planks with my knapsack, Clifford offered me one of these hands and glanced at me shyly. But then, shifting his eyes away to the muddy water of the canal, he withdrew the hand before I had a chance to extend my own. "I think my hand's too dirty to shake; I been workin' with them rats." He made a sweeping gesture toward them.

Animal corpses were everywhere in various attitudes of death—on the benches, on the floor, along the wharf, and in the boats tied to the wharf. There were more nutrias among them than muskrats. The nutrias' huge incisors were a shining orange, and their ratlike tails splayed out from the piled-up skins like seaweed from rocks. A heap of skinned and gutted carcasses lay bunched up near one door of the shed, their gunmetal-blue entrails in a plastic tub next to them, while the pelts soaked in a washbasin near by. More pelts hung on racks outside, swinging to and fro as they dried in the chilly wind, the sun glinting off the guard hairs.

Three of Clifford's five sons—Randall, Wyndal, and Blaine—were also in the shed. Standing before a bench, each had a knife in his hand and a nutria lying in front of him. Their sidelong glances at me were timid but ill-concealed. Beyond the most meager greeting, they scarcely said a word. Their work hid their shyness. Randall made quick cuts around the paws of a nutria. The movements of his knife were no more traceable than flashes of light. His visored cap was awry and his cigar stub was awash with saliva. After making the four cuts, he sliced between the back paws and the base of the tail, shoving his hand underneath the skin of the animal's back to separate it from the flesh. With the pelt suddenly loosened from its body, the nutria appeared to be draped in a luxurious fur coat. Randall picked up the animal and heaved it across the shed. It landed on the bench near Wyndal or Blaine with the heavy thud of a bag of laundry.

Every so often one of the brothers murmured something in French and received a guttural reply, also in French, sometimes followed by a belly laugh. This was particularly noticeable in Randall, whose ample stomach bounced up and down. This was Cajun French, some of whose clipped staccato phrasing dates back to seventeenth-century usage. Verb endings sounded different from those of contemporary French. The pronouns would confound the teachings of any French grammar book. It was only the frequent interspersal of English words that permitted me to follow the movement of the talk.

Blaine, a round-faced nineteen-year-old with a penchant for sudden observations, was talking about catfish. "Mo pense qu'il fait trop cold pour les catfish."

"Mais non, man," retorted Randall, "m'en ai attrapé hier. Good ones." He threw his cigar stub into the canal. "Plus grand que ça, anyway." His belly shook with laughter.

"M'espère, 'cause if they was smaller, serait difficil skin, non."

Amid the bantering, the second stage of the skinning fell to Wyndal and to Blaine, who stood side by side at another bench. Wyndal plunked each animal down on its hindlegs so that it sat upright and, for one split second, had the winsome look of a pet. Then, with movements too fast to follow, his hand shoved the head down between the shoulders so that the back arched. The skin seemed to fly up and over the contorted body. He whirled the half-naked body around, flung its hindfeet into an iron chock, and pulled the skin over the head. Then he cut the skin away from the skull—gently around the eyes, nose, and mouth—pulled it free, gave it a shake, and tossed it into the washbasin, later to be stretched and dried.

The denuded corpses ended up on the floor. Mink ranchers from Michigan and Wisconsin would buy them as food for their animals. But they could be sold only after being gutted and having their paws and teeth cut away. This task fell to Charlyne, one of the three Stelly daughters. She spent every morning on the cold wharf, stoically cutting and chopping with a hatchet and dumping the entrails and appendages into the canal.

I commented to Wyndal about the pace of the work. He looked up at me with a shy smile. "Yeah, you jus' git used to it; that's all. I been doin' this ma whole life."

The three brothers can skin fifty nutrias in half an hour, but this is not really fast work. The little town of Cameron, perched on the edge of the Gulf, holds an annual fur festival that brings trappers from miles around. Side by side with a beauty contest is the muskrat- and nutria-skinning contest. The winners each year will be able to skin three muskrats in well under a minute and a nutria in about half a minute. Their reputations spread all through the marsh. But this kind of speed is short-lived. Trapping as a serious business requires some pacing, and anyway, trappers are rarely in a hurry.

The Stellys' cabin is connected to the shed by a boardwalk on stilts. The cabin stands perched on the levee above Boston Canal; behind it stretches the vast Louisiana marsh. Three children's swings that hang from a metal frame just to the left of the cabin are the only geometrical arrangement about the place; everything else is simply an accumulation. An old gas stove sits in the grass near a corner of the cabin, with a rusted frying pan on one burner. Derelict electricity generators occupy the muddy grass in back of the cabin. "We uses six every year," Clifford tells me, with a note of pride. "We works 'em real hard out here." Oil drums are also scattered about. Narrow aluminum boats, some partially filled with water, line a little canal at the edge of the marsh behind the cabin. One adornment particularly strikes me—a table whose frame was once the dashboard structure of a car. The ancient steering wheel, speedometer, and throttle are still in place. The children who are forever scampering about compete for the honor of traveling to imaginary places in this strange vehicle. But their imaginations can carry them no further than a few miles out into the marsh or up Boston Canal; that is all they know. The remains of steel traps are everywhere—rusting jaws, broken springs, chains, and pans litter the ground under the cabin so thickly that the hut appears built on a heap of traps.

The cabin itself is orderly enough to give some relief from the clutter around it, though one would guess that construction came to a halt just as soon as the roof and the four walls were secure. Strips of tar paper shield the back and sides from damp winter winds. Sheets of plywood painted gray give the front the look of an army barracks. But this is an impression that quickly ends upon entering the dwelling. It is dark and perpetually cool inside, the light from the small windows reflecting dully off the bare linoleum underfoot. Battered furniture crowds against the simulated wood paneling of the living room/kitchen. The number of chairs and scattered bits of personal property lying about—cigarette packs, shoes, hats, and jackets—bear witness to a sizable congregation here, fully occupying the darkened bedrooms whose doors stand ajar. Decorations are few, a sign that the camp is a place of work rather than leisure. A couple of paintings of wildlife by a sixteen-year-old daughter, Dena, show an untrained hand but an eye sensitive to color. The only other noticeable adornments are a gleaming, stylized representation of ducks in flight on one of the walls, deer antlers that serve as a hat rack, and over a sofa a plate on which is inscribed: "When I works, I works hard. When I sits, I sits loose. When I thinks, I falls asleep."

The family spends every autumn and most of each winter here, far out in the marsh. In coming here, Clifford and his sons follow a tradition established generations ago. In November, when the summer's heat and humidity give way to cooler winds, thousands of Louisiana fur trappers head for the marsh with their families, leaving their inland homes and jobs until the following spring. The migration is so deeply instilled that many people in south Louisiana regard it as instinctive. Clifford jokes about it in his quiet way. "Ah don' know why ah likes it out here. Trappin's a terrible business. Lookit all the blood an' mess. All the money's gone out of it. But if ah could, ah'd stay right here all year 'round, where ah don' have no one to bother me an' ah got all the food ah needs right here at ma feets."

Even though few trappers articulate the reasons why they do it, this occupation is the common denominator of Louisiana marsh life. Those who follow it seem to mimic the movements of hundreds of thousands of migratory birds that flock to the marsh and leave it on an annual cycle. In the spring, trappers scatter once again. Some, like Clifford, go back to their fields of rice or sugarcane. Others return to jobs with some branch of the omnipresent petroleum and natural gas industry. Wyndal and Randall are among these people. Wyndal is a welder who puts together the behemoth-sized oil-well platforms that are now fixtures of the Gulf. Randall is a foreman in a pipe yard, but says he doesn't do anything but "sit aroun' until they need some pipe an' then work for a couple of hours an' then sit aroun' again until ah goes crazy gittin' bored."

Older trappers go back to occupations that let them harvest the nearby resources. A man who traps a freshwater marsh may merely change equipment and lay some hoop nets in the bayou for catfish, or he may turn to crawfishing. Some who trap near the edge of the Gulf will dredge for oysters or trawl for shrimps. Others do nothing except odd jobs. There is really no need to do anymore, since the marsh provides them a living. A chicken neck tied to a string will fill a bucket with crabs in half an hour. Catfish bite on almost anything. Oysters line the banks of many bayous. Rabbits thrive on the levees, and sometimes the marsh is over-run with ducks and geese.

The Stellys, particularly the sons, could certainly make more money if they didn't trap. The hours are long and the returns can be meager. But most other occupations would not allow them to stay in the marsh for weeks at a time. The family greets each dawn in a state of low-keyed excitement tempered by skepticism concerning the weather, whose mood can change with remarkable speed during the winter. Clifford and his three sons mill about the cabin in their stocking feet. They down cup after cup of coffee and mumble comments about the weather, the coming day's trapping, their planned whereabouts, and their expectations. Clifford's wife, Della, stands quietly at the stove, frying huge portions of bacon and eggs. A dull light filters through the frost-clouded window above the stove and onto her frizzy gray hair. The tilt of her head betrays a careful attention to what is being said. Occasionally she turns around and in a singsong voice asks a question that clearly reveals her anxiety about the departure of her husband and sons into the marsh.

The talk is slow, a step or two behind the brightening sky. "I bet them nutr'a ran some las' night. It sure was cold 'nough for 'em," says Wyndal.

"It's gonna be cold 'nough for me out there this mornin'," observes Blaine. "Hey, didya hear that Virgil got his fingers fros'bit yesti'dy mornin'? That's what I heared on the radio."

"Me, ah think maybe the marsh be iced over this mornin'. She dropped down to twenty-five las' night," Clifford adds. "There's gonna be ice out there unless the sun come out good. A couple of more days of this an' the ice gonna freeze up them nutr'as' tails." He sidles up a little closer to the cabin's single gas heater and says with a sheepish grin, "Ah goin' wait a little bit 'fore ah goes out."

Clifford's leadership of the family is so detached and unostentatious as to be almost automatic. His wife, children, and grandchildren look to him for direction, and he provides it with a murmur or a gentle wave of the hand. He may say, while he warms himself at the stove, "Blaine, check the trotline later an' see if we got us any catfish, huh." Blaine barely acknowledges the request. But it is sure to be obeyed.

The meandering conversation subsides entirely with the appearance of the bacon and eggs, which are consumed in a matter of minutes. It is as though the food signaled the real beginning of the day, bringing a certain tension into the cabin. Randall wipes his mouth with his sleeve and tugs on his boots. Blaine bustles about collecting a variety of gear— additional traps, a .22 rifle, life jackets, and a torn slicker. He invites me to go with him.

An artificial channel—*trainasse* in local French parlance—leads from the rear of the cabin to Lake Hébert, about a mile across the marsh. Blaine dumps his gear into the ice-coated bottom of an outboard at the head of the channel. He is about to jump in, but suddenly he pauses. "Almost forgot to feed Newt," he says, running over to a cage near the shed where skins are stretched and dried. In the cage, an almost full grown nutria is already moving its incisors up and down in anticipation of the carrots and lettuce Blaine is about to bring. But before he feeds it, Blaine takes the animal out of the cage, holds it in his arms, and caresses its thick fur.

"I catched his mammy in a trap last year. I didn't knowed she had little ones, but the nex' day I come by an' seed two little babies settin' on a clump of grass. I brought 'em both back, but one died. But Newt here, he good an' strong. I think he's gonna have babies, but it's hard to tell with these animals. The males and the females, they looks jus' about the same."

His hand travels up and down the nutria's back, around the neck behind the ears, and down the back again in a single steady movement. The nutria shifts its beady eyes ceaselessly. Its long whiskers gyrate back and forth, set in motion by the movement of the incisors, and its tail hangs limply toward the ground.

"He don' like children though. He'll try to take a bite right outta their fingers. At times I let him outta the cage at night an' he goes into the marsh. But in the mornin', he's settin' right in front of his cage waitin' for a carrot."

After giving the animal a last scratch on the head, Blaine puts the animal back into the cage and throws in a couple of carrots. We watch for a moment as Newt sniffs them and then begins nibbling on one with quick bites. Then Blaine trots back to the boat and we start off down the channel. The marsh grass flashes by, ducks lift from potholes, and fish swirl out of our path. The channel is no more than five feet wide, leaving about six inches of water on either side of the boat. Narrow passages such as this crisscross the marsh. Most of them were made long ago by trappers who wanted easy access to its interior. The older ones were hewn out by hand. In the 1920s, marsh buggies came along—treaded monsters with bargelike bodies that hauled great plows behind them and heaved the muck to one side. Now, most such channels are dredged out with draglines that gobble up all the ooze and vegetation in a straight line and dump it beside the channel. The Stellys' ditch was made that way. It runs straight and true, five feet wide and three feet deep in high water, like a part down the middle of a scalp. When Blaine is not trapping, he operates a commercial dragline. But he rarely talks about this; it's just a way to earn money.

The traps are set along the edge of the ditch and around the shore of Lake Hébert—one hundred sixty of them—a line of deadly steel jaws ready to snap closed on the legs of animals. A tall pole topped by a strip of white cloth marks each trap. The poles also serve to anchor the traps. As we come up to some of them, white flags thrashing back and forth show that an animal is struggling to free itself.

Blaine seems oblivious to the jerking flags. I guess that he is going to the end of the trapline on the other side of the lake and will then work his way back. The first trap at the end of the line holds a big nutria. A mature animal weighs about sixteen pounds, solidly built with about the proportions of a beaver or a groundhog. Its broad rear paws are webbed except between the fourth and fifth toes, making it possible for the animal to get a grip on slippery mud banks and to clutch blades of grass. The head is square and solid looking. The nose is firmly planted, the forehead wide, and the teeth so prominent as to draw all one's attention.

As we approach the first nutria on foot, the gnashing of those teeth makes even the shrill cry of killdeer rising from the mudflats inaudible.

The animal is caught high up on the right rear leg. Coated in mud, it has worn a circle around the pole during the long night of thrashing about, with no chance of escape. Now it paces back and forth around the perimeter of the circle on the far side of the pole. It gives a series of mighty tugs in an effort to wrench its body away, grinding its teeth all the while.

When we are almost on top of it, the animal lunges. Blaine leaps aside shouting, "You git too close to them teeth, an' he'll take yer leg off."

Trappers club their captured animals to death. It's not a nice sight. Perhaps nutrias are fortunate that their skulls are so thin, despite a massive appearance. At any rate, they die quickly. Otters and raccoons have tough skulls that sometimes require five or six blows to crack. A nutria's head will split under just one.

Blaine holds out the end of his club, the "killing stick" as he calls it, and the nutria goes for that. "I always do this. If you git 'em with their heads out, you got a good target. But when they's all huddled up an' snarlin' at you, an' you hit 'em, you can miss the heads an' hurt the fur."

The nutria strikes at the end of the club and Blaine raises the stick behind his shoulder, leaving the animal still straining, neck extended, and almost motionless with eyes bulging. In the next split second, it is thrashing on the ground, blood spurting from the top of its head and nostrils and soaking into the dark mud, legs thrusting out crazily in all directions. Blaine brings the club down again and takes the limp body out of the trap. The skin and muscle on the leg near where the jaws snapped have been scoured through to the bone.

Louisiana fur trappers, not unexpectedly, are the targets of sporadic campaigns to ban the use of leg-hold traps. Most of them just shrug the matter off. "If those peoples ever came out here and saw all them nutr'a, they'd think different," Clifford told me. But the Louisiana Wildlife and Fisheries Commission takes the protests more to heart than do the trappers. In 1976, staff biologists introduced some trappers to a type of trap designed to kill an animal almost instantly by crushing it. The trappers didn't like these traps one bit. "They broke on us all the time," Clifford says, "an' they was too big to put in the nutr'a runways. We weren't catchin' nothin' in them." The same consensus coursed through the marsh, arming the commission with pro-leg-hold lobbying ammunition if the animal welfare people ever really press the issue: they can say, correctly, that the new traps will put trappers out of business.

Even so, a bill to prohibit leg-hold traps would make little headway in the state legislature if examples of past attitudes toward animals suggest anything. Some years ago, efforts were afoot to ban cockfighting, and a bill to that effect was introduced. By thirty-one to seven, the state senate voted that chickens were not animals; the senators never saw fit to reclassify chickens, but the point was brought home that participation in cockfighting was the inalienable right of every Louisianan.

Blaine found forty-odd nutrias in his traps that morning. A few of them were young ones that he let go. They hobbled away to shelter in clumps of marsh grass. He also got half a dozen muskrats. They were all dead, the victims at some time during the night of either trauma or drowning. Some of the traps were sprung but quite empty, others empty except for the claws of nutrias or muskrats. When we came to a sprung trap, the look on Blaine's open face changed to one of bewilderment, as though encountering an undeserved slight. He always moved carefully around the area, searching the grass and mud for some clue to how the animal had escaped. During these searches, he muttered to himself in a tone of chastisement before resetting the trap. But when he came on a trap that held a nutria or a muskrat, he rarely expressed pleasure at his own success, only at the beauty of the fur. "Lookit the pelt on that animal," he would observe. "That'll make someone a purty coat. I don' know how they make those. It must take a lot of animals. They must cost somethin' though, huh?"

As we headed back to the cabin, Blaine suddenly began shouting above the roar of the outboard. "Ya know, I only went up to the seventh grade. When I tol' my daddy I was quittin' school, he was mad. Maybe I shoulda stayed, but if I had I wouldn't be comin' out here. I'd probably have a different job somewheres an' they wouldn't let me take the trappin' season off. I sure couldn't take that."

As the men return with their catches during the day and dump them in the small shed, the conversation takes on an edge of rivalry. Victors or losers, they hang over the benches, spit into the canal, and smoke their cigarettes.

"Man, was it cold out there this mornin'," says Randall, pushing his forever drooping eyeglasses up on the bridge of his nose.

"Well, you shoulda waited like ah done." Clifford hoists his body upright from its customary tilted position. The change in posture fore-warns of humor. "When ah got out there, ah thought ah was 'bout to die from heat stroke."

"Sure, jus' like one of them what you call 'em, polar bears up nor'. If I been with you, I coulda cooled you off with a bucket of water. Yessir, what's that temperature say now? Forty-five degrees. That's hot." Pleased with this response, Randall pulls his sagging pants up on his rounded stomach and struts around the shed in a little circle.

"Well, we sure got us some animals las' night, though. They was runnin' good," Wyndal says, breaking a few minutes of silence.

"Yeah, an' ah almost got an' otter, me," Clifford says with a note of regret. "Ah seen his tracks all roun' one of my sets. But he didn't go in. They's too smart. You gotta be settin' for 'em if you want to catch any."

Conversations start up and trail off into silence. Soon someone takes out a knife and picks up a nutria. Clifford begins skinning the muskrats. Older trappers prefer to work with muskrats, leaving the nutrias to their sons. A muskrat requires less work to skin but more expertise in cutting, for its skin is delicate. People like Clifford grew up skinning muskrats. He scarcely looks at the animal while he does it.

As the skinning continues, Della and the wives of the three sons come out of the cabin and watch the men, or perhaps wash some of the skins and hang them up to dry in the sun. Children are forever in and out of the shed and are always being watched over by the adults. Della assumes the role of supervisor over the children and the other women as well as the guardian of the men. The set of her wide blue eyes in a round, soft face gives her a gentle, caring look.

Just as Clifford directs the family in its use of the marsh, Della reigns over the kitchen. It is her pride to lay a good table; the more food on it, the better. She spends most of the hours of the day in the kitchen, either cutting or stirring. One afternoon when she was hovering over a pot of gumbo, she turned to me and handed me a spoon. "Here, you tastes that and tells me what you think. We're going to add some crabs later on, but we don't have 'em yet. So you jus' take a taste the way it is now. Go ahead."

I dipped into the thick stew, in which floated bits of a bell pepper, onion, okra, and shrimp, and took a taste.

"It's good, non?" She lowered her voice and confided, in a voice barely containing its pride, "We eats good here. Mais yeah, cher. No one goes hungry here."

Della cherishes being able to feed her family well, just as Clifford cherishes the marsh. The combination is fortunate, for much of the food she cooks comes from the marsh and is gathered by Clifford and his sons. Food gathering is the usual afternoon activity. Blaine goes out to

Lake Hébert to check and bait the catfish trotline. Wyndal pulls in the crab traps and gingerly removes a dozen big blue claws for the gumbo. Randall wrestles some garfish from the gill net's mesh, their slack gaping jaws lined with needlelike teeth. During the shrimping season, Clifford trawls in Vermilion Bay.

The results of the afternoon's harvest bring the men together in the shed, usually to clean fish. Each catfish is strung up on a hook and its skin is pulled off with pincers, usually while it is still alive. The bloody thing flaps grotesquely from the hook until someone takes it down and hammers it to death. The garfish are laid out on the benches and skinned in more delicate fashion.

Della or one of her daughters-in-law comes out with a washbasin to collect the ingredients for the evening meal. The men remain in the dying light of the shed for a while longer, talking in gentler tones and comparing notes on the day's activities. At this time of day, a stillness settles over the marsh. The boarded-up summer cabins along Boston Canal blend into the deepening colors of the marsh. The grasses stop waving, and the canal is now so calm that the water has an icelike sheen all the way to Vermilion Bay. Reluctantly, the men begin to gravitate toward the cabin. They may pause for a moment to sit on the doorstep, using the excuse of taking off their boots to linger outside a moment longer.

This is the time of day when they seem content to just sit. Inside, they tilt back in their chairs and listlessly watch the television screen, keeping an ear always cocked toward the CB radio, which likewise stays on from before daybreak until well into the night. No one pays much overt attention to either TV or radio, but neither is totally ignored. Both offer instant companionship. When gossip and shop talk run thin, all eyes turn to the television until a distraction of another sort draws their combined attention. It might be the voice of a friend on the CB radio, full of French and static and the boastful talk of shrimpers returning from the Gulf. Occasionally a call comes in for a member of the family. For each one of them, there is an identifying CB name, given by a friend or relative, that amounts to a crystallized image of the person. Clifford's CB name is Big Parain, and Della's is Big Nanan—Cajun French for godfather and godmother, respectively. Randall is the Muskrat; Wyndal is the Forked Island Welder.

Children are another distraction. They are the family clowns, and they constitute the glue that binds families together. With their actions constantly followed, they learn early how charm earns lavish displays of affection. Toby James, Randall's toddling son, is usually the star of the pre-dinner family gathering. As a result of an ear infection that left him deaf for a time, he is a strangely quiet child, absorbed in a private world. Before an operation that cured his deafness, the family communicated to him by signs; even now they still gesticulate to attract his attention. Frequently, when the CB radio is quiet, conversation momentarily exhausted, and when eyes have not yet turned to the television, Toby James steps forth on little legs so plump they do not quite straighten. Instantly becoming the center of attention, he stares at the circle of faces as half a dozen or more hands rise in the air in greeting. "Hi ya, Toby James; hi ya," echoes through the cabin. The child looks up uncertainly at the faces. Clifford pads over to him with an outstretched hand. "Gimme five, Toby James," he says, "gimme five." Toby James stares into Clifford's grizzled face, blinks, and tentatively lifts his tiny hand as Clifford's huge one gently encircles it.

The distractions that unite the family at this time of day are climaxed by the meal. But if it is the evening's main event, it is also the quietest one. Della and the other women pile the little kitchen table high with gumbo, rice, boiled vegetables, fried catfish, and garfish balls, as well as a selection of homemade jams and hot sauces and the inevitable loaf of Evangeline Maid—white bread so soft that it hangs limply over the table's edge. Once the plates are filled, members of the family scatter to the chairs around the living area. They are silent, hunching over to gobble down the food.

In the tiredness that now prevails, the allure of the television screen is strong, even though no one is entirely seduced by it. This is also a time for affection. Wyndal's children crawl onto his lap and he swings them in the air. Husbands and wives sit side by side on a couch, talking in low tones. They smile at each other; some hold hands or rest a palm on the other's thigh in a somewhat awkward closeness.

The interlude does not last long. One by one the men drift out through the door, followed by the older children, toward the warmth of the stretching and drying shack. Here the next few hours will be spent tacking nutria skins to wooden molds and slipping muskrat skins over wire stretchers. The end of the day, the big meal, the close heat from the two kerosene stoves in the shed prompt a mood of joviality, a babble accompanied by the ceaseless tap-tap of the hammers as they work.

Dena, sidling up to Randall and Wyndal, says playfully, "You hit them nails like that an' you goin' to pound yer thumb."

"That's what you said las' night an' it didn't happen, did it?" Wyndal retorts with his shy smile.

"That's what she done said las' night and the night afore that an' the one afore that," Randall declares with a chuckle. "Her voice box starts repeatin' itself at this time a night, I guess."

Dena giggles, "That's jus' what you says to me every night, so I guess it's yer voice box that's broke."

Clifford is in the next room with Shelly, his youngest son, who is fourteen years old. They are taking dried skins off the molds and arranging them in a stack. They both listen to the conversation and smile. Each time another skin is added, everyone looks at it. At the end of the evening, when the stack is waist-high, the family in the shed stands back to admire it. Blaine stretches his arm out at eye level and says, "If them nutr'a are runnin' tonight, she be up to here tomorrow."

No one says anything in particular, but there are nods as one by one they go back to the cabin. The women and most of the children have long since gone to bed. Before he comes in, Clifford turns the generator off. The silence of the marsh pervades the cabin as the generator's last chug and sputter die away.

Seven Songs of Modern Montana

Greg Keeler

The Ballad of Billy Montana

> *He was born near Big Timber where the Yellowstone runs deep;*
> *His daddy was a drifter, his mother was a sheep;*
> *The doctor said the people there would never understand,*
> *But his daddy said he'd pass him off as a North Dakota man.*
> > *And the wind comes up, and the grass lies down,*
> > *And the wind don't care if they put Billy in the ground,*
> > *And the grass lies down. . . .*

> *On October first of '61, a truck rolled into town.*
> *If Billy'd knowed the driver, he'd of never thumbed it down.*
> *But as it was he fell in with a rhinestone-studded man,*
> *Became the inadvertent member of a country-western band.*
> > *And the clouds roll up and the rain falls down,*
> > *And the clouds don't care if they put Billy in the ground,*
> > *And the rain falls down. . . .*

> *One day near Missoula as he went into his act*
> *A pretty girl named Millicent with her hair tied up in back*
> *Proposed that he should drive her home that night after the show,*
> *And Billy, bein' innocent, just couldn't wait to go.*
> > *And the trees grow up, and the roots grow down,*
> > *And the trees don't care if they put Billy in the ground,*
> > *And the roots grow down. . . .*

Well she took him to her trailer and she opened up a book
Wrote by a guy named Karl Marx and flashed a knowing look;
She said she understood his plight, just how he didn't ask,
But later on he found out that her daddy was a Basque.
      And the geese fly south, and the snow flies down,
      And the geese don't care if they put Billy in the ground,
      And the snow flies down. . . .

Well early that next morning he got up and quit his job.
He hit his boss and called him a fat capitalist slob.
Then he took off with that filly who taught anthropology
And joined her in a seminar at the university.
      And the hills roll up and the plains roll down,
      And the hills don't care if they put Billy in the ground,
      And the plains roll down. . . .

But as luck would have it, Millicent turned out to be bad news:
She didn't trust the Catholics and she didn't trust the Jews,
She didn't trust Ralph Nader, and as if that weren't enough
Some fellows in white coats came up and dragged her off in cuffs.
      And the smoke drifts up, and the fire burns down,
      And the smoke don't care if they put Billy in the ground,
      And the fire burns down. . . .

He tried loggin' up near Callaspell, he tried ranchin' down near Butte,
He tried building condominiums in the southern Bitter Root;
But the land he worked was never his, and the friends he made are gone;
Now he sells real estate near Helena and evenings mows the lawn.
      And the sun comes up, and the sun goes down,
      And the sun don't care if they put Billy in the ground,
      And the sun goes down. . . .

Fossil-Fuel Cowboy

I'm proud to be a fossil-fuel cowboy,
A diesel-burnin', meat-consumin' man;
I ain't got to have no brains,

I'm at the top of the food chain,
And the way I see it now,
There ain't bound to be no change.
Yes, when I was young, my daddy was a loser:
He tried to make it on the family farm.
We didn't have a dime, we was workin' most the time,
So I left him there at home and made a fortune on my own.

Yes, I learned the ins and outs of agribusiness,
And how to take the watertable down.
In spring I fertilize, in fall my crops is oversized,
And I don't lift a finger 'cause it's all computerized.

Oh my Lord, I got petroleum in my system;
It's in the air I breathe and in my blood.
I burn it up in stacks and I wear it on my back
In my dacron leisure suit and my double-knitted slacks.

Yes, I'm proud to be a fossil-fuel cowboy,
And I say this prayer before I go to bed:
"God help me if I need it, give me oil till I deplete it,
Then I won't give a shit, 'cause I'll be dead."

Yes, I'm proud to be a fossil-fuel cowboy,
A diesel-burnin', meat-consumin' man;
I ain't gotta have no brains,
I'm at the top of the food chain,
And the way I see it now,
There ain't bound to be no change.

Montana Cowboy

Well I couldn't be cooler, I come from Missoula,
And I rope, and I chew, and I ride,
But I'm a heroin-dealer, and I drive a four-wheeler
With stereo speakers inside.
My old lady Phoebe's out rippin' off CB's
From rigs at the Wagon Wheel Bar

Near a Montana truck stop, and a shit-out-of-luck stop
For a trucker who's driven too far.

And there ain't no such thing as a Montana cowboy:
They's all dead or they's fixin' to die.
And there ain't no such thing as a Montana cowboy because . . .
What you think's a cowboy's most likely a plowboy
So you better not ask for a hand.
The plowboys ain't friendly and all the cowboys is Indians,
And the Indians just don't give a damn.

  And where are the sons of the Montana cowboys?
  They've all gone to ski the Big Sky;
  They're ridin' gondolas and eatin' Grainolas
  And lookin' for a piece of the pie.

Last night I was deep in an uneasy sleep,
And I dreamed Crazy Horse had returned,
Ridin' 'cross the damp grounds and the KOA campgrounds
Till the last Winnebago was burned.
Then I awoke in a fever, just like Dennis Weaver
As Chester before a gunfight,
And I pulled my Tony Lamas up over my pajamas,
And I stumbled out into the night.

And there ain't no such thing as a Montana cowboy:
They's all dead or they's fixin' to die,
And there ain't no such thing as a Montana cowboy because. . . .
What you thinks a cowboy's most likely a plowboy
So you better not ask for a hand.
The plowboys ain't friendly, and all the cowboys is Indians,
And the Indians just don't give a damn.

Miles City Buckin' Horse Sale

Last summer in Wyoming I was mendin' fence
For a rancher named Orville Hale.

Days was so hot, and the nights long enough
Make a tough son-of-a-bitch turn pale.

So I asked my boss for a few days off
Just to get me some peace of mind;
But I had to admit that the weather wasn't it,
I had a bad case of women on my mind.
Then his face puckered up and he spit a wad
Of Day's Work on the ground,
Said, "When I was young, every once in a while,
I had to take off and fool around.

"If I was you, I'd head up north
Toward the Eastern Montana line
Where the bars are wild and the women are too—
The combination make a man feel fine."

I said, "That sounds real good, but eastern Montana's got
A hell of a lot of trail."
He said, "As far as I'm concerned, there's just one place that counts,
That's the Miles City Buckin' Horse Sale."

Didn't know about him, but a bucking horse
Wasn't my idea of fun.
He said from what he knew that was just an excuse
For the gals to go out and get undone.

So a couple days later I found myself
Headin' on into town
With a fifth of Black Velvet and a bottle of Old Spice
And mind full of foolin' around.

I checked into the hotel room and headed for a bar
And proceeded to get me a buzz,
But no sooner had I started than I looked back in a corner
By the jukebox and there she was

With her Dolly Parton hairdo and her Dolly Parton smile
And her Dolly Parton god knows what else.
As I stumbled toward the jukebox, I don't know what possessed me,
I could hardly control myself.

Before I knew it, I was buyin' her drinks
And invitin' her up to my room.
And she was playin' right along, while in the background a sad song
Made me wonder if I'd made my move too soon.

But later on that night it all seemed to be all right
As we slipped in between the sheets
And made wild, abandoned love in that hotel room above
All the cussin' and fightin' in the streets.

Well I never met a woman that made me feel
Like such a pistol-packin' son-of-a-gun,
As I drifted off all satisfied, I dreamed about her Dolly eyes
And knew that I had finally found The One.

Early that next morning, I was feelin' my oats,
So I reached across the bed;
That lady wasn't there, but at the mirror combin' her hair,
And here's what she said:

"Listen, buckaroo, I'm splittin' from this scene,
'Cause last night was just a waste of my time;
You may be tall in the saddle, but you're short in your jeans,"
And she turned around and flipped me a dime.

Well in all of my life, I've never heard words that sent
So much blood into my face.
As I chased her to the door, she dropped me to the floor
With a swift kick in just the wrong place.

So if you're ever mendin' fence near Casey, Wyoming
for a rancher named Orville Hale,
Don't take his advice 'bout what he says is mighty nice
If you want to stay a full-fledged male.

Montana Banana Belt Cowboy

I'm a Montana Banana Belt, Theodore Roosevelt, rough-ridin', quiche-
   eatin' cowboy,
I'm a rounder of means, and I wear L.L. Beans, where's that Telex
   machine, anyhow, boys?
I've looked everywhere, and I can't find the Barron's, I've got to check
   in on the Dow, boys.
I'd swear before dark that there'll be a bull market, I got to buy Exon
   right now, boys.

I jog in my Walkman and walk to the sun-tanning booth the first
   month of each winter.
It's Key West for starters, then Puerto Vallarta; Montana can freeze
   you to splinters.
Now I'm off to Jamaica, who says you can't make a silk purse from the
   ear of a sow, boys?
A tough life, yessirree, but someone's got to be a Montana Banana Belt
   Cowboy.

To stay hale and hearty at wine and cheese parties, I skip wine and
   drink Perier water.
I try to stay trim on my Nautilus gym, and chase girls the same age as
   my daughter.
Yes, I prowl the fern bars, and I deal in fast cars, my Ferrari is really
   a wow, boys.
It costs ninety grand, and it matches the tan on Montana Banana Belt
   Cowboys.

I sit on my sundeck and glance at my Rolex; the truck should pull up
   any minute.
You rent a safari, we'll unload my quarry, I'll shoot it, they'll gut it
   and skin it.
It's five thousand at least just to shoot threatened species; I paid for this
   moment, and how, boys!
Hell, it's nothin' but the best for this son of the West, this Montana
   Banana Belt Cowboy.

P-U-B-L-I-C   L-A-N-D-S

I found a way to make big bucks
If you promise not to tell
From the public that must be
So damned dumb they can't spell;
So just in case they overhear,
I'll spell out what works best,
yes I'll tell you the S-E-C-
R-E-T of my success.

Oh yes, now P-U-B-L-I-C
L-A-N-D-S,
M-I-L-K them for all they're worth
And screw the rest.
Just find you some connections for an
L-E-A-S-E,
And if you play your cards right, it's
Damned near F-R-E-E.

The Bureau of Land M-A-N-A-G
E-M-E-N-T
Will let you bring your herd of
C-A-T-T-L-E
And turn the verdant meadows and
The meadows green and wide
Into piles of P-O-O-P
Down the mountainside.

Oh yes, now P-U-B-L-I-C
L-A-N-D-S,
M-I-L-K them for all they're worth
And screw the rest.
Just find you some connections for an
L-E-A-S-E,
And if you play your cards right, it's
Damned near F-R-E-E.

The F-O-R-E-S-T
S-E-R-V-I-C-E
Wants to sell off grizzley
H-A-B-I-T-A-T,
So get your C-H-A-I-N
S-A-W-S—
What the hell, it's easy but
Some Freddie, he knows best.

Oh yes, now P-U-B-L-I-C
L-A-N-D-S,
M-I-L-K them for all they're worth
And screw the rest.
Just find you some connections for an
L-E-A-S-E,
And if you play your cards right, it's
Damned near F-R-E-E.
Watch out for E-N-V-I-R-
O-N-M-E-N
T-A-L-I-S-T-S, they'll
Try to stop you when
They see you coming with your saws,
Your 'dozers and your trucks,
But in the West, them whimps is S-
H-I-T out of luck.

Oh yes, now P-U-B-L-I-C
L-A-N-D-S,
M-I-L-K them for all they're worth
And screw the rest.
Just find you some connections for an
L-E-A-S-E,
And if you play your cards right, it's
Damned near F-R-E-E.

Oh yes, now, M-I-L-K them
For all they're worth, and screw the rest.
Yes, P-U-B (Be a long time 'fore this grows back)
L-I-C (See all the cow flop and clear cuts?)
L-A-N-D-S

What's Left of the West

Manifest Destiny ain't had a rest
Since Horace Greeley said, "Young Man, go west."
So we chewed up the mountains and spit out the plains
While we get indigestion with each acid rain.
It's gotten so bad, the West ain't any place;
I'll ask you how are you, and you stare into space.
What's left of the West where we've already been?
So I'll ask ya, how are ya, again.

> *Honolulu's no lulu, Fairbank's ain't so fair;*
> *Take a sip of the water, take a whiff of the air,*
> *Take some pictures of the wildlife, take a leak in a stream,*
> *Take a jet back to Cleveland and dream.*

If trees ran for Congress and forests could vote,
Our chances of survival might not be so remote;
Since we don't give a damn about who they'd elect
Their absentee ballots have a greenhouse effect.
What's a boatload of timber, what's the whole human race?
I'll ask you how are you, and you stare into space.
What's left of the West where we've already been?
So I'll ask ya, how are ya, again.

> *Honolulu's no lulu, Fairbank's ain't so fair;*
> *Take a sip of the water, take a whiff of the air,*
> *Take some pictures of the wildlife, take a leak in a stream,*
> *Take a jet back to Cleveland and dream.*

We scrub up with phosphates and flush down the suds
Till the banks of our rivers are bubbles and mud;
Just to stay sanitary we've gone to these lengths—
Now our whole ecosystem is industrial strength.
It's so simple to screw up what can't be replaced.
I'll ask you how are you, and you stare into space.

What's left of the West where we've already been?
So I'll ask ya, how are ya, again.

> *Honolulu's no lulu, Fairbank's ain't so fair;*
> *Take a sip of the water, take a whiff of the air,*
> *Take some pictures of the wildlife, take a leak in a stream,*
> *Take a jet back to Cleveland and dream.*

·10·

Buffalo

Barry Holstun Lopez

IN JANUARY 1845, after a week of cold but brilliantly clear weather, it began to snow in southern Wyoming. Snow accumulated on the flat in a dead calm to a depth of four feet in only a few days. The day following the storm was breezy and warm—chinook weather. A party of Cheyenne camped in a river bottom spent the day tramping the snow down, felling cottonwood trees for their horses, and securing game, in response to a dream by one of them, a thirty-year-old man called Blue Feather on the Side of His Head, that they would be trapped by a sudden freeze.

That evening the temperature fell fifty degrees and an ice crust as rigid, as easily broken, as sharp as window glass formed over the snow. The crust held for weeks.

Access across the pane of ice to game and pasturage on the clear, wind-blown slopes of the adjacent Medicine Bow Mountains was impossible for both Indian hunters and a buffalo herd trapped nearby. The buffalo, exhausted from digging in the deep snow, went to their knees by the thousands, their legs slashed by the razor ice, glistening red in the bright sunlight. Their woolly carcasses lay scattered like black boulders over the blinding white of the prairie, connected by a thin crosshatching of bloody red trails.

Winds moaned for days in the thick fur of the dead and dying buffalo, broken by the agonized bellows of the animals themselves. Coyotes would not draw near. The Cheyenne camped in the river bottom were terrified. As soon as they were able to move they departed. No Cheyenne ever camped there again.

The following summer the storm and the death of the herd were depicted on a buffalo robe by one of the Cheyenne, a man called Raven on His Back. Above the scene, in the sky, he drew a white buffalo. The day they had left camp a man was supposed to have seen a small herd of buffalo, fewer than twenty, leaving the plains and lumbering up the Medicine Bow River into the mountains. He said they were all white, and each seemed to him larger than any bull he had ever seen. There is no record of this man's name, but another Cheyenne in the party, a medicine man called Walks Toward the Two Rivers, carried the story of the surviving white buffalo to Crow and Teton Sioux in an effort to learn its meaning. In spite of the enmity among these tribes their leaders agreed that the incident was a common and disturbing augury. They gathered on the Box Elder River in southeastern Montana in the spring of 1846 to decipher its meaning. No one was able to plumb it, though many had fasted and bathed in preparation.

Buffalo were never seen again on the Laramie Plains after 1845, in spite of the richness of the grasses there and the size of the buffalo herds nearby in those days. The belief that there were still buffalo in the Medicine Bow Mountains, however, survivors of the storm, persisted for years, long after the disappearance of buffalo (some 60 million animals) from Wyoming and neighboring territories by the 1880s.

In the closing years of the nineteenth century, Arapaho and Shoshoni warriors who went into the Medicine Bow to dream say they did, indeed, see buffalo up there then. The animals lived among the barren rocks above timberline, far from any vegetation. They stood more than eight feet at the shoulder; their coats were white as winter ermine and their huge eyes were light blue. At the approach of men they would perch motionless on the granite boulders, like mountain goats. Since fogs are common in these high valleys in spring and summer it was impossible, they say, to tell how many buffalo there were.

In May 1887 a Shoshoni called Long Otter came on two of these buffalo in the Snowy Range. As he watched they watched him. They began raising and lowering their hooves, started drumming softly on the rocks. They began singing a death song, way back in the throat like the sound of wind moaning in a canyon. The man, Long Otter, later lost his mind and was killed in a buckboard accident the following year. As far as I know this is the last report of living buffalo in the Medicine Bow.

It is curious to me that in view of the value of the hides no white man ever tried to find and kill one of these buffalo. But that is the case. No detail of the terrible storm of that winter, or of the presence of a herd of enormous white buffalo in the Medicine Bow, has ever been found among the papers of whites who lived in the area or who might have passed through in the years following.

It should be noted, however, by way of verification, that a geology student from Illinois called Fritiof Fryxell came upon two buffalo skeletons in the Snowy Range in the summer of 1925. Thinking these barren heights an extraordinary elevation at which to find buffalo, he carefully marked the location on a topographic map. He measured the largest of the skeletons, found the size staggering, and later wrote up the incident in the May 1926 issue of the *Journal of Mammalogy*.

In 1955, a related incident came to light. In the fall of 1911, at the request of the Colorado Mountain Club, a party of Arapaho Indians were brought into the Rocky Mountains in the northern part of the state to relate to white residents the history of the area prior to 1859. The settlers were concerned that during the years when the white man was moving into the area, and the Indian was being extirpated, a conflict in historical records arose such that the white record was incomplete and possibly in error.

The Arapaho were at first reluctant to speak; they made up stories of the sort they believed the whites would like to hear. But the interest and persistence of the white listeners made an impression upon them and they began to tell what had really happened.

Among the incidents the Arapaho revealed was that in the winter of 1845 (when news of white settlers coming in covered wagons first reached them) there was a terrible storm. A herd of buffalo wintering in Brainard Valley (called then Bear in the Hole Valley) began singing a death song. At first it was barely audible, and it was believed the wind was making the sound until it got louder and more distinct. As the snow got deeper the buffalo left the valley and began to climb into the mountains. For four days they climbed, still singing the moaning death song, followed by Arapaho warriors, until they reached the top of the mountain. This was the highest place but it had no name. Now it is called Thatchtop Mountain.

During the time the buffalo climbed they did not stop singing.

They turned red all over; their eyes became smooth white. The singing became louder. It sounded like thunder that would not stop. Everyone who heard it, even people four or five days' journey away, was terrified.

At the top of the mountain the buffalo stopped singing. They stood motionless in the snow, the wind blowing clouds around them. The Arapaho men who had followed had not eaten for four days. One, wandering into the clouds with his hands outstretched and a rawhide string connecting him to the others, grabbed hold of one of the buffalo and killed it. The remaining buffalo disappeared into the clouds; the death song began again, very softly, and remained behind them. The wind was like the singing of the buffalo. When the clouds cleared the men went down the mountain.

The white people at the 1911 meeting said they did not understand the purpose of telling such a story. The Arapaho said this was the first time the buffalo tried to show them how to climb out through the sky.

The notes of this meeting in 1911 have been lost, but what happened there remained clear in the mind of the son of one of the Indians who was present. It was brought to my attention by accident one evening in the library of the university where I teach. I was reading an article on the introduction of fallow deer in Nebraska in the August 1955 issue of the *Journal of Mammalogy* when this man, who was apparently just walking by, stopped and, pointing at the opposite page, said, "This is not what this is about." The article he indicated was called "An Altitudinal Record for Bison in Northern Colorado." He spoke briefly of it, as if to himself, and then departed.

Excited by this encounter I began to research the incident. I have been able to verify what I have written here. In view of the similarity between the events in the Medicine Bow and those in Colorado, I suspect that there were others in the winter of 1845 who began, as the Arapaho believe, trying to get away from what was coming, and that subsequent attention to this phenomenon is of some importance.

I recently slept among weathered cottonwoods on the Laramie Plains in the vicinity of the Medicine Bow Mountains. I awoke in the morning to find my legs broken.

·11·

Meditations on a Small Lake

Norbert Blei

FOR REASONS OF MY OWN, I will call it Little Lake, as some of the oldtimers still remember it. One of a handful of small inland lakes on the Door Peninsula, each possessing a special insular attraction, as small bodies of water often do.

Little Lake I know best, longer and more intimately, within range of where I reintegrate my world each day with words.

The nearness of water attracts.

To go down to the little lake for a spell.

Lake Michigan is within my domain too. To seek solace, though, in the universe of blue, one should make a path, set his mind on smaller wonders first.

A great lake can be an ocean.

The difference between Lake Michigan and Little Lake is the difference between

. . . the Morning Star and the Milky Way

. . . a raven on a branch and crows in cornfields

. . . a man in a red rowboat on a small lake and a sea of Sunday worshippers in a white church.

It's an oldtimer's lake anyway. A small body of water the settlers, the Indians once knew. And one can only re-imagine that. The uncommonness of wonder. Unobtrusive. A small body of water perfectly in place. More importantly: unpossessed. Waiting to be undiscovered.

It was all there, once. The small mind of man, the diminisher of dreams.

Possession is the serpent most self-consuming in the Eden of men's souls.

I must have it.

I must make it mine.

No matter. No man can own any more of it than he holds in his hands.

A small body of water possesses only its beholder.

A small body of water, its back against the earth, trains its vision heavenward.

We look into water and see the color of sky, the shape of clouds, the heat of the sun.

At night we bathe our hands in stars, lift a languid yellow moon to our lips for sustenance.

We will return again. Into water.

The lake, undiscovered, was to itself, thickly ringed with trees: pine, maple, beech, birch, poplar. Beyond that, in distance, came the fields.

The Indians at first filtered through the forest unobtrusively, making their way to water.

Lumbermen felled a pathway through the virgin timber.

The forest floor moist, pine needle soft and fragrant.

The lure of clear, fresh water ahead. Just follow your nose.

While the Indian advanced and retreated leaving no trail, the lumberman made his access certain, clearing the way for others to follow.

Pathways, trailways, roadways.

Who knows when the first fisherman came?

The oldtimers picked up the scent of the small body of water at the end of the dirt path, down the dirt road.

"I cut timber around Little Lake," one of them recalls. "I made wooden crates to sell. I tapped maples in March for syrup. The whole summer long I fished for perch. Come winter I chopped a hole in the ice and fished for perch some more. I cut big blocks of ice and hauled them to market on a sled.

"All a man needs to live is a small lake."

All a man needs to love is a small lake.

The Old Fisherman put the tackle box, minnow bucket, poles, rods, net, worm box, and two cans of beer in the bed of the black, 1938 pickup truck, tightened the hitch of the boat trailer, and motioned to climb in the cab.

It was still early in the morning. It was time to leave. The sun had been up hours ago. Now was the best time to fish, it had been said.

"Anytime's the best time to fish," said the Old Fisherman.

It was summer, the 1960's. I was a stranger renting a place for the next two months from the man who loved to fish. "I dug up some nice nightcrawlers behind the raspberries," he said. He was going to show me something I had never seen before. Little Lake.

The back roads of the county remain more than half of its charm. The unexpected vision of water appearing when you least expect it. The land lies flat, climbs, even rolls in one long stretch. Mired in farmland for miles and miles, you can't believe that just behind that barn you're looking at Lake Michigan.

The Old Fisherman poking his way in the pickup past cherry orchards, herds of Holsteins, abandoned farm machinery, stone fences, a working windmill, the smell of cornfields, of earth, of wildflowers . . . the dry air giving way to a breezy moistness that can only mean a lake nearby.

When the old man talks, he talks of fish. "I know a fella once caught a six-pound bass where we're going. Lots of perch, some small, some big. To land a northern, use a spoon. The red and white one, that's the ticket. I brought a net along just in case. Bullheads ain't so bad to eat. Taste like chicken. You gotta nail their tail down to a board and skin 'em. The main thing is, we don't get skunked."

At the end of a gravel road lay Little Lake.

The Old Fisherman just smiled. I was not prepared for what I saw, and he knew it.

A small body of water so blue and green and still in morning light; so innocent of much of the trappings of modern man as he secures his place on, in, beside the water.

I was content to leave it as I discovered it. To fish it in my own mind, from the shore.

We were the only boat on the lake that morning, just the Old Fisherman and I.

What we caught I can't quite remember.

What I began to learn with him on water is with me yet.

"I don't suppose it matters much what a fella believes as long as it can be like this," the Old Fisherman said.

We drifted over limestone the color of cream. There were shadows, there was darkness, there was holy light below moving in levels of color like Paul Klee's paintings of magical fish.

Or so it appeared to the man who fished without his heart in it, who mostly dangled an empty hook. While the Old Fisherman, I suspect, filled our bucket with perch.

Each man knew the lesson of water, but neither felt the need to speak.

Often the Old Fisherman pulled anchor. We went with the water.

Silence was our sacrament.

These things are passed down, friend to friend, father to son, instinctively.

When the time came to make my home in this landscape, I moved near the small body of water.

Near, not on its shore, for fear much of the water's mystery might be lost.

We see least what stares us in our face.

We enjoy less what we finally possess.

The truest pleasure is the unfulfilled dream.

If a man does not desire, he does not live.

I desired to be near water.

One day the Old Fisherman left me a red wooden rowboat tied to a cedar on the shore of Little Lake.

These things are passed down, friend to friend, father to son, instinctively. Memories truest to the heart are best unspoken.

The time came for my own son's rite-of-passage. I began to teach, as most fathers do, from the shore. A simple cane pole, line, bobber, weight, and tiny hook. The tender connection. A man's first grasp of the floating world. All the mystery in motion out there.

I do not tell him. These things in time may be revealed to him. Life is simply this: casting into the unknown. A tenuous connection to uncertainty. You receive more, the less you put your mind to it. Be like water.

I taught him almost nothing, then placed him in the hands of the Old Fisherman who might guide him in the silence of water, the luminosity of ice, the lessons of the lake.

He returned when he was still.

My friend the Old Fisherman is dead.

My son, a man, is drawn to places far away from here, yet knows what he must do some day when he returns to Little Lake.

I no longer fish.

The man in the red rowboat drifts in the center of the small body of water contemplating the movement of two fish, one black, one white, head-to-tail, all one circle. Heaven and earth, fire and water, thunder and wind, mountain and mist.

'He is fishing,' whispers a visitor to a child from the shore.

There is no rod, no tackle box, no bait in the boat. The only line, a thick rope attached to a heavy stone anchoring him to the water.

Drops of water still glisten from the oars. The boat gently turns upon itself.

He sees perch and rock bass, an empty can, parts of trees gone soft. He sees the undulating shadows of the bottom. He knows the darkness only water holds. And the baptism, the absolution.

For some years, spring, summer, and autumn, the man in the red rowboat glides across the water into dawn, the oar locks squeaking. Drops the stone anchor with a splash. Waits for the water to reclaim its own silence. Watches the sun first touch the tops of the trees on the west shore, the liquid colors upon water, the spreading light. And remains that way a while, the man in the red rowboat, motionless.

Rows in when there is too much light. Only to return in the deep orange of some later afternoon to wait for the oncoming darkness, first stars, the invocation of the night.

Mornings and evenings of mist, too, when even the man in the red rowboat visits the final, spacial dimension of being and not being there.

To row home finally in moonlight so bright both the boat and the man's reflections seem the colors of day.

Sometimes on a night like that, a need to be near the water, I follow a moonlit path to Little Lake and remember the red row boat, now abandoned in a woods, its bottom in communion with the forest floor of leaves, pine needles, plants, and small trees.

I recall it was the perfect vessel for one man.

A small lake.

Alone.

To recall that feeling from shore, I hold the image of man upon water like a prayer.

Carry it back to the desk with me, failing to give it words.

Conjure the image again and again, anywhere in the world I may find myself. Even the desert.

Especially the desert.

Wilderness Letter

Wallace Stegner

Los Altos, Calif.
Dec. 3, 1960

David E. Pesonen
Wildland Research Center
Agricultural Experiment Station
243 Mulford Hall
University of California
Berkeley 4, Calif.

Dear Mr. Pesonen:

I believe that you are working on the wilderness portion of the Outdoor Recreation Resources Review Commission's report. If I may, I should like to urge some arguments for wilderness preservation that involve recreation, as it is ordinarily conceived, hardly at all. Hunting, fishing, hiking, mountain-climbing, camping, photography, and the enjoyment of natural scenery will all, surely, figure in your report. So will the wilderness as a genetic reserve, a scientific yardstick by which we may measure the world in its natural balance against the world in its man-made imbalance. What I want to speak for is not so much the wilderness uses, valuable as those are, but the wilderness *idea*, which is a resource in itself. Being an intangible and spiritual resource, it will seem mystical to the practical-minded—but then anything that cannot be moved by a bulldozer is likely to seem mystical to them.

I want to speak for the wilderness idea as something that has helped form our character and that has certainly shaped our history as a people.

It has no more to do with recreation than churches have to do with recreation, or than the strenuousness and optimism and expansiveness of what historians call the "American Dream" have to do with recreation. Nevertheless, since it is only in this recreation survey that the values of wilderness are being compiled, I hope you will permit me to insert this idea between the leaves, as it were, of the recreation report.

Something will have gone out of us as a people if we ever let the remaining wilderness be destroyed; if we permit the last virgin forests to be turned into comic books and plastic cigarette cases; if we drive the few remaining members of the wild species into zoos or to extinction; if we pollute the last clear air and dirty the last clean streams and push our paved roads through the last of the silence, so that never again will Americans be free in their own country from the noise, the exhausts, the stinks of human and automotive waste. And so that never again can we have the chance to see ourselves single, separate, vertical and individual in the world, part of the environment of trees and rocks and soil, brother to the other animals, part of the natural world and competent to belong in it. Without any remaining wilderness we are committed wholly, without chance for even momentary reflection and rest, to a headlong drive into our technological termite-life, the Brave New World of completely man-controlled environment. We need wilderness preserved—as much of it as is still left, and as many kinds—because it was the challenge against which our character as a people was formed. The reminder and the reassurance that it is still there is good for our spiritual health even if we never once in ten years set foot in it. It is good for us when we are young, because of the incomparable sanity it can bring briefly, as vacation and rest, into our insane lives. It is important to us when we are old simply because it is there—important, that is, simply as idea.

We are a wild species, as Darwin pointed out. Nobody ever tamed or domesticated or scientifically bred us. But for at least three millennia we have been engaged in a cumulative and ambitious race to modify and gain control of our environment, and in the process we have come close to domesticating ourselves. Not many people are likely, any more, to look upon what we call "progress" as an unmixed blessing. Just as surely as it has brought us increased comfort and more material goods, it has brought us spiritual losses, and it threatens now to become the Frankenstein that will destroy us. One means of sanity is to retain a hold on the natural world, to remain, insofar as we can, good animals. Americans still have that chance, more than many peoples; for while we were demonstrating ourselves the most efficient and ruthless environment-busters in history, and slashing and burning and cutting our way through a wilderness continent, the wilderness was working on us. It remains in us surely as Indian names remain on the land. If the abstract dream of human liberty and human dignity became, in America, something more than an abstract dream, mark it down at least partially to the fact that we were in subtle ways subdued by what we conquered.

The Connecticut Yankee, sending likely candidates from King Arthur's unjust kingdom to his Man Factory for rehabilitation, was over-optimistic, as he later admitted. These things cannot be forced, they have to grow. To make such a man, such a democrat, such a believer in human individual dignity, as Mark Twain himself, the frontier was necessary, Hannibal and the Mississippi and Virginia City, and reaching out from those the wilderness; the wilderness as opportunity and as idea, the thing that has helped to make an American different from and, until we forget it in the roar of our industrial cities, more fortunate than other men. For an American, insofar as he is new and different at all, is a civilized man who has renewed himself in the wild. The American experience has been the confrontation by old peoples and cultures of a world as new as if it had just risen from the sea. That gave us our hope and our excitement, and the hope and excitement can be passed on to newer Americans, Americans who never saw any phase of the frontier. But only so long as we keep the remainder of our wild as a reserve and a promise—a sort of wilderness bank.

As a novelist, I may perhaps be forgiven for taking literature as a reflection, indirect but profoundly true, of our national consciousness. And our literature, as perhaps you are aware, is sick, embittered, losing its mind, losing its faith. Our novelists are the declared enemies of their society. There has hardly been a serious or important novel in this century that did not repudiate in part or in whole American technological culture for its commercialism, its vulgarity, and the way in which it has dirtied a clean continent and a clean dream. I do not expect that the preservation of our remaining wilderness is going to cure this condition. But the mere example that we can as a nation apply some other criteria than commercial and exploitative considerations would be heartening to many Americans, novelists or otherwise. We need to demonstrate our acceptance of the natural world, including ourselves; we need the spiritual refreshment that being natural can produce. And one of the best places for us to get that is in the wilderness where the fun houses, the bulldozers, and the pavements of our civilization are shut out.

Sherwood Anderson, in a letter to Waldo Frank in the 1920's, said it better than I can. "Is it not likely that when the country was new and men were often alone in the fields and the forest they got a sense of bigness outside themselves that has now in some way been lost . . . Mystery whispered in the grass, played in the branches of trees over-head, was caught up and blown across the American line in clouds of dust at evening on the prairies . . . I am old enough to remember tales that strengthen my belief in a deep semi-religious influence that was formerly at work among our people. The flavor of it hangs over the best work of Mark Twain . . . I can remember old fellows in my home town speaking feelingly of an evening spent on the big empty plains. It had taken the shrillness out of them. They had learned the trick of quiet . . ."

We could learn it too, even yet; even our children and grandchildren could learn it. But only if we save, for just such absolutely non-recreational, impractical, and mystical uses as this, all the wild that still remains to us.

It seems to me significant that the distinct downturn in our literature from hope to bitterness took place almost at the precise time when the frontier officially came to an end, in 1890, and when the American way of life had begun to turn strongly urban and industrial. The more urban it has become, and the more frantic with technological change, the sicker and more embittered our literature, and I believe our people, have become. For myself, I grew up on the empty plains of Saskatchewan and Montana and in the mountains of Utah, and I put a very high valuation on what those places gave me. And if I had not been able periodically to renew myself in the mountains and deserts of western America I would be very nearly bughouse. Even when I can't get to the back country, the thought of the colored deserts of southern Utah, or the reassurance that there are still stretches of prairie where the world can be instantaneously perceived as disk and bowl, and where the little but intensely important human being is exposed to the five directions and the thirty-six winds, is a positive consolation. The idea alone can sustain me. But as the wilder-ness areas are progressively exploited or "improved," as the jeeps and bulldozers of uranium prospectors scar up the deserts and the roads are cut into the alpine timberlands, and as the remnants of the unspoiled and natural world are progressively eroded, every such loss is a little death in me. In us.

I am not moved by the argument that those wilderness areas which have already been exposed to grazing or mining are already deflowered, and so might as well be "harvested." For mining I cannot say much good except that its operations are generally short-lived. The extractable wealth is taken and the shafts, the tailings, and the ruins left, and in a dry country such as the American West the wounds men make in the earth do not quickly heal. Still, they are only wounds; they aren't absolutely mortal. Better a wounded wilderness than none at all. And as for grazing, if it is strictly controlled so that it does not destroy the ground cover, damage the ecology, or compete with the wildlife it is in itself nothing that need conflict with the wilderness feeling or the validity of the wilderness experience. I have known enough range cattle to recognize them as wild animals; and the people who herd them have, in the wilderness context, the dignity of rareness; they belong on the frontier, moreover, and have a look of rightness. The invasion they make on the virgin country is a sort of invasion that is as old as Neolithic man, and they can, in moderation, even emphasize a man's feeling of belonging to the natural world. Under surveillance, they can belong; under control, they need not deface or mar. I do not believe that in wilderness areas where grazing has never been permitted, it should be permitted; but I do not believe either that an otherwise untouched wilderness should be eliminated from the preservation plan because of limited existing uses such as grazing which are in consonance with the frontier condition and image.

Let me say something on the subject of the kinds of wilderness worth preserving. Most of those areas contemplated are in the national forests and in high mountain country. For all the usual recreational purposes, the alpine and forest wildernesses are obviously the most important, both as genetic banks and as beauty spots. But for the spiritual renewal, the recognition of identity, the birth of awe, other kinds will serve every bit as well. Perhaps, because they are less friendly to life, more abstractly nonhuman, they will serve even better. On our Saskatchewan prairie, the nearest neighbor was four miles away, and at night we saw only two lights on all the dark rounding earth. The earth was full of animals—field mice, ground squirrels, weasels, ferrets, badgers, coyotes, burrowing owls, snakes. I knew them as my little brothers, as fellow creatures, and I have never been able to look upon animals in any other way since. The sky in that country came clear down to the ground on every side, and it was full of great weathers, and clouds, and winds, and hawks. I hope I learned something from knowing intimately the creatures of the earth; I hope I learned something from looking a long way, from looking up, from being much alone. A prairie like that, one big enough to carry the eye clear to the sinking, rounding horizon, can be as lonely and grand and simple in its forms as the sea. It is as good a place as any for the wilderness experience to happen; the vanishing prairie is as worth preserving for the wilderness idea as the alpine forests.

So are great reaches of our western deserts, scarred somewhat by prospectors but otherwise open, beautiful, waiting, close to whatever God you want to see in them. Just as a sample, let me suggest the Robbers' Roost country in Wayne County, Utah, near the Capitol Reef National Monument. In that desert climate the dozer and jeep tracks will not soon melt back into the earth, but the country has a way of making the scars insignificant. It is a lovely and terrible wilderness, such a wilderness as Christ and the prophets went out into; harshly and beautifully colored, broken and worn until its bones are exposed, its great sky without a smudge or taint from Technocracy, and in hidden corners and pockets under its cliffs the sudden poetry of springs. Save a piece of country like that intact, and it does not matter in the slightest that only a few people every year will go into it. That is precisely its value. Roads would be a desecration, crowds would ruin it. But those who haven't the strength or youth to go into it and live can simply sit and look. They can look two hundred miles, clear into Colorado; and looking down over the cliffs and canyons of the San Rafael Swell and the Robbers' Roost they can also look as deeply into themselves as anywhere I know. And if they can't even get to the places on the Aquarius Plateau where the present roads will carry them, they can simply contemplate the *idea*, take pleasure in the fact that such a timeless and uncontrolled part of earth is still there.

These are some of the things wilderness can do for us. That is the reason we need to put into effect, for its preservation, some other principle than the principles of exploitation or "usefulness" or even recreation. We simply need that wild country available to us, even if we never do more than drive to its edge and look in. For it can be a means of reassuring ourselves of our sanity as creatures, a part of the geography of hope.

Very sincerely yours,
Wallace Stegner

Biographies

Ed Abbey (1927–1989) was born in Home, Pennsylvania, although education at the University of New Mexico (B.A., 1951; M.A., 1956) turned his heart early to the desert Southwest. Abbey described himself as "agrarian anarchist" in politics, "Piute" in religion. His new journalist style thrust his provocative personality directly at readers, alienating some, entrancing more. His death in 1989 was genuinely untimely, although *Desert Solitaire* and *The Monkey Wrench Gang* remain as modern American classics.

Sherwood Anderson (1876–1941) led, until that famous day in 1913 when he walked out of his office in a paint manufacturing company, the quintessentially normal American life: born in small-town Camden, Ohio, educated at Wittenberg Academy, service in the Spanish-American War, a stable and middle-class job, wife, house . . . the full catastrophe. In 1913 he left everything—including job, house, and wife—for a new and far more bohemian life as a writer. Anderson's stories reflect a developing twentieth-century interest in sexuality and the unconscious mind. His work was widely admired by readers and other writers alike, often imitated, and often rejected by former disciples who believed they had passed beyond what Anderson had to teach. He had the misfortune to write his best work (*Winesburg, Ohio*, 1919) early in his career, and subsequent stories and novels, including the auto-biographical *Tar, a Midwest Boyhood* and *A Story Teller's Story*, never fulfilled his early promise.

Wendell Berry (1934–) left his native Kentucky hills for a brilliant career as distinguished professor of English at the University of Kentucky, then returned to rural Kentucky to write (essays, poems, novels) and restore a small part of the depleted landscape. Today a farmer-poet in the classic tradition, Berry works his farm with absolutely minimal technology (animal power, no chemicals), writes prolifically, speaks frequently on environmental issues. In life, philosophy, and written style, Berry is quiet and old-fashioned, persistently making the case for old and proven traditions. His books include *The Gift of Good Land* and *A Continuous Harmony* (essays), *The Memory of Old Jack* (fiction), and *Farming: A Handbook* (poems).

Norbert Blei (1938–) was born and raised in Cicero, Illinois, an urban-ethnic community best remembered as the home of Al Capone. After several years as a Chicago-area teacher and journalist, Blei moved to Door County, Wisconsin . . . the peninsula northeast of Green Bay celebrated mostly for fishing, cherry orchards, dairies, and tourism. He travels frequently, to the American Southwest and to Eastern Europe. Blei's writing—poetry, journalism, fiction, serious essay—reflects his ethnic heritage (Bohemian), his wild imagination, and his many worlds. His best work is *Door Way* (the first book in his Door County trilogy), *Neighborhood* and *The Ghost of Sandburg's Phizzog* (the first two books of his Chicago trilogy), *The Hour of the Sunshine Now* (his first collection of stories), *Adventures in an American's Literature* (a novel which might have been the original *Dead Poets Society*), and *Paint Me a Picture/Make Me a Poem* (word-and-image poems).

Carol Bly (1930–) has spent most of her life in Minnesota, first as a child in Duluth, then married to Robert Bly in Madison, and more recently in Sturgeon Lake and the Twin Cities. She worked long hours and in many capacities on *Fifties/Sixties/Seventies* magazine and press, and tirelessly in a long string of social, political, educational, and civic projects. Bly has been especially generous as a teacher of writing (workshops and at universities) and as a resource for various humanities projects. Her own best writing is found in *Letters from the Country* (controversial essays on life in small-town Madison) and *Backbone* (short stories).

Frederick Busch (1941–) was born in Brooklyn, educated at Muhlenberg and Columbia, and presently teaches at Colgate. He has written short stories, novels, and essays both informal and scholarly. His books include a critical work on the fiction of John Hawkes, a fantasy novel spun around the life of Charles Dickens (*The Mutual Friend*), a thirteen-episode family chronicle (*Domestic Particulars*), and other novels and collections of stories, including *Hardwater Country*, from which "Widow Water" is taken.

Carolyn Chute (1947–) is the daughter of a Portland, Maine, electrical parts salesman and the wife first of a factory worker and later of a woodcutter-firewood salesman. She attended the University of Southern Maine between 1972 and 1978 while raising her daughter and working at various odd jobs: waitress, chicken factory worker, hospital floor scrubber, shoe factory worker, canvasser, social worker, school bus driver. Since then she has taught creative writing and worked as a newspaper correspondent for the *Portland Evening Express*. After publishing short stories in a number of little magazines, Chute published her first novel in 1985 with Ticknor & Fields: *The Beans of Egypt*, from which the selection in this book is taken.

Michel-Guillaume Jean de Crèvecoeur (1735–1813), a native of France, emigrated in his late adolescence to Canada, where he fought as a lieutenant in Montcalm's army. Later he worked as a surveyor up and down the American coast, settling, with an American wife, on a farm in Orange County, New York. The American Revolution—which he opposed—interrupted this bucolic idyl, and Crevecoeur left the colonies (alone) for England in 1781. The following year saw British publication of his *Letters from an American Farmer* under the pseudonym Hector St. John; in 1783 a larger French edition was published. His enthusiasm for the rural life made Crevecoeur a favorite with followers of Rousseau and won him an appointment as French consul general to New York. Upon his return to America, however, he discovered that his home had been burned, his wife killed, and his children carried off in an Indian raid. In 1790 he returned to France, where he lived until his death.

Leo Dangel (1941–) spent his youth in South Dakota before attending colleges in Minnesota, South Dakota, and Kansas. Like many midwestern poets, Dangel has been influenced more than a little by the work of Dave Etter and Bill Kloefkorn: He writes easily accessible story poems with a wry sense of humor and tight social commentary. To date, his work has appeared in two collections: *Keeping Between the Fences* and *Old Man Brunner Country* (from which are reprinted the poems in this collection).

Annie Dillard (1945–), a Phi Beta Kappa graduate of Hollins College and a contributing editor to *Harper's*, publishes frequently in the best American magazines, including *Harper's*, *Atlantic Monthly*, *Cosmopolitan*, and *Sports Illustrated*. Her *Pilgrim at Tinker Creek* (1974), from which "Seeing" is excerpted, was one of the first post-sixties letters from the country, an attempt in the tradition of Thoreau to see the world in a grain of sand. It struck a resonant chord with a generation of Americans and became almost overnight a classic of the 1970s.

Richard Dokey (1933–) was born and raised in the San Joaquin Valley of California. At Berkeley he majored in journalism, but his writing has been short stories (*August Heat*, from which "Birth" is reprinted, and *Sundown*) and drama (*Funeral* and *Craps*). His fiction has appeared in many literary magazines and several times been cited as "distinctive" in *Best American Short Stories*.

Dave Etter (1928–) was born in California, but early adopted the Midwest—Illinois in particular—as his spiritual and literary homeland. His degree is from the University of Iowa (*not* the Writers' Workshop). He served in the U.S. Army in Korea, then worked as a copy editor/writer for a number of midwest publishers. He is a prolific writer of poetry, for which he has won a string of prizes and awards, and averages a new paperback collection each year. The "essential Etter" is *Selected Poems* (1987) and *Alliance, Illinois* (1983).

Truman C. Everts (1816–1902) was born in Burlington, Vermont, son of a ship captain. He accompanied his father on several voyages around the Great Lakes, grew up, moved west, married, and served from 1864 to 1870 as assessor of internal revenues for the Montana Territory. When he lost that position (with the Grant administration), Everts joined the first white expedition into what is now Yellowstone Park, precipitating the adventure recounted in his story for *Scribner's Monthly*. Everts not only survived to write about the ordeal, he went on to live a very long life, returning east to a job in the post office, marrying for a second time, and fathering a daughter at the age of seventy-six.

Zona Gale (1874–1938) spent most of her life in Portage, Wisconsin, except for a brief decade in New York where, around the turn of the century, she worked as a reporter and a professional writer. Gale grew up in a close and indulgent family, married her childhood sweetheart, and—even though she crusaded vigorously for women's suffrage, international peace, prohibition, and progressivism in general—lived the pleasant, warm life depicted in *Friendship Village* (1908) and subsequent Friendship novels and stories.

William Gass (1924–) is widely recognized as a writer of fiction and literary essays and was for a time visiting professor of English at the

University of Illinois. He has taught philosophy virtually all of his adult life, first at Purdue and, since 1969, at Washington University in St. Louis. Possessing a writing style which is dense, multifaceted, and fecund, his words at times reflect the mainstream American tradition from Twain to Faulkner, at times suggest the styles of various foreign surrealists and experimentalists. Most of the time, Gass's style is the author's own voice articulating the author's own vision. His major works include *Omensetter's Luck* (1966), *In the Heart of the Heart of the Country and Other Stories* (1968), and *Willie Masters' Lonesome Wife* (1971).

Paul Gruchow (1947–) retired in 1986 as editor of the *Worthington Globe* to pursue a full-time career in writing. He is a regular contributor to *Minnesota Monthly*, a past president of the Minnesota Humanities Commission, and a tireless worker in environmentalist and preservationist causes. His *Journal of a Prairie Year* is the source of material reprinted in this collection; the *Journal* has since been joined by another book, *The Necessity of Open Spaces*.

Donald Hall (1928–) has written prolifically, well, and in a wide range of literary forms virtually all his life. At Harvard he edited the *Advocate*; at Oxford he won a Newdigate Prize for poetry. After leaving Harvard and Oxford (and Stanford), he taught for a decade at the University of Michigan, then retired to his family farm in Danbury, New Hampshire, to write. His many published books include *Andrew the Lion Farmer* (a juvenile), *Exiles and Marriages* (poetry, winner of the Lamont Prize), *Contemporary American Poetry* (an anthology, one of more than a dozen Hall has edited), *Fathers Playing Catch with Sons* (essays on sport), *String Too Short to Be Saved* (autobiography, from which the essay in this book is taken), *To Read Literature* (textbook), and the great classic textbook on style, *Writing Well*.

Christopher Hallowell (1945–) was born in Boston, Massachusetts, educated at Harvard and Columbia. He pursued a career in journalism, including a position as senior editor of *Human Nature*, and a stint as a freelance writer. As a writer, he once claimed, he feels most comfortable "in writing about man's relationship to his environment, and on anthropological and ecological subjects." *People of the Bayou*, from which the selection in this anthology is excerpted, was published in 1979.

Linda Hasselstrom (1943–) lives in Hermosa, South Dakota, writing poetry and essays and managing the ranch on which she was born. Tireless in the causes of environmentalism and literature, she embodies for many in the Midwest that ideal woman who has not compromised herself while surviving in the (often hostile) male world, who has taken repeated blows of outrageous fortune only to remain economically and spiritually unbowed, combining the art of writing and living well. Her poetry collections include *Caught by One Wing* and *Roadkill*; her prose writings include *Windbreak* and *Going over East*. In July, 1989, she somehow managed to publish a poem (along with excerpts from a journal) in *Life* magazine.

Jim Heynen (1940–   ) was born and raised in Sioux County, Iowa, in the strict Dutch Calvinist tradition. Although he has spent much of his adult life in the far more cosmopolitan Northwest, it is on his rural midwestern roots that Heynen draws for much of his best material in his collection of poetry (*A Suitable Church*) and the delightful prose pieces on farm life contained in *The Man Who Kept Cigars in His Cap* (1978) and *You Know What Is Right* (1985).

Bill Holm (1943–   ) was born in Minneota, Minnesota, the grandson of Icelandic immigrant farmers. He escaped his hometown to Gustavus Adolphus College and the University of Kansas, later to teach at Hampton Institute in Virginia. He was a Fulbright lecturer to Reykjavik, and taught for a year in China. However, Holm came home. His books are strongly scented with the odors of western Minnesota: *The Music of Failure* (prose) and *Boxelderbug Variations* (poetry and songs).

Greg Keeler (1946–   ) is a professor of English at Montana State University in Bozeman, Montana. He is also an avid fly fisherman and outdoorsman, increasingly concerned (as are most outdoorsmen in Montana) about the present development of the American West. Keeler has published a book of poems (*American Falls*), created a comic book character (*Poetryman*), and scripted a centennial dramatic celebration titled *Rewinding Montana*. He is, however, best known as an underground singer-performer of topical/satirical songs, somewhat in the vein of the early Bob Dylan or Phil Ochs. (The songs reprinted in this book are collected on five audio tapes [available from Mastadon Productions, P.O. Box 6272, Bozeman, Montana], including *Songs of Fishing*, *Sheep and Guns in Montana*; *Bad Science Fiction*; *Talking Sweet Bye and Bye*; *The Nuclear-Dioxin Queen*; and *Post-Modern Blues*.)

Garrison Keillor (1942–   ) is a rural Minnesota product, although not entirely as rural as the two million weekly fans of *A Prairie Home Companion* might suspect. While still a student (B.A. and some graduate study) at the University of Minnesota, Keillor began working as a staff announcer for Minnesota Public Radio, a career which led eventually to the weekly program he hosted and (mostly) scripted for over a decade. The program's casual tone and folksy music, coupled with Keillor's genial, down home humor and rich, reassuring voice, tempered what was in fact a relatively austere portrait of rural America. The program went national in a big way. Meanwhile, Keillor was also contributing prose pieces to the *Atlantic Monthly*, the *New Yorker*, and other magazines. The radio material—even more brilliant on the air than it is in print, thanks to Keillor's remarkable sense of timing—produced in 1985 a truly blockbusting best seller, *Lake Wobegon Days*, an instant landmark of rural American literature that resurrected Keillor's previous book (*Happy To Be Here*), spawned further Lake Wobegon books (and tapes) and made Keillor a reluctant multimillionaire.

William Kloefkorn (1932–) lives in Lincoln, Nebraska, where he is professor of English at Nebraska Wesleyan University, and is the Nebraska State Poet, and former state champion hog caller. He is a prolific and popular poet, combining a wry sense of humor with a penetrating but kindly understanding of human nature. His collections of poetry include *Alvin Turner as Farmer* (from which come the poems herein reprinted), *Uncertain the Final Run to Winter*, *Not Such a Bad Place to Be*, and, most recently, *Where the Visible Sun Is*.

Mark Kramer (1944–), son of a publisher and attorney, holds degrees from Brandeis, Columbia, and Indiana University. He has farmed in western Massachusetts, lectured at U. Mass., and played flute with Shehan's Reel Contradance Orchestra. He cowrote and codirected an award winning film, "Crisis in Yankee Agriculture," and held a Ford Foundation fellowship in 1980–81. In addition to *Three Farms* (from which the essay in this book is taken), Kramer's books include *Mother Walker and the Pig Tragedy* and *Invasive Procedures: A Year in the World of Two Surgeons*.

Verlyn Klinkenborg (1952–) grew up in small town Iowa, son of a farm boy turned teacher, among relatives who were farmers and friends who farmed. Klinkenborg took a Ph. D. from Princeton and a teaching job at Fordham University, publishing in *Esquire*, *Rod & Reel*, the *Washington Post*, and elsewhere. On a visit home during the present agricultural crisis he began writing *Making Hay* (1986), from which the account in this book is excerpted.

Maxine Kumin (1925–) received both her B.A. and M.A. from Radcliffe, and has taught at Tufts, the University of Massachusetts, and Princeton. She has written more than twenty children's books, more than half a dozen books of poetry, and half a dozen novels. She is a former chairperson of the Literature Panel of the National Endowment for the Arts, and the 1973 winner of the Pulitzer Prize in poetry. Although Kumin's focus has always been the middle-class, mostly suburban experience, in *In Deep*, from which "Life on a Hill" is excerpted, Kumin recounts her experience living, for a while at least, out in the country.

Patricia Leimbach (1927–   ) was born the daughter of an Ohio farmer and, after study at Case Western Reserve and McGill, married another Ohio farmer. She is a frequent contributor to farm newspapers and magazines, and writes a column, "The Country Wife," for the Elyria (Ohio) *Chronicle Telegram*. Her first book of essays, *A Thread of Blue Denim*, was published in 1974; a second collection, *All My Meadows: A Harvest of Country Wisdom*, appeared in 1987.

Meridel LeSueur (1900–   ), daughter of populist politician Arthur LeSueur and his crusading partner, Marion LeSueur, has herself been a powerful champion of the people all her long life. She began her writing early, recording in her journals the speech of farmers and small businessmen congregated around the watering troughs of the small towns in which she lived. During the thirties she wrote for the *New Masses* and bore two daughters as a protest, she has said, against the dark times. LeSueur was blacklisted by big commercial publishers in the fifties, reemerging in the 1960s as one of the great matriarchs of rural American literature. Her best work includes the short stories of *Salute to Spring*, *Harvest*, and *Song for Our Time*; a novel, *The Girl*; her people's history of north country titled *North Star Country*; juvenile books on Nancy Hanks and Abraham Lincoln; and a magnificent autobiographical essay, "The Ancient People and the Newly Come," contained in *Growing Up in Minnesota*.

Barry Holstun Lopez (1945–   ), son of publisher Adrian Bernard, has been a freelance writer and photographer, working out of the Northwest, since 1970. He writes for literary magazines and for travel and natural history journals, including *Audubon* and *North American Review*. His books include *Desert Notes: Reflections in the Eye of a Raven*, *Winter Count* (which contains "Buffalo"), *Arctic Dreams*, and, most recently, *Crossing Open Ground*.

Bobbie Ann Mason (1940–   ) grew up the daughter of a dairy farmer, took her B.A. at the University of Kentucky. Her career as a writer began with some New York fan magazines, interviewing Fabian, Annette Funicello, Ann-Margaret, and others. Dissatisfied with the direction her life was taking, she took a Ph.D. in literature at the University of Connecticut and began a college teaching career at Mansfield State College in rural Pennsylvania. Her dissertation on Nabakov produced one book; her childhood reading of Nancy Drew and the Bobbsey Twins another. Then her first published book of fiction, *Shiloh and Other Stories*, won the PEN Hemingway Award and was a finalist for the National Book Critics Award and the American Book Award. And Bobbie Ann Mason woke up famous.

Noel Perrin (1920–   ) holds degrees from Williams College, Duke, and Trinity Hall, Cambridge . . . and a Phi Beta Kappa key, and a Bronze Star for his military service in Korea. He taught at Dartmouth College, beginning in 1959, and authored numerous books including *Dr. Bowlder's Legacy: A History of Expurgated Books in England and America*, *Amateur Sugar Maker*, *Vermont: In All Weathers*, and the trilogy *First Person Rural*, *Second Person Rural*, and *Third Person Rural*.

Gary Snyder (1930–   ) studied literature and anthropology at Reed College, oriental languages at Berkeley, and Zen Buddhism in Kyoto, Japan. He has worked as a seaman, logger, and forester and has taught at Berkeley. He has also received numerous study fellowships, grants, and prizes, including the 1975 Pulitzer Prize in literature. Snyder's poetry derives as much from his work experiences as from his academic studies: It is unusually (for post-modern American writing) celebratory. The influence of his Zen studies is everywhere apparent, particularly in Snyder's attention to the little matters of earth and animal, and in his concern for the ecological consequences of civilization. Snyder's many books include *Riprap & Cold Mountain Poems*, *The Back Country*, *Earth House Hold*, *Passage Through India*, *Turtle Island*, and *The Real Work: Interviews and Talks*.

Wallace Stegner (1909–   ) was born in Lake Mills, Iowa, but spent his boyhood on the family homestead in Saskatchewan, Canada, in the Cypress Hills along the Montana border. His memoir of those years, *Wolf Willow* (1955), is subtitled "A History, a Story, and a Memory of the Last Plains Frontier." Stegner holds a B.A. from the University of Iowa and a Ph.D. from Berkeley, but his novels and other writing are permeated with his love of frontier life, and he is regarded as a major western writer. Other books include *All the Little Living Things*, *The Big Rock Candy Mountain*, *Mormon Country*, *The Sound of Mountain Water*, and *American West as Living Space.*.

Henry David Thoreau (1817–1862) lived most of his life within a very small radius of his native Concord, Massachusetts, although he traveled somewhat farther than many readers believe, and he read extensively, aided by the Harvard education he was fond of deprecating. After a rather successful stint in the family pencil-manufacturing concern and a less successful effort at school teaching, Thoreau built himself a cabin at Walden Pond, where he lived from July 4, 1845, to September 6, 1847, reading, observing, meditating, attempting to discover what was essential in life. The record of that stay, much revised, became *Walden*, on which rests half of Thoreau's present reputation (although his journals are classics of the journal form, and Thoreau did also write poetry). The other half of his modern reputation stems from his famous essay on "Civil Disobedience," a spirited assertion of the individual's rights in a state which, in 1849, condoned slavery and was busy pursuing a war in Mexico. Thoreau's tight style, his strong moral imperative, and the admixture of naturalistic observation and social thought defined one form of rural writing still common in American literature.

Ann Zwinger (1925–   ) was born in Muncie, Indiana, educated at Wellesley, Indiana University, and Radcliffe. The mother of three, Zwinger also taught art and art history at several institutions (she drew her own illustrations for *Beyond the Aspen Grove*), and has emerged in the past couple of decades as one of the country's leading naturalist writers. Other books include *A Conscious Stillness*, *A Desert Country Near the Sea*, *Land Above the Trees*, and *Run, River, Run*.